FOOD Lover's GUIDE
TO THE WORLD
Experience the Great Global Cuisines

FOREWORD

I suppose I was already plotting my getaway even when I was a kid. Sprawled on the floor of my suburban California bedroom with a copy of the latest National Geographic magazine, I would disappear for hours into the photographs I saw between its glossy pages. The images that always held me captive the longest, though, weren't of exotic landscapes or archaeological digs. They were of people in distant places doing that most simple of things: eating.

There's one photo I remember particularly well. It showed a village in rural India, a woman in a turquoise sari using a stick to stoke a sparking fire, a blackened pot hanging over it. I remember closely inspecting the mysterious ochre-colored curry inside the pot, the meal she was preparing, enchanted. This place seemed so foreign but I wanted to be there, smelling that fire, hearing it crackle, eating what I thought must be the most unimaginably delicious, exotic food. The photo was a doorway into another world, a world far removed from the pot roast and frozen dinners that I grew up eating.

At 19, I had my first real opportunity to travel to a place like the ones I'd fantasised about since I was a kid. I was in college; it was 1982. One afternoon, Tanya, a fellow student who came from Indonesia, asked rather matter of factly, 'Why don't you visit my family in Jakarta sometime?' Within days, I booked a ticket. Within weeks, I was staying in Tanya's family's home.

Then, as now, Jakarta was about as overwhelming as a place can be for a newcomer: crowded, hot, a cacophony of smells and sounds, none of them familiar or particularly friendly. My first few weeks were spent in a kind of sweaty stupor. One day, though, Tanya's mother, Ann, held a *selamatan,* a traditional Javanese feast, as a benefit for a charity organization she was involved in. 'It's our version of a potluck', Tanya told me. A parade of women soon arrived in silk sarongs with foods they'd prepared for the occasion. I counted 32 dishes in all. My jaw dropped. There were glistening coconut milk curries, pickled vegetables tinted yellow with fresh turmeric, whole grilled fish topped with lemon basil, sticky-rice sweets in every colour of the rainbow – and that's just what I saw on the first table. A woman in orange batik spotted me.

'Tell me, do you know any of these foods?' she asked.

Over the course of the next few minutes she took it upon herself to act as guide, steering me toward different dishes – a beef *rendang,* meltingly tender and scattered with finely shredded lime leaves, from West Sumatra; Javanese *opor ayam,* a chicken curry fragrant with cinnamon and cilantro – filling in my mental map of Indonesia with distinct flavours and aromas. Of a dish from the Spice Islands, of tuna braised with tomatoes and whole spices, she said, 'The locals use cloves and nutmeg in everything.' I began to tease out the layers of spice, chilli, lime leaf, and lemongrass in the dishes I was eating, and to grasp how a few simple, fresh foods like pineapple, cucumber, palm sugar, and peanuts can come together to make something that awakens your palate. I'd found a way to understand – and to love – Indonesia.

In the years since that trip I've travelled to more places than I can count in hopes of seeking out similarly revelatory meals. I've eaten rustic *char kuey teow* (wok-fried noodles with cockles and shrimp) at night markets in Malaysia. I've sampled thick, chewy *huaraches* (foot-long, handmade tortillas) covered with searing hot arból chilli salsa and a tangle of sautéed cactus at street stalls in Mexico City. I've gorged on thalis of a dozen different dishes, including lentil dhals and salty pickles, in Kerala, India. For me, there is no better way to understand a place – to literally get it inside you – than by eating its food. Through food, I always find my way.

James Oseland is the editor-in-chief of *Saveur* magazine.

TRAVEL TO EAT

When we travel we discover a place – its people, land and culture – through its food. We bring back not just mouthwatering memories but inspiration. Mark Bittman explains.

There is a Japanese place in midtown Manhattan, of the kind we used to call a greasy spoon, whose name I barely know. I go there monthly at least, and I send friends there as well. Not everyone: just people who I think will appreciate the funky, playful, non-sushi side of Japanese food – for the most part, these happen to be people who've been to Japan. And, for the most part, they love it. Afterwards, they'll call me and say, 'It was amazing! We were the only non-Japanese people in the place! Everyone was speaking Japanese! The food was unlike anything else! It was just like being in Tokyo!'

Actually, no. It's not. I'm not a Tokyo expert, but I can tell you that as authentic as the representations of 'foreign' food have become in our native cities, the experience isn't the same. A bistro outside of France, a *pho* stand in a country other than Vietnam, a trattoria that isn't in Italy, a taco shack even 100 miles from Mexico ... without taking anything away from any of those places – and, really, the food itself can be just as good as it is in its home – the experience is different.

That's because food, of course, is only one of several keys to a fantastic restaurant experience in an unfamiliar place. What veteran traveller doesn't remember stumbling on an eatery that wasn't recommended by a friend (or a guidebook, for that matter), a discovery that's somehow owned by ourselves – that is, a real discovery? We all know that in those instances the food isn't even the most important thing; it becomes a representation, an integral and essential part of so much else, of an experience that cannot

possibly be duplicated by eating at the most authentic Turkish, Moroccan or Argentinian place in your home city. Three examples:

• On the way back from an early morning run in a village (I never knew its name) near Soc Trang in the Mekong Delta, I came across a *pho* cart. I'd been eating *pho* daily for a week (and I never stop to eat when I'm in a post-run situation), but something about this cart – the aroma, the look, the older woman serving the hot broth – was alluring. I sat with my early-morning comrades and enjoyed that *pho* more than any other.

• Wandering on foot in Istanbul, lost – not hopelessly but seriously – I found myself quite befuddled, and recognised that I was beyond hungry. I stopped at the next restaurant I saw, a steam table joint, the type of place I'd never choose at home, and chose a soupy stew of overcooked rice, carrots, onions, and peas. Sounds abominable, right? Since then, I make it myself, all the time. In fact it's one of my favourite comfort foods.

• In East Berlin, on a snowy, blustery day, walking through oddly grey neighbourhoods at a time after reunification but before gentrification, I was in quest of something real, although I didn't quite know what that was. Without guidance (without a clue, really), I plunged down a few steps into an old bar and ordered the only dish offered with sauerkraut – *Schweinshaxe*, or pork shank (or 'knuckle') – and hunkered down with a couple of beers and a crew of new friends.

Was this the best food I've ever eaten, or even the best examples of these particular dishes? I can't say. They were

enjoyable, serendipitous, wonderful experiences that created (as you can tell) lasting memories, memories comparable to a first day in Rome, that glimpse of Big Ben, the Golden Gate.

That stuff doesn't happen to me in New York (which is where I grew up, and where I live), and no matter where you live I'll bet it doesn't happen to you. It couldn't possibly: we never wander in our own cities the way we wander when we're in someone else's. We never set out to get lost, to make random discoveries, to go to restaurants that we haven't read or heard about. Those kinds of experiences are precisely why we travel.

It's not only that food tastes better when it's indigenous, it's the reasons why it tastes better when it's indigenous. And, as you probably know, those reasons are largely 'psychological': in other words, they're in your head. And, more and more – as international ingredients improve, as immigrants from everywhere wind up in all developed countries, as it becomes easier and easier to run a restaurant – they really are in your head. If you could judge it in a vacuum, the food often would be as good, as authentic, as rich, in your local *pho* joint as it was on the sidewalk that day when I ate it.

But you can't judge it in a vacuum: the food is one of the very

real ways in which you experience an unfamiliar place, as real as the landscape and the people, and intertwined with both. Food is one of the windows into culture, and the experience of getting to a restaurant, of ordering the food, or seeing those same ingredients you might have seen in the market that morning, of hearing citizens chat in a tongue you may or may not understand, or seeing what they order, of figuring out what you're going to eat, of relating to the waiter – all of this and much more, a list you can readily make yourself – means that what's in your head has a huge impact on the way you experience the food you're eating.

And yet another wonderful thing may happen when you bring memories of eating home from your travels: you may be inspired to cook it, or – perhaps more common – to use ingredients in ways you've not done previously, and to use them more frequently. (No one who's been to Vietnam, for example, can ever think of fragrant herbs in the same way they did before.) Of this I could give literally hundreds of examples (then again I've made a living doing this). Again, I'll settle for three:

• On my first visit to Rome, now nearly 40 years ago, I dutifully ordered *spaghetti alla carbonara,* knowing that that was a dish

that Americans had not yet experienced and which was reported to be amazing. (As practically everyone now knows, it is.) And yet that's not the story: the story is that a man at a neighbouring table had ordered a bowl of mussels, and the sight of those so excited me that I called my waiter over and, in fractured Italian and sign language, explained that I did not want *carbonara* but mussels. (We had to get past the point where he thought I was ordering 'mosquitos'.) Since that time, I have cooked mussels – just like that, with garlic, basil, and tomatoes – scores of times, never failing to thank that gentleman at the next table. (I ate *carbonara* at lunch the next day, of course.)

• In Progreso – the Gulf port of the Yucatán, and the primary outlet to the sea for Mérida – there is (or was, on my last visit), a huge variety of seafood. And yet, it's almost all prepared with the same flavours: lime, chilli, and cilantro. After a few days of eating this way, it's impossible to think of cooking fresh fish simply without considering 'lime, chilli, cilantro.' And you could do a lot worse.

• On a trip to northern India, meal in and meal out, I was served dhal; no two were the same. For me, a rich tourist, the dhal were usually served as side dishes. But it would've taken wilful ignorance to not recognise that the simple dhal, with roti or chapatti or rice, was the backbone, if not the whole of breakfast,

lunch, and dinner, for millions of people surrounding me. I came home with a new appreciation for pulses, and have cooked them more often and far better in the years since that happened.

As important as are these first two reasons to experience food *in situ* – the argument that it's as powerful a vehicle for experiencing culture as any other, and that it creates experiences and memories that you can't otherwise get – to me, a cook, I think that the third is really critical. As Western diets have moved in precisely the wrong direction over the course of the last couple of generations, our bringing back experiences, flavours, ingredients, cooking techniques (really, what I'm saying here is inspiration), is actually a means of salvation, yet another way in which the traditions of both the developed and so-called developing world can not only remind us about what's really valuable but show us how to integrate it into our own lives. Every time every one of us introduces dhal, or corn tortillas and beans, or a stew of vegetables and rice, to our friends and family, we're bringing the wisdom of the ancients back into the modern world, and perhaps saving a little piece of it.

Mark Bittman is the lead food writer for *The New York Times Magazine* and is the author of the best-selling book *How To Cook Everything*. His website is www.markbittman.com

COUNTRIES

The view to central Shanghai
from a traditional tea house

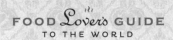

CHINA

Tuck into tofu, heads and tails, spices that numb and eye-watering vinegars. In China, hardened foodies soar to new culinary limits and squeamish diners are seduced into leaving their comfort zones behind.

China covers too much territory to have a national cuisine. Instead, regional cuisines have developed over the centuries into eight specific styles: *huicai* from Anhui, *yuecai* from Guangdong, *mincai* from Fujian, *lucai* from Shandong, *xiangcai* from Hunan, *sucai* from Jiangsu, *chuancai* from Sichuan and *zhecai* from Zhejiang.

Each style has its own vocabulary of spices, herbs and sauces, particular to that landscape. In fact, eating your way around China can feel like a voyage to eight different countries. To simplify things, it helps to think of a north–south rivalry. Northerners are known as wheat eaters; southerners, rice eaters. People who eat wheat are physically large but provincial in their outlook. People who eat rice are small and soft-willed. Or so they say: the 'you are what you eat' concept is taken very seriously in China.

Both north and south claim superiority in their culinary heritage, and each is justified in its bombast. The north is home to imperial cuisine, dishes influenced by Shandong's

lucai and refined to fit an emperor's palate. But the fertile south is where you'll find the great regional cuisines, such as the delicate seafood of *yuecai*, the mind-blowing hot sauces of *chuancai* and the elegance of *sucai*, the cuisine of the gastronomes. With such a rich food culture, one would think that Chinese diners are kept busy enough just exploring their own diversity.

But a love for world cuisines is blossoming and with it come restaurants serving Italian, French and Japanese crowd-pleasers, and the new fads of Ethiopian, Persian and Nordic food. In Beijing alone, there are 40,000 restaurants, although Hong Kong offers the world's lowest priced Michelin-starred restaurants. Wine is almost a must at upscale Chinese dining tables, no matter what's on the menu. Chinese drinkers consume an average of 300 million bottles of wine a year with a penchant for heavy reds. While the days of mixing a Bordeaux with Sprite are not entirely behind us, it is no longer a norm.

COMFORT FOOD

China's version of chicken soup for the sick and the soul is *congee*, a thin, easily digestible gruel made from rice boiled with plenty of water. For many, *congee* is also breakfast, a thin rice porridge served with fried *youtiao* (dough sticks), pickles and fresh soy milk. *Congee* can also be dressed up with all manner of additions to sate a gourmand's cravings, from slices of abalone to *pidan*, the preserved duck eggs with green yolks and black albumen. A luxurious *congee* should be boiled until the rice 'blooms', like fluffy popcorn. The resulting porridge is a viscous white wonder, resembling a cloud in a bowl.

EATING FOR HEALTH

According to Chinese tradition, all foods have a medicinal effect. When you are feeling unwell, your body is out of balance – too hot, too moist, too dry, too cold. Finding the food with the right elements can help remedy and rebalance the body. This practice is known as *shiliao*. Cooling foods such as bitter melon can nix a sore throat, a symptom of an overheated body. A medicinal meal, *yaoshan*, is a combination of nutritious foods and therapeutic herbs, such as ginseng or cordyceps, that Chinese believe prevents or heals illnesses and promotes longevity. The most typical are tonics boiled for hours, rich stews with a chicken base or the sex organs of animals.

RICE
THE GRAIN ON EVERYONE'S PLATES

Not everyone eats rice in China, but the grain plays a central role in Chinese food culture. In China, the word for rice means 'meal' in a general sense. The customary polite greeting of *'Chifan le ma?'*, used all over the country, literally translates as 'Have you eaten rice yet?'

Rice was once the hero of a meal, with other dishes merely adding flavour. Nowadays, the appreciation of rice has been taken to the next level, and some consider themselves rice critics. If the grains are fragrant, soft and retain their pearly white wholeness, guests will pay compliments. But if the rice is poorly cooked and of a low grade, it is shunned.

China produces more than a quarter of the world's rice, primarily along the fertile banks of the Yangtze River where it was first domesticated. The best place to see traditional rice cultivation is at the spectacular Unesco-listed Hani rice terraces in Yunnan Province. The Hani ethnic people in Yuanyang County still live a traditional way of life in this isolated area. Up to a thousand species of rice were once cultivated in their fields, and these days the Hani are partial to purple rice, which is said to have huge health benefits. It's typically used to make *baba*, a chewy rice cake wrapped in a banana leaf with cured meats.

Chinese-inspired fried rice is a well-loved dish around the globe. Luxurious ingredients like scallops, crab roe and an inauthentic dash of black-truffle oil elevate it from stomach-filler to a banquet-worthy dish. Every grain should be coated in oil but not greasy, and a wash of egg should be spread throughout. Fried rice tests the strength of a chef's wrist, as the heavy wok is continuously tossed to keep the rice separated and evenly cooked.

⚓ WHERE TO EAT SPRING PAPAYA DAI ETHNIC RESTAURANT 3 MENGHAI RD, JINGHONG, XISHUANGBANNA, YUNNAN

Yunnan is famous for stuffing rice into bamboo with slivers of mushrooms and for its pineapple rice, a whole pineapple stuffed with sticky rice and sometimes nuts.

RIGHT Water-intensive rice terraces growing the most imporant ingredient in Chinese cuisine **ABOVE** A perfectly portable snack: rice wrapped in a dried banana leaf with noodles **ABOVE LEFT** Congee for the soul

〰

XIAOLONGBAO
BITE-SIZED DUMPLINGS

Meaning 'little basket buns', *xiaolongbao* are Shanghainese pork dumplings traditionally steamed in the namesake baskets. They're also dubbed 'soup dumpling', for the rich pork broth that floods into your mouth as soon as you bite into the delicate morsel.

Essentially a triple-whammy pork experience, the tightly packed pork meatball and soul-warming pork soup are concealed in a wheat wrapper. Shaped like twisted domes, the dumplings are grasped carefully but firmly by *xiaolongbao* connoisseurs, as breaking the skin will meaning losing the precious soup. The dumplings are then dunked into black Zhenjiang vinegar mixed with slivers of fresh ginger, the tear-jerking acidic sauce reviving the senses after an overload of delicious pork. Using a spoon to catch any spillage, *xiaolongbao* experts nibble off a piece of the wrapper and suck out the broth from the dumpling before eating the lot. If you're a *xiaolongbao* virgin, give in to your hedonistic instincts. First, allow the dumpling to cool off for a good five minutes, or the cascade of soup will scald your taste buds. Then just pop the whole thing in your mouth. Allow your tongue to bathe in the juices as you chew on the meat. Try not to moan.

The secret to getting that soup into the dumpling lies not in syringes or other surgical equipment. The rich pork broth is simply chilled to form aspic, which is then cut into small blocks and tucked into the dumplings together with the meat. The beauty of dumplings like *xiaolongbao* is that just about anything can be stuffed into a wheat dough casing, sealed, boiled and popped into the mouth, and China has come up with a huge variation.

🍲 **WHERE TO EAT NAN XIANG XIAOLONG MANTOU
85 YUYUAN LAO LU, SHANGHAI**

Near Chenghuang Temple in Shanghai's old town, this dumpling restaurant is more than 100 years old, and the classic introduction to the city's iconic *xiaolongbao*.

ABOVE Bamboo baskets are used to steam and present pork dumplings **LEFT** It's not uncommon to see a family elder working all afternoon in the kitchen, stuffing and wrapping traditional dumplings by hand

JIAO ZI
Craft pork and cabbage dumplings.

INGREDIENTS
300g/11oz Chinese cabbage

2 tsp salt

250g/9oz minced pork

1 tbsp minced ginger

3 tbsp chopped chives

½ tsp white pepper powder

1 tbsp rice wine

1 tbsp sesame oil

1 tbsp cornflour

FOR THE WRAPPER
2 cups plain flour

½ cup water

PREPARATION
Shred and salt the cabbage and set aside for 20 minutes.

If making your own wrappers, mix the flour and water and knead until smooth and elastic, adding flour or water to achieve a firm but pliable texture. Cover tightly with plastic wrap and set aside.

Squeeze the moisture from the cabbage, rinse in cold water, repeat. Then squeeze again – you want the cabbage to be reduced to a dry handful or two. Mix the remaining ingredients with the cabbage.

For the wrapper-makers... pinch a good teaspoon of dough and roll into a ball. With a flour-dusted roller and a well-floured bench, roll the ball into a flat, thin disk 10cm/4in in diameter. Repeat until you have a stack.

Place a teaspoon of the filling into the centre of a wrapper. Wet the outside edges with water, fold in half and pinch the edges of the half moon you've made, to make it a tight, airless parcel. Repeat until out of wrappers or filling – it will happen eventually!

Fill a large pot with water and bring it to the boil. Drop in your dumplings and cook for about 10 minutes. Serve with a dipping sauce of two parts black vinegar, one part soy sauce and roasted chilli paste to taste.

TOFU WITH SHIITAKE AND GINGER

INGREDIENTS

5–6 large dried shiitakes, soaked in a little warm water until soft

250g/9oz silken tofu, cubed

1 cup water

1 tbsp soy sauce

Pinch salt

Pinch sugar

1 tbsp cornflour

Several drops sesame oil

2 tbsp peanut or vegetable oil

1 small red capsicum, sliced

3cm/1in ginger, shredded or grated

1 small red chilli, deseeded and sliced

3 green onions in 2cm/1in lengths

PREPARATION

Squeeze the shiitakes and reserve soaking water. Cut off stems and discard. Slice the caps finely. Make a sauce by boiling the water, soy, salt and sugar. Use a little of the mushroom-soaking liquid to dissolve the cornflour, and whisk this runny paste into the simmering sauce. Bring back to the boil whisking constantly, stir in sesame oil then keep to one side.

In a wok or very hot pan heat the oil and fry strips of the red capsicum. Add the ginger and chilli and stir-fry a minute longer. Pop in the onion and stir-fry for another 30 seconds. Add any remaining mushroom-soaking water and boil dry, add tofu, sliced shiitakes and sauce you made earlier. Bring to a simmer and serve with steamed rice. Serves two or three.

TOFU
THE ULTIMATE VEGETARIAN PROTEIN

After paper, gunpowder and the compass, tofu is China's greatest invention. Eaten on a daily basis all over China, the easily digestible, highly nutritious and cheap plant-based protein is one of the country's most versatile foods. Soft, solid, watery, fermented, dried, fried and sweetened, it can be transformed into any number of dishes.

Tofu is simply coagulated soy milk. The curds are pressed into the desired density and shape, most typically into smooth white blocks. The texture can be manipulated to become hard as bricks or soft as a semisolid porridge. Far from being bland and unappetising, tofu in China is never humdrum. It's a comfort food, whether as a bowl of *douhua* for breakfast, a spicy *mapo doufu* with rice for lunch, or a stir-fried *dougan* (dried tofu) for dinner. The tofu pudding *douhua* is tiny pieces of soft tofu in water flavoured with strong pickles and pork floss, or in a thin syrup with granulated sugar as a dessert. Eating the delicate silken *douhua* is like eating pieces of butter that's just starting to melt.

Then there's stinky tofu, a popular street food that's prepared slightly differently around the country. Traditionally, stinky tofu is fermented, but what you find on the streets of China nowadays is mostly fresh tofu that's been steeped in brine for a few days to absorb the smell, described as somewhere between sewage and garbage. Urban legends of stinky tofu being made from actual garbage are unwarranted. The fermented brine is in fact a hodgepodge of herbs, vegetables and seafood shells left to sit. Stinky tofu is usually deep-fried to a golden brown and served with various condiments.

♨ WHERE TO EAT HUOGONGDIAN RESTAURANT
78 POZI ST, TIANXIN DISTRICT, CHANGSHA

Changsha specialises in a black version of stinky tofu, thanks to the signature fermented brine. Order a plate at Huogongdian with a bright red chilli sauce.

TOP LEFT Delicate and light, shiitake mushroom and tofu broth is the perfect winter warmer **ABOVE** Tofu varies in flavour, density and texture depending on how it is produced

HOT POT
CHINESE-STYLE FONDUE

Hot pot is a communal dining experience with a 1000-year-old history. Friends and family gather around a wide, shallow pot full of boiling-hot broth and take turns to dip raw food into the oil to cook. It can be a humble winter meal for a time-squeezed family, the boiling pot doing double duty as a space heater, or it can be an extravagant feast with a buffet of raw foods including abalone, *Wagyū* beef or rare mushrooms sliced into bite-sized pieces. Meat needs to be paper-thin to reduce the cooking time; green leafy vegetables are saved for the end of the meal; and noodles go in last to absorb the broth, which becomes a rich stock after a night of dipping meat and seafood into it.

Chongqing-style hot pot is in a class of its own. The numbingly spicy *ma la* soup base is so addictive, it should come with a warning. While Cantonese *da been lo*, literally meaning 'to strike the edge of the pot', doesn't have the headiness of *ma la*, it spotlights ultrafresh seafood, small dumplings and meatballs.

Mongolian-style mutton hot pot sent men off to war. According to legend, Genghis Khan's army chefs improvised a meal of paper-thin lamb blanched in boiling water that could be eaten quickly before battle. When Kublai Khan established the Yuan Dynasty in 1279, he brought mutton hot pot with him. Traditional Mongolian hot pot is eaten using a copper cooking vessel heated by coals. Slivers of mutton marbled with fat are dipped in boiling water for just a few seconds. Condiments are typical of the north: pickled onions, raw scallions, sesame paste, tofu and coriander.

🍲 **WHERE TO EAT DALONG HUOGUO**
DIANTAI LANE, XIAOLONGKAN, SHAPINGBEI DISTRICT, CHONGQING
Hard-to-find Dalong Huoguo is Chongqing's famed hot-pot spot. It doesn't have signage; follow the crowds who flock here for the spicy broth and fresh ingredients.

ABOVE Taking communal eating to the next level, diners take turns dipping fresh ingredients into the steaming broth to consume them as they're cooked

MA LA

Eating *ma la* puts you somewhere between pain and pleasure. *Ma* means 'numbing' and *la* means 'spicy', and that is exactly what this sauce is – a hot and spicy flavouring that creates a numbing sensation. The Sichuan peppercorns make your lips tingle and swell, and a generous amount of chilli provokes a surge of endorphins, leaving you panting as your tongue is set on fire. No wonder the Chinese are completely hooked on this irresistible sauce.

Sichuan and Chongqing regional cuisines are famous for their *ma la* sauce, which headlines any feast in the region. There are flavours of fermented bean sauce, and a bouquet of star anise, cardamom and fennel provides a sweet aftertaste even as the chilli onslaught continues.

A popular way to try *ma la* is *shuizhuyu*. Slices of fish are poached in a broth, then covered in chilli oil and heaps of Sichuan peppercorns. Another crowd-pleaser is *fuqi feipian* – slices of beef and offal covered in a Sichuan-style chilli sauce that's high on the spice meter. A plate of *mapo doufu* will convert anyone who doesn't like tofu into a fan. Super-soft tofu is cooked with minced pork and a *ma la* sauce that should be powerfully hot. For those who want to take it down a notch, try the *laziji*, fried chicken pieces flavoured with Sichuan peppercorns and hidden under a mountain of red chillies. It looks intimidating but is relatively forgiving.

For authentic Sichuan food in Chengdu, visit Chenmapo Doufu, literally 'Pockmarked grandma Chen's tofu shop'. Apart from the *mapo doufu*, this purveyor of all things *ma la* also serves excellent *fuqi feipian*, Sichuan cold noodles, *kungpao* chicken and *shuizhuyu*.

School children break
from their lessons to enjoy
a hot bowl of noodles

≈≈

NOODLES
MEAN MIAN

Mian **are noodles** served throughout China, and the regional variations are legion. Hand-pulled, the noodles are made by repeatedly stretching and folding the dough. The chef divides the dough into ever-finer strands, pulling them over and over again, using the dough's own weight to stretch the strands longer and thinner. Dedicated *la mian* masters perform the famous noodle dance, where strands of noodles fly around like ribbons, much like a pizza chef throwing pizza dough. The resulting noodles are then cooked *al dente*.

In northern provinces, noodles are white, glutinous and made from wheat flour. The water from boiling the noodles, called *miantang* or 'noodle soup', is drunk as a digestive. In the south, noodles are made with rice or mung-bean starch, and worked into fine threads. *Mian* can be anything from a quick fix from a styrofoam bowl to food for auspicious events: on birthdays longevity noodles, *changshoumian,* are eaten to symbolise a long, healthy life.

The world's oldest bowl of noodles dates back 4000 years, unearthed at the Lajia archaeological site on the banks of the Yellow River. Considering their age, the noodles are surprisingly refined. Made from two types of millet, a similar noodle can be found today in China's noodle province, Shanxi, where China's most obsessive noodle chefs can be found. It's said that even regular home cooks in Shanxi know how to make dozens of types of noodles from scratch. Being a northern province, Shanxi's noodles are made from basic wheat-flour dough. But there is nothing basic about the resulting noodles. There are 300 types of Shanxi noodles, each made with a different tool and a different action. Cat's ear noodles, *mao'erduo,* are made by pinching off tiny pieces of dough to resemble little ears. Another noodle is made by using a chopstick to simply flick off small pieces of the dough.

The most famous Shanxi noodle is *daoshaomian,* knife-cut noodles. A block of dough is supported by the noodle master's forearm while the other hand rapidly shaves off flat, short noodles into a pot of water at a rolling boil. Shaving off about 200 noodles per minute, a *daoshaomian* master is a whirlwind in action, with one noodle hitting the water, one flying through the air and one just leaving the knife, creating a show for customers. Many upscale Shanxi noodle restaurants feature open kitchens specifically so customers can watch the *daoshaomian* master in action. The noodles are typically eaten without a soup base, and are instead tossed with diced meat, pickles, sprouts and Shanxi's other famous product, *laochencu,* aged Shanxi vinegar.

A classic mixture of Sichuan flavours is used to make fiery *dandanmian* noodles: pickled mustard, sprouts, chilli oil, Sichuan peppercorn, minced pork and sometimes sesame paste. These Sichuan noodles were traditionally sold from baskets dangling on the ends of a long bamboo pole that the noodle vendor would carry on his shoulders.

Jook sing noodles are a fast-disappearing type of noodle from Guangdong. Made with duck eggs and flour, the noodle must be pressed with a long bamboo pole. The noodle chef balances on one end of the pole and hops up and down on it to apply pressure to the dough. The acrobatics of this method make it highly labour intensive and few people practise it today – making *jook sing* noodles all the more coveted.

🍲 **WHERE TO EAT TAI YUAN NOODLE SHOP**
5 JIEFANGJUN RD, YINGZE DISTRICT, SHANXI
The sight of chefs making noodles by hand is a Shanxi signature in China's noodle capital, Taiyuan, and this is a classic place to order a bowl of traditional *daoshaomian*.

DANDAN NOODLES
Spicy, numbing, satisfying... these Szechuan noodles are a must in your comfort-food repertoire.

INGREDIENTS
800g/28oz fresh Shanghai-style noodles or udon

500g/17oz minced pork

3 tbsp peanut oil

2 tbsp minced garlic

3 tbsp minced ginger

2 tbsp Chinese rice wine

300mL/10fl oz chicken stock

3 tbsp soy sauce

3 tbsp Chinese sesame seed paste (or tahini)

2 tbsp ground Sichuan peppercorns

3 tbsp chilli oil (or to taste)

3 tsp sesame oil

1 tsp sugar

Salt to taste

½ cup roasted peanuts, finely chopped

3 spring onions, finely sliced

PREPARATION
Bring a large pot of water to boil and cook the noodles according to package instructions.

Drain the noodles, rinse under cold water, and drain again. Put to the side.

Heat oil in a large frying pan or wok, add pork, and stir to break up lumps of meat separate until lightly browned.

Add ginger and garlic; and cook for another 3 minutes or so.

Stir in remaining ingredients except the salt, spring onions and peanuts; simmer until reduced to a thick meaty gravy. Taste for salt and add accordingly.

Refresh noodles under hot running water then put into bowls and top with a generous serve of the pork.

Garnish with spring onions and pork mixture over noodles; garnish with peanuts and scallions. Serves 4.

DIFFERENT DUMPLINGS

At their most basic, dumplings are known as *jiao zi* (see p17). Many Chinese families gather at midnight on the eve of Chinese New Year to make these dumplings resembling gold ingots and symbolising prosperity for the coming year.

Pan-fried dumplings are *guotie* – literally, 'pot stickers'. When pork is incorporated into the wrappers and the dumplings are the size of a thumbnail, they are Fujianese *rouyan*.

In Hong Kong, people gobble down half a dozen shrimp wontons in a sitting. In Sichuan, it is all about the crescent-moon-shaped *longchaoshou* swimming in chilli oil.

Dumplings have travelled too. In Japan you'll find *gyoza* (a word related to Chinese *guotie*), generally a daintier version of its Chinese forbear. In Nepal, you won't go far before meeting *momos* (see p311), the ubiquitous high-altitude dumpling. It's also not a stretch to see where a connection can be found with ravioli, the queen of Italian pasta.

⁀
DIM SUM
THE TRIUMPH OF THE SNACK

These little steam baskets of dumplings were originally created as snacks to accompany tea, the drinking of which was the main event. The term dim sum means 'to gently touch the heart' – not stuff the stomach. Over time, the supporting act stole the show, and while good-quality tea is still important for a dim-sum meal, the food itself has become a fully fledged subcuisine particular to Guangdong and Hong Kong.

Until recently, dim sum was sold from mobile carts pushed around a restaurant. This dictates a slow pace of eating as steam baskets of food are ordered one by one from passing carts. It made the dim-sum meal an ideal format for long family brunches on weekends. Few restaurants use cart service nowadays but the family gatherings continue and the rowdy atmosphere remains.

In a dim-sum meal, southern Chinese culinary wisdom is on full display like a peacock on the make. There are too many classic dishes to squeeze on a page, but they include the notoriously difficult to make shrimp dumplings, *har gow,* that arrive at the table looking like plump oversized pearls, the pink glow of the shrimp showing through the translucent white skins. Another classic is *cheung fun,* the bundles of meat and vegetables wrapped in silk-like sheets of rice noodle that unbelievably resist tearing. Any remaining appetite is usually sated with a fluffy, white steamed bun filled with sweet and smoky barbecue pork or velvety lotus-seed paste and preserved egg yolks.

Dim-sum restaurants compete to create the best new dish, inventing food combinations and creations that sound exotic even to Chinese people. Dumplings and buns take the shape of swans, rabbits, hedgehogs and goldfish, or take your pick of pickled mustard barbecue-pork buns, deep-fried sticky rice (*nuomiji*), lobster and shark's fin dumplings, soup dumplings stuffed with bamboo shoots and bird's nest, foie-gras pastries...

🍴 WHERE TO EAT

Enjoyed 24 hours a day, from a light snack from a streetside vendor to a meal that stretches over several hours, Hong Kong is a city of dim sum. For an old-school experience, check out Lin Heung Teahouse at 160–164 Wellington St, Central. Opened in 1912, it is renowned for its old-fashioned pork dim sum, such as pork-liver *siu mai,* and has the best lotus-seed-paste buns in town.

Or visit Tim Ho Wan at Shop 12A, Hong Kong Station, Central. Known as the world's cheapest Michelin-starred restaurant, this no-frills dim-sum eatery makes shockingly good *lo mai gai,* the sticky rice that is wrapped in a lotus leaf, and barbecue pork stuffed in a sweet pastry.

For some pampering, the service is incomparable at Lung King Heen, a swanky dim-sum restaurant with a panoramic view of Victoria Harbour. Lobster dumplings are served in individual steam baskets and *cheung fun* are stuffed with grouper.

RIGHT Dumplings shaped like money bags **ABOVE LEFT** Dim-sum dining is one of China's most popular exports, but Hong Kong is the place to sample the best

TEA
MORNING, NOON AND NIGHT

Tea permeates life in China. Often, a freshly brewed cup to wake the senses is the first liquid people drink upon rising, and tea is drunk constantly throughout the day. Instead of sipping water, people stuff a bunch of green tea leaves into a large glass that is continuously topped up with hot water, the tea growing weaker as the day progresses. In the evening, after dinner, black fermented teas believed to aid digestion are drunk.

For Tibetans and Mongolians, tea is almost a staple food. Drunk salty, with pungent yak butter for the former and cream for the latter, the *suyoucha* provides many calories and nutrients.

The tea connoisseur's appreciation of tea is as complex and detailed as that of wine. Tea can be dried, heated, smoked, pressed, fermented and scented with flowers, and the more than 320 strains of tea in China are categorised according to way they are processed.

And tea isn't just for drinking. In tea-rich areas, tea imbues food with grassy, floral and smoky notes. The prized Hangzhou *longjing cha,* 'dragon-well tea', has one of the richest flavours of China's green teas. The best crop is *mingqian longjing,* harvested before the Ching Ming festival that falls in April. It is processed by a sort of dry stir-frying to extract the moisture. As a result, the flavour is slightly smoky and savoury, perfect for cooking with prawns in *hangzhou longjing xiaren* or thrown into scrambled eggs.

In Yunnan, *pu'er* is the sought-after tea. The dark fermented tea is drunk plain, appreciated for its mellow taste and heavy mouth feel, and is believed to aid digestion and weight loss. The latest fad in Yunnan is to use *pu'er* tea to cook rice, imbuing it with the purported slimming benefits as well as a subtle woodsy aroma. China's *oolong* tea mecca is arguably Fujian, home to *tieguanyin*, Iron Buddha. It is also where you can find the Wuyi Mountains. This protected area is the native land of lapsang souchong, *wuyi yancha* and the last remaining mother trees of *dahongpao*. Naturally, Wuyi cuisine incorporates tea leaves into dishes, the best of which is an incredible tea-smoked duck.

🍽 WHERE TO DRINK HU XIN TING
YU YUAN XIN LU, SHANGHAI, HUANGPU DISTRICT

Sip from a glass or porcelain cup at Hu Xin Ting Teahouse. Situated in the middle of a lake, this two-storey tea house is nearly 150 years old. Sure, it's smack in the center of Shanghai's most touristy, crowded Yu Yuan Garden, but that is what makes the serenity inside Hu Xin Ting that much more striking. When in Hangzhou, any tea house is a good bet for variety and service, but head to Taiji Teahouse at 184 Hefang Street for a kung fu tea show where the server will literally bend over backward to pour your tea.

📖 LEARNING

INTREPID TRAVEL
This Western tour operator offers culinary tours of China, including the China Gourmet Traveller where you can sample and learn to cook a variety of regional cuisines.

MARTHA SHERPA'S COOKING SCHOOL
In Hong Kong, head to Martha Sherpa's Cooking school. Located in Mongkok where the street eats are plentiful, the school teaches students how to make dim sum, Chinese bread and more.

XINJIANG GRAPE FESTIVAL
Head to the grape valley in Turpan, Xinjiang, in August and help harvest grapes. The arid region produces some of the sweetest fruit in China, sold fresh, dried into raisins or made into a sickly sweet dessert wine.

HUTONG SCHOOL
The Hutong School in Beijing is hosted in a traditional courtyard home and teaches regional cuisines. Private classes and wet market tours can be arranged.

LEFT Tea pouring is a performance at Lao She tea house in Beijing **TOP RIGHT** Harvesting grapes in the Bortala Mongol prefecture

PEKING DUCK

China's emperors may be long gone but you can appreciate their legacy at home with the help of a fat duck.

INGREDIENTS

1 whole duck
3L/100fl oz water
5 tbsp honey
2 tbsp minced ginger
4 tbsp dark soy sauce
150mL/5fl oz Chinese cooking wine
3 star anise
2 spring onions (sliced)
Peking duck pancakes

PREPARATION

Take the duck and trim any excess fat and skin from around the cavity openings. Pat it dry with paper towels.

Gently slip your fingers between the skin and the flesh of the duck and probe your way around until the skin is as unattached as you can make it without actually removing it.

Pierce the neck end of the duck with a meat hook (or thread a doubled length of strong twine through the neck skin to create a strong hanging loop).

Combine the water with the honey, ginger, dark soy, star anise and cooking wine in a large pot and bring the mixture to the boil.

Holding the duck by the hook or string over a bowl, ladle the boiling liquid over the body. It should take on a light brown colour.

Find a cool dry place to hang the duck for five hours or so. The skin should be firm and dry to touch.

Place the duck on a rack in a baking dish. Add a couple of cups of water to the dish and put in a 240°C/465°F oven for 20 minutes. Decrease the oven temperature to 180°C/350°F and cook for another hour.

Break or cut the skin into pieces, likewise the meat. To eat, wrap a morsel of meat and skin in a pancake with chopped spring onions and dip into hoisin sauce. Serves four.

PEKING DUCK
IMPERIAL FAVOURITE

If China had to be represented by one dish, it would be Peking duck. Everything about Beijing's iconic dish screams decadence, from the tableside carving of the bird to the fact that only the best parts – skin, fat and a bit of meat – are eaten. No wonder the imperial courts kept Peking duck to themselves. The recipe was developed in the Yuan dynasty, and the expertly roasted birds only made their way to the tables of China's gentry in the 1700s.

Preparing Peking duck is a lengthy, laborious craft, testament to the genius of northern Chinese cooking. The magic starts with the careful breeding and force-feeding of young ducks, hence the Chinese name *beijing tianya* – literally, 'Beijing stuffed ducks'. Once the duck is slaughtered, air is blown under the skin to separate it from the fat. A glaze is then applied, made according to each restaurant's secret recipe. After hanging to dry for a day, the duck is roasted, hung by its neck, in either an open or closed oven powered by wood. Every so often, the duck must be shifted by hand so it is evenly exposed to the heat. The result is red-lacquered skin like the varnish of an ancient violin, and tender juicy meat.

All that labour doesn't end with the preparation of the duck. To serve, the meat is carved into bite-sized slices, then rolled in a paper-thin pancake with spring onion, sweet bean sauce and julienned cucumber. Use your hands to roll and eat Peking duck – chopsticks are impossible – and savour the slight burst of fat as you bite into the crackling duck skin, the sharply pungent spring onion and nutty sweet sauce.

☙ WHERE TO EAT

Authentic Peking duck can be found in nearly any Beijing restaurant worth its salt, but there are a few household names to keep in mind. Bianyifang on the historic old street Xianyukou is the oldest Peking-duck restaurant, established in 1416. Another tip for excellent duck is Da Dong Restaurant at Jinbao Dasha, Jinbao Jie, Dongcheng District.

ABOVE Carved in front of diners and assembled by hand, Peking duck pancake has become synonymous with Chinese cooking and has won die-hard fans across the globe

̰̰̰
HONGSHAO ROU
RED-COOKED PORK

Red is considered an auspicious colour in China, and the hue comes into its own with *hongshao rou*. Although more brown than crimson, *hongshao rou* is pork that's been slow-cooked in soy sauce, Shaoxing wine, sugar and spices. Hence the euphemistic name 'red-cooked pork'. You can use the *hongshao* cooking method to prepare all kinds of meats and meat cuts, as is the case in Wuxi where the *hongshao* cuisine has a sweeter, more caramelised flavour. Wu-style spare ribs are so sweet they're practically candied meat.

Each household has its own closely guarded *hongshao* recipe, and cooks argue over which flavour to add first, sugar or soy sauce, and whether to include star anise or chilli or keep it spice-free and mild. Another version is *dongpo rou,* a red-cooked pork-belly dish named after the Song-dynasty poet Su Dongpo. A gourmand, the poet allegedly made it his mission to improve traditional *hongshao rou* by adding Chinese yellow wine to create the resulting sweet, salty and aromatic meat.

A star of Hangzhou's highly refined cuisine, *dongpo rou* is served as one large chunk of pork belly cut into a near perfect cube. The alternating layers of fat and meat should glisten with sauce, but not be mushy or falling apart. It should look solid, yet when the chopsticks hit the meat, it should give way as easily as tofu. The pork will have absorbed the sauce and turned almost purple. The best *dongpo rou* is never stodgy, and the dish is as much about the fat as the meat. The ideal *dongpo rou* fat is light and full of flavour, leaving the mouth feeling clean, not greasy – like an intensely pork-flavoured gelatine.

⬦ WHERE TO EAT HUODIANGONG
93 WUYI EAST RD, FURONG DISTRICT, HUNAN

Changshu's must-try restaurant remains Huodiangong, once a temple to the fire god. Order gloriously fatty Mao-style hongshao rou.

ABOVE Slow cooked *hongshao rou* is usually low on chilli and spices, making it gentle on the taste buds
TOP RIGHT The refreshing and light Tsingtao beer is the perfect accompaniment for many Chinese dishes

ALCOHOLIC DRINKS
Beer is cheap, refreshing and goes well with any type of Chinese food, so no wonder the country is the world's biggest consumer of lager. Many provinces have their own label, without much discernible difference in the mild and generally weak taste. Tsingtao is the most famous, made from a brewery in Qingdao, a former German concession that inherited beer culture. Black beers from Xinjiang and Heilongjiang, called *heipi*, have a pleasant wheatiness, while Inner Mongolia makes milk beer and Beijing has a pineapple beer. *Baijiu* is the banquet drink. A spirit made from sorghum, it can reach 65% proof. The taste has been compared to rubbing alcohol, but better brands, like Maotai, can be sweet and aromatic.

MAO'S HONGSHAO ROU
Proving the allure of *hongshao rou*, the Great Helmsman himself was one of its fans. Mao-style *hongshao rou* is a rustic variation: the skin of the pork belly isn't cooked to as soft a texture as elsewhere, and less sugar is used.

Mao Tse-tung believed that fatty meats help nourish the brain, and in his native province Hunan, the official line is that the Chairman owed his entire success to this one heart-stopping dish. The Hunan provincial government has tried to standardise the recipe for this dish, though diners have largely ignored its efforts.

Making noodles is a performance at the International Noodle Festival, Shanxi

CHINESE FESTIVALS

Noodles, grapes, edible chrysanthemums and even the humble hairy crab: all get their own festival in China and its regions. For the vistor these are opportunites to not only try the dish of the day but experience the distinct local culture.

JANUARY

Long Street Banquet
In the Honghe Prefecture of Yunnan Province, a street banquet is held by the Hani ethnic people, complete with singing and dancing.

APRIL

Shanxi Jinshang (Shanxi Merchant) Flour Food Festival
Locally famous chefs make dishes from flour for competition, and also for festival goers to taste.

MAY–JULY

Sichuan International Delicacy Festival
In Sichuan's capital, Chengdu, the local hotel and restaurant associations feature famous Sichuan dishes and snacks. There's a contest to vote for the best Sichuan hot-pot dishes.

JUNE

Colourful International Delicacy Festival (Shandong)
At Yantai, where much of China's better wines are produced, China's eight major cuisine styles are highlighted. There's also the Zhonghua Shandong Cuisine Culture Symposium and a tour showcasing Shandong cuisine.

National Dragon Boat Invitation Tournament & Zongzi Delicacy Culture Festival (Jiangsu)
In the ancient canal of Changzhou (Dragon City), six dragon-like boats race each other across White Cloud Stream. The local government holds the Zongzi Delicacy Culture Festival to promote traditional local foods.

AUGUST

Ordos Delicacy Festival
At Ordos near Dongsheng in Inner Mongolia, the Zhama Banquet re-creates the grandest palace banquet of the ancient Mongolians, combining food, singing, dancing and sport.

Grape Festival
In Xinjiang Autonomous Region, this season finds many Uyghur wedding ceremonies, as well as a Hami melon contest and Turpan's grape festival. A street of grapes and melons stands on the northern end of the former Silk Road.

Qingdao International Beer Festival
On the second weekend of August, Qingdao hosts Asia's largest beer festival. Brewers from around the world come here to celebrate China's beer-drinking culture, and taste Tsingtao, brewed locally.

SEPTEMBER

International Noodle Festival
Shanxi shows off its expertise in handmade noodles with cooking demonstrations and crash courses available for participants.

Yangcheng Lake Hairy Crab Festival
From September to December is the time to eat fat hairy crabs from Yangcheng Lake, prized for their rich-tasting reproductive organs.

OCTOBER

Shantou 'Chaoshan Delicacy Festival'
The largest food festival in east Guangdong showcases Chiu Chow cuisine.

Henan Kaifeng Chrysanthemum Banquet
The annual chrysanthemum fair focuses on the folk culture of the Song Dynasty. Part of the festival is the traditional chrysanthemum banquet, including chrysanthemum dumplings, cakes and tea.

NOVEMBER

Hong Kong Food & Wine Month
The month-long eating fest includes a food expo and wine festival attracting hundreds of exhibitors from around the world. Take advantage of the free tastings of gourmet foods and fine wines.

Where once fish were landed at Saint-Goustan's port in Brittany, now diners enjoy the setting

FRANCE

Home is where the heart is, and France is it for food lovers everywhere. Its creation of the concept of cuisine, the famed produce, the equally famous chefs – it may not have invented cooking, but it sure put the art into it.

Take a sensual waltz through aromatic street markets bursting with local produce, sun-baked olive groves tended by third-generation farmers, ancient truffle estates and vineyards that mirror to exacting perfection the beauty of each season. Cruising around the country that coined the word 'cuisine' – no other language could handle all the nuances – inspires hunger, gastronomic know-how and experimental adventure.

Few Western cuisines are as envied, so aspired to, or as seminal as the food of France, celebrated for its use of fresh ingredients, regional variety and signature cooking methods. And no country so blatantly bundles up its cuisine with the notion of *terroir* (land), or makes dining an experience so tightly tied to place and people.

'*Le jardin de France*' (the garden of France) has been exploited ever since the writer Rabelais coined the poetic phrase in the 16th century to describe his native Touraine.

Yet it is the serene valley tracing the course of the River Loire west of the French capital that remains most true to the Rabelaisian image of a green and succulent landscape laden with fruits, flowers, nuts and vegetables. It was in the Renaissance kitchens of this region's celebrated chateaux that French cooking was refined: poultry and game dishes were the kitchens' pride and joy, and once or twice a year a fattened pig was slaughtered and prepared dozens of different ways – roasts, sausages, *boudin* (black pudding), *charcuterie* (cold meats) and pâtés. No single part, offal et al, was wasted.

Two natural factors determine the brilliant diversity of contemporary French food: season and geography see the hot south favour olive oil, garlic and tomatoes; the cooler, pastoral regions of northern France turn to cream and butter; while the Mediterranean and Atlantic coasts are awash with mussels, oysters, saltwater fish and other seafood.

FONDUE SAVOYARDE

The ultimate après-ski treat is from the Savoie region of the Alps.

INGREDIENTS

1 garlic clove

200g/7oz Gruyère cheese

200g/7oz Beaufort cheese

200g/7oz Comté cheese

Half a bottle of Savoie white wine

1 tsp nutmeg (freshly grated)

Shot glass of Kirsch

Black pepper

Baguette

PREPARATION

Peel the garlic clove and rub it around the inside of a *caquelon* (a glazed ceramic pot with a thick handle – a cast-iron saucepan is fine). Discard the clove.

Pour in the wine and bring it to a boil before turning down the heat to a simmer. Grate the cheeses and add them to the pot, stirring continuously with a wooden spoon as it melts. Ensure it doesn't boil or burn (this is why a heavy-bottomed pan is essential).

When the cheese is melted, add a few grates of nutmeg, some ground pepper to taste and the dash of kirsch. If you don't have a fondue pot, stand and spirit lamp (it's not the 1970s so why would you?) you can reheat the fondue when it cools.

Swirl cubes of the bread around the pot to stop the cheese solidifying. Enjoy with a nice Savoie white wine (but not water, which can cause indigestion). Serves four.

CHEESE
BLESSED ARE THE CHEESEMAKERS

No food product is a purer reflection of *terroir* than cheese, an iconic staple that – with the exception of most coastal areas – is made all over the country, tiny villages laying claim to ancient variations made just the way *grand-père* did it.

Chèvre, made from goat's milk, is creamy, sweet and faintly salty when fresh, but hardens and gets saltier as it matures. Among the best is Ste-Maure de Touraine, a mild creamy cheese from the Loire Valley; and Cabècou de Rocamadour from Midi-Pyrènèes, often served warm with salad or marinated in oil and rosemary.

Roquefort, a ewe's-milk veined cheese from Languedoc, is the king of blue cheeses and vies with Burgundy's pongy Époisses for the strongest taste award. Soft, white, orange-skinned Époisses, created in the 16th century by monks at Abbaye de Cîteaux, takes a month to make, using washes of saltwater, rainwater and Marc de Bourgogne – a local pomace brandy and the source of the cheese's final fierce bite.

Equal parts of Comté, Beaufort and Gruyère – a trio of hard fruity, cow-milk cheeses from the Alps – are grated and melted in a garlic-smeared pot with a dash of nutmeg, white wine and kirsch (cherry liqueur) to create fondue Savoyarde. Hearty and filling, this pot of melting deliciousness originated from the simple peasant need of using up cheese scraps and has become the chic dish to eat on the ski slopes.

Louis XV adored Vacherin Mont d'Or, a soft cheese packed in a box and the only one in France to be eaten with a spoon. Made with *lait cru* (raw milk) from August to March, it derives its unique nutty taste from the strip of spruce bark in which it's wrapped. In the 18th century it was called fat cheese, wood cheese or box cheese. Today, it bears the name of the mountain village in the Jura from which it originates. Connoisseurs spoon a hole in the soft-crusted cheese, fill it with finely chopped onion and garlic, cover it in white wine, wrap it in aluminium foil and bake it for 45 minutes to create a *boîte chaude* (hot box) – the perfect, alternative cheese fondue.

ABOVE Saint Nectaire cheese ripening in a cave in the Auvergne **ABOVE LEFT** The word fondue derives from the French word *fondre* (to melt) **RIGHT** There are more than 350 types of French cheeses

POILÂNE
ORIGINAL FRENCH BREAD

The bread line forms early at Poilâne, a Parisian *boulangerie* of doll's-house dimensions in the well-to-do 7e. The old-fashioned shop with its neat rows of sweet apple tartlets, raisin buns and croissants like crabs in the window is retro chic – as is the yesteryear ritual of buying its bread.

Nothing is more French than *pain* (bread). Starved peasants demanded bread on the eve of the French Revolution, when the ill-fated Queen Marie-Antoinette is purported to have said, 'Let them eat cake'. And bread today – no longer a matter of life or death but a cultural icon – accompanies every meal. Wheat fields shade vast swaths of agricultural land a gorgeous golden-copper hue in northern France.

Standing in line at Poilâne, its interior dating to 1932, is to experience bread-making history first-hand. Rows of round, sourdough *miches* sit on open shelves like a medieval still life. A mural illustrates step-by-step how the bread is made. From the ancient grindstone insisted upon by Poilâne's boutique miller to the flawless *sel de Guérande*, harvested from salt pans that shimmer silver in the Breton sun, little has changed. An electric mixer to knead dough is the only concession to modernity by this third-generation baker. Dark and gold-crusted, bread here is baked for an hour in wood-fired, brick bread ovens pioneered by Loire Valley Renaissance chateaux in the 16th century. Its taste: tangy, tart, nutty and deliciously chewy. Purchasing the 1.9kg loaf, emblazoned with a 'P' and sold by weight, is a gastronomic ritual. Female staff, dressed in linen beige dress-coats, wrap loaves in paper and pop them in brown bags with a satisfying crunch.

⚓ WHERE TO EAT LA CUISINE DE BAR, 8 RUE DU CHERCHE MIDI, PARIS

This modern space near the Poilâne bakery is an ode to the way its bread tastes best: as a *tartine* (toasted, open sandwich). Creative toppings include velvet foie gras, Bayonne ham drizzled with marjoram-infused olive oil, or simply sardines with butter and herbs.

UNE BAGUETTE, S'IL VOUS PLAIT MADAME

The iconic baguette is a modern creation that took off after WWII when the French, fed up with scant food and dark bread, rejoiced in the new-day freshness of the 250g white stick with a thick, flavoursome, well-baked crust and soft chewy interior.

No ritual is as dear to the French as the daily trip to the *boulangerie* where Madame holds court behind the counter, wrapping baguettes to go in thin, undersized white paper, while Monsieur works the ovens to ensure fresh bread all day. Ripping off the crunchy end and eating it on the way home is part of the charm.

The short knife-slits slashed diagonally across the obligatory 55cm-to-70cm length appeared in the 1850s, when bakers realised the need to release heated carbonic gas inside hot rising dough. In 1919 a law forbade bakers to work between 10pm and 4am, hence the need for a loaf that could be cooked quickly at dawn. Hail *la baguette!*

Top five tastings: fresh and on the rocks; smothered in Breton butter; next-day dry for breakfast dunked in a bowl of *café au lait* (milky coffee); stale, cubed and dipped in a cheese fondue; sliced, smothered in melted cheese and afloat traditional onion soup.

LEFT Bread-proofing baskets or *bannetons* **ABOVE** Lionel Poilâne gives a baking demonstration **ABOVE RIGHT** Baguettes have few preservatives and go stale within 24 hours – eat them while fresh

FOOD LOVER
ERIC RIPERT

French cuisine has had the most influence on me. **I learned the basics and techniques in France** at school and in French restaurants. When I go home I always have my mother's coq au vin.

At an early age, I lived in Andorra. Being so close to Barcelona, **Spanish food was also a huge part of my diet** and I love Mediterranean flavors.

Black truffle inspires me. I love cooking with it. It's a **mythical and mysterious** ingredient.

I have always been **attracted to Japanese cuisine and culture.** We get a lot of Japanese ingredients in New York and we learn a lot of techniques from their chefs. **Eric Ripert is head chef at Le Bernardin, New York, and a regular guest on *Top Chef.***

LEARNING

DOMAINE TRUFFIER DE SALEIX
Domaine de Saleix, Sorges
Hunt fresh truffles on this estate, championed as 'world truffle capital'.

FLOCONS DE SEL
Megève
Take a two-hour cookery workshop in the Alps with chef Emannuel Renaut.

2CV EXPERIENCE.COM
Ventabren
Grab the picnic basket and cruise vine-laced lanes in a Citroën 2CV.

TERRE DE SEL
Guérande
Wild walks through salt-rich marshes with a salt harvester or naturalist.

ÉCOLES DE TREBLEC
Maure-de-Bretagne
One-day crêpe-making courses, southwest of Rennes.

OMELETTE AUX TRUFFES
HUMBLE AND HEADY

Beat three eggs, season with salt, pepper and 15g of grated black truffle, then cook in a hot frying pan with a little olive oil or melted butter until set. To scramble, cook in a *bain-marie* with cream. Sprinkle with truffle shavings and serve. No recipe is simpler or more seductive than truffle omelette if you know the housewives' tricks like stashing raw egg and truffle mixture in an airtight container for several hours first. Two centuries ago, families celebrated New Year's Day with a *coq* (rooster; symbolising the coming year) stuffed with truffles or, in wealthier circles, served alongside 12 partridges (one for each month), truffles (symbolising night) and eggs (day).

A fungus that takes root underground at the foot of an elm or oak tree, the *truffe noir* (black truffle) is France's most luxurious and elusive culinary product, sniffed out by highly trained dogs in Provence and Dordogne in southern France. Unlike two centuries ago, truffles are fiendishly difficult to find today, hence their nicknames *diamants noir* (black diamonds) or *perle noir* de Périgord (Dordogne black pearl). The truffle-hunting season runs from late November to March; white French truffles, *truffe blanche d'été white* (summer truffle), are found between June and August, and are less tasty and cheaper.

⚇ WHERE TO EAT MARCHÉ DE TRUFFES
RICHERENCHES, 65KM NORTH OF AVIGNON

This wealthy village within a 12th-century Templar fortress hosts Provence's leading wholesale truffle market. On Saturday mornings in winter, listen for the furtive whispers of *rabassaïres* (truffle hunters) selling their harvest to dealers from Paris, Italy and beyond. The dealers inspect, weigh and bargain for the precious fungi from the back of their cars. *Courtiers* (brokers) mingle with the truffle hunters to scout out the best truffles – stashed away, mud-caked, in a decidedly unglamorous grubby plastic bag.

ABOVE One man and his trusty pig search for truffles in the Dordogne – pigs, like dogs, have an exceptional sense of smell and are similarly greedy, making them ideal truffle hunters

≈

ANDOUILLETTE LYONNAISE
LYON FOR FOOD LOVERS

Often dubbed France's gastronomic capital, the elegant city of Lyon, built by the Romans from two rivers and two hills near the Alps in southeast France, holds its own with inventive dishes and unique dining. As a prelunch *apéritif,* meander the kaleidoscopic aisles of Les Halles, an indoor food market where *charcutiers* (pork butchers) tempt with chewy slices of *saucisson de Lyon* (air-dried sausage) and salmon-pink *rosette* to taste. Knowing locals queue at Fromagerie La Mère Richard for a pongy round of St-Marcellin, ripened to gooey perfection. In winter there is no finer Sunday-morning pilgrimage than a glass of chilled white and a dozen shucked oysters at a *coquillage* (shellfish) stand.

At noon, grab a table with checked tablecloth in a *bouchon* (traditional Lyonnais bistro) and decipher the handwritten menu over a *communard,* a blood-red apéritif named after the fated supporters of the 1871 Paris Commune that mixes red Beaujolais wine with blackcurrant liqueur – a combo criminal elsewhere. Lovers of roast pork crackling will swoon over the *grattons* (chunks of pork fat fried to a crisp) to nibble.

Tablier de sapeur (breaded, fried tripe) is a meaty starter packed with character, but not a patch on the feisty main course: a beast of an over-sized sausage, *andouillette Lyonnaise* packs a punch with its rough-cut, pig-intestine-packed body and overwhelming, meaty aroma. Served in a cream or red wine sauce, the dish is rich – a love or hate affair.

······································

⚓ WHERE TO EAT MÈRE BRAZIER
12 RUE ROYALE, 1ER, LYON

Savour culinary history: Lyonnais *mère,* Eugène Brazier – one of several women who left bourgeois families to open kitchen-restaurants in Lyon and forge its reputation – opened here in 1921. Chef Mathieu Vianney has since reinvented the restaurant that earned Lyon's first trio of Michelin stars in 1933 (a copy of the original guide takes pride of place).

ABOVE *Charcutier* slicing cured ham at Bellota-Bellota restaurant and food store in Lyon – considered by many to be the culinary capital of France

CUISSES DE GRENOUILLES

They are one of the great icons of the French kitchen, yet in an ironic twist, the fiddly mass of pint-sized, finger-licking frog legs that end up on your plate in France – either *à la Provençale* (in garlicky, tomato sauce), *à la Grenobloise* (with lemon and capers) or pan-fried in butter the original way with garlic and parsley – are imported: to protect the green amphibian and its habitat, frog farming and wild harvesting has been banned in France since 1980.

Frog legs took off in the 10th century when monks persuaded church authorities to consider frogs as 'fish' to spice up meatless fast days. They became a national delicacy in 1908 after French chef Auguste Escoffier served them to the Prince of Wales at London's Savoy. With typical French flair, Escoffier called the dish *cuisses de nymphe à l'aurore* (dawn nymph thighs), a poetic name that naturally seduced every diner at the banquet, royalty included.

Soggy parts of France with lakes and marshland, such as Les Dombes in eastern France and the Vosges in northern France, remain loyal to culinary tradition. Frogs are imported from Southeast Asia and cooked as they have always been – in casseroles, on skewers or swimming in a dozen different sauces. '*Grenouilles fraîches*' (fresh frogs) on a menu indicates that the frogs arrived in France alive and kicking, and were then prepared locally. To try them at their best, hop over to chef Georges Blanc's Michelin-starred, 19th century auberge (inn) between Bresse and Les Dombes, where his homage to his grandmother Élisa has always been *cuisses de grenouilles en persillade* (frog legs sautéed in butter, garlic and parsley.

À LA PROVENÇALE
THE SUN-KISSED CUISINE

Lush with tomatoes, melons, cherries, peaches, olives, Mediterranean fish and Alpine cheese, Provencal cuisine emerged centuries ago out of the humble rhythm and natural cycle of a warm, mistral-blown land where farmers still gather at the weekly market to sell their fruit and vegetables, olives, woven garlic plaits and dried herbs displayed in stubby coarse sacks.

Olive oil, pressed in December from olives that start life as soft pink springtime blossoms, is vital. Savour its deep richness in *socca* (chickpea-flour pancake from Nice) or delight in its fruity greenness drizzled over fresh *chèvre* (goat's cheese). From the 5th century AD until the French revolution, the kings of France were baptised with olive oil from St-Rémy de Provence.

Garlic weds olive oil in Provencal cuisine. Planted in August, plucked from the soil the following June and strewn across the fields to dry for a few days before harvesting, woven garlands are piled high at summer markets. With oil it lets rip in ratatouille, that perennial Provencal favourite of stewed eggplant, zucchini and tomatoes; and in a clutch of fantastic strong-tasting sauces served with raw vegetables, soups and fish dishes. *Anchoïade* is an anchovy paste laced with garlic and olive oil; *brandade de morue* is a don't-mess-with-me mix of crushed salt cod, garlic and olive oil; and tapenade is a sharp, black-olive-based dip seasoned with garlic, capers, anchovies and olive oil.

On the coast, *aïoli* (potent garlic mayonnaise) is smeared over fish dishes and is essential to *aïoli Provençal complet* – a mountain of vegetables (including artichokes), boiled potatoes, a boiled egg and small shellfish. Fiery pink *rouille* (garlic mayonnaise with breadcrumbs and crushed chillies, hence its wild colour) is best friend to *soupe de poisson* (fish soup), served with bite-sized toasts, a pot of *rouille* – and a garlic clove. Rub the garlic over the toast, spread the *rouille* on top, bite it and breathe fire.

In 1929, chef Alain Bourguignon mapped France's regional specialities in his *Carte Gastronomique*, now a collector's item. Bourguignon located 279 dishes specific to Provence – *fruits confit* in Carpentras, *brandade* between Aubagne and Cassis – making it perhaps France's most diverse corner. But don't take his word for it; there's no more delicious way of spending a week or two than doing your own culinary cartography.

♨ WHERE TO EAT LA TABLE DE VENTABREN
1 RUE CÈZANNE, VENTABREN

Get lost in cobbled lanes watched by gold-stone cottages with wooden shutters to find this restaurant, hidden in a sleepy hilltop village west of Aix-en-Provence. Both cuisine (modern) and setting (canvas-canopied terrace looking out to mountains and starry horizon) are magical.

LEFT Lavender is not traditionally used in southern French cooking, but it's a common ingredient in the popular herb mix *herbes de Provence*

PISSALADIÈRE

This Provencal onion tart is thought to have been introduced by Roman cooks but it's become an iconic dish of southern France.

DOUGH
200g/7oz strong white-bread flour
1 tsp salt
2 tsp easy-blend dried yeast
150mL/5fl oz warm water
1 tbsp olive oil

TOPPING
4 tbsp olive oil
1kg/2lb onions, thinly sliced
Sprigs of thyme
2 tomatoes, skinned and chopped
2 x 80g/3oz cans of anchovy fillets
Handful of black olives

PREPARATION
Tip the flour, salt and yeast into a bowl. Pour in the water and oil and mix to a soft dough. Turn out on to a lightly floured surface and knead for five minutes until the dough is smooth and no longer sticky. Return the dough to the bowl, cover with cling film or a damp tea towel and leave it to rise for 45 to 90 minutes or until it springs back when pressed. Don't worry if it takes more or less time.

While the dough is rising, heat the oil in a large, deep frying pan, throw in the onions and fry gently for about 10 minutes until softened but not browned. Sprinkle in the thyme, salt and pepper and add the tomatoes. Stir well, cover and leave to cook for 45 minutes, until the onions are soft. Remove the lid for the last 10 minutes to reduce any liquid. Leave to cool.

Preheat the oven to 220°C/430°F. Lightly oil a shallow baking tray. Knead the dough again briefly, roll it out and press into the tin. Spread the onion mixture on the dough and arrange the anchovies in a criss-cross pattern on the top. Stud each window between the anchovies with an olive and bake for 25 to 30 minutes, until golden. Serve hot or cold.

RILLETTES

Walk into a back-to-basics wine bar in Paris – Le Baron Rouge in Bastille, for example – and the barman may push a plate of crusty bread and a pot of rillettes across the counter to accompany your glass of wine. Rillettes is shredded and preserved pork (or duck or goose) and makes perfect snack food. Stored under a layer of fat in an airtight Kilner jar, rillettes will keep in a cool pantry for months.

INGREDIENTS
1.5kg/3lb pork belly (rind removed)
Good-quality sea salt
Flavourings can include juniper berries or pepper corns, a bouquet garni with bay leaves, thyme and parsley or garlic

PREPARATION
With a very sharp knife, cut the pork belly into inch-wide strips. If you use boned shoulder of pork, you will need to add fat (in the form of caul or leaf lard). Put the meat and fat into a large, heavy-bottomed pan, with a bouquet garni, garlic or other flavourings, cover with water and bring to a very gentle simmer. Poach for about four hours.

When cool, shred the meat and fat (it should fall apart easily) into the pan, adding salt and pepper. Mash the fat into the meat to form a rough paste and transfer to individual ramekins, a larger dish or a sterilised Kilner jar for storage. Melt more pork fat or use lard to cover the top of the rillettes. Serve with a crusty baguette, some cornichons and a glass of wine.

TARTARE DE CHEVAL
ORIGINAL BISTRO DINING

On Friday morning in Paris' working-class 11e arrondissement, market vendors at the Marché Popincourt sell their produce with raucous shouts and cheeky smiles. Up the street at Aux Deux Amis, Mathieu Perez prepares lunch. Manipulating a butcher knife with precision and finesse, the bistro chef dices slabs of ruby-coloured rump steak at a speed that would have made his grandmother proud. His family recipe is the envy of many a gourmet carnivore who venerates his *tartare de cheval* as the tastiest in town.

Sweeter and milder-tasting than beef, horsemeat is the original ingredient for *tartare*, a 150g mound of raw chopped meat flavoured with finely cut shallots, capers, anchovies, fresh parsley, salt, pepper, wholegrain mustard and ketchup. The hard-core bistro classic gets its kick from the flick of a wrist of Worcester sauce and Tabasco, and its grace from a dash of olive oil. Pile the mix on a plate, sink an unbroken quail egg on top and serve with a green salad and pan-fried boiled potatoes. Few gastronomic thrills rival that of cracking open the egg, piercing the bulbous yolk and watching it spill marigold across the rich red *tartare. Viande de cheval* (horsemeat) – cheaper than beef, it was the poor man's red meat at the end of the 19th century – is enjoying a renaissance, and its historic contribution to the very specific culinary experience of Parisian bistro dining is unrivalled. *Pieds de cochon* (pig trotters), *soupe à l'ognion* (onion soup) and *rillettes* are other ancient pauper dishes that democratised dining out.

☕ WHERE TO EAT AUX DEUX AMIS
45 RUE OBERKAMPF, 11E, PARIS
Well-worn tiled floor, handwritten price list stuck in the window, menu scrawled on vintage mirrored wall behind the bar – this is your quintessential Parisian cafe-bar-bistro, retro enough to be hip and serving Paris' best *tartare de cheval* – only on Friday.

ABOVE The French bistro is where to taste simple farmhouse classics and affordable wine
ABOVE LEFT Serve rillettes with bread or toast

ESCARGOTS DE BOURGOGNE
CUISINE DU TERROIR

Clumsily manipulating snail tongs around a dozen black *escargots de Bourgogne*, the table lit by an 11th-century candlestick – dining in Burgundy is a gastronomic romp through history. The Romans planted vines, grain crops and mustard seed here, and in the 14th century the Dukedom of Burgundy, a land of ecclesiastical grandeur and celebrated vineyards in eastern France, was richer and more powerful than the kingdom of France itself. Its culinary legacy is *cuisine bourgeoise*, its holy trinity: beef, wine and Dijon mustard.

Snails – the shells stuffed with garlic and parsley butter, and baked in the oven – are a classic Burgundy starter. Prise out the earthy gastropod with the twin-tong snail fork, then mop up the puddle of oil with bread. Know the snail had a good life: *escargots de Bourgogne* feed on lush grape leaves. .

Handsome Charolais cows dot green fields white in southern Burgundy. Bred since the 18th century, the breed is famed for its beef, said to be so flavoursome because of the extra year of life these elegant white cattle are granted (six instead of five years before slaughter). Fortunately for world gastronomy, the meat of their hard-working predecessor, the Morvan cow, was not so baby-tender, hence the need for Burgundy peasants to tenderise the beef by simmering it in red wine with mushrooms, onions and bacon – enter *boeuf Bourguignon*. To completely overindulge in the rich earthy taste of this signature French classic, marinate the beef overnight in red wine before braising.

🍽 WHERE TO EAT LA BEURSAUDIÈRE
CHEMIN DE RONDE, NITRY

From copper pots strung on whitewashed walls to waiting staff in long black dress to chunks of beef sizzling on the farmhouse grill, this restaurant in rural Burgundy is a celebration of tradition.

ABOVE There are many edible snail species, but Burgundy snails are the most common in French cooking

BOEUF BOURGUIGNON

Burgundy's eponymous beef dish marries its light, low-tannin wines with the local Charolais cattle to create the ultimate in winter-warming stews. Buy a cheap cut such as braising (chuck) steak or shin; lean cuts will dry out during slow cooking, but fat and collagen in meat helps keep it moist. Add flavour by marinating the meat overnight in the wine, which is traditionally a Burgundy.

INGREDIENTS

1kg/2lb braising steak, roughly cubed

2 carrots, sliced

1 celery stalk, sliced

500g/1lb button mushrooms (cut larger mushrooms into squares)

1 onion, chopped

2 cloves of garlic, finely sliced

Bottle of light red wine

Bouquet garni (bay leaves, thyme, parsley)

Olive oil

PREPARATION

Heat olive oil in a large frying pan and add a few chunks of the beef at a time to brown. (Dry the meat with a paper towel first. Adding all the meat at once won't brown it.)

When all the meat is in the pan and brown, add the onion and garlic. When they have some colour, add the wine gradually so it boils, reduces and deglazes the pan. Transfer the contents of the pan to a large casserole dish, adding the bouquet garni, the mushrooms, and the sliced celery and carrot. Top up the casserole dish until the liquid is the same level as the meat. Cover and place in an oven preheated to around 160°C/320°F to cook gently for about two hours.

Check periodically and add more liquid if it's drying out. Season to taste. Serve with boiled potatoes, rice or pasta, accompanied by a bottle of good Burgundy red wine. Serves 4.

CASSOULET

No culinary dish better evokes the kitchen of Languedoc in southwest France than cassoulet, an earthy peasant stew of white beans and meat that fires passionate debate and should be treated with the reverence it deserves: Everyone knows exactly which type of bean and meat hunk should be thrown in the *caçolet* (in Occitan, *cassole* in French, hence the name), the traditional earthenware casserole dish in which this iconic dish is cooked and brought to the table, and it is bordering on blasphemy to dismiss it as just another stew. In the oft-quoted words of culinary author Prosper Montagné writing in 1929, it is 'the god of Occitan cuisine. The Castelnaudary version is God the Father, that of Carcassonne is God the Son, while Toulouse's is the Holy Spirit.'

The essence of any cassoulet, always served piping-hot, is lingots, prized white beans grown locally and soaked so that they just start to germinate and begin to taste a tad sweet. With them come juicy pork cubes, even bigger cylinders of meaty sausage and, in most variants, a hunk of duck or, in season, partridge. But each region and each chef who takes pride, will have their own variant. In Castelnaudary, it tends to be only pork. Carcassonne will add mutton. And the eclectic Toulouse variant will have both of these plus a wedge of its own, very special *saucisse de Toulouse*. Many a discerning chef will slip in goose or goose fat, a pig's trotter, pork rind or a hock of ham.

Whatever the ingredients, cooking is a long, slow simmer to ensure the different flavours meld, blend and mix harmoniously.

CONFIT DE CANARD & FOIE GRAS
SOUTHWEST SPECIALITIES

Never is there such a noise or commotion in Périgueux as on market day in winter. The chaotic sound of honking sets the tempo as ducks, geese, automobiles, vendors and buyers flock to the twice-weekly Marchés au Gras (literally 'Fat Market') on Place Saint Louis to surrender, sell and shop for fattened duck and goose livers – as has been done since the Middle Ages on this old-town square in the gourmet heart of Dordogne, a rolling countryside littered with historic castles in southwestern France.

Merchants set up their culinary wares on tables beneath vast tarpaulins, humming with the pungent smell of fat and smoked poultry. Unplucked geese and ducks go on sale, their scrawny wrung necks hanging long off the table like a thick white fringe. In one corner, what appears to be an anserine anatomy lesson is in progress, with every part of the cranky creature on offer: giblets, breast meat, wings, pinions, necks with or without skin, fat either whole or rendered (a dream for roasting potatoes in), skin (yes, just skin), and of course fresh fattened *foies* (livers) – huge, smooth and delicate pale pink from a goose, smaller and redder when plucked from a duck. Aficionados eat them raw and chilled with a glass of sweet Monbazillac wine or *mi-cuit* (half-cooked) with lemon, salt and pepper. Out of season, they are eaten cooked and conserved.

For those who can't handle the butcher's knife, packets of *pâté de foie gras* (a sublime, silky-smooth creamy pâté of foie gras and pork, eaten with sweet toasts) sit on tables ready to go alongside glass jars of *confit de canard* (preserved duck) and *confit d'oie* (preserved goose). Traditionally cracked open at Christmas, these duck and goose joints would have been simmered very slowly with seasoning in their own fat, then left to stand for several months. At the end of the festive feast, the *confit* and fat scraps were fried up in the farm kitchen to make *grillons*, a type of chunky pâté best eaten piled on small toasts. No part of the precious family fowl was wasted.

The Egyptians were the first to realise the sublime taste of enlarged duck and goose livers. The Romans force-fed their gaggles with figs, and by the 16th century the French were doing it with corn: *gavage* (force-feeding) triples or quadruples a bird's liver size. *Gavage* is not without controversy. The practice is banned in several of France's European neighbours, and foie gras, famously, has been banned in California and, for a while, in the city of Chicago. A growing trend for traditional methods of producing 'ethical' foie gras (the geese are not force-fed with a tube) reflects strong demand for the delicacy and an awareness of how it is produced.

🍽 WHERE TO EAT **LA TOUR DE VENTS**
MOULIN DE MALFOURAT, MONBAZILLAC

Savour foie gras dozens of different ways at this dreamy address amid vines, 50km south of Périgueux. Born-and-bred Dordogne gal Marie Rougier is the Michelin-starred tour de force in the kitchen, and the summer terrace overlooking Monbazillac vineyards is *la belle France* at its romantic best.

RIGHT Geese in the Lot valley: the Toulouse goose is the most common variety used to produce foie gras

₰₰
BOUILLABAISSE
FISHERMEN'S STEW

The Mediterranean port of Marseille is a frenzy of sights, sounds, smells and flavours, with a culinary history harking back to the Greeks who came ashore around 600 BC. Follow the beat of African drums, clinking masts and fishwives to the fish market at the Vieux Port, where eels flip in buckets and seagulls squawk overhead. Walk and gawk at seething piles of squid, octopus, sole, whiting, turbot, eel and mackerel – or join locals waiting for the next boat to moor in case its catch includes an essential fish for *bouillabaisse*.

Humble fishermen first cooked up Marseille's pungent and aromatic fish stew centuries ago to get rid of their scraps. And little has changed in the cooking method or in the way it is eaten – in two parts, as soup starter then fish main course. No two *bouillabaisses* are identical and debates rage as to which fresh fish constitute a true *bouillabaisse*. Most agree on at least four types – scorpion fish, white scorpion fish, weever, conger eel, tub gurnard, John Dory or monkfish perhaps – thrown in the pot with a stock made from rockfish, onions, tomatoes, garlic, parsley, bay leaves, thyme and other Provencal herbs.

Saffron gives *bouillabaisse* its vivacious, deep-yellow colour. Its name derives from *bouillir* ('to boil' in French) and *baisser* ('to lower', as in a flame), reflecting the cooking method: bring it to the boil, bubble ferociously for 15 minutes, then serve. The *bouillon* (broth) is served first, as a soup, followed by the fish flesh in the company of a local wine such as a crisp white Cassis or dry Bandol rosé.

⊜ WHERE TO EAT CHEZ FONFON
140 RUE DU VALLON DES AUFFES, MARSEILLE
Of Marseille's many *bouillabaisse* kitchens, this address near the Vieux Port is a reliable choice. Stroll quay-side past buildings of ripened apricot and blanched almond hues to Vallon des Auffes – a tiny cove wrapped around fishing boats, nets drying in the sun.

LEFT Seafront restaurants on the Vieux Port in Marseille are the best place to find traditional *bouillabaisse* **ABOVE** Serving *bouillabaisse* **ABOVE RIGHT** Sea urchins are considered a delicacy in France

SEA CHESTNUTS
Slice the bottom off the spiny ball, which can be anything from deep purple to eggplant, chocolate brown or jet black in colour, and serve like oysters by the dozen or half. To taste and eat, scrape off the foul-looking guts and rather unsightly brown grit to uncover the startling rusty-orange coloured ambrosia inside – the roe of the sea urchin, exquisitely arranged by nature in five delicate sweet-salty strips. This is what you eat and what gourmets wax lyrical about.

Savouring *oursins* (sea urchins), nicknamed *châtaignes de mer* (sea chestnuts), is a delicacy that falls in the same love-or-hate realm as oysters and foie gras. They are fished September to April, and are best served with fresh lemon and glass of chilled white Cassis wine.

Other catches to impassion taste buds on the French Riviera – an impossibly glamorous and romantic part of France where blue-rimmed coastal roads chicane around sun-scorched coves and sandy beaches – include clamlike *violets* (sea squirts) whose iodine-infused yellow flesh tastes like the sea, *supions frits* (squid pan-fried with fresh garlic and parsley), or the catch of the day flambéed in pastis.

TARTE TATIN

Where the macaron is a precisely engineered sweet of fiendish difficulty to cook, the same can't be said of France's most famous tart. Born of a mishap when the Tatin sisters of Lamotte-Beuvron in the Loire were making an apple pie for a customer in their eatery, tarte Tatin is an upside-down, caramelised delight.

INGREDIENTS
210g/7.5oz plain flour
1 egg
105g/4oz butter
1 tbsp sugar
1 tbsp water
pinch of salt

FOR THE FILLING
120g/4oz butter
180g/6oz icing sugar
1¼kg apples, peeled and quartered

PREPARATION
Put the flour into a large bowl, make a well in the centre and break the egg into it. Add the butter, sugar and salt and mix together with a wooden spoon. Sprinkle some of the water to moisten the mixture and form into a ball. Put it in the fridge.

Melt the butter in a high-sided skillet and sprinkle in the icing sugar. Add the apples and stir to combine. Cook for 20 minutes and then turn up the heat for 10 minutes more, or until the apples turn golden brown. Do not let the mixture burn.

Place the apples in a large glass baking dish, filling in any gaps with large slices. Roll out the dough and place it on top of the apples, tucking the dough around the edge into the dish. Bake the pie at 180°C/350°F for 20 minutes then remove from the oven and allow to stand for a few minutes. Place a serving platter over the baking dish flip it over quickly. Serve plain, with a dollop of whipped cream or ice cream. Serves 8.

MACARONS
GASTRONOMIC ART

No first bite is so shattering. Polished smooth like smarties, round and lurid enough to belie their egg-shell fragility, *macarons* (nothing to do with coconut) evoke the essence of French *pâtisserie* (cake-making) – elegance, sophistication and zany creation. No other French cake or pastry is made in such a rainbow of colours or, as in the world of fashion, unveils a new flavour each season: contemporary pastry and *macaron* maestro Pierre Hermé is a master of this art.

Indulged in over a *café gourmand* (gourmet coffee) or afternoon tea, the *macaron* is a pair of crisp-shelled, chewy-inside discs – egg whites whisked stiff with sugar and ground almonds – sandwiched together with a smooth filling. Flavours are inexhaustible (rose petal, cherry blossom, caramel with coconut and mango, mandarin orange and olive oil...) and seemingly any marriage of tastes is possible. Call it the gastronomic application of that *art de vivre* the French do so well.

Macarons are the legacy of Catherine de Médicis, who came to France in 1533 with an entourage of Florentine chefs and pastry cooks adept in the subtleties of Italian Renaissance cooking, and armed with such delicacies as aspic, truffles, *quenelles* (dumplings), artichokes and *macarons*.

⚘ WHERE TO EAT LADURÉE
16 RUE ROYALE, 8E, PARIS

In Paris in 1871, a miller from southwest France called Louis Ernest Ladurée started serving tea in his pastry shop near the new Garnier opera. The height of Second Empire elegance, the shop remains a glorious feast of polished wood panelling, mirrors and winged fairies fluttering across the frescoed ceiling. A pale green Ladurée box filled with *macarons* is the last word in Parisian romance.

ABOVE *Macarons* were originally simple almond pastries until somebody in the early 20th century had the clever idea of filling them

ِ‹‹
BRETON BUTTER
A BITE OF BRITTANY

Tucking into a wheat-flour crêpe after a windswept, wave-washed frolic between rocks on a ginger sand beach or a bicycle ride past fields dotted with ancient megaliths is to taste Brittany. Salt harvested by hand since the 1st century from marshes fringing this rugged Atlantic coastline speckles the creamy *beurre salé* (salted butter) that goes into Breton crêpes – France's finest. Unlike the rolled-up crêpes sold at stalls on Paris' street corners, Brittany's crêpes are folded envelope-style at the edges, served flat on a plate and eaten using cutlery. Paired with a stubby *bolée* (terracotta goblet) of local apple-rich cider, they are exceptional.

It is the same Breton butter, handcrafted for centuries in tiny family dairies like that of Jean-Yves Bordier in St-Malo (his retro-wrapped packets of *Le Beurre Bordier* supply top chefs worldwide), that makes *kouign amann* so dangerously irresistible. Breton butter cake is the world's butteriest, syrupiest cake – twirls of sweet, butter-loaded dough baked into a salty-sweet caramelised bliss. Georges Larnicol, a Breton *chocolatier* with boutiques in Quimper, Paris and elsewhere, considerately makes *kouignettes* (mini butter cakes).

Glass jars of vivid, copper-coloured *caramel au beurre sale* (that come with a tiny spoon should you be unable to wait until you get home to rip it open and consume) is the other Breton product to die(t) for. Indulgent, decadent and sublimely sweet, salted butter caramel from Brittany risks becoming an obsession: spoon it straight from the jar, suck as an old-fashioned lollipop or warm gently and drizzle over a Breton crêpe.

⏧ WHERE TO EAT AU PRESSOIR
LIEU DIT MÉNEC, CARNAC
Follow the trail of mystifying megaliths to this artisan *crêperie* in a traditional Breton longhouse with whitewashed walls and wooden tables on the grass out front. Carnac is on the Morbihan Coast, a wild haven of islands and bird life on Brittany's south coast.

ABOVE Mont St Michel is iconic of the Breton coast – despite actually being just over the border in Normandy
ABOVE RIGHT Buckwheat has a stronger flavour than wheat and goes well with savoury fillings

GALETTES BRETONNES AU SARRASIN
Brittany's buckwheat galettes – soft, nutty and delicious crêpes – are a savoury fast-food snack worth replicating at home. Fillings are often a combination of ham, cheese, mushrooms and spinach.

INGREDIENTS
225g/8oz buckwheat flour
225g/8oz plain flour
4 eggs
1 tsp salt
500mL/17fl oz whole milk
100g/3.5oz butter (clarified)

PREPARATION
For clarified butter, melt the butter in small pan and skim off the froth. Allow the clear melted butter to cool. Sift the flours and salt into a large mixing bowl. The buckwheat (a hardier seed than wheat) benefits from being blended with other flour; you can use white or wholemeal or a combination. Crack the eggs into the flour and whisk well.

Add milk gradually, beating as you go, and the melted butter. Continue whisking until the batter is smooth and set it aside for an hour or two.

Heat some sunflower oil (or butter) in a skillet or pancake pan. Pour half a cup (or a ladle) of batter into the pan and swirl around until evenly distributed. Cook until golden brown, usually for two to three minutes for the first side and a minute or two for the second. Stack cooked crêpes somewhere warm then fill with some wilted spinach and cheese or ham.

Fruit displays in the main streets of Menton on the French Riviera, during La Fête du Citron

FRENCH FESTIVALS

No country in the world can match France's calendar of festivals celebrating regional foods. Every town and village has a day when its local speciality takes pride of place, from the wrinkled walnut to the mighty tuna. Here are some of our favourites.

JANUARY & FEBRUARY

Fête de la St-Antoine, Richerenches
Villagers in this Provencal village celebrate the patron saint of truffle-harvesters each year with a truffle Mass in church, during which truffles (instead of cash) are offered to the Lord. The Mass falls on the closest Sunday to 17 January.

Fête du Citron, Menton
Once Europe's biggest lemon producer, this seaside town on the French Riviera stages a real bonanza of a Lemon Fair in February. Exotic carnival floats laden with gargantuan characters sculpted from zillions of lemons parade through the streets.

L'Oursinade, Carry-le-Rouet
On the first three Sundays of February, a giant open-air picnic spills across quays in the old port Carry-le-Rouet near Marseille. The festival is a rare opportunity to taste sea urchins with locals around shared tables.

APRIL & MAY

Bayonne Ham Fair, Bayonne
No ham rivals Parma more than *jambon de Bayonne,* a prime salt-cured Basque ham from southwest France celebrated by townsfolk in Bayonne at Easter since 1462.

Fête de la Coquille St-Jacques, Erqy
Some of France's finest *coquilles St-Jacques* (scallops) are fished in the bustling Breton port of Erqy and sweet neighbours St-Quay-Portrieux and Logyuivy – alternative April hosts to the tastiest gourmet street party in Brittany.

Fête du Fromage, Banon
May sees the mountain village of Banon in Haute-Provence pay homage to Provence's best-known cheese, *chèvre de Banon* – a delicate round of goat's cheese wrapped in chestnut leaves.

JULY & AUGUST

Fête de Melon, Cavaillon
Mountains of sweet, orange-fleshed cantaloupe melons fill the Provencal market town of Cavaillon during this colourful, four-day melon fest in July.

Fête du Cassoulet, Castelnaudary
A cassoulet stronghold if ever there was one: the Languedoc town of Castelnaudary, smart on the watery banks of the pea-green Canal du Midi, makes a magnificent host for this giant of a food fest to which 70,000-odd food lovers flock each August.

SEPTEMBER

Braderie de Lille, Lille
Mountains of empty mussel shells engulf the streets after three days of mussel-munching in the handsome northern French town of Lille. Europe's largest flea market, held on the first weekend in September, is the excuse.

Fête de Tomate, Montlouis-sur-Loire
Château de la Bourdaisière in the regal Loire Valley, west of Paris, is the cinematic setting for this gourmet celebration of tomatoes – red, yellow, black, every colour under the French sun, ancient variety and experimental new – in September.

Fête de la Crevette, Honfleur
Prawns, scallops and mackerel are the main catch in the postcard pretty, fishing port of Honfleur, chic port of call in Normandy for weekending Parisians. For gourmands crazy about prawns, this autumn fest is a must.

Fête de la Figue, Banyuls-sur-Mer
Pebbly beach resort Banyuls in southwest France is synonymous with wine, notably dessert wine made from grapes grown in terraced vineyards propped up by dry stone walls. Marry it with figs at the town's annual fig fest in mid-September for a sweet treat.

Fête du Vin, Perpignan
Of the hundreds of wine fairs celebrated all over France after the autumnal grape harvest, what makes this one stand out is the barrel of new wine that is borne to the city's cathedral to be blessed. Join the merrymakers during the third weekend in September.

OCTOBER

Piment d'Espelette, Espelette
The Basque region is famous for its large, rust-red dried chilli peppers and for one weekend they get their day in the sun. Garlands of the peppers decorate this village and a Mass at the 16th-century church celebrates the harvest. There's music, dancing and plenty of eating.

Fête du Miel, Roquebrune-sur-Argens
Hear that buzzing sound? That's some of Provence's 350 beekeepers and their nectar-seeking friends in town to show off their flavoured honeys and demonstrate how to collect it from a hive without angering the occupants.

~~~
CHEESE

Some superstar cheeses get all the accolades but each has several delicious understudies. Claudia Bowman of cheesemongers McIntosh & Bowman profiles the cheese world's headline acts and related cheeses that deserve more of the spotlight.

MUNSTER AOC
FRANCE, ALSACE AND LORRAINE
Thought to be the oldest of all French washed-rind cheeses, Munster dates from around the 7th century and has monastic origins. It is traditionally produced in the Vosges Mountains of Alsace and matured for 21 days.
TYPE Cow **STYLE** Washed **TEXTURE** soft, open to fudgey **AROMA** pungent **FLAVOUR** meaty, yeasty, savoury **SERVE** With a hoppy Pilsner or strong Belgian beer or an acidic Alsatian riesling

PONT L'EVEQUE AOC
France, Normandy
Pont L'Eveque, mentioned in a 12th century manuscript, is one of the oldest cheeses still produced by monks in a Norman abbey.
Flavour robust, savoury

ARDRAHAN
Ireland, Kanturk, Co. Cork (origin)
The mild and damp climate of Cork where the Atlantic's salty spray sweeps across the fields makes for favourable conditions for producing washed-rind cheese.
Flavour rich, buttery, meaty with a tang

EPOISSES AOC
France, Burgundy
First produced by Cistercian monks in the 15th century, Epoisses is washed with a local liqueur, Marc de Bourgogne, which adds a fruit complexity to the rind.
Flavour robust, savoury

LIVAROT AOC
France, Normandy
Livarot has monastic origins, and is washed with annatto to enhance the striking orange colour of the bacterial rind.
Flavour robust, savoury

ITALY, VAL TALEGGIO
Lombardy
Named after the limestone caves of Valtaleggi, Taleggio is one of the oldest soft cheeses in Italy. It's mild yet aromatic and not as challenging as other bacterial, washed-rinded cheeses.
Flavour meaty with a lingering fruitiness

STINKING BISHOP
England, Gloucestershire
Stinking Bishop is regularly washed during its maturation with Perry; a liquor made from local 'Stinking Bishop' pears. **Flavour** milder and fruitier than the pungent aroma suggests

STILTON
ENGLAND, DERBYSHIRE, NOTTINGHAMSHIRE AND LEICESTERSHIRE
England's iconic blue cheese is licensed to be produced by six dairies in three English counties. Its blue veins come from the same penicillium mould as Roquefort.
TYPE Cow **STYLE** Blue **FLAVOUR** rich, sometimes salty, yeasty, mellow **TEXTURE** buttery, crumbly **SERVE** On an oat biscuit with a glass of port

STICHELTON
England, Collingthwaite Farm, Welbeck Estate, Nottinghamshire
Stichelton is one of a few unpasteurised English blue cheeses, made with organic milk.
Flavour nutty, toasty, sweetly spiced

SHROPSHIRE BLUE
England, Nottinghamshire
Essentially Stilton with annatto colouring, Shropshire Blue was invented by Cheshire cheese grader Dennis Biggins in the 1930s.
Flavour savoury, yeasty

CASHEL BLUE
Ireland, Beechmount, near Fethard Co.Tipperary
Cashel Blue is to Ireland what Stilton is to England – the national blue. It's at its best between 15 and 25 weeks' maturation.
Flavour savoury, yeasty and creamy

HALLOUMI
TURKISH-CYPRUS
Halloumi has been around since the days of the Byzantines. It is traditionally produced using raw sheep's or goat's milk, and kneaded to create a stretchy, rubbery texture similar to mozzarella. Halloumi has a higher melting point, making it perfect for cooking.
TYPE Sheep, cow or goat **STYLE** Fresh **TEXTURE** Rubbery, squeaky **FLAVOUR** Plain, salty, unchallenging **SERVE** Straight off the barbecue, thinly sliced with a slice of fresh watermelon and a sprig of mint, paired with a pale ale

PROVOLONE
Italy, Po River valley, Lombardia, Veneto
Provolone originated in southern Italy and is a 'stretched-curd' cheese, produced in a similar way as mozzarella and bocconcini. It has a characteristic round knob for hanging and can be flavoured or smoked, fresh and soft or matured and firm. **Flavour** mild, milky, slightly sweet when young

MOZZARELLA DI BUFALA
Italy, Campania
Mozzarella made from buffalo milk is produced exclusively in Campania. Mozzarellas made in other areas of Italy or with cow's milk are known as *fiore di latte*. **Flavour** slightly sweet, milky

BURRATA
Italy (origin)
Meaning 'buttered' in Italian, burrata is a mozzarella ball filled with fresh cream and mozzarella before being knotted at the top and cut. It's eaten fresh and at room temperature. **Flavour** creamy, milky

VACHERINE MONT D'OR AOC
FRANCE, FRANCHE-COMTE, JURA-SWITZERLAND
The AOC accreditation for Vacherin demands the use of raw milk from Montbéliard and Simmentaler breeds. Set in a ring of spruce bark, it's a seasonal cheese using autumn and winter milk.
MILK Cow **STYLE** Soft, washed rind **AROMA** Pungent, meaty **FLAVOUR** Earthy, savoury, warm milk and vegetal **TEXTURE** Creamy **SERVE** Melt in the oven on high for 15 minutes, then ladle onto boiled potatoes and serve with a crisp, fruity, dry white wine

WINNIMERE
USA, Vermont
Winniemere is an American Vacherine-style cheese made to harness the high-fat winter's milk of the Ayrshire heifers at Jasper Hill Farm. Similar to Vacherine Mont d'Or, Winnimere is wrapped in spruce bark before being washed in a Lambic-style of beer from a nearby brewery then aged for 60 days in the farm's cellar. **Flavour** pungent, meaty with warm milk overtones

EDEL DE CLERON
France, Franche-Comte
The next best thing if you can't get your hands on Vacherin, Édel de Cléron is described as 'faux Vacherin' thanks to its year-round commercial production with pasteurised cow's milk, instead of the traditional raw milk.

CLARINES DES PERRIN
France, Franche-Comte
Clarines des Perrin is boxed in pine without the aromatic spruce bark of Edel de Cleron and also has a less pungent or challenging flavour than Edel des Cleron.

MONTGOMERY'S CHEDDAR
ENGLAND, SOMERSET
Cheddar is named after a Somerset village famous for limestone caves and the dramatic Cheddar Gorge. Montgomery's Cheddar is considered king of all English cheddars and is one of three truly traditional cheddars made in England. **TYPE** Cow **STYLE** Hard-pressed **AROMA** Damp earth and cellar floor **FLAVOUR** Sharp, musky-sweet grassy pasture **TEXTURE** Crumbly, crunchy flecks **SERVE** With an Indian Pale Ale and a Ploughman's lunch

CABOT CLOTH CHEDDAR
USA, Vermont
Cabot's Cloth is an English-inspired cloth-bound cheddar. **Flavour** balanced sharpness, slight nuttiness, and a caramelized, long-lasting earthy tang

ISLE OF MULL CHEDDAR
Scotland, Isle of Mull, near Tobermory
Isle of Mull Cheddar is a moist, soft, crumbly cheese born in the bleakly beautiful Isle of Mull. **Flavour** wild, farmy, fruity

CANTAL AOC
France, Various.
Named after the province, Cantal is one of France's oldest cheeses, served at Louis XIV's table, and is an ancestor to contemporary cheddar. **Flavour** complex, deep, savoury

PYENGANA CLOTH-MATURED CHEDDAR
Australia, Pyengana, Tasmania
Pyengana Cheddar is one of Australia's oldest specialist cheeses, using the traditional English style of cloth binding and maturation. **Flavour** rich, earthy, cellar floor, musky, becoming butter-scotchy

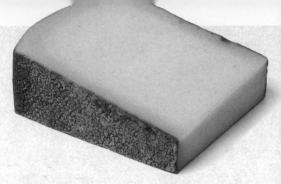

ROQUEFORT
FRANCE, ROQUEFORT-SUR-SOULZON

Roquefort is considered the king of blue cheese. The story goes that a young shepherd was lunching on rye bread and fresh ewes' milk cheese under a cool rocky overhang when he saw a beautiful girl in the distance. Distracted, he left his sandwich in the cave and did not return for months, by which time the wild mould spores of the local environment, *penicillium roqueforti,* had transformed his plain cheese into Roquefort.
MILK Sheep **STYLE** Blue **FLAVOUR** complex, punchy, spicy, fruity **TEXTURE** rich but melt-in-your-mouth light **SERVE** With honeycomb and champagne

CROZIER BLUE
Ireland, Beechmount, Co.Tipperary
Crozier Blue is made by brother cheese-makers Henry and Louis Clifton Browne with milk from their flock of Friesland sheep.
Flavour savoury, buttery flavour and a rich, long-lasting texture

HOOK'S LITTLE BOY BLUE
America, Mineral Point, Wisconsin
This seasonal Roquefort-inspired blue cheese is made from sheep's milk collected from neighbouring Amish farms.
Flavour fruity, piquante

BEENLEIGH BLUE
England, Sharpham Barton, Devon
Beenleigh Blue is a modern relative of Roquefort produced by UK cheesemaker Robin Congdon, who planted the French herbs found in Aveyron for his sheep to feed on and introduced mould spores he collected from the caves of Roquefort-sur-Soulzon. **Flavour** fruity, tangy

BRIE
FRANCE

Brie de Meaux is named after the Brie region and the town in which it was originally produced.
MILK Cow **STYLE** Bloomy **TEXTURE** Soft, smooth **FLAVOUR** Creamy milk, mushroomy grass. **SERVE** With a crusty baguette and a glass of champagne

BRIE DE MELUN
France, Ile-de-France
Brie de Melun AOC is a more traditional but less popular Brie, distinguished by red or brown blushes and a receding penicillin mould rind. **Flavour** stronger, saltier than Brie de Meaux

CAMEMBERT DE NORMANDIE
France, Normandy
Legend has it that camembert was invented in 1791 by Marie Harel, a dairy farmer from Normandy, after a brief liaison with a priest who had fled the village of Brie.
Flavour pungent, mushroomy, cauliflower

NEUFCHATEL
France, Normandy
Neufchatel is one of the oldest French cheeses, often produced in a heart shape for Valentines' Day.
Flavour mushrooms, damp earth

TUNSWORTH
England, Hampshire
Tunworth was created by two mums who initially met at the school gate and decided to go into business together. Their Camembert-style cheese is made from the fresh milk of an Ayrshire herd that grazes on the Hampshire Downs.
Flavour mellow, buttery, mushroomy

GRUYERE
SWITZERLAND

Gruyere is named after the Swiss town. Both France and Switzerland produce AOC-accredited Gruyeres with slight differences.
MILK Cow **STYLE** Hard-pressed **FLAVOUR** Balanced, elegant, nutty, slightly sweet, predominantly savoury **TEXTURE** becomes more granular with age **SERVE** In a classic fondue and drink a crisp, fruity, dry white wine

COMTÉ
France, Franche-Comté
Comté has been made in the mountainous Jura region since the 12th century.
Flavour elegant, nutty, long-lasting, savoury, deepening with age

SWISS EMMENTALER
Switzerland
Named after the valley Tal of the river Emme in the Canton of Bern, where it was first produced. The 'eyes' (holes) are formed by carbon dioxide produced during maturation.
Flavour mild, nutty becoming more spicy, aromatic with age

BEAUFORT CHALET D'ALPAGE
France, Savoie (origin)
Named after a town in the French Alps and the ancient breed of Beaufort cows whose milk it uses, Beaufort is perfect for cooking and is often used in fondue.
Flavour nutty, grassy, well balanced with floral hints

APPENZELLER
Switzerland, Courtelary, La Neuveville and Moutier
Named after the Swiss region of Appenzell, this cheese is known as the spiciest, most herbaceous cheese in Switzerland.
Flavour strong, rich, with a spicy finish

CHABICHOU DE POITOU
FRANCE
Chabichou de Poitou takes its name from the Arabic word 'cheblis' meaning 'goat'. Poitou is considered to be the most significant goat cheese–making region in France.
MILK Goat **STYLE** Bloomy **FLAVOUR** nutty, slightly sweet, earthy **SERVE** With a chunk of dark chocolate and a glass of red wine

CROTTIN DE CHAVIGNOL
France, Sancerre, Loire
Crottin de Chavignol is named after the village where it has been produced since the 16th century in the shape of a small, flattened ball. As the Crottin de Chavignol matures it becomes harder and browner; 'crotte' means 'animal droppings' in French.
Flavour subtle, slightly nutty, sweet

VALENCAY
France, Berry
Valencay's pyramid shape and ash-dusted coating gives it a distinctive appearance.
Flavour nutty, slightly citric

RAGSTONE
England, Herefordshire
Ragstone is named after the Ragstone Ridge and is cheesemaker Charlie Westhead's, original soft cheese.
Flavour savoury, lemony

HOLY GOAT LA LUNA
Australia, Victoria
La Luna is produced on a bio-dynamic organic farm. Holy Goat's cheeses emulate the traditional French slow lactic fermentation of the curd.
Flavour tangy, delicate, earthy

LA TUR
Italy, Piedmont
La Tur, meaning 'the tower' in the local dialect, is one of several mixed milk cheeses made with a blend of sheep, goat and cow milk by three brothers from the Alta Langa region.
Flavour delicate, floral, mellow tang

TYMSBORO
England, Somerset
Tymsboro is produced from the milk of a much-admired herd Saanens, Anglo-Nubians, Alpines, Boers and cross-breed goats. Farmer and cheesemaker, Mary Holbrook, rests their milk before hand ladling the delicate curd into Valencay-style moulds. The soft curd is coated with ash before being left to mature and develop a rind.
Flavour citric, nutty, goaty

MONTENEBRO
Spain, Avila
Montenebro is a cave-matured cheese that has been treated to the same penicillin mould used in Roquefort.
Flavour slightly acidic, lemony, clean

CALIFORNIA CROTTIN
America, California
Redwood's California Crottin is produced in the style of a traditional French Crottin cheese and has a wrinkly, *geotrichum candidum* rind. **Flavour** robust, nutty

RICOTTA
How to make your own ricotta.

INGREDIENTS
4 cups milk
4 cups cream
3 tbsp vinegar OR half cup of lemon juice
Salt to taste

EQUIPMENT
Sauce pan for heating milk/cream
Spatula
Second saucepan or heat-resistant mixing bowl
Colander
Muslin or cheese cloth

PREPARATION
Hygiene is of the utmost importance in the cheese-making process.

Ensure that all equipment and preparation surfaces are sterilised prior to cheese making in order to kill bacteria, viruses, fungi and spores, and ultimately avoid spoilage of cheese and illness. This can be done in one of two ways:

1. Boiling water sterilisation
2. Milton sterilising solution in a large condominium that equipment can be submerged into for 3 minutes.

To sterilise the cheese cloth that will be used for straining the ricotta, boil the cloth in a pot of water to rid it of washing detergent, dirt, dust.

Mix the milk with the cream in the saucepan and heat on a high stove.

Add a generous pinch of salt and keep mixing until it is just about to come to the boil.

At this point add the vinegar or the lemon juice (whichever you prefer or have to hand) and turn the heat off.

You will be see a dramatic change in the milk as nutrients clump together.

Once curdled, place the muslin or cheese cloth on top of the colander and strain the mixture through and into the second saucepan or bowl.

Eat warm on toast with honey on top or place in an airtight container and keep in fridge for up to one week.

Shop for sustenance at the winter market in Berlin's Gendarmenmarkt

GERMANY

Cured meats and sausages, dense dark breads, sauerkraut and beer: these hallmarks of traditional German cuisine are how a food-loving people met the challenge of eating well through cold winters.

Black Forest cake, the Frankfurter, the Berliner doughnut...Germany is a nation of many regions, each with its own culinary traditions. To travel through them is to discover a feast of intensely local foods, many of which bear their geographic origins proudly in their names. And like many great European cuisines, German cooking is at its heart rural and peasant.

In Saarland, bordering France, goose liver and coq au vin share the menu with potatoes and grilled pork. Fish is a staple of the north, so much so that the locals are called *Fischköpfe* (fish heads) by their meat-eating southern neighbours. The Hanseatic port cities made their fortunes from herrings, which they learned to salt; further north, on the Baltic Sea coast, smoked whole sprats are the Scandinavian-style speciality.

Germany's fish-loving regions are a deviation from the norm, for Germany is one of the world's more carnivorous nations. Meat, and particularly pig, is the national staple, consumed in hearty variations of braised and roasted cuts. In Bavaria, nose-to-tail eating has been in vogue for centuries, from *Schweinshaxe* (pork knuckle) and *Rippchen* (ribs) to *Züngerl* (tongue) and *Wammerl* (belly).

The closest Germany comes to a national dish is *Sauerbraten* (literally, sour roast). The ingredients of the sweet-and-sour marinade vary by region; the constant is time – the beef marinates for three to four days before being cooked to a melt-in-your-mouth softness.

But with stodgy food no longer a seasonal necessity, chefs in Munich, Berlin and other cities are bringing lighter, livelier versions of German classics to the table.

NEW GERMAN CUISINE

Traditional German cuisine is often dismissed as reliant on meat and potatoes but, as elsewhere in Europe, a new breed of chef is reinterpreting historical dishes and reintroducing a focus on local and seasonal ingredients.

At three-Michelin-star Vendôme in Bergisch Gladbach, heirloom vegetables and ancient livestock breeds have been resurrected by chef Joachim Wissler, who delights diners with his take on German haute cuisine with dishes like oyster with 'pearls' of sauerkraut and Holzberghof veal braised for 24 hours, with polenta 'drops'.

In Munich, that stolid city of laptops and lederhosen, the retro interior of Michelin-starred Tantris may reference the 1970s but chef Hans Haas's food is anything but dated; his signature dish is dove with marinated cabbage and black salsify, a witty take on sauerkraut.

At Volt, in hip Kreuzberg, Berlin, chef Matthias Gleiß gives a modern makeover to German classics using fresh, seasonal vegetables, served in a former electrical sub-station.

◌◌◌
BROT
BRÖTCHEN AND BRETZELN

When in exile in California in 1941, German playwright Bertolt Brecht confessed that what he most missed about his homeland was the bread. Considering the quality and diversity of German baked goods, with anywhere from 400 to 600 varieties of *Brot* across the country, and 1500 *Brötchen* (bread rolls) and pastries, there's a lot to miss. Many German breads include rye flour, which has low levels of gluten and a dense texture; the most popular mix rye and wheat flours. Those most emphatically German are the *Schwarzbrot* – darker, rye-dominated breads that can be stored for long periods without going stale. Pumpernickel, a rich, dark bread made with coarse rye flour, is the most intense *Schwarzbrot*. Deep brown and dense, a result of a long cooking time, the bread's traditional recipe demands the dough be steamed for up to 24 hours after its initial baking. Pumpernickel has been made this way for centuries in Westphalia, northwest Germany, whose medieval character, with crooked lanes of half-timbered houses, has been preserved with its baking heritage.

The German bread product that left home and struck it rich is the pretzel, or *Brezel*. A soft, yeasty dough is given a salt bath and sprinkled with coarse salt (or in regional variations, sunflower, poppy or sesame seeds) before baking. Bavarian legend has it that this type of pretzel was invented by accident in 1839, when a baker mistook a sodium hydroxide cleaning solution for the sugar-water intended for sweet pretzels, and served the results to great acclaim. Other pretzel-related legends concern the meaning of its shape: was it made to resemble a Roman ring-bread, or a praying monk?

🔔 WHERE TO EAT BÄCKEREI HAVERLAND
OPMÜNDER WEG 65, SOEST

Founded in 1570, this bakery has been producing genuine pumpernickel for a dozen generations, making it the oldest family bakery in Germany.

LEFT Back to the future: the interior of Tantris Restaurant in Munich **ABOVE** Hard pretzels are easy to make and accompany German lager perfectly

⸎
WURST
GERMAN INVENTION

The food most identified with Germany is the humble sausage. But with more than 1500 different varieties on offer, there's little room for humility. Within the three broad types of wurst – *Brühwurst* (scalded or parboiled sausage, like the Frankfurter), *Kochwurst* (fully cooked sausage, such as blood or liver sausage) and *Rohwurst* (raw cured sausage like *Mettwurst*) – there's a dizzying array of regional variation. And, of course, out on its own category-defining branch there's the bratwurst, which comes in over 50 regional guises featuring different ingredients as well as dimensions – from the petite *Nürnberger Rostbratwurst* at just 8cm to 10cm long and served in platefuls of six or 12, to the seriously intimidating northern Bavarian *Mainfränkische Meterbratwurst* measuring a full metre!

The radical young tearaway of the wurst family is the *currywurst*. Swimming in ketchup and dusted in curry powder, the sliced pork wurst is Germany's most popular fast food, with 70 million consumed each year. Commonly served from *Imbiss* (fast-food stands), the *currywurst* was invented by a Berlin *Imbiss* worker in 1949 after she obtained Worcestershire sauce, ketchup and curry powder from British soldiers. Ever since she started selling the calorific and outrageously spicy snack to hungry construction workers, Germany's sausage-loving citizens have never looked back.

⊖ **WHERE TO EAT KONNOPKE'S IMBISS**
UNDER THE U-BAHN TRACKS, CNR DANZIGER STRASSE AND SCHÖNHAUSER ALLEE, PRENZLAUER BERG, BERLIN
A classic *Imbiss*, under the same family management since 1930 and serving some of the city's best *currywurst*. If it leaves you with unanswered questions, the Deutsches Currywurst Museum (Kurfürstendamm 46), with exhibitions and a Snack Lounge featuring you-know-what, pays tribute to the nation's favourite snack.

ABOVE It may not be the most elegant of culinary concoctions but Berliners are proud of the spicy currywurst

SPARGEL
While for the most part their dietary favourites are from the meat and carb categories, when Germans find a vegetable they like they really make a big deal of it. So don't be surprised if, when travelling between April and June, particularly in the country's southwest, you find entire towns given over to a mania for *Spargel* – asparagus. Restaurants all over the country will offer at least one asparagus dish on a special *Spargelkarte*, or asparagus menu. Some will feature almost nothing else, offering the fresh-cut spears slathered in Béarnaise or Hollandaise sauces.

The finest white asparagus comes from an area in Baden-Württemberg known as the 'asparagus triangle', centred on the aristocratic old town of Schwetzingen, the self-proclaimed asparagus capital of the world. This is the home of the most famous asparagus festival of the season, with parades, an asparagus banquet, and the crowning of an Asparagus King and Queen. All hail the asparagus!

ఓ

BEER
REVERE THE BEER

The *Reinheitsgebot,* or Beer Purity Law, passed in 1516, decreed that only barley, hops and water could be used in the production of beer (yeast was added later). Until the EU struck it down as uncompetitive in 1987, this was the world's oldest food-purity regulation. Beer was a part of German life as early as 800 BC, and the country has one of the world's proudest beer traditions – and some of its best beers.

Given the strict regulations over beer production for the past five centuries, the rich regional variation is astounding. Some of these deviations arose from necessities of climate and season in a world before refrigeration. Historically, top-fermented beers like wheat and malt beers, requiring a higher brewing temperature, developed in areas with a mild climate such as the Lower Rhine. Bottom-fermented beers like pilsner and bock, requiring a lower temperature, could only be brewed over long cold winters, in places such as Bavaria.

While Germans have beer in common, regional favourites set them apart. Bavaria's *Hefeweissbier,* strongly aromatic and cloudy, is one of the country's best wheat beers; a more acquired taste is the dark, smoky *Rauchbier,* tasting a little of bacon. *Altbier,* a dark amber, spicy top-fermented beer, is mostly brewed in Düsseldorf. Berliners drink *Berliner Weisse*: low-alcohol, very sour, wheat-based beer, usually served with juniper or raspberry syrup. But, thanks to the Beer Purity Law, wherever you are in the world, Germany's beers are very highly regarded.

🍽 WHERE TO DRINK OKTOBERFEST

Munich's Oktoberfest is a booze-up like no other. Over six million people from around the world show up every September to gather in enormous tents and drink *Wiesn-Märzen* (a lager brewed especially for the occasion) out of 1L steins hefted in lots of 10 by beefy waitresses dressed in dirndls. Lederhosen, Tiroler hats, oompah music, spontaneous song and extreme drunkenness – all the German stereotypes are present and accounted for in this 16-day extravaganza which started in 1810 as a party to celebrate the marriage of Prince Ludwig I.

Traditional Oktoberfest foods are designed to soak up alcohol and enable continued drinking: giant *Brezel,* potato pancakes, roasted meats. Beer tents are dedicated to particular foodstuffs – the *Ochsenbraterei* serves up a dazzling range of ox-based specialities, including an enormous ox-sized rotisserie; the *Wildstuben* does venison. There are tents for veal, roast duck, cheese, dumplings, bratwurst, fish-on-a-stick, and more. It's a strictly salad-free zone, unless you count warm potato salad, served with suckling pig and a beer sauce.

Staying in Munich, Starkbierzeit – Oktoberfest's secret, hardcore cousin – celebrates only the most lethal amber ales, the *doppelbocks* (over 7% alcohol). The timing, around mid-March, reflects the invention of the brew by Paulaner monks to give them strength through Lent. The festival kicks off with the tapping of the first keg at Paulaner Keller.

LEFT Exercise your drinking arm lifting beer-filled steins at Munich's Oktoberfest; more than seven million litres of beer are drunk during the festival

GERMAN FESTIVALS

EBBELWOI-FEST, LANGEN
This small town in Hesse celebrates *Apfelwein* (apple cider) on the last weekend in June. With streets closed to traffic, revellers stroll through the old town sampling cider at taverns, enjoying the fireworks and witnessing the crowning of the Ebbelwoi King.

STUTTGARTER WEINDORF
In late August, Stuttgart city centre is transformed into a festive *Weindorf* (wine village), with traditionally decorated stalls serving hundreds of wines from around Baden-Württemberg, as well as local delicacies like *Schupfnudeln* (potato noodles) with pickled cabbage.

DITHMARSCHER KOHLTAGE
In the agricultural district of Heide on the north coast, the harvest of 80 million cabbages each September is marked with a festival celebrating sauerkraut, with costumed Cabbage Queens, farmers markets and cabbage dishes.

WURSTMARKT, BAD DÜRKHEIM
Despite its name, the main drawcard is the wines of Rhineland Palatinate, particularly its riesling. Starting as a local fair almost 600 years ago, it has evolved into an event attracting over 600,000 visitors but retaining its traditional feel, celebrated on the second and third weekends in September.

ONION MARKET, WEIMAR
Proudly the world's largest onion market, this may also be the oldest, with the first held in 1653. Historically a dealers' market, it's now a popular festival attracting around 300,000 people in early October and boasting souvenir onion garlands and, naturally, the coronation of an Onion Queen.

LEBKUCHEN

Christkindlmarkt are a magical German type of Christmas: snow (if you're lucky), twinkling lights, glittering ornaments, handcrafted gifts and delicious Christmas treats. To keep you warm as you shop, sip *Glühwein*, red wine heated and spiced with cinnamon sticks, vanilla pods, cloves, star anise, citrus and sugar. The spicy scent of *Lebkuchen* biscuits fills the air.

INGREDIENTS

250g/9oz plain flour
85g/3oz ground almonds
2 tsp ground ginger
1 tsp ground cinnamon
1 tsp baking powder
½ tsp bicarbonate of soda
Pinch of ground cloves, grated nutmeg and black pepper
200mL/7fl oz clear honey
85g/3oz butter
1 lemon , finely grated zest

FOR THE ICING

100g/3.5oz icing sugar
1 egg white , beaten

PREPARATION

Tip the dry ingredients into a large bowl. Heat the honey and butter in a pan over a low heat until melted. Pour into the flour mixture with the lemon zest. Mix until the dough is combined and fairly solid.

Cover and leave to cool. Heat oven to 180°C/350°F. Roll dough into about 30 balls with your hands, each 3cm/1in wide, then flatten each ball into a disk. Divide the biscuits between two baking trays lined with baking parchment, leaving room for them to expand. Bake for 15 minutes, then cool on a wire rack.

To ice the biscuits, mix the icing sugar, egg white and 1 to 2 tbsp water to form a smooth icing. Dip the top of each biscuit in the icing and spread with the back of a knife. Leave to dry.

⟨⟨⟩ SCHWARZWÄLDER KIRSCHTORTE
THE SWEET STUFF

The German food most likely to get sweet tooths salivating is *Schwarzwälder Kirschtorte:* the Black Forest cake. Like the fever-dream of a deprived chocoholic, the rich gateau overdoes it on every level: lofty with layers of chocolate cake, lavished with fresh cream and cherries between the layers, boozy with the strong *Kirschwasser* (cherry schnapps) made in the Black Forest that gives the cake its name and, finally, topped with more cherries and chocolate shavings. Truly, a Kaiser among cakes.

But there's more. Lübeck, the Unesco-listed town once at the centre of the all-powerful trading bloc, the Hanseatic league, discovered marzipan in the 16th century when it made its way from the Middle East. A confection of almonds and sugar, it was a delicacy that only the nobility could afford for centuries due to sugar's high price, and until the 19th century it was seen mostly as medicinal. The opening of the Niederegger factory in Lübeck in 1806 marked the beginning of marzipan's march towards mass consumption – Lübeck marzipan is now a protected brand, and Cafe Niederegger is Germany's marzipan mecca.

Bavaria's Nuremburg, strategically positioned on the Middle Ages' spice routes, was poised for an influx of exotic ingredients: cloves, ginger, cardamom, allspice, cinnamon. By 1395 the first bakeries were taking these spices – along with aniseed, mace, nuts and candied peel – and creating the iconic *Lebkuchen* (gingerbread). A guild of gingerbread bakers was established in 1643, and *Lebkuchen Nuremberg* is also protected by the EU.

🍽 WHERE TO EAT CAFE DECKER
HAUPTSTRASSE 70, STAUFEN IM BREISGAU

Its origin is a matter for debate, but eating *Schwarzwälder Kirschtorte* in the Black Forest is an unbeatable place-plus-food combination. Cafe Decker is a shrine to the great German tradition of *Kaffee und Kuchen,* heady with the aroma of fresh-baked cakes.

RIGHT *Lebkuchenherz,* or gingerbread hearts, baked for Oktoberfest **ABOVE** Sweet temptation: the Black Forest cake is an over-the-top tribute to cherries, chocolate and whipped cream

Du bist das süßeste Mädel der Welt

A Herzerl fürs Herzerl

hab Dich sooo lieb

Ich bin verliebt in Dich

Gruß vom Oktoberfest

Du bist mein süß Bärche

Ich hab Dich lieb

Kleiner Schm kät

Sitting on the dock of a bay on the island of Lesbos

GREECE

With long summer days and sparkling seas, Greek cuisine needs be no more complicated than a table laden with roasted lamb, sizzling calamari and crusty bread.

The culinary traditions of Greece reflect the bounty of the Greek homeland and its surrounding seas. A succession of invaders and trading partners have added their influences, from the Romans to the Ottomans.

A long and often harsh history has made the Greek chef resourceful, and the cuisine is simple and unfussy. Living through difficult times has fostered an inspired ability to create mouth-watering dishes using only what is immediately available, with little need for additional relish or adornment. The majority of Greek dishes are simply seasoned with salt, pepper, lemon juice and dried oregano. Vegetables, pulses and legumes (key elements of the healthy Mediterranean diet) are made tastier by plentiful use of olive oil and herbs.

The Greeks are fussy eaters and sticklers for fresh produce. They'll go out of their way to eat in the village taverna if the meat is local and the produce comes from the cook's own garden, or to dine on the day's catch in a remote fishing village. They aren't big on breakfast, but they see lunch and dinner as opportunities to gather and partake in food, news, gossip and the simple joy of conviviality. Dining communally with family and friends is an integral part of social life, and whether rich or poor, the Greeks eat out regularly.

Lunch is the main meal of the day. It tends to be eaten late, as befits the laid-back Mediterranean lifestyle, and it can turn into an extended event, particularly on weekends. An eat-and-run approach is unthinkable to the Greeks; instead, meals unfurl at a gentle pace, all the better to savour the tastes, banter and atmosphere.

Nothing conjures up the essence of a Greek holiday like the simple pleasure of sitting under a vine-shaded trellis while enjoying a succession of tasty dishes, surrounded by cheerful chatter and ebullient families in the dappled sunshine.

THE GOOD OIL

Greeks consume more olive oil per capita than any other people: 30L annually. Olive oil is used as a cooking medium, but also as a dressing, garnish and relish. A preliminary step in virtually any Greek recipe is to add olive oil (a good slug of it) to the pan. Once the particular dish is prepared, it is likely to be given a further drizzling to enhance the flavour... then another for good measure. Oil is drizzled on cheese, adds lustre to dips, is used as a moistener for crusty bread or is poured on as a simple dressing for salads.

And olive oil is an important part of the healthy Mediterranean diet: it contains high levels of antioxidants, and is thought to lower cholesterol levels and reduce the risk of heart disease.

LOW-FAT FETA

With its weathered shepherds and restless hordes of sheep and goats, Greece produces a range of tangy cheeses, but the one for which it is famous is feta. Taking its name from the Italian word for slice, it has been a part of the Greek diet since at least the 16th century. Feta is always made from sheep's milk, but may contain up to 30% goat's milk.

Its flavour is a product of the mountainous mainland and sparse islands of Greece. Sheep have to venture far and wide to find sufficient foraging, eating a variety of grasses and accumulating little fat, thus producing the pure-white, low-fat milk that gives feta its colour, zest and bite.

There are plenty of ways to eat your feta. It can be simply splashed with oil and coupled with fresh bread, as the centrepiece of the classic *choriatiki* (Greek salad), crumbled on omelettes or stews, or baked in a pie.

HORTA
FRUITS OF THE EARTH

Bound up in the rhythms of the land and the seasons, Greek food has an undeniably earthy quality. Many culinary traditions stem from the peasant lifestyle, a reminder of times when populations had to survive on the few resources at hand. Game, such as hare, rabbit or quail, is roasted to mouth-watering perfection. Goat, often overlooked in European cuisines, is sumptuous when spit roasted or baked with potatoes and spices. Even snails, prepared with garlic and herbs, make it onto the Greek table. The Greeks can rustle up a fabulous meal at the drop of a hat.

Other recipes are a reflection of an intimate knowledge of the land. One dish peculiar to Greece is *horta,* a catch-all term for wild greens, which can vary between regions and seasons. *Horta* may include poppy shoots, milk thistle, wild asparagus, or nettle, or, on the Aegean islands, certain types of seaweed. It can be pickled, lightly fried in olive oil to bring out flavour and crispness, or put in a pie. Whatever and however, *horta* demonstrates an inherent Greek resourcefulness – only a Greek could spy something edible amid what may appear to be miscellaneous greenery and in an instant transform it into something delicious.

Simple and unpretentious, a tavern meal of succulent roasted goat and crisp sautéed *horta* captures the Greek culinary genius at its down-to-earth best.

🍽 WHERE TO EAT MYRSINI
TSOPELA 2, THESSALONIKI

This simply adorned restaurant, with worn wooden floors and authentic accoutrements, serves tasty *horta* and other traditional fare.

ABOVE Traditional tavernas – this one is in Thessaloniki – are the place to eat your greens

❧
KOUNELI STIFADO
A GREEK VARIETY SHOW

Sprawled across a large swathe of the eastern Mediterranean, Greece encompasses markedly different landscapes and this has had a corresponding impact on regional cuisines. Each region – in fact, each island, each city, each village – will have its specialities and idiosyncrasies. You may have a general idea of what constitutes Greek cookery, but rest assured that the adventurous diner will find a stunning variety of dishes, traditions and culinary experiences from the alpine villages of the Pindus to the sun-drenched islands of the Dodecanese.

All this regionality makes for controversy, because even what may be considered a standard dish will vary considerably from place to place. Take *kouneli stifado* (rabbit stew with baby onions): in one region, cooks will add cinnamon, in another cloves; tomatoes will be a must-have inclusion in some parts, while elsewhere they will be replaced with currants. And so it goes.

Cooks in mountainous Epirus tend to use butter rather than olive oil; in Crete, just north of the north African coast, dates feature in many dishes. In the Ionian islands, once lorded over by the Italians, you'll find salamis and dishes flecked with red pepper.

🍽 WHERE TO EAT TAVERNA VAKHOS
APOLLONOS 31, DELPHI
Dive into a substantial meal of *kouneli stifadho* at this excellent family taverna in historic Delphi on the Greek mainland.

ABOVE *Stifado* made with beef, rabbit, or lamb, is usually served with *hilopittes* (egg pasta) or with rice, garnished with a bay leaf or rosemary.

ARNI OFTO
The perfect Greek meal takes place outdoors, where a whole spring lamb can be prepared and spit-roasted. You'll need to arrange for the lamb some days ahead of time, even as you would in Greece. And you must plan the shape, size and depth of your fire pit. Electrically powered spits, as well as hand-driven ones, are available at rental stores. It will take anywhere from four to six hours to roast the little beast. Your butcher can advise you. Time the arrival of your guests so that the air is thick with the aroma of roasting lamb. *Retsina,* if you can get it, is the best thing with which to grease the wheels at this point. If not, some dry white wine, a pale beer or water will keep folk refreshed. When the lamb is done, there is no particular Greek method of carving. See that each guest gets something well done from the outside and something rare from the inside. Serve with salad, bread and more wine.

INGREDIENTS
1 lamb prepared for the spit
1–2 lemons
250mL/8.5oz olive oil
Sprigs of rosemary

PREPARATION
Rub the lamb generously with lemon juice and olive oil, and sprinkle with chopped rosemary. Skewer it onto the spit. When your fire has reduced to a bed of glowing coals, position the lamb about 25cm/10 in above it.

Be prepared to adjust the height if the lamb cooks too fast or too slow.

Turn the spit and from time to time baste the meat with oil and lemon (you'll also need to replenish your fire every 30 minutes or so).

For an added touch, throw whole rosemary sprigs on the fire and let the aroma rise to the meat. Serves a large group.

FOOD LOVER
TESSA KIROS

Even before I lived in Italy I was impressed by the Italian way. I am inspired in every aspect – starting from coffee right through to gelati and digestives. I love the way the ingredients and seasons are honoured. And the simplicity of presentation.

A memorable food experience – my grandfather in Cyprus comes straight to mind. **I can see him frying chips and artichoke bottoms,** turning the souvlakia and *sheftalia* on the coals while the rice pudding is cooling in the fridge.

Next on my travels I'm heading to the north. Salmon, Arctic char, dill, various smoked and barbecued fish: three-tiered platters of seafood.

I think that the favourite dish I have tasted abroad is *cozido* **on the island of San Miguel in the Azores.** A mixed meat and vegetable casserole flavoured with chorizo and cooked in the earth by the heat of the volcano. I recreated this dish when I got back in the oven, but for me the fact that it was cooked by volcano as a traditional Sunday dish wins the prize.

Tessa Kiros is the author of *Limoncello and Linen Water*

SWEETS
WELCOME GREEKS BEARING LOUKOUMADHES

Rare is the Greek who doesn't have a sweet tooth – you'll find cakes, biscuits, sweets and desserts in countless tempting variations wherever you go in Greece, from Epirus to the Peloponnese, the Ionian Sea to the southern Mediterranean. The original Greek sweet is honey. Distinctively dark in colour and rich in taste, Greek honey is a combination of the intense Greek sunshine, the diverse native wildflowers and fruit trees, and their extended flowering period. It is often eaten for breakfast, drizzled over yoghurt, and it is a central ingredient in goodies as diverse as *melomakarona* (honey cookies); *koliva*, a combination of boiled cracked wheat, nuts and dried fruits; and *ghlika tapysu* (cakes, pies or pastries).

A Greek peculiarity is spoon sweets (*ghlika kutalyu*), an element of hospitality thought to date back to old Constantinople, whereby visitors were treated to a glass of water and spoonful of fruit conserve. In some homes, the custom continues, with guests being presented with a cut-crystal glass of water and a silver spoon laden with preserved orange flavoured with bergamot, or jellied quinces, to be nibbled over polite conversation.

Other sweets include baklava, *loukoumadhes* (mini doughnuts with honey and cinnamon), *kataïfi* (chopped nuts inside shredded angel-hair pastry), *rizogalo* (rice pudding) and *galaktoboureko* (custard-filled pastry). It's worth keeping an eye out for regional sweet specialities, such as *amygdhalota* (almond sweets) from Andros, and Thessaloniki's famed *bougatsa* (custard pudding wrapped in a pastry envelope, baked and sprinkled with icing sugar), as well as for places selling *politiko pagoto* (Constantinople-style ice cream).

⌖ WHERE TO EAT KOTSOLIS
ADRIANOU 112, PLAKA, ATHENS
In the heart of Athens, this well-loved institution offers an array of mouth-watering goodies in atmospheric surrounds. Choose from *galaktoboureki,* baklava and *kataïfi*.

ABOVE *Melomakarona,* a honey and walnut cookie usually enjoyed at Christmas **RIGHT** Sweet as honey: Greek bees make some of the world's most delicious honey from wild herbs and flowers

Hung out to dry: the pink
tentacles of the octopus are
closely tied to Greek cuisine

BITE-SIZE DIVERSIONS

Along with philosophy, the Greeks also invented
'authenticity' (from *authentikos*, meaning genuine). For a taste
of genuine Greek cuisine, try the following.

SLOW-ROASTED LAMB
From the spit or the wood-fired oven, dusted
with salt, lemon juice and a hint of rosemary,
this is the most Greek of all meals.

PICKLED OCTOPUS
A popular meze, with a tender fleshy
texture and vinegar bite.

SAGANAKI
Fried cheese; a salty fried crust yields to
melting richness.

FISH AND SEAFOOD
Pulled snapping from the Mediterranean,
fish, octopus and squid are fried, pickled,
baked or grilled – and always delicious.

SPANAKOPITA
A pie of layered filo pastry, feta, spinach
and herbs – simple perfection.

DOLMADHES
Another popular meze, combining aromatic
rice and herbs, and the resinous texture
and tang of fan-shaped vine leaves.

YEMISTES
Oven-baked trio of tomato, eggplant and
red capsicum, individually stuffed with
rice, garlic and herbs.

FRAPPÉ
Hardly a high-brow experience, but this
iced and highly sugared coffee is the
must-have beverage in any of Greece's
buzzing cafes.

YAURTI
Ultracreamy yoghurt drizzled with locally
collected *meli* (honey) is a simple yet
indulgent treat (that may even be good
for you).

BAKLAVA
The Mediterranean sweet par excellence,
bursting with chopped nuts and doused
with syrup or honey.

KEFALOGHRAVIERA
Once you can pronuonce it, you'll be
addicted. This sharp, satisfying cheese is
best fried, but can be used in a wide range
of dishes.

WINE
Greek wine has moved on from holiday-
favourite *retsina*, as new-generation
winemakers are producing fine wines from
age-old indigenous varietals with unique
flavours. A rosé *agiorgitiko* is the perfect
summer wine.

PASTA
Pasta is widely used in Greek cooking,
from *pastitsio* (a thick spaghetti and meat
bake) to the hearty *youvetsi*, slow-cooked
lamb or beef in a tomato sauce with
kritharaki (orzo or rice-shaped pasta).

SOUVLAKI
Arguably the national dish, this comes in
many forms, from cubes of grilled meat
on a skewer, to *gyros* (kebab-style meat
cooked on a vertical rotisserie.

It's a family affair: food is at the heart of community life in India

INDIA

**India's gastronomic terrain is as diverse as its landscape.
Both are steeped in history and intensely more-ish. And for vegetarians,
the vast country is heaven on a plate.**

Like Mother India herself – economic powerhouse and home to some of the world's poorest people – Indian food isn't easy to define. Forming a national topography of tastes are unique regional dishes, each with its own preparation techniques and jumble of ingredients. The religious communities that make up India's cultural tapestry also add diversity to the dining table – apart from the country's Hindu majority, they include Muslims, Sikhs, Jains, Christians, Buddhists and Parsis. Drawing upon an extraordinary array of regional, religious and global influences, from rotis cooked in dusty village kitchens to traditional recipes flaunting contemporary twists in Mumbai's glamorous high-end restaurants, India's carnival of flavours fires the imagination and taste buds.

The basis of most Indian meals is grain: rice in the southern states, and wheat in the form of roti in the north. Most meals include a lentil-based dish and a selection of curried vegetables and/or meat specialities. Apart from its myriad mains, Indian cuisine is also famous for its street snacks. The aromas of crispy *bhajia* (vegetable fritters) and succulent meat-on-a-stick takeaway offerings are as much a part of the general mayhem of Indian street life as the crowds, petrol fumes and clamour.

From the smorgasbord of vegetarian creations to the seafood of the South, the marinated tandoori fare of the north, the Euro-Indian fusions of former colonies and the mind-bending mix of *mithai* (sweets), eating your way around India is a deliciously rewarding trip.

BUTTER CHICKEN

This rich and flavoursome favourite is delicious with freshly baked roti. Make it spicy or mild, depending on your taste.

INGREDIENTS

1kg/2lb cooked and jointed tandoori chicken

200mL/7fl oz tomato purée

1 tbsp ginger paste

1 tsp garlic paste

1 tsp red chilli powder (use paprika if you do not want it hot)

2 tsp salt

100g/3.5oz butter

125mL/5fl oz thick cream

PREPARATION

Simmer the chicken in tomato purée, ginger and garlic paste, chilli powder and salt for around 10 minutes (until the chicken is tender). Add the butter and simmer for another five minutes. Mix the cream in and serve. Serves five to six.

PICKLES, CHUTNEYS & RELISHES

No Indian meal is complete without the accompanying tang of pickles, chutneys and relishes. A relish can be anything from a tiny pickled purple onion to a delicate fusion of fruit, nuts and spices. One of the most popular accompaniments is raita, a mildly spiced, chilled yoghurt that's often mixed with shredded cucumber or diced pineapple to provide a tongue-cooling counter to spicy food. *Chatnis* can come in any number of varieties, sweet or savoury, and can be made from many different vegetables, fruits, herbs and spices. Truly, these are crucial condiments at the Indian dining table.

₰₰₰
KABAB
KABABS TO KORMAS

'Kabab' is a loose term in India, applied equally to ground beef or marinated chunks of lamb, cooked on a skewer, fried on a hot plate or seared under a grill. In fact, you could probably use the term to describe just about any small cut of meat that doesn't already have a name.

There are two basic forms of kabab: skewered barbecued meat, especially popular in Punjab and Delhi, and Muslim specialities made with mince. A signature mince variety from Uttar Pradesh is the *Kakori kabab*, named after the town near Lucknow, made from meat pounded into a fine paste, which is then spiced, wrapped around a skewer and quickly charred until crispy on the outside and almost creamy within. Another UP mainstay is the *shami kabab,* made with boiled mincemeat ground with chickpeas and spices, with raw papaya added to make the meat so tender that it melts in the mouth. Other common varieties you might come across are *galavat* (balls of mincemeat), *sheekh* (mincemeat wrapped around iron spikes) and *ghute* (mincemeat stirred into a fine paste in the pan).

As very few people have a *tandoor* in their homes, tandoori-cooked meats are favourite restaurant fare all over India, especially in the north. Marinated meats become kababs in the tandoor, succulent chunks of chicken transform into the famous tikka, and *paneer* squares provide a vegetarian alternative to meat.

Another North Indian speciality is korma, where cubes of goat, lamb or chicken are cooked in a rich, spicy sauce, usually with the addition of onion. Contemporary kormas are often cooked over a stove like stews but they were traditionally made via the *dum pukht* method of steaming, in which the vessel is sealed with dough, placed over glowing embers and slowly 'baked'.

Two very popular methods of cooking goat, beef and lamb are *kheema,* which means mincemeat, and koftas, or meatballs.

ABOVE Let them rest for a moment – freshly grilled skewers can retain a fair bit of heat – then gently remove the meat and vegetables, before attempting to eat kababs

SAMOSAS
TAKEAWAY TRIANGLES

With its crisp pastry shell encasing a soft filling, these plump, triangular deep-fried pockets stuffed with spicy vegetables are one of India's most iconic street snacks. The most common fillings are spiced potato, onion, peas, coriander and green chillies, served hot with fresh tamarind, coriander or mint chutney on the side. Southern twists to the typically northern samosa include slight variations in how the pastry is folded, as well as differences in the filling – potato may be replaced with cabbage, onion, carrot, peas and curry leaves.

It's thought samosas originated in pre-10th-century Central Asia, where they were known as *samsas*. Thanks to flourishing trading routes between Central and South Asia, they were introduced to India somewhere between the 13th and 14th centuries. Traditionally, they were cooked around campfires during night halts on overland trade journeys, not only because they were nutritious and easy to prepare, but also because they could be transported cold and eaten en route. Old manuscripts describe subsequent 'royal' versions of the little pastry parcels being filled with everything from walnuts and pistachios to prime cuts of minced meat.

In South India, the traditional snack is the *idlis*, a spongy, round rice cake that you dip in *sambar* and coconut chutney. Other southern stalwarts include *vadas* (doughnut-shaped deep-fried lentil savouries) and *appams* or *uttappams* (thick, savoury rice pancakes with finely chopped onion, green chillies, coriander and coconut). These snacks tend to be fruitier and more mildly spiced than elsewhere in India.

⊜ WHERE TO EAT

Samosa vendors are widely found in bazaars and on street corners throughout India. Watching samosas being sizzled in front of you is part and parcel of the Indian experience.

ABOVE Perhaps the perfect street snack, Indian samosas tick every box for fast food: served hot with vegetables, sometimes meat, inside a deep-fried pastry parcel, they can be dipped in chutney for extra tang

FOOD LOVER
MARK HIX

I visited the Catalan region of Spain a lot about 20 years ago and loved their use of seasonal ingredients and unfussy approach, which has influenced me a lot.

My first meal in Japan was dancing prawns. They fish them out of the tank, peel them in front of you and serve the wriggling flesh. While you are tucking into that, they deep-fry the shells and scatter them with sea salt for the next course, just like real scampi fries.

I've always wanted to explore India, especially Kerala. That's next on my travel menu.

Cumin is the addictive ingredient in curry, but for me **it has many uses in flavouring,** and giving dishes a gentle spicing.

My travels to Spain years ago took me **on a mission to find the best black rice,** *arroz negro,* made with squid ink. I never quite found the perfect one but they were all pretty good, and since then I have perfected it.

A chef, restaurateur and food writer, Mark Hix opened his own restaurant, Hix Oyster & Chop House, in London in 2008. He writes a weekly column for the Independent newspaper in the UK and a monthly column for Esquire magazine. He is the author of several cookbooks, most recently *HIX on Baking.*

PORK VINDALOO

Vindaloo is a spicy speciality of Goa, which has a large Christian population permitting the use of pork. It tastes equally good with rice or some soft bread such as the Goan, *pao*. It is never served with Indian breads. The name is a corruption of the Portuguese words for wine and garlic, but despite its European roots, the dish is one of the spicier curries. Versions of vindaloo served in Western restaurants tend to be hotter than the Goan original, which uses the sharp, sour taste of vinegar to add an extra layer0 of flavour.

INGREDIENTS

1kg/2lb pork in 5cm/2in dice

10 dried red chillies (slit and the seeds removed)

10 peppercorns

8–10 garlic cloves

5cm/2in piece of ginger

2 tsp cumin seeds

1 tsp mustard seeds

½ tsp turmeric powder (optional)

8 cloves

5cm/2in piece cinnamon

2 tsp salt

1 tsp sugar

125mL/5fl oz malt vinegar

2 onions, finely chopped

2 tbsp vegetable or sunflower oil

PREPARATION

Put all the ingredients (except pork, onions and oil) in a food processor and grind to a fine paste.

Coat the pork with this paste and leave to marinate for two hours.

Now heat the oil in a heavy-bottomed pan and sauté the onions until light pink. Add the pork and stir well.

Just about cover the pork with water and cook it until a thick gravy forms (about 30 minutes). Serves six.

SPICES
SPICE UP YOUR LIFE

Spices have played a central part in Indian life for centuries, as food and as medicines in Ayurvedic treatments. In fact, when Christopher Columbus stumbled upon America, he was actually in search of the black pepper of Kerala's Malabar coast. Today, when gourmands are on the hunt for best-quality black pepper, it's these southern Indian varieties that they go for, and black pepper is fundamental to many savoury Indian dishes. Used whole or ground, for flavour, aroma or colouring, for vegetables, fish, meat or dessert, each spice has its own culinary and medicinal use and is typically used in blends called *masalas*.

The majority of Indian curries rely on turmeric as their essence, but coriander seeds are the most widely used spice, providing a boost of flavour to just about every savoury dish. Indian 'wet' dishes – known as curries in the West – usually begin with the crackle of cumin seeds in hot oil. Tamarind is sometimes known as the 'Indian date', and is a popular souring agent in the South. But the queen of Indian spices is cardamom. Green cardamom of Kerala's Western Ghats is considered the world's best, and you'll find it in savouries and desserts. It can also be used as a mouth-refreshing digestive. The larger black cardamom, grown in the northeast, is stronger in flavour and commonly added to meat dishes. *Amchur,* or mango powder, is made from green mangoes that are peeled, sun-dried and powdered. The tart, fruity powder adds bite to many dishes. Saffron, the dried stigmas of crocus flowers grown in the northern region of Kashmir, is so light that it takes more than 1500 hand-plucked flowers to yield just 1g. Because of its high prices, saffron can sometimes be adulterated (usually with safflower) to be sold at cheaper rates in and beyond India.

🍽 WHERE TO EAT

Take a stroll through a spice market, ablaze with powdery piles of crimson chilli powder, burnt-orange turmeric and masses of other colour-charged, aromatic spices. Don't forget your camera!

ABOVE Hot work: women sorting harvested red chillis in Orissa for drying **RIGHT** Turmeric thrown by Jain devotees clouds the air at a ceremony held every 12 years in Shravanabelagola, Karnataka

♨
JALEBIS
SWEET TREAT

A standout among India's medley of *mithai, jalebis* are orange (or red) coils of deep-fried batter, prepared from *maida* (all-purpose flour) and dunked in a sugar syrup. Saffron and rose water lend a delicate undertone to this otherwise robust Indian fritter, which is a popular year-round sweet snack and especially popular during festive occasions. Sizzled in ghee or vegetable oil, *jalebis* are eaten piping hot from a wok-like vessel called a *kadai*.

Jalebis are believed to trace their origins to ancient Persia, where they were known as *zoolbia*. The earliest literary record of their existence has been discovered in 13th-century manuscripts. Historically, during Ramadan, *zoolbia* was one of several sweets that were traditionally distributed among the poor. It's thought that the sweet first came to the Indian Subcontinent at least 500 years ago with the Mughals.

Biting into a *jalebi* is almost orgasmic. The interplay of textures – the crisp but chewy outer shell then the sweet warm syrup within – is tempered by hints of fragrant rose water or *kewra* (derived from flowers of the *pandanus fascicularis* shrub). After an energy-zapping afternoon haggling in India's packed bazaars, nothing is quite as reviving as the sugar hit of a *garam garam* (hot hot) *jalebi*. Half the fun is watching a street side *jalebi-wallah* swirl the batter and, with a deft flick of the wrist, flip the frying sweets until both sides are honey brown. With another flick the *jalebis* are plunged into sugar syrup before being popped onto a plate. *Jalebis* are best eaten hot from the *kadai,* so don't be sweet-talked by a vendor into buying leftovers from an earlier batch; they'll lack the crunch of freshly sizzled ones. Watch out: these squiggly delights – traditionally eaten by hand – are super-sticky.

♨ WHERE TO EAT JALEBIWALA
DARIBA CORNER, CHANDNI CHOWK, OLD DELHI

Famed Jalebiwala sells the fattest, sweetest, most scrumptious *jalebis* you'll sink your teeth into.

LEFT AND ABOVE Sweet stop: after being fried in oil, jalebis are left to absorb sugar syrup, making them a perfect pick-me-up on a trip around India

MITHAI

Need a sugar fix? Look no further than *mithai*. With its kaleidoscope of sticky creations, *mithai* satisfy the sweetest of sweet-tooths. The main types of *mithai* are *barfi* (a fudgelike milk-based sweet), soft *halwa* (made with vegetables, cereals, lentils, nuts or fruit), *ladoos* (sweet balls made with gram flour and semolina) and those derived from *chhana* (unpressed *paneer*), such as *rasgullas* (cream-cheese balls flavoured with rose water). *Kheer* (called *payasam* in the South) is one of the most popular. It's a creamy rice pudding with a delicate flavour, enhanced with cardamom, saffron, pistachios, flaked almonds, chopped cashews or slivered dried fruit. Other favourites include *gulab jamuns*, deep-fried balls of dough soaked in rose-flavoured syrup, and *kulfi*, a firm ice cream made with reduced milk and flavoured with nuts (often pistachio), fruits and berries.

SWEET GOA

Goa specialises in elaborate cakes and desserts. Apart from postcard-perfect beaches and lush coconut groves, this coast-hugging state's Portuguese past is still alive in both home and restaurant kitchens, with traditional Iberian-inspired dishes still hot favourites. The Portuguese came to Goa in the early 16th century to control the region's profitable spice routes. It was only in 1961, 14 years after British independence and 450 years after Portuguese occupation that India annexed this tropical enclave from Portuguese rule.

Some of Goa's must-try sweet treats include *bathique* (a cake made of semolina, coconut and eggs), *dodol* (a black cake made of jaggery, rice flour and coconut cream) and famous *bebinca* (the layered 40-egg sweet).

FESTIVALS

HOLI

This colourful Hindu festival, which celebrates the beginning of spring (in February or March, depending on the lunar calendar), is a great time to indulge! Sweet specialities include *karanjis* (crescent-shaped flour parcels stuffed with sweet *khoya* (milk solids), *malpuas* (wheat pancakes dipped in syrup), fudgelike *barfis* and *pedas* (multicoloured pieces of *khoya* and sugar). Some festival goers also partake in *bhang* (cannabis) mixed with vegetables and fried into pakoras or drunk in 'special' *lassis*.

PONGAL

Pongal – an important Tamil harvest festival in January – is most closely associated with the dish of the same name, made with the season's first rice, along with jaggery, nuts, milk, raisins and spices (symbolic of prosperity and abundance).

DIWALI

Consumption of *mithai* reaches a festive frenzy during this joyous Hindu festival of lights which falls on auspicious days in October/November. Each year, an estimated 15 tonnes of pure silver is converted into the edible silver foil that decorates the masses of sweets produced specially for this occasion.

RAMADAN & EID AL-FITR

Ramadan (Ramazan) is the Islamic month of fasting whereby Muslims abstain from eating during daylight, replenishing themselves only before daybreak and at night. Traditionally, the day's fast is broken with dates – considered an auspicious food in Islam – followed by a more substantial meal. Eid al-Fitr, the final day of Ramadan, is celebrated with grand feasts that include some particularly elaborate biryanis and sweets.

PAAN
THE CHEWABLE DIGESTIF

One of India's postprandial gems, *paan* is a fragrant mixture of betel nut (also called areca nut), lime paste, spices and condiments wrapped in an edible *paan* leaf. Dating back almost 5000 years, the various types of *paan* peddled today are incarnations of those concocted for royal palates seeking an after-meal digestive and mouth freshener. Back then, not only was the blend of betel nut and betel leaf believed to assist with digestion, it was also thought to have therapeutic properties, for instance lowering blood pressure.

There are two basic types of *paan: mitha* (sweet) and *saadha* (with tobacco). The betel nut is mildly narcotic and some aficionados eat *paan* the same way heavy smokers consume cigarettes – over the years these people's teeth can become rotted red and black.

Mitha paan usually includes *choona* (slaked lime) and *kattha* (acacia-bark extract) pastes as its base. Added to these are coconut flakes, candy-coated fennel, a variety of spices (most often cardamom and clove), *gulkand* (a rose-petal jam) and assorted dried fruits which are neatly wrapped in a glistening betel leaf.

Often strategically positioned in makeshift stalls outside popular restaurants, *paan-wallahs* sit cross-legged amid masses of bright green betel leaves and jars crammed with an array of colourful ingredients. Made to order, you simply pop the plump wad in your mouth and let the intense symphony of tastes and textures – from the mushy dried fruits to the crunchy candy-coated seeds – work their magic on your taste buds.

ABOVE The best *paan* is rolled to order in a betel nut leaf

֍

BHELPURI
MUMBAI'S MUNCHIES

This feisty savoury snack – assembled on a mound of crunchy *sev* (fried chickpea-flour noodles) and puffed rice, tossed with diced tomato, onion, coriander leaves, green chillies, potato, assorted spices, tamarind chutney and a generous squeeze of lemon juice – is as exhilarating as the city that invented it: Mumbai (Bombay). India's financial powerhouse, Mumbai is a dynamic kaleidoscope of Subcontinental culture, thanks to its mishmash of religions and diverse regional traditions. When we're talking food, the result is a rich repertoire of cuisines. And when it comes to street food, *bhelpuri* is one of the coolest kids on the block. It's said that this spicy snack was brainstormed when the revered 17th-century Maratha leader Chhatrapati Shivaji Maharaj instructed his cooks to come up with something easy to prepare and consume en route to battle.

Bhelpuri kicks taste buds into overdrive. The first sensation is the crunch of the spindly *sev* and rice puffs, followed by the mouth-tingling tang of tamarind chutney interspersed with waves of fiery green chilli. It's nothing short of a flavour festival in your mouth, which will have you hankering for more.

🍲 WHERE TO EAT
Nibbling *bhelpuri* at one of the many hawker stands found at Mumbai's convivial Chowpatty Beach – while watching people watching the sun set – is the de rigueur way to savour this locally loved snack.

ABOVE Grab a bite to eat from Mumbai's street vendors

MASALA DOSA
The masala dosa hails from the South, but the popular crêpe has now gone global. A dosa is a large, papery rice-flour crêpe, believed to have been mentioned in classical Indian poems way back in the 6th century AD. Its origins lie in the town of Udupi (Karnataka) – an area renowned for vegetarian fare.

Watching a dosa being prepared is nothing short of a spectacle and shouldn't be missed. Cooks deftly swirl the smooth batter across a hot plate in concentric circles, using the underside of a steel bowl.

For many dosa aficionados, the belle of the bunch is the classic masala dosa, a conical crêpe filled with a hearty mixture of curried potato, onion and dried red chillies. Served with a side order of coconut chutney and *sambar*, a soupy but fragrant lentil dish, start from the crispy outer edges and move inwards to the spongy centre. Pieces are ripped off and dipped into the piquant sambar and cool coconut chutney.

ON THE MOVE
One of the thrills of travelling by rail in India is the culinary circus that greets you at every station. Roving vendors accost arriving trains, racing through the carriages with their trays of sweets, chai or fried snacks; fruit, *namkin* (savoury nibbles), omelettes and sweets are offered through window grilles; and platform cooks lure passengers from the train with the sizzle of spicy snacks. Savvy rail travellers know which station is famous for which food item: Lonavla station in Maharashtra is largely known for *chikki* (rock-hard toffeelike confectionery), Agra for *peitha* (a square sweet made from pumpkin and glucose, usually flavoured with rose water, coconut or saffron) and Dhaund, near Delhi, for biryani.

ιὶι

MASALA CHAI
THE NATIONAL DRINK

Across India and the Subcontinent, the morning starts with the rhythmic clang of stoves being primed and the chai-wallahs' mantra, *'Ek chai, ek chai?'* Without that morning cuppa, rickshaw-wallahs would lose the will to pedal, rice-pickers would abandon the paddy fields, and the bureaucracy on which the Subcontinent depends would grind to a halt.

To prepare this essential brew, tea leaves are flash-boiled with sugar and milk, and long-poured into shot-glass measures. The ritual of preparation is almost as important as the act of drinking. Gourmets spice up the brew with cardamom, *dalchini* (cassia, or Indian cinnamon), cloves, *adrak* (ginger), and pepper, creating masala chai – a beverage that lingers on the palate like liquid gingerbread.

Most chai-wallahs use blends from lowland estates in Bangladesh and Assam, but connoisseurs pay premium prices for the first-flush single-estate teas produced in highland estates like the plantations of Ilam in Eastern Nepal. As a rule, top-flight teas are served black – only a philistine would pollute the flavour of the world's finest tea leaves with sugar and milk. Chai, on the other hand, is the drink of the masses, with lashings of sugar to kick-start the day.

Watching the chai-wallah ply his trade is half the fun. The tea is steeped with sugar, spices and milk in a large pot, then poured through an old-fashioned cotton strainer. The *dalchini* gives the tea its robust body, the cardamom proffers the perfume and the *adrak* lends a lingering bite. Sipping the wallah's frothy masala chai from a steaming glass is a welcome antidote to the vicissitudes of life on the dusty road, and his call one of the most familiar sounds on a long train journey.

LEFT Letting the flavours infuse after boiling up a brew **ABOVE** A warm glass of spiced chai tea is one of the enduring flavours and memories of any India adventure

CHILLING OUT

To quench the most savage summer thirst, try *masala soda* – fizzy soda water pepped up with lime, spices, salt and sugar. The drink is sold by mobile vendors at bazaars and transport hubs. Other traditional home-grown beverages include *jal jeera* (lime juice, cumin, mint and rock salt) and sweet or savoury *lassi* (a chilled yoghurt-based beverage, sometimes with fruit flavouring). *Falooda* is a delicate rose-flavoured drink made with milk, cream, nuts and strands of vermicelli, while *badam* milk (served hot or cold) is infused with almonds and saffron.

MILK TREATS

Milk makes a huge contribution to Indian cuisine: *dahi* (curd/yoghurt) is commonly served with meals and is terrific when it comes to subduing heat; *paneer* (unfermented cheese) is a godsend for the vegetarian majority; *lassi* is one of a host of nourishing sweet and savoury beverages; ghee (clarified butter) is the traditional and pure cooking medium; and some of the finest sweet *mithai* are made with milk.

EATING INDIAN-STYLE

It's customary to eat with the right hand. In the South, people tend to use as much of the hand as is necessary; elsewhere just the tips of the fingers are used. The left hand can be used for holding drinks and serving yourself.

Once served, food is mixed with the fingers. If you are having dhal and *sabzi* (vegetables), only mix the dhal into the rice and have the *sabzi* in small scoops with each mouthful. If you are eating fish or meat curry, mix the gravy into the rice and take the flesh off the bones from the side of the plate.

BEST BREADS

PURI (POORI)
Especially popular in the north, these small deep-fried discs of dough puff up into soft, crispy balloons.

PHULKA
Literally 'puff', this is a mini *puri* made with whole-wheat flour and cooked on a naked flame.

KACHORI
Like *puri,* only the dough has been pepped up with corn or dhal, which also renders its texture thicker.

PARATHA
Paratha is unleavened, fried, flaky bread, eaten as is or stuffed with a spiced vegetable such as potato.

NAAN
Originally from the Middle East, Punjabis opened their hearths to the tear-shaped naan. Cooked on the walls of a tandoor oven, it is especially good when smothered with garlic butter.

SHIRMAL
Flaky *shirmal's* ingredients are flour, ghee, salt, sugar and milk. It's cooked inside the walls of tandoor-like ovens and drizzled with saffron-infused milk to add fragrance and keep it moist.

PAPPADAM
Thin and crispy, pappadams (commonly referred to as pappad) are circle-shaped lentil- or chickpea-flour wafers served either before or with a meal.

KULCHA
This soft, round leavened bread traces its origins to Hyderabad, in Andhra Pradesh, and may be filled with onion, spices, vegetables or meat.

BHATURA
Bhatura is a Punjabi speciality. It is a deep-fried, puffy version of the naan, and is popularly eaten with spiced chickpeas.

⸜⸝
BREADS
NORTHERN INDIA'S DAILY STAPLE

While rice lords it over the South, wheat is the mainstay in the north. Roti and chapati are used interchangeably to describe the most common variety of bread, the unleavened round flatbread made with whole-wheat flour and cooked on a *tawa* (hot plate), then smothered with ghee or oil.

There are many variations of Indian bread, and even staples like chapati are made according to different recipes depending on the region, neighbourhood or household. Most breads are unleavened and made with *atta* (whole-wheat flour), although you'll also come across *makki* (cornmeal), *bajri* (millet) and *jawar* (barley).

No matter how it is made or served, bread is always eaten with the right hand, dexterously used to scoop food and soak up sauces.

⊜ WHERE TO EAT PARATHA WALI GALI
OFF CHANDNI CHOWK, OLD DELHI
If you're in Delhi, head to the foodstall-lined lane of Paratha Wali Gali in Old Delhi, which flips up a tempting assortment of traditional flatbreads stuffed with everything from *mooli* (white radish) to crushed *badam* (almonds).

ABOVE Unleavened roti or chapati piled on a plate ready to be used to consume a feast of flavours
RIGHT Traditional bread making in Rajasthan

℣
BIRYANI
HYDERABAD'S REGAL LEGACY

When it comes to making a masterpiece out of the humble rice grain, nothing beats biryani. This aromatic dish traces its origins to ancient Persia, and has been adapted over the centuries to become one of the Subcontinent's signature rice dishes. Rice – usually basmati, a high-quality long-grain variety – forms the foundation of biryani, along with vegetables, meat or seafood. But the magic of biryani ultimately lies in its pot-pourri of spices, which usually includes (but is not restricted to) cardamom, cinnamon, nutmeg, bay leaves, cloves, mace, coriander and saffron. What sets biryani apart from most of its rice-based sisters (such as *pulao*) is the method in the magic: the spiced rice is cooked separately from the meat/vegetables/seafood, which is later layered into the rice.

Regional recipes vary, but Hyderabad – capital of Andhra Pradesh – is hailed as the biryani master. This part of India was the seat of power for several dynasties, including the mighty Mughals. The legacies of Hyderabad's past include graceful 16th-century buildings like Golconda Fort, but it's the regal cuisine that gets pulses racing. The region's rulers put their chefs to work to create dozens of variations on the biryani theme, from fish and shrimp to hare and quail. One of Hyderabad's signature biryani dishes is *kacchi yeqni*, which breaks customary biryani convention by cooking the meat and rice together.

Biryani reaches festive heights on occasions such as Eid al-Fitr at the end of Ramadan, when it's decorated with dried fruits, nuts and layers of *varq* (edible silver foil). Sample the styles of Hyderabadi biryani at ramshackle roadside *dhabas* (basic eateries) or swanky city restaurants. Pickles and a cooling bowl of raita are served as accompaniments.

⚇ WHERE TO EAT **PARADISE PERSIS RESTAURANT**
CNR SD & MG RDS, SECUNDERABAD, HYDERABAD

For the best biryani, Hyderabadis will direct you to Paradise, which has five decades of practice.

LEFT Terraced rice fields in the Kullu Valley of Himachal Pradesh; India produces about 100 million tonnes of rice each year **ABOVE** A biryani's spiciness is more aromatic than hot

HYDERABADI BIRYANI
INGREDIENTS

1kg/2lb lamb shoulder with the bone kept on, cut in 5cm/2in pieces
1kg/2lb basmati rice
100g/3½oz ghee
3 large onions halved and sliced
1 tsp saffron
250mL/8½fl oz milk
1 tbsp raw papaya paste
250mL/8½fl oz plain yoghurt
1 tsp red chilli powder (or paprika)
2 tsp ginger paste
1 tsp garlic paste
1 tsp garam masala
1 tsp caraway seeds, ground
Seeds of 4 cardamom pods, ground
6 cloves
2 cinnamon sticks
½ cup coriander, chopped
½ cup mint, chopped
6 green chillies
Juice of 4 limes

PREPARATION

Fry the onions in ghee until golden brown. Set aside half the onions. Dissolve the saffron in milk and set aside. Rub the papaya into the lamb and marinate it with the yoghurt, chilli powder, ginger, garlic, garam masala, caraway seeds and the drained onions. Soak the rice for 20 minutes. Add the cardamom, cloves, cinnamon and 1 tsp salt to 10 cups of water and cook the rice until half done. Drain the rice, saving 1½ cups of the water. Spread the marinated lamb at the bottom of a deep pan. On it pour half the saffron-milk mix, the rice water, the onions with the ghee, coriander, mint and chillies. Spread the rice over and on it sprinkle the remaining saffron-milk mix, lime juice and 1 tsp salt. Cover with a tight lid, seal with foil and place over medium heat. If the water sputters, place a thick skillet on the flame and put the pan on this. Cook for 30 minutes or until the water is absorbed. Serves eight.

BREAKFAST OF CHAMPIONS

Breakfast is the most important meal of the day, and also a tasty shortcut to getting to know a country's culture. Here are Brett Atkinson's top 10 recommendations for getting the day started around the globe, whether you're waking up to fiery sambal in Kandy or ordering a full English breakfast in London.

BUN RIEU CUA IN HANOI

Jettison your hotel's breakfast buffet, and secure a sidewalk spot for a Hanoi classic. This street stall is pretty basic but its *bun rieu cua* (crab noodle soup) is one of the best ways to start the day before diving into the organised chaos of Hanoi's Old Quarter. Made from tiny rice-paddy crabs, the rich broth is laced with fried spring onions and garlic, then topped with shrimp paste and chilli.
40 Hang Tre, Hanoi's Old Quarter

STRING HOPPERS IN KANDY

Forget dining and dashing when you're having breakfast in Sri Lanka. In the simple guesthouses in the lakeside city of Kandy, the meal is usually a multiplate affair combining *idiyappam* (string hoppers) with a curry, dhal and spicy *sambal* chutney. The recommended form is to use your right hand to dip compact mounds of the spaghetti-like rice pasta into the other tasty side dishes. They're best enjoyed with the refreshing juice of a fresh *thambili* (king coconut).
Palm Gardens Guesthouse, 18 Bogodawatte Rd, Kandy

HUEVOS RANCHEROS IN MEXICO

Mexico's classic spin on fried eggs is rustic *huevos rancheros:* a couple of fried eggs on lightly fried corn tortillas, topped with cheese and a tomato-chilli sauce, and served with refried beans and guacamole. Variations include *huevos revueltos,* scrambled eggs with cheese, garlic, coriander, chilli and chorizo; and *huevos motuleño* with ham, peas and plantains.
Café El Popular, Avenida 5 de Mayo 52, Centro Historicó, Mexico City

A FULL ENGLISH BREAKFAST IN LONDON

After eating breakfast with the lot at a traditional cafe, you'll definitely need a spot of exercise. A 'full English' usually features a plate groaning with eggs, bacon, sausages and baked beans, partnered with a couple of slices of toast and a mug of sweet, milky 'builders tea'. The retro-style Regency Café is one of London's iconic spots to order this 1000-calorie feast. Negotiate the fast-moving queue, order your meal at the counter, and wait to hear your name and order announced *very loudly*.
Regency Café, 17-19 Regency Street, Westminster, London

KAYA TOAST IN SINGAPORE

Ya Kun Kaya Toast in Chinatown's Far East Square serves up the quintessential Singapore brunch. Try the more-ish butter sugar toast with Singapore-style *kopi* (coffee with condensed milk) or an iced lemon tea. Ya Kun's been around since the early 1940s, and is now more popular than ever. Park yourself amid the city's iPad and smartphone-toting locals and consider other Singapore variations including peanut toast and French toast. Add a side order of deliciously runny soft-boiled eggs and get dipping. You'll also find other *kaya* toast stalls around Chinatown. Just look out for where the local taxi drivers are eating.
Ya Kun Kaya Toast, Far East Square, 45 Peking St, Singapore

TURKISH BREAKFAST IN VAN

Breakfast anywhere in Turkey is always a leisurely affair, but in the eastern city of Van they've elevated the meal to an art form. *Kahvaltı salonu* (breakfast restaurants) are dotted around town, but the centrally located Eski Sümerbank Sokak is a tasty procession of eateries that only offer the most important meal of the day. Bring along

a couple of dining companions and order a spread of freshly baked flatbread, local cheeses flavoured with mountain herbs, and the irresistible combination of chunky honeycomb and *kaymak* (clotted cream)..
Eski Sümerbank Sokak, also called Kahvaltı Sokak (Breakfast St), Van, Turkey

COFFEE & CROISSANTS IN PARIS

The French don't do lingering breakfasts, preferring instead to invest in a leisurely lunch. But for visitors to Paris, the classic morning combination of coffee and croissants at a sidewalk cafe is an essential experience. Rather than heading to Montmartre or the Marais, make your way to Aux Folies in bohemian Belleville – it's the Parisian real deal, crammed with local colour in a pleasantly grungy neighbourhood..
Aux Folies, 8 rue de Belleville, Paris

FUUL MEDAMES IN CAIRO

One of the world's oldest breakfast dishes is also one of the healthiest. Dating back to the Egyptian pharaohs, *fuul medames* combines slow-cooked fava beans mashed with olive oil, parsley, onion, garlic and lemon juice. The addition of warm flatbread, pickled vegetables and crisp rocket leaves completes an experience common across all of Egyptian society.
Al-Gahsh, near the Sayida Zeinab mosque, Cairo, every taxi driver knows it

SHAKSHOUKA IN JERUSALEM

Originally introduced by Tunisian Jews, North African–influenced *shakshouka* is a favourite brunch dish throughout Israel. In Hebrew, *shakshouka* means 'all mixed up', a tastily accurate description of this dish of eggs poached in a sauce of tomatoes, peppers, onion and spices. If you like spicy flavours, order your *shakshouka charif,* and don't forget to ask for extra crusty bread to mop up the hearty sauce.
Tmol-Shilshom, Solomon St. Jerusalem

XIAOLONGBAO DUMPLINGS IN SHANGHAI

Breakfasting on Shanghai's iconic 'soup dumplings' using the incorrect technique can get messy. Get it wrong, and you're looking at a mini explosion of steaming broth. Start by using chopsticks to place the *xiaolongbao* on a spoon. Carefully bite a small hole in the edge of the dumpling and let the glorious broth spill out onto the spoon. Do not under any circumstances bite directly into the middle of the dumpling. Let the broth cool in the spoon before drinking it, and then you're free to eat the pork-filled *xiaolongbao* in a couple of tasty bites. Good luck.
At Jia Jia Tang Bao, 90 Huanghe Lu near Fengyang Lu, Shanghai

The undulating landscape around Bologna produces some of Italy's definitive foods

ITALY

Italy is a food lover's dream destination. Leave the stereotypes behind and embrace *cucina povera*, Arab-inspired desserts and a buffet of cheeses, cured meats and antipasti.

Mouth-watering sights, sounds and smells surround you wherever you travel in this food-mad country – noisy markets blazing with colour, restaurants spilling onto historic piazzas, the scent of freshly ground coffee. But while a passion for food is a national trait, the flavours are largely regional.

Until Italy was unified in the late 19th century, the Italian peninsula was a patchwork of kingdoms, states and republics, each with its own geography, history and traditions. As a result, regional cuisines developed according to local conditions. In the richer northern areas, produce from the fertile Po Valley plain and Alpine valleys gave rise to a cuisine based on staples such as butter, cheese, rice, polenta and meat. In the south, a hot, dry climate and rugged geography led to a reliance on local vegetables and long-lasting pastas and legumes.

Poverty also played a part, particularly in central and southern Italy, where *cucina povera* (peasant cooking)

lies at the heart of the food culture. Many regional dishes were developed to use up leftovers and incorporate cheap, easily available ingredients. Hence there are Tuscan soups thickened with stale bread, Puglian pastas paired with wild greens and Roman recipes for meat offcuts and offal.

Modern Italian cuisine is based almost entirely on ingredients produced in the *bel paese* (beautiful country), as Italians call their country. But it wasn't always so, and many staples that are now considered Italian were originally imported by foreign invaders. Most notably, the Arab Saracens introduced dried pasta, rice and citrus fruit to Sicily in the 9th century, and the Spanish masters of southern Italy imported the tomato from their New World colonies in the 16th century.

Alongside these treasured imports, other essentials of *cucina Italiana* include bread, fruit, seafood, and the ever-present and much-worshipped olive oil.

VINO

From aristocratic reds to rosés, crisp sparkling whites and sweet dessert wines, Italy is the world's largest wine producer, with a drop for every palate.

Many big names hail from Piedmont, where barolo and barbaresco rule, and Tuscany, whose wine list includes Chianti classico and Brunello di Montalcino. Veneto is another big wine region, boasting reds such as Valpolicella and amarone, and sparkling white prosecco. At the other end of the country, Sicily produces a full range of *vino*, but is best known for its Marsala, malvasia and moscato dessert wines.

Wherever you go in Italy, you'll find a tipple to tickle your taste buds: Montepulciano d'Abruzzo, a versatile food-friendly red; sparkling Lambrusco in Emilia-Romagna; full-bodied primitivo in Puglia; Vermentino di Gallura, a highly respected white, in Sardinia.

Italian wines are classified according to strict guidelines, with the best denominated *Denominazione di Origine Controllata e Garantita* (DOCG), followed by *Denominazione di Origine Controllata* (DOC), *Indicazione di Geografica Tipica* (IGT) and *vino da tavola*.

᎓᎓᎓ APERITIVO
HAPPY HOUR ITALIAN STYLE

In Italy an *aperitivo* (aperitif) is much more than a predinner drink with a few salty nibbles. Rather, it's an early-evening ritual, complete with cocktails and a bar buffet. Italy's *aperitivo* capital is Turin, where locals have been enjoying predinner cocktails ever since the local Cinzano brothers invented vermouth in 1757. Martini & Rossi and Campari set up for business in the city, and the two companies' drinks continue to dominate cocktail menus across the country, appearing in favourites such as Negroni (Campari, red vermouth and gin), Americano (Campari, red vermouth and soda) and Spritz (Aperol or Campari and prosecco, a sparkling white wine). But *aperitivo* is all about the setting and the food. And nowhere sets a grander stage than Turin's historic cafes with their stucco work, gilded mirrors and dripping chandeliers. The buffets are equally as lavish, from canapés and cured meats to cheese, salads, pastas, pizzas and grilled vegetables.

Over on the eastern side of northern Italy, Venice does a great line in tapas-like bar snacks, known as *cicchetti*. These are served in *osterie* (inns) and range from simple bites like meatballs in tomato sauce to more sophisticated offerings such as lagoon shrimp wrapped in pancetta or *crostini* (toasted baguette) with local salami.

⊜ WHERE TO EAT CAFFÈ SAN CARLO
PIAZZA SAN CARLO 156, TURIN

Turin's stately centre is full of bars and cafes serving *aperitivi* from 6pm to 9pm. Caffè San Carlo is one of the oldest and most opulent cafes, under the porticoes on the piazza of the same name. Dating to 1822, it was a favourite hang-out of Risorgimento nationalists and 19th-century intellectuals, and now serves the city's smart set. For a younger, more laid-back scene head to the bars and cafes around Piazza Emanuele Filiberto. For *cicchetti* in Venice, try All'Arco (Calle dell'Arco, San Polo 436), a local favourite near the Rialto market.

ABOVE The immaculate service is part of the performance at Caffè Torino in Turin **ABOVE LEFT** Decanting wine **RIGHT** Appointment for an aperitif at the historic Caffè Mulassano on Turin's Piazza Castello

TOMATO SAUCE

Italy's tomato purée, *passata*, is the base for many classic Italian sauces. Most Italians buy theirs ready-made, but some families still gather in early September to prepare their year's supply, a communal task that can take up to three days.

First, the tomatoes – ideally the San Marzano variety – are cleaned, cooked and, if necessary, peeled. Once ready, they are put into glass containers, either whole as *pelati* (peeled tomatoes) or pressed to produce *passata*. The glass containers are wrapped in tea towels (to stop them smashing together) and boiled in a cauldron of water to sterilise for about 45 minutes, after which they're left to cool. No oil or salt is added.

SUGO DI POMODORO
INGREDIENTS
15 ripe tomatoes
1 large red onion, finely chopped
2 tbsp olive oil
4 garlic cloves, chopped
1 tbsp basil, finely chopped
1 dessert sp sun-dried tomato paste
1 dessert sp tomato paste
1 tbsp black pepper

PREPARATION
Place the tomatoes, garlic, basil and black pepper in a blender and liquidise. Gently fry the red onion in a large pan with the olive oil, until golden.

Pour the tomato mixture into the pan and bring to a simmer, adding the tomato pastes.

Season to taste, and stir regularly for 15 minutes until the sauce has reduced.

PIZZA
THE ULTIMATE STREET FOOD

The world's favourite takeaway is also a national icon. Italians of all ages eat pizza, and pizzerias are as central to the country's landscape as ancient ruins and hilltop towns. But if anywhere can claim the pizza as its own it's Naples, the brash southern city where pizza *Margherita* was born. According to city folklore, a local chef, Raffaelle Esposito, created it in 1889 as a gift for the then queen of Italy, using the colours of the Italian flag as the inspiration for his ingredients – red (tomato), white (mozzarella) and green (basil).

A derivation of the flatbreads baked by the ancient Greeks and Egyptians, the dish was already a popular snack by the time the tomato was introduced to Italy by Naples' Spanish rulers in the 16th century. These days there are hundreds of toppings, but Italians like to keep it simple, and their pizzas rarely have more than two or three. Pizza aficionados go further, claiming you can't beat the *Margherita*, especially if it's made with *mozzarella di bufala* (buffalo mozzarella) and cooked in a *forno a legna* (wood-fired oven). A true Neapolitan pizza – which differs from the thinner, crispier Roman pizza – should always be served bubbling and blisteringly hot straight from the oven.

But the pizza is not the only street food adored by Italians. The Genoese specialise in focaccia and *farinata*, a kind of pancake made with chickpea flour, while in Emilia-Romagna they go mad for *piadine*, flatbreads cut open and stuffed with cheese or cured meats. Sicily is the place to go for *arancine*, delicious deep-fried rice balls made with rice, saffron, a smidgen of *ragù* (meat sauce), peas and a few cubes of cheese.

WHERE TO EAT NAPLES' PIZZA STREET
For the full-on pizza experience, Via dei Tribunali in Naples' historic heart boasts three popular pizzerias – at No 32, Pizzeria Sorbillo; at No 94, Di Matteo; and at No 120, Il Pizzaiolo del Presidente, where chef Heston Blumenthal visited for a TV series.

ABOVE Fast food: catch the ballet of the pizza chefs at Trianon Pizzeria in Naples **ABOVE LEFT** Italians won't tolerate a tomato that isn't fresh, red and ripened in the sun

ܓ
RISOTTO ALLA MILANESE
THE MAIN GRAIN

In Italy, rice means risotto. There are hundreds of risotto recipes but the most famous is Milan's signature *risotto alla milanese*, a rich, creamy classic that's cooked with beef bone marrow and given a yellow hue by the addition of saffron. According to foodie folklore, the dish was created in 1574 by a young apprentice, Valerius, who was working on the construction of the city's Gothic cathedral. His job was to colour the stained-glass windows and he apparently used saffron to brighten his pigments, much to the amusement of his teasing colleagues. Fed up with the stick he was getting, Valerius threw some saffron into a batch of risotto that had been prepared for his master's wedding. The joke backfired, though, and the dish proved a hit. Some 500 years on and it's one of Italy's most recognisable dishes. But risotto's true appeal lies in its simplicity. Depending on the season, a basic *risotto bianco* can be the vehicle for wild mushrooms, or fresh peas with mint and parsley, or whatever else the home cook has in the larder.

Rice was originally brought to Sicily by the Saracens in the 9th century. Local conditions weren't favourable in Sicily, and by the 15th century Italian *risicoltura* (rice growing) had moved north to the Po Valley plains of Piedmont and Lombardy. These days, Italy is Europe's largest rice producer, with the focus on three short- and medium-grain varieties: *arborio*, *carnaroli* and the Veneto region's *Vialone nano*.

⚓ WHERE TO EAT ANTICA TRATTORIA DELLA PESA
VIALE PASUBIO 10, MILAN

There's no shortage of Milanese restaurants offering their versions of the city's namesake dish, but for an authentic and delicious experience, try Antica Trattoria della Pesa, a Milan institution since 1880.

ABOVE The humble risotto is the perfect vehicle for any ingredients you have in the larder
ABOVE RIGHT *Orecchiette alle cime di rapa* features ear-shaped pasta and greens

CUCINA POVERA

Over the centuries, poverty has been one of the driving forces of Italian history, particularly in the rural south. This poverty led to the traditions of *cucina povera* (peasant cooking), a cuisine based on cheap, readily available ingredients and leftovers.

A classic case in point is Puglia's signature dish, orecchiette alle cime di rapa (little ears of pasta with *cime di rapa* (rapini – you can use turnip tops if you can't find this leafy green), garlic, chilli and anchovies). In richer parts of the country, no one would have dreamed of eating rapini, but the Pugliese peasantry were in no position to be choosy.

ORECCHIETTE ALLE CIME DI RAPA
INGREDIENTS

200g/7oz dried orecchiette
400g/14oz *cime di rapa* (rapini)
4 tbsp olive oil
2 garlic cloves, sliced thinly
Pinch of dried chilli flakes
1 small can of anchovies

PREPARATION

Roughly slice the rapini into 5cm- (2in) strips, discarding the thicker stems. If using turnip tops use only the leaves. Boil in salted water for five minutes (or 10 minutes for older leaves). Strain, and cook the pasta in the water. In a pan, fry the garlic in olive oil, add chilli flakes, anchovies and then the rapini. Sauté and season with salt and pepper. Add the cooked pasta and a splash of the pasta water. Mix and cook for another minute or two.

﹏ PASTA
SPAGHETTI AND STEREOTYPES

For once, the stereotype is true: Italians adore pasta and eat inordinate amounts of the stuff – about 28kg per year, almost three times more than the average American. The origins of this long-standing love affair have been much debated, but most food historians agree that dried pasta was originally introduced to Italy by the Saracens in the 9th century – and not by Marco Polo, as some romantics have claimed. It soon caught on, and by the 17th century it was a popular and affordable staple.

Pasta can be divided into two groups: *pasta secca* (dried pasta) and *pasta fresca* (fresh pasta). Dried pasta, made from *semola di grano duro* (durum wheat semolina) and water, is what most Italian eat on a daily basis, while fresh pasta is mostly kept for Sundays and special occasions. A further distinction is between regular pasta and *pasta all'uovo* (egg pasta), a favourite in northern Italy, where it's often served in broth or with rich sauces.

In all, there are about 350 different shapes and sizes of pasta, each suited to a particular dish and many associated with a specific region. Emilia-Romagna is famous for egg pastas such as tagliatelle, thin ribbons of pasta, and tortellini, pockets of meat-stuffed pasta. Liguria has thin spindly *trofie* that go well with pesto, while Umbria is known for its *strangozzi*, a kind of rectangular spaghetti that's named after the leather cord that locals reputedly wanted to strangle tax collectors with. Down in Italy's heel, Puglia is the land of *orecchiette*, little ears of pasta that are traditionally served with *cime di rapa* (turnip tops).

♨ WHERE TO EAT TRATTORIA DEL ROSSO
VIA A RIGHI 30, BOLOGNA

To taste the real tagliatelle alla Bolognese, Bologna's red-bricked medieval centre teems with trattorias. Said to be the oldest in town, Trattoria del Rosso is a wonderful, no-frills restaurant that does a brisk business in soul-warming pastas and authentic meat dishes.

ABOVE Taste a traditional bolognese in the shadow of St Petronio cathedral in Piazza Maggiore, Bologna
LEFT No tangles here: the very best tagliatelle is freshly made and cut by hand

SPAGHETTI BOLOGNESE

Bologna will always be associated with spaghetti bolognese. In reality, spag bol served outside Italy is very different from the original. In Italy, the meat sauce – *ragù* – contains no garlic and no herbs, just meat, onion, carrot, celery, tomato paste and red wine. And it's mixed with strips of tagliatelle rather than spaghetti.

INGREDIENTS

2 tbsp olive oil
100g/3.5oz pancetta
1 onions, finely chopped
2 carrots, finely chopped
1 celery stick, finely chopped
2 garlic cloves, crushed
250g/9oz mushrooms sliced
750g/26oz lean minced beef
2 cans chopped tomatoes
1 tbsp tomato puree
Large glass red wine

PREPARATION

Heat the oil in a large saucepan. Gently cook the pancetta, onions, carrots and celery for 20 minutes until golden. Add the garlic, mushrooms and cook for two minutes more.

Heat a large frying pan until hot. Crumble in enough mince to cover the pan and cook until brown. Add to the veg. Continue to brown the mince until it is used up.

Tip the tomatoes and purée in with the mince and veg. Rinse the cans out with red wine and add to the pan. Season and simmer slowly for one hour, until thick and the mince is tender. Serves 4, with tagliatelle.

LUXURY FOODS
Italian cuisine boasts some truly decadent foods.

TRUFFLES
Truffles are among the world's most expensive foods. The *tartufo bianco* (white truffle) from Alba commands astronomical prices, selling for about €200 per 100g. White truffles are rare, elusive and only available for a few months of the year. Growing underground near tree roots in the Langhe hills south of Alba and around Monferrato, they fruit from September to December. *Trifulai* hunters (truffle) head to their secret spots and set their specially trained sniffer dogs to work. White truffles should never be cooked but shaved raw onto risottos, pastas, salads and egg dishes.

FORMAGGIO
Parmigiano reggiano has been made in the countryside around Parma and Reggio Emilia for 700 years, and is considered the king of cheeses, its nutty, complex taste the result of careful production and meticulous ageing. Lombardy also produces a pair of excellent cheeses: blue-mould gorgonzola and grana padano, a close relative of parmesan.

BALSAMIC VINEGAR
The prince of balsamic vinegars is *aceto balsamico di Modena* from Emilia-Romagna. It is made by boiling unfermented juice from Trebbiano grapes grown around Modena, and then ageing the vinegar in a series of barrels made of different woods – cherry, mulberry, oak, chestnut.

GIANDUIA
Turin's passion for chocolate dates back to the 16th century when a Savoy general brought cocoa back from the New World. But it wasn't until 1867 that a local confectioner came up with the idea for *gianduia*. A mix of hazelnuts from the Langhe hills and cocoa paste, it was a hit and remains a prized local speciality.

PARMA'S PROSCIUTTO
HAM IT UP

Italian regional pride finds full expression in the nation's smorgasbord of cured meats (*salumi*). Every region has its specialities, and towns across the country take enormous pride in producing their own hams, sausages and salamis.

Of the hundreds of Italian hams, the most celebrated is *prosciutto crudo di Parma* from Parma in Emilia-Romagna. Parma is something of a superstar in Italy's culinary firmament, producing not only the country's finest ham but also its most famous cheese, parmigiano reggiano. Prosciutto is usually eaten as antipasti, the savoury starters that wake up the taste buds before the main dish (the *secondi*). Its rich, salty flavour works well with sweet fruit and a glass of prosecco. Try the ham with fresh figs (cut a cross in the top of each fig and squeeze to open), with asparagus (sear the spears on a griddle, sprinkle with sea salt, pepper and olive oil and wrap in ham) with bundles of rocket and shavings of parmigiano reggiano, or just paired with slices of buffalo mozzarella. As always in Italian cuisine, simplicity and sublime ingredients go a long way

Other standout regional meats are mortadella (or baloney) from Bologna, and culatello, a salted spiced ham, from Zibello. To the north of Emilia-Romagna, Italy's Alpine regions produce some fine ham, including prosciutto di San Daniele, a sweet ham from Friuli-Venezia Giulia, and speck, a dry-salted ham from Trentino Alto-Adige. Lombardy is home to *bresaola*, an air-dried beef.

⊜ WHERE TO EAT SALUMERIA GARIBALDI
VIA GARIBALDI 42, PARMA
A bountiful delicatessen in central Parma, Salumeria Garibaldi is a treasure trove of regional delicacies with dangling sausages, shelves of Lambrusco wines, slabs of Parma ham and wheels of parmigiano reggiano.

ABOVE A match made in heaven: mozzarella and Parma ham are two of Italy's tastiest products
RIGHT Curing legs of ham worth thousands of euros in Langhirano, Emilia-Romagna

OLIO DI OLIVA

Olive oil has been prized in the Mediterranean for thousands of years. In ancient times it was used in religious rites and as a medicinal rub. Nowadays, it's Italy's cooking oil of choice. After Spain, Italy is the world's second-largest producer, with Puglia, Calabria, Sicily and Tuscany the major regions. Some of the finest oils, however, come from Liguria. The best oils are designated *extravergine* (extra virgin), which means that they were mechanically extracted (as opposed to chemically extracted) and contain no more than 0.8% oleic acid; virgin olive oils contain up to 2% oleic acid. Lower acid generally means more flavour and a stronger aroma.

SPAGHETTI ALLA VONGOLE

Fresh clams and tomatoes doused in olive oil create a zesty dish.

INGREDIENTS

140g/5oz spaghetti
500g/1lb fresh clams in shells
2 ripe tomatoes
2 tbsp olive oil
1 fat garlic clove, chopped
1 small fresh red chilli, finely chopped
Splash of white wine
2 tbsp chopped parsley

PREPARATION

Rinse the clams, discarding any that remain open. Cover the tomatoes with boiling water, leave one minute, then slip off their skins, remove the seeds and chop the flesh.

Cook spaghetti in the boiling water. Heat oil in a large pan, add garlic and chilli and fry gently for a few seconds. Stir in the tomatoes, clams, wine, salt and pepper. Bring to the boil, cover, cook for three to four minutes, until the clams open.

Discard any closed clams. Drain the pasta, tip into the pan and toss with parsley. Serve in bowls with bread to soak up the juices. Serves 4.

ᘜ
SEAFOOD
FRESH FROM THE SEA

Food shopping becomes street theatre at La Pescheria, Catania's historic fish market. Tables groan under the weight of swordfish, ruby-pink prawns, clams, mussels, sardines and sea urchins, while fishmongers gut fish and high-heeled housewives step daintily over puddles of blood-stained water.

The sea has long been a source of food for Italians, and the country's four seas – the Ligurian, Tyrrhenian, Ionian and Adriatic – have been fished for millennia. Traditionally, fish and *frutti di mare* (a generic term referring to mussels, clams and other molluscs) were eaten as a cheap alternative to meat on Fridays and Christmas Eve.

Italians like their seafood served in a thousand different ways. Typically, an antipasto of *insalata di polpo* (octopus salad) or *alici marinate* (marinated anchovies) might be followed by *spaghetti alle vongole* (with clams, olive oil and a dash of chilli) or *pasta con le cozze* (with mussels) and a main course of baked *spigola* (sea bass) or *fritto misto* (battered and fried squid, prawns and other small fish) or grilled *seppia* (cuttlefish). *Pescespada* (swordfish), sardines and *tonno* (tuna) are also popular, particularly in Sicily. Cod is a surprise find on Italian menus but a taste for *stoccafisso* (air-dried cod) and *baccalà* (salted cod) has survived from times when sailors would spend long periods at sea eating preserved fish for months on end.

♨ WHERE TO EAT OSTERIA ANTICA MARINA
VIA PARDO 20, CATANIA

In the Sicilian city of Catania, seafood aficionados head to Osteria Antica Marina for *spaghetti ai ricci di mare* (spaghetti with sea urchins) and other fishy treats.

ABOVE Changing times: once a poor fishing village, Positano is now a jewel of the Amalfi Coast

 due

BISTECCA ALLA FIORENTINA
FLORENTINE STEAK

Florence might be the cradle of the Renaissance and guardian to some of the world's greatest masterpieces, but when it comes to food, the locals like to keep it simple. And nothing is as simple as the city's iconic *bistecca alla fiorentina*, a thick T-bone of local Chianina beef that's rubbed with olive oil, seared on the char grill, seasoned and served *al sangue* (bloody).

For centuries, meat was something of a rarity for Italy's toiling masses, reserved for Sundays and traditional holidays. However, prosperity has brought a marked increase in consumption and modern Italians, though not Europe's greediest carnivores, are enthusiastic meat-eaters.

Another of the country's big meat-eating regions is Sardinia, despite being an island. The locals generally consider themselves *pastori, non pescatori* (shepherds not fishermen). Until fairly recently, Sardinia's inland communities were cut off from the coast and dishes evolved according to shepherds' needs. Pork and lamb were spit roasted over juniper fires to save on equipment; *pane carasau* (bread) was baked light so shepherds could carry it; and pecorino cheese was made from ewe's milk.

The island's most famous dish is *porceddu*, also spelt *porcheddu* (suckling pig). This is usually spit roasted but some old-fashioned recipes call for it to be cooked in a hole in the ground, just like bandits used to cook theirs to cover their tracks.

◉ **WHERE TO EAT L'OSTERIA DI GIOVANNI**
VIA DEL MORO 22, FLORENCE

For a meaty fill-up in Florence, head to L'Osteria di Giovanni, a neighbourhood favourite specialising in earthy Tuscan staples – including, of course, *bistecca alla fiorentina*.

ABOVE Rare treat: cuts from the historic Chianina beef breed, named after a Tuscan valley

PEPOSO

This peppy, slow-cooked beef dish is a Florentine classic, once feeding the workers building the Duomo of the city's cathedral. You'll need a hearty appetite, lots of wine and a terracotta casserole dish – but a medieval masterpiece isn't required.

INGREDIENTS

1kg/2lb beef shank
2 tbsp (minimum) black pepper
1 tbsp sea salt
1 head of garlic
1–1.5 bottles of Chianti

PREPARATION METHOD

Preheat the oven to 150°C/300°F. Cut the beef into rough chunks. Smash the garlic head with your hand or the flat blade of a knife, discarding the excess papery skin. Put both in a large casserole dish. If you have black peppercorns, crush them. Add salt, as much pepper as your guests can handle and the wine. Place in the hot oven until it has heated up then turn down the oven to 95°C/200°F. Cook gently for between four and eight hours. Serve with crusty bread.

DOLCE & GELATO
THE SWEET FINALE

A love of *gelato* is ingrained in the Italian DNA. No one is quite sure where ice cream came from but it was probably introduced to Italy by the Saracens, who brought techniques for freezing fruit juices to Sicily in the 9th century. Today, *gelato* is part of Italy's summer scene – holidaymakers slurp on cones on seafronts; kids go gaga over their favourite flavours; slick urbanites lose their cool over *coppe* (tubs) at elegant cafes. Flavours include *bacio* (chocolate hazelnut), *zabaglione* (creamy mix of egg yolks and sweet Marsala wine) and *stracciatella* (cream with chocolate chips). Whatever your choice, the best *gelato* is always made in small-scale artisanal *gelaterie* from seasonal fruits and fresh local ingredients.

For a cooling summertime treat, try a semi-frozen Sicilian granita made from sugar, water and a syrup or fruit juice. For truly memorable taste go for a *granita di mandorla* (almonds) or *granita di gelsi neri* (black mulberries). Italians also take their *dolci* (a word that covers everything from biscuits to cakes) seriously. Each town has its specialities: Naples is celebrated for *sfogliatelle* (flaky pastries stuffed with ricotta and candied fruit); Turin is the home of *gianduia*, a velvety chocolate hazelnut paste. Treviso is the birthplace of tiramisu, that creamy marriage of mascarpone, coffee and *savoiardi* sponge biscuits.

For the sweet of tooth, Sicily is a veritable promised land. Chief among the island's sugary pleasures is the *cannolo*, a heavenly tube of biscuity-pastry stuffed with creamy ricotta and candied fruit or chocolate chips. Next up is cassata, the queen of Sicilian desserts, a sweet cake of ricotta, sugar, vanilla, diced chocolate and candied fruits.

⊜ WHERE TO EAT CAPPELLO
VIA NICOLOÒ GARZILLI 10, PALERMO

Cappello is one of Palermo's best *pasticcerie* (pastry shops). Other than the classic cannoli and cassata, its dreamy showstoppers include a seven-layer chocolate cake called *setteveli*.

ABOVE Italian ice-cream makers ply their trade around the world but it tastes best at home
LEFT Gorgeous Grand Canal: dine alfresco in Venice and it's not only the food that looks great

---

▥ LEARNING

Whether you want to hone your culinary talents in a Tuscan villa or visit a parmesan cheese-maker, there are plenty of opportunities to learn about Italian food.

CITTÀ DEL GUSTO
www.gamberorosso.it
Run by Gambero Rosso, Italy's top foodie publisher, the City of Taste is a six-storey temple to food offering courses taught by Rome's top chefs, live cooking demonstrations, wine courses and workshops.

MODENATUR
www.modenatur.it
A Modena-based tour operator that organises gastronomic tours of the city and its environs, including visits to a local balsamic-vinegar producer, a parmesan cheese-maker and a Lambrusco vineyard.

TUSCOOKANY
www.tuscookany.com
Two rustic Tuscan villas, one about 50km from Florence and one near Arezzo, provide the idyllic settings for week long and three-day cooking courses.

ANNA TASCA LANZA
www.annatascalanza.com
Anna Tasca Lanza runs her residential cookery school on the Regaleali estate, southeast of Palermo. Courses range from five-day packages including accommodation to a day-long lesson and lunch.

APICIUS
www.apicius.it
For a more career-minded approach, sign up at the International School of Hospitality in Florence. The school also offers short courses and wine-tasting instruction.

Food fight: protective
headgear is advised at the
Battaglia della Arance

FESTIVALS

Traditions run deep in Italy, a country where each city, town and village has its own customs and festivals. Many are religious in origin or fuelled by ancient rivalries, but some are simple celebrations of food. These *sagre* are popular community events, drawing enthusiastic crowds and local producers.

FEBRUARY & MARCH

Mandorlara, Agrigento
For 10 days in early February, chefs in the Sicilian town of Agrigento pay homage to their local almonds with special menus and nut-based menus.

Battaglia delle Arance
In the run-up to Lent, the Piedmontese town of Ivrea stages Italy's wildest food fight. Up to 3500 citizens take part in the Battle of the Oranges, pelting each other with 400,000kg of Sicilian oranges, specially imported for the occasion.

NeroNorcia: Mostra Mercato del Tartufo
The black truffle is the star of this Umbrian food fest, held in Norcia on the last two weekends in February. Producers gather to display their hams, salamis, cheeses, and, of course, truffles.

Cioccolatò
Turin is Italy's chocolate capital, as you'll discover at this mega celebration of all things chocolaty. Events kick off in early March and last for about 10 days.

Vinitaly, Verona
Get to grips with Italian *vino* and international vintages at Italy's top wine fair, held over four days in late March or early April in Verona.

APRIL

Mille e 2 Formaggi
The charming Lombard town of Mantua provides the stage for this three-day homage to Italian cheese and the artisans who make it.

Fritto Misto all'Italiana
As the birthplace of *olive all'ascolana* (deep-fried meat-stuffed olives), Ascoli Piceno is the perfect place for a festival dedicated to fried food.

Sagra dei Tarallucci e Vino
Get to grips with Pugliese wine while snacking on *tarallucci*, pretzel-like baked biscuits, amid Alberobello's characteristic *trulli* (conical-capped houses).

MAY & JUNE

Slow Fish
Head to Genoa for everything you always wanted to know about fish at Slow Food's biennial seafood jamboree.

Girotonno
Islanders of Isola San Pietro, a tiny islet off Sardinia's southwest coast, celebrate their yearly tuna catch in June with a four-day festival of cooking competitions, tastings, seminars, concerts and nautical-themed events.

SEPTEMBER

Pizza Village
Naples is the proud home of the pizza *Margherita* and rarely misses any opportunity to advertise the fact. This five-day bonanza attracts teams of swaggering *pizzaioli* (pizza makers) and crowds of hungry visitors. In 2011 some 60,000 pizzas were made by 20 participating pizzerias.

Gusta Minori
Minori, a small town on the Amalfi Coast, hosts this annual festival of art, culture and food. Expect plenty of juicy local lemons, lashings of *limoncello liqueur*, and locally caught tuna and anchovies.

Cheese
One of the world's largest cheese festivals, this biennial event is held in Bra, the birthplace of the Slow Food movement. Thousands flock to the town's medieval centre to taste, sniff and prod cheeses from all over the world.

OCTOBER & NOVEMBER

Salone Internazionale del Gusto
Slow Food's big showcase festival is held every other year in Turin. Small-scale organic producers come from across the globe to promote their goods and debate sustainability and environmental issues.

Fiera Internazionale del Tartufo Bianco
For much of October, Alba revels in white truffles with street stalls at the weekends and truffle-based specialities in restaurants. A highlight is the Donkey Palio, which takes place on the first Sunday of the month.

Eurochocolate
A big international chocolate fair in the hilltop town of Perugia, home of Perugina chocolate.

Asta Mondiale del Tartufo Bianco d'alba
Restaurateurs from as far afield as Hong Kong tune into the international white-truffle auction held in Grinzane Cavour every November. It's big business – in 2011, a dozen truffles sold for a mind-boggling €227,000.

For a flashback to eating and drinking
in '50s Japan, hit the alleyways of
Omoide Yokocho in Tokyo

JAPAN

The beauty of a Japanese dish draws you in with its simple elegance – you're likely to end up in zen-like contemplation of every detail. Then you taste it and simplicity takes on a power you could never have imagined ...

It's hard to believe that barely a generation ago, Westerners considered Japanese cuisine strange, exotic and – dare we say – off-putting. Raw fish? Fermented soybeans? Slurping noodles from a bowl? Green tea? 'Unusual' would have been polite. Yet the world has since come to know and love the exquisite zing of wasabi on sushi, the tang of teriyaki, the silkiness of tofu and the soothing warmth of a bowl of soba.

Japanese cuisine tells the story of Japanese history, from samurai to world economic domination. For millennia, Japanese people survived on just three staples: rice, soybeans and pickled vegetables. Today, these humble foods are often passed over in favour of fish and meats, yet their presence continues to be felt at virtually every meal.

Like the country's culture, Japanese cooking is deeply seasonal, with some seasons lasting for just a week. *Shin-mai* (new rice) is especially prized for the moisture it retains in the first months after harvest, and its clumpy character is a great match for other dishes. But this ephemeral treasure isn't for export: by the time it could be shipped, the extra moisture would be gone.

Revered as a stealth ingredient in Japanese cuisine, the humble soybean is versatile and monstrously good for you. It's the main component of the *miso* in your soup and the tofu gently bubbling in the pot of your vegetarian lunch. And *edamame*, quickly boiled, deep-green whole soybean pods, go so well with Japanese beer.

Tsukemono (pickled vegetables) were essential to the diet of the Japanese, who until recently had no way of procuring fresh vegetables for much of the year. Whether made up of *daikon* (a long white radish), eggplant, cucumber or mixed greens, the bold colours of *tsukemono* are specially chosen to offset each other.

This artful presentation mirrors Japan's aesthetic sense, as bowls, plates and bento boxes are precisely matched to the foods served on them.

THE ORIGINAL FUSION CUISINE

The western port of Nagasaki has been a crossroads since Portuguese missionaries and Chinese and Dutch traders arrived in the 1600s, and that history carries through to its modern food scene. *Champon* is a local take on rāmen, featuring squid, octopus, pork and vegetables in a white, salt-based broth. Chinese and Portuguese influences converge in *shippoku-ryōri*, Nagasaki-style *kaiseki*, while *kakuni-manju* is a Chinese import, a slab of pork belly in a thick, sweet sauce, served in a steamed wheat bun and often found at street stalls.

SAKE NO TERIYAKI
Salmon sautéed Japanese-style.

INGREDIENTS

4 unsalted salmon fillets

1 or 2 white leeks

2 or 3 *togarashi* (red chilli peppers)

A little salad oil

1 tbsp sake

3 tbsp *shoyu*

PREPARATION METHOD

Sprinkle salt on to the salmon fillets and allow them to sit for 30 minutes. Cut the leek diagonally in 5cm-to 6cm/3in-long pieces. Heat the salad oil in a frying pan, add the fillets and leek and fry gently until golden brown. Add the sake and shoyu, cover the frying pan and cook for a further two to three minutes. Serve immediately. Serves four.

KOBE BEEF
MARBLED MAGIC

Tender, silky and with a buttery mouth feel, Kōbe beef (and other varieties of *wagyū*, Japanese beef) has been elevated to a fetish in much of the world. But until the 19th century, beef was not eaten in Japan. It's a textbook example of how Japan takes something from elsewhere, makes it its own, and beats the rest of the world at its game.

The turning point was 1868, when a teenager named Meiji ascended to the throne as emperor. Japan was in the last throes of its feudal period, having just come through some 225 years of isolation from the rest of the world, under the s*hogun* (military overlord). It dawned on Meiji that Japan, impoverished and undeveloped, could adopt the ways of the world's leading nations to become a leading nation itself. Clothes, education, music and architecture were brought in from the West. And Meiji is quoted as saying, 'I shall eat meat.'

The problem is that compared to other nations, Japan has virtually no grazing land. The solution? Take the cattle for daily walks and give them massages. No grasses for them to feed on? Tofu lees work just great (and give cows a lower saturated fat content), and feeding cows beer helps stimulate their appetite. The playing of classical music? Why not?

It all resulted in the graceful marbling of Japanese beef, which the Western world is now scrambling to imitate. Japanese eat their beef lightly seared, sometimes even sashimi-style. Then there's *shabu-shabu;* a boiling pot of water is placed at the table in front of you – add vegetables, dip paper-thin slices of meat into the water, and swish them to cook in seconds.

WHERE TO EAT IMAHAN
3-1-12 NISHI-ASAKUSA, TAITŌ-KU, TOKYO

Try *wagyū shabu-shabu* at Imahan in Tokyo's Asakusa district. It's old-school and friendly, and after the beef is dipped in sesame sauce, it may be a head-spinning experience.

ABOVE LEFT Chinese-style noodles and fresh seafood meet in *champon* **ABOVE** A w*agyū* steak sizzles on a griddle, its fat providing more flavour than steak from a less-pampered beef herd

SOBA, UDON AND RAMEN
CHOOSE YOUR NOODLES

There you are, in one of Tokyo's most crowded train stations, and next to the magazine stand and snack kiosk is a tiny counter with no seats, selling bargain-priced bowls of *soba* or *udon* to blue-suited businessmen who stand while they eat.

Or maybe you're walking down a country lane and come across a chef in a restaurant window, rolling out dough the colour of sand. From a soccer-ball-sized lump, he ends up with a metre-wide sheet no more than a couple of millimetres thick. It's mesmerising as he dusts the sheet with flour, folds it in half and then in half again, then uses a pastry cutter to cut *soba* noodles with unmatched precision, to end up in broth mere minutes later.

Or maybe you're in the Rāmen Alley of Sapporo – while other nightlife districts are known for drinking, this one is for noodles.

Japan may have been raised on rice, but it runs on noodles. *Soba*, the thin, brownish buckwheat-based noodles, are closely associated with the Kantō region (around Tokyo) and the mountains of the Japan Alps, where the harsh climate and lack of arable land made it all but impossible to raise wheat. *Udon,* meanwhile, are the pencil-thick white wheat noodles typical of Osaka and western Japan. Many restaurants serve both.

Then there's rāmen, which originated in China but whose popularity in Japan is epic, with entire neighbourhoods and floors of department stores and office towers dedicated solely to rāmen restaurants. Basic rāmen is a big bowl of noodles in broth, served with toppings such as *chashu* (sliced roast pork), *moyashi* (bean sprouts) and *negi* (leeks).

🍜 WHERE TO EAT SHIN-YOKOHAMA RAUMEN MUSEUM

There are rāmen theme parks throughout Japan, where some of the nation's finest shops sell their wares. The first was the Shin-Yokohama Raumen Museum in Yokohama.

ABOVE Few meals are as comforting as a steaming bowl of *udon* noodles with whatever extras you can find

HOW TO ORDER NOODLES

First, choose your restaurant. While *soba* and *udon* are often served in the same restaurant, you can't count on it, and in many cases you'll want to go to a speciality shop to order your favourite.

- **Kake-soba** – served in a large bowl of light, bonito-flavoured broth

- **Mori-soba (aka seiro-soba)** – served cold and piled on a bamboo mat; dip the noodles in a soy-sauce-based broth, fortified with wasabi and slices of green onion

- **Zaru-soba** – *mori* or *seiro* soba topped with slivers of dried *nori* (seaweed); very refreshing in warm weather

- **Tsuke-men** – cold noodles served with a bowl of broth and a plate of vegetables, which cook when they're dunked in the bowl with the noodles

- **Sobayu** – at the end of the meal, the hot water used for boiling the noodles is mixed with the leftover broth, and drunk like tea

EATING ETIQUETTE

- Say '**itadakimasu**' (literally 'I receive') before digging in. At the end of the meal, thank your host or server by saying, '*Gochisō-sama deshita*' ('It was a feast').

- **Chopsticks in rice** Do not stick your *hashi* (chopsticks) upright in a bowl of rice. This is how rice is offered to the dead in Buddhist rituals. Similarly, do not pass food from your chopsticks to someone else's, which recalls another funeral ritual.

- **Slurp** When eating noodles in Japan, it's perfectly OK, even expected, to slurp them. This cools hot noodles, and many aficionados say it enhances the flavour. In fact, one of the best ways to judge a rāmen restaurant is to listen for the loud slurping sound!

IZAKAYA

Izakaya translates as drinking house, and these rowdy little shops, historically identified by the red lanterns out front, are great places for a casual meal, with a wide selection of food, a hearty atmosphere and plenty of beer and sake to lubricate conversation – enter as a stranger, and you may end up with a new friend.

Patrons typically order a few dishes at a time, from a selection of *yakitori* (skewers of grilled chicken, in teriyaki sauce or sprinkled with salt), *kushiyaki* (other grilled skewers), sashimi and grilled fish. Say *'toriaezu'* (that's all for now) when you've finished ordering each set of dishes.

SHŌCHŪ

Forget *sake* – *shōchū* is king in the southern prefecture of Kagoshima. This distilled spirit can be made from sweet potato (in which case it's called *imo-jōchū*), barley (*mugi-jōchū*) and even green tea (*cha-jōchū*). Unlike vodka, which is distilled multiple times to remove flavours, part of the fun of drinking *shōchū* is tasting those overtones.

In recent years, *shōchū* has been resurrected from its previous lowly status (it was used as a disinfectant in the Edo period) to become a trendy drink nationwide. Try it *oyu-wari* (diluted in hot water), *rokku* (on the rocks), or in a *chūhai* (highball with soda and lemon).

SAKE
JAPAN'S NATIONAL DRINK

Sake is simple, requiring only three ingredients – rice, water and *koji* (brewer's yeast) – yet its impact on Japanese culture is far reaching. No wonder the more formal name of *sake* (pronounced sah-keh, not sah-kee, please) has a more proper name in Japanese: *Nihonshu*, the 'drink of Japan'.

With more than 1500 *sake* breweries in Japan, *sake's* presence can be felt almost everywhere. It seals vows in traditional wedding ceremonies, sipped from three saucers of red lacquer, stacked on tiny pedestals. It is so enmeshed with ceremonies of Shinto, Japan's native religion, that almost every Shinto shrine displays huge *sake* casks. And an entire ceramics culture, from *tokkuri* flasks to tiny *chokko* cups, grew up around drinking the fermented rice beverage.

On balmy summer nights during the Edo period, nobles and their courtesans gathered on the verandah to pay tribute to the glowing moon, said to be visible in four places. First, the sky, and second, its reflection off the ground or a pond below. The third location: in the *sake* cup. And the fourth? In the eyes of your beloved, made all the more dreamy by the *sake's* afterglow.

Though it's often called rice wine, *sake* is actually brewed more like beer. In winter, when the rice crop is fresh, the breweries are in full swing: steaming rice, mixing in *koji*, letting it ferment, pressing out the lees and filling massive 1.8L bottles. The rest of the year, *sakagura* (*sake* breweries) can be spotted by the balls of cedar fronds hanging above their doors, selling their production to make way for the next year's supply; unlike grape wines, *sakes* are not meant to be aged.

As with many other things in Japan, the gradations of *sake* are myriad and detailed. It starts with the rice – the more of the kernel that is polished away, the more refined the taste is said to be: from *futsu-shu* (ordinary *sake*, with little to none of the outer layer gone) to *daiginjo* (as little as 30% of the original kernels, until they're like tiny white ball bearings). While *sake* is often drunk *atsu-kan* (piping hot), purists say that a high-quality *sake* should never be served warmer than *reishu* (very cold). Top-drawer stuff is normally served well chilled (the classification depends on how much the rice is refined before fermentation).

Then there's *sake's* communal nature. The first rule of drinking: don't do it alone. The second: watch out for others. Fill their glasses with both hands, then let them reciprocate, and raise your glass a little off the table while it is being filled. Once everyone has some *sake* in their glass, wait for the chorus of '*Kanpai!*' ('Cheers!') before putting glass to lips. Don't use the Mediterranean toast of *cin-cin* unless you want to induce peals of laughter – it's slang for what little boys have and little girls don't! Should you make a gaffe, it's OK. *Sake* is one way many normally staid Japanese let off steam.

🍴 WHERE TO EAT OMOIDE YOKOCHO, TOKYO

Sake and yakitori always seem to go together. A great place to sample them is Omoide Yokocho, next to Tokyo's Shinjuku Station. This warren of tiny shops, with tiny counters and smoke wafting through the air, is like a step back to the Japan of 50 years ago – its name means Memory Lane, but locals also call it Shōben Yokochō (Piss Alley). We'll let you figure out why.

ABOVE LEFT An *izakaya* in Tokyo is the perfect place to try sake for the first time **RIGHT** It is considered auspicious to break open by hand a cask of sake at important occasions

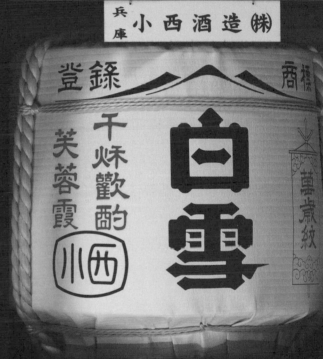
兵庫 小西酒造㈱

兵庫 大関株式会社

兵庫 菊正宗酒造㈱

兵庫 櫻 正宗 ㈱

SUSHI ETIQUETTE

- Pour just enough soy sauce to cover the bottom of the saucer.

- Mix a pinch of wasabi into the soy sauce, to taste.

- Ask the chef if this piece of sushi should be dipped, as some are already flavoured.

- Dip the sushi into the soy sauce–wasabi mixture for a split second, with the fish side down (not the rice side). The idea is to accent the fish, not overwhelm it.

- Each piece of sushi is meant to be eaten in one bite.

- Sushi is one of the few Japanese foods that's acceptable to eat with your fingers. Just be sure you first wipe your hands carefully with the *oshibori* (hot towel) you've been provided – or use your chopsticks if you prefer.

SUSHI
RAW TALENT

Sushi marries two Japanese icons – fish and rice – but the central ingredient of sushi is not raw fish, which when served alone is called sashimi, but the sweetened, vinegared rice it's served with. In addition to raw fish, the rice is often paired with vegetables and egg.

As with any skill worth mastering in Japan, the training to prepare raw fish is laborious. In a top restaurant, it may be months, if not years, of mixing rice with vinegar and sugar in precise proportions and slicing pickled ginger, before a trainee is allowed before a customer. By the time he (or she, but only rarely) becomes an *itamae* (sushi chef), the making of the *nigiri* (little pillows of sushi rice) and the slicing of the fish to top them are second nature.

To let your *itamae* shine, order *omakase*, a chef's-choice course of the freshest, most seasonal fish. Then there's *fugu* (aka globefish, puffer fish or blowfish), whose silvery flesh is usually arranged like a chrysanthemum, and is actually rather bland – it's eaten more for the thrill than the taste, since most of its internal organs (especially the liver) are highly poisonous. The danger of *fugu* poisoning is negligible, since, as you've probably figured by now, only chefs who have a licence and have undergone extensive training are allowed to prepare it. That said, Japanese joke that you should let your dining companion try the first piece of *fugu*. If they are still talking after five minutes, the dish is safe.

In the home, fish is used for more than sushi. *Dashi*, a broth made from paper-thin flakes of dried bonito, is the base for everything from miso soup to a sauce for soba and egg custard.

ABOVE LEFT Presentation, representing precision and harmony, is a core part of the sushi experience
RIGHT ABOVE & BELOW The Japanese idea of watching chefs at work has spread to Western kitchens

TSUKIJI MARKETS

Hectares of fish and seafood (around 450 varieties, 2000 tonnes, altogether worth over US$20 million) change hands daily at Tokyo's Tsukiji Central Fish Market, in an atmosphere of controlled chaos. A quick scan of the wholesalers' stalls seems to reveal half the contents of the ocean, with mountains of octopus, rows of giant tuna, endless varieties of shellfish and tank upon tank of live fish. Some of the hundreds of merchants at work here have been in the business for as many as 20 generations.

The famous tuna auctions take place before dawn, with a riot of bell ringing and the sort of yelling rarely heard elsewhere in Japan. Access for visitors has been an on-again off-again affair for the last few years, so before you head in, confirm via your hotel concierge or www.tsukiji-market.or.jp.

After 9am, though, anyone is free to wander along the seemingly endless rows of wholesalers; be sure to keep your distance though, as it's very much a place of business. By late morning, the action will have pretty much wound down.

Tsukiji's Outer Market is neither as famous or as breathtakingly busy as its inner counterpart. But most people will find that a blessing, allowing time and space to browse the produce and admire displays of prepared foods you may never have seen before. There are sushi and noodle shops here, tiny cafes and suppliers of boots, baubles, baskets, plates, picks (of the tooth variety) and pottery, all at reasonable prices.

Not going to Tokyo? Two other well-known food-market streets to visit are Nishiki in Kyoto and Omicho in Kanazawa.

A SUSHI GLOSSARY

- **Nigiri-zushi** – a small slice of fish served on a small pillow of rice
- **Maki-zushi** – served in a seaweed roll
- **Chirashi-zushi** – a bowl of rice covered in a colourful confetti of fish, vegetables and julienned egg
- **Oshi-zushi** – fish pressed in a mould over rice
- **Inari-zushi** – rice in a pocket of sweet, fried tofu
- **Omakase** – chef's choice
- **Kaiten-zushi** – sushi served on a conveyor belt

ẁ
Sado
THE WAY OF TEA

On a craggy path, in the middle of a forest, you come across a tiny, thatch-roofed hut, its walls a mottled brown. As you pause outside, admiring its rustic simplicity, you hear the singsong '*Ohairi kudasai*' ('come in') from within. Where you expect a door, there's only a sliding window made of a paper *shoji* screen. You leave your pack outside (it won't fit through the *shoji* window), bow and enter...

And suddenly you're in a separate world.

That is the essence of tea, or more accurately, the tea ceremony, whose Japanese name *sadō* (the Way of Tea) is probably more fitting. In this land of elegant arts, the presentation of tea is king. Yes, there's tea involved, but that's only one component of the ceremony. *Matcha* (powdered, whisked green tea) is deeply intertwined with traditions of the samurai and Zen meditation. Over the centuries, it's spawned a host of related arts and crafts: ceramics, kimono, calligraphy, *ikebana* (flower arrangement), traditional architecture and garden design among them.

It starts with that tea house, where you're now comfortably seated on a cushion. The room is exactly four and a half *tatami* mats in size, and in front of you a special alcove, the *tokonoma*, is set aside for art: a just-picked flower in a bamboo bud vase, a scroll inscribed with swooshes of calligraphy evoking the host's emotion about this moment.

It's this simplicity and humility that create a spirit called *wabi-sabi*. Most importantly, the outside world stays outside the tea house. Just as your pack couldn't fit through the entrance, nor could a samurai's sword; for centuries, the teahouse was a place where peace was made between enemies.

The ceremony begins with ritualised movements of its preparation, serving and partaking. On the *tatami* before you, sits a sleek lacquered tray or rough-hewn ceramic dish topped with a single, perfectly creased sheet of *washi* paper and a solitary sweet, a work of art in its own right. '*Itadakimasu*', you say to your host with a bow, the first bite sweet and a bit chalky.

As the tea bowl is heated with water from a cast-iron kettle on a charcoal-fired *hibachi*, the sparseness of the tea room lets you pick up on the subtle *buku-buku* boiling of the water in the kettle. Then, with rituals codified by tea-master Sen no Rikyu in the late 16th century, water is poured, the bowl wiped clean, the tea powder and water added and whisked to a froth before the bowl is set before you with ultimate grace. Being equally gracious, you bow, drink the tea in three sips and admire the character of the bowl.

Each individual piece of hardware used, from the artwork to the bamboo whisk to the tea bowls, may be priceless – easily into the tens of thousands of dollars – but price is forgotten against the backdrop of this luxury of time to appreciate this single moment that has never been before and will never come again. Your host opens another *shoji* screen, onto a garden that, had you passed by the tea house, you'd never have realised was there.

🍵 WHERE TO DRINK ŌKŌCHI SANSŌ
8 TABUCHIYAMA-CHŌ, OGURAYAMA, SAGA UKYŌ-KU, KYOTO

Stroll through a bamboo forest in the Arashiyama district of western Kyoto, and you'll come across Ōkōchi Sansō, villa of silent film star Ōkōchi Denjirō. A bowl of *matcha* and a sweet are included in the price of admission and provide fortitude to ramble up and down stone paths in the villa's garden.

LEFT Every aspect of Japan's tea ceremony, from the craft and design to the etiquette is highly refined
ABOVE RIGHT There are dozens of different types of *wagashi*, not all so beautifully sculpted

THE SWEETEST THING

Dessert is not a Japanese mainstay but there is no lack of sweets. *Wagashi*, are popular gifts, many as artful as flowers. Some balance the bitter taste of the *matcha* served during the tea ceremony. An earthy filling of red *adzuki*-bean paste called *anko* turns up in *manju* (dumplings). Visitors expecting chocolate can be surprised, not always unpleasantly, to find *anko*.

YUZU NO SHABETTO

The yuzu is a grapefruit-like citrus fruit used in a zesty sorbet.

INGREDIENTS

1 large yuzu
⅓ cup sugar
2 cups water
2 tbsp Cointreau

PREPARATION

Wash the yuzu and grate the zest finely, without including the fruit's white flesh. Squeeze the yuzu and reserve the juice.

Put the sugar, juice and water into a thin-bottomed pan and heat over a moderate heat until the sugar dissolves. Cool this mixture.

Add the grated zest, Cointreau, and freeze. Prior to serving, place the frozen block in a food processor and whisk it into a mouldable consistency.

Serve in small ball shapes, garnished with fresh mint. If yuzu is not available, use lemon and orange zest.

Chopped *ao-jiso* (green beefsteak plant) leaf can be used; substitute the Cointreau with white wine. Serves 4.

Stirring soy sauce: the beans
ferment for 18 months

BITE-SIZE DIVERSIONS

Japanese food famously appeals to all your senses: strap in for a gastronomic odyssey to their outer-reaches.

WAGYŪ
Kōbe beef is just one variety of *wagyū* (literally, Japanese beef), cattle bred for the fatty marbling of their meat; other regions have their own, highly prized cattle. Due to its intense richness (and price), portions are small, seared quickly then cooked to medium rare. As you savour each bite, you may well agree that sometimes less is more.

CASTELLA IN NAGASAKI
These perfect yellow bricks of pound cake pay homage to the Portuguese influence in Nagasaki. Pick one up at Fukusaya, which has been making Castella since 1624, or Shōkandō, Castella supplier to the Japanese Imperial family.

OKONOMIYAKI IN OSAKA
The name of Osaka's signature dish means 'cook what you like'. These pancakes of cabbage and your choice of meat, seafood or vegetables, combined in an egg batter, sizzle on a *teppan* (iron griddle). Top them with *katsuo bushi* (bonito flakes), *ao-nori* (a sea green similar to parsley), Japanese Worcestershire-style sauce and mayonnaise.

ALFRESCO IN FUKUOKA
The Californian climate of Kyūshū's largest city is well suited to outdoor dining at *yatai*, mobile food stalls with simple counters and stools, serving cuisines from noodles to French. Fukuoka claims well over 200 *yatai*, more than the rest of Japan combined. The aromas and chatty conversation lead you to the best cooking.

SUSHI FROM A CONVEYOR BELT
Combining two Japanese obsessions, sushi and automation, *kaiten-zushi* (conveyor-belt sushi shops or sushi train) lets the sushi come to you as you sit at the counter.

SHABU-SHABU AT YOUR TABLE
Shabu-shabu is Japanese onomatopoeia for 'swish-swish', the sound thin slices of beef make when you swirl them in light broth in a pot at your table. Dip the beef, along with vegetables cooked in the same pot, in a variety of special sesame-seed and citrus-based sauces.

YUDŌFU IN KYOTO
Taking its cues from Buddhist vegetarian cuisine, *yudōfu* (boiled tofu) is, for many Japanese, a must-eat on a visit to one of Kyoto's 2000 temples. Blocks of hot tofu, fresh from a pot on your table, explode with flavour when dipped in a soy-based sauce mixed with chopped spring onion, dried bonito flakes and ground ginger.

NATTŌ IN KANTŌ
Admittedly, *nattō* is not for everyone, but fans are manic for these brown pearls of fermented soybeans connected with stringy goo. Residents of Kantō (Tokyo and surrounds) eat it for breakfast, mixed into rice with a dab of hot mustard.

HOBA-MISO IN TAKAYAMA
While in this historic samurai town in the Japan Alps, try *hoba-miso*, sweet miso paste grilled at the table on a magnolia leaf on your own personal *hibachi*.

ONIGIRI AT A CONVENIENCE STORE
Nutritious, filling and portable, these palm-sized rice triangles were said to be road food for itinerant samurai; today's road warriors carry them in briefcases or backpacks. Deep inside is a thimble-sized morsel of broiled salmon, simmered *konbu* (kelp), tuna mayo or more, all wrapped in a sheet of crispy *nori* seaweed.

Snow has fallen on red chilli pepper ristras drying in the sun

MEXICO

**Say a hearty 'hola' to Latin America's culinary backbone:
from Cuba to Tierra del Fuego, nowhere offers food with as many tastes,
traits, colours and complexities as Mexico.**

Mexican cuisine is hugely diverse, thanks to the 60-odd indigenous groups scattered across the country, each with its own legacy of recipes. Mexico's vast deserts, mountain ranges and jungles have isolated, accentuated and preserved these differences, resulting in a mouth-watering mosaic of flavours and traditions.

Mexico's northern cuisine rustles up beef and goat specialities; central Mexican dishes incorporate nopales (cacti); in the south, poultry and vegetables predominate in a throwback to ancient Mexico. Nationwide, fiery chillies are a standout seasoning, alongside the equally distinctive use of fresh coriander and the bitter, lemony, camphor-like *epazote,* also known as Mexican tea.

The roots of Mexico's cuisine lie in two of the most influential pre-Columbian civilisations: the Mayans and the Aztecs. Maize (corn) was the lifeblood of these cultures. Ground and whipped into *masa* (dough), it was cooked on a skillet to make tortillas, now enjoyed worldwide.

Delicious accompaniments might have included lentils, tomatillos (small green relatives of the cape gooseberry, and distant relatives of the tomato), squashes, avocados, seeds and fish. Pineapple and papaya were common fruits but the ultimate sweet treat was chocolate: the Mayan's great gift to the world, and so revered by the Aztecs that they used cacao beans for currency.

Conquistadors liked what they saw (or ate), and a culinary collision ensued as Mesoamerican food mingled with Old World cattle, sheep, pigs, chickens, rice, wine and olive oil. It only seems fitting, therefore, that Mexico's signature dish, *mole poblano,* is a fusion of pre-Columbian and Spanish ingredients. The rich, dark red sauce is imbued with chillies, tomatoes, a medley of spices and a kick of dark chocolate. Fast-forward several centuries from the Spanish conquest, and Mexico's traditional cuisine is one of the world's few to attain Unesco's coveted Intangible Cultural Heritage (ICH) status. *Buen provecho, amigos!*

OAXACA MARKETS

Buckets are filled with *chapulines* (grasshoppers) fried with chilli powder. Still-sizzling *tlayudas* (plate-sized tortillas) are ladled with salsa concocted from some of the region's 60 endemic chillies, ranging from the rare stumpy black chilhuacle negro to scarlet onzas. Gusanos, the worms in the mezcal for which Oaxaca is famous, droop from awnings. Strings of quesillo cheese are wound into balls by gossiping *abuelas* (grandmothers). In the fruit section stand pyramids of papayas. Mole paste in black or *coloradito* (red) awaits in sacks, as everyone from local food vendors to internationally renowned restaurateurs (who know Mexico's worst-kept culinary secret: that Oaxaca, land of seven moles, is the place to purchase the country's top produce) haggle over prices.

Simmering mole dishes are close by: try the sought-after, chilhuacle-based *chichilo negro, mole amarillo* (made with tomatillos and cloves) and *mancha manteles* (served with tropical fruit). Fittingly for Mexico's chocolate capital, outside the main food market of Mercado Benito Juárez you'll glimpse cocoa beans being pummelled into paste and mingled with almonds and sugar in pools of creamy-brown to make the finished product.

This food frenzy is set against the rainbow hues of stall canopies and the multicoloured clothing of the women running the show, the clamorous bartering, the bleating livestock and, above all, the vendors' cries of 'que quiere?' (what do you want?).

Many writers, notably DH Lawrence in Mornings in Mexico, have tried to capture the vivid atmosphere of Oaxaca's markets. Words, though, can only do this sensory overload so much justice...

CHILLIES
RED-HOT CHILLI PEPPERS

Mexican food's feistiness comes courtesy of chillies, head honchos of colour and taste for much of the country's cuisine. The Yucatán is the main producer of habaneros: officially the world's hottest chillies and a common flavouring thereabouts. But Mexico has over 150 native chillies, far more varieties than it gave to the world when Mexico was Spain's main New World trading post with Asia.

Mexican chillies are incredibly versatile, alternating from red to black, spicy to smoky. It was the Mayans who came up with the idea of eating these fiery devils with the unlikely accompaniment of chocolate. Chillies add spice to moles, they prop up the country's salsas and they also get stuffed to make chilli relleno, a meal in itself.

Among the 60 chillies native to Oaxaca are the licorice-like chilhuacles, mulatos and pasillas used in the highly prized mole *chichilo negro*. The hotter serrano is what you'll often taste in guacamole, while the guajillo is added to meat before cooking. When you taste chocolate, nuts or fruit in your soup or salsa in Mexico, the flavour could be coming from chillies.

Chillies will sometimes blow your mouth off, rather than your mind, especially in salsas, but things quieten down a little when they're cooked.

⬙ WHERE TO EAT **MEXICAN CHILLI COOKOFF**

Ajijic, on Lake Chapala near Guadalajara, hosts the capsicum extravaganza that is the National Mexican Chilli Cookoff. Expect margarita, salsa and chilli competitions and more.

ABOVE Hot stuff: Mexico's many varieties of chilli are dried and sold in markets **RIGHT** Choose your own mole to add to your Mexican staples such as rice and eggs

COCHINITA PIBIL
INGREDIENTS

1 tsp salt

1 tsp white pepper

1kg/2lb pork loin

2L/68fl oz water

2 bay leaves

Prepared achiote paste*

Juice of 1 lime

3 cloves garlic, crushed or minced

300mL/10fl oz orange juice

100mL/3fl oz apple cider vinegar

1 large chipotle chilli in adobo sauce

2 tbsp brown sugar

1 sliced onion

FOR THE ACHIOTE PASTE

½ cup achiote (annatto) seeds

1 tbsp cumin seeds

1 tbsp black peppercorns

1 tbsp coriander seeds

5 allspice berries

1 cinnamon stick

8 cloves garlic

100ml/3fl oz orange juice

100ml/3fl oz white vinegar

50ml/1.5fl oz lemon juice

2 tbsp salt

PREPARATION

Grind the spices to a powder and mix with orange and lemon juice, vinegar, garlic and salt to make a paste. Let it sit for a couple of hours.

Put the pork in a pot with seasoning and bay leaves and cover with water. Simmer with the lid on for about two hours. Blend all the remaining ingredients, except the onion.

Remove pork and place on a plate, keeping the cooking stock. Shred the meat with a pair of forks. Keep 3 or so cups of the stock and discard the rest. Return the pork to the pot and add the blended mix of ingredients

Return to a simmer and slow cook with the lid on for about four hours (or until the liquid has mostly evaporated), adding the sliced onion for the last hour. Serve with tortillas, guacamole and coriander.

♨
COCHINITA PIBIL
MAYAN PORK

The Yucatán's most famous meal is a slow-cooked, leaf-wrapped pork speciality, marinated in brick-red achiote-seed sauce. Cochinita literally means 'little pork' but chicken is frequently used instead. The meat the Mayans would most likely have used was turkey, which, incidentally, Mexico was first to domesticate. And *pibil* dishes are so Mayan. The achiote, or annatto seeds, were once used by Mesoamerican tribes for body paint, which conveys an idea of their extract's potent red colouring. And nowhere do they provide more of a theme for a region's food than in the Yucatán.

The achiote seed's earthy, peppery flavour dominates the marinade, which these days incorporates bitter Seville oranges for a citrus kick. The dish is wrapped in banana leaves before being cooked, which should leave the meat falling apart when the leaf casing is removed. This cooking process would traditionally have been carried out over smoking coals in a *pib* (the pit) but these days, in possibly the only change to the dish since Mayan-era *pibil,* food vendors at Yucatán markets prefer to use everyday cooking pots. *Pollo pibil* is the chicken version of the dish, with the marinaded chicken wrapped and steamed in a banana leaf before serving.

⊜ WHERE TO EAT ELADIOS
MÉRIDA

Mérida is Yucatán's *pibil* capital: try it in a restaurant such as one of the several branches of family-friendly Eladio's or, better still, at the Mercado Santa Ana market.

ABOVE Rich, earthy achiote powder is the basis for many distinctive Mexican dishes

ANTOJITOS
MEXICAN FOR MUNCHIES

In this happy family are some of the world's most-loved snacks: *quesadillas*, enchiladas, tacos and tamales. *Antojitos* are as often served as main meals, although their portable nature makes them the ideal quick fix (*antojito* actually means 'little whim'). While World War Food might erupt in Latin America if you intimated that Mexico was the birthplace of any *antojito*, they are at their most gloriously diverse in the Mayan homeland. Mayans worshipped maize – they even severed their newborns' umbilical cords over a layer of corn husks. The best-known *antojitos* are tacos: cornflour-dough tortillas wrapped around meat, cheese or vegetables. *Quesadillas* are tortillas folded over cheese and cooked over a griddle. Enchiladas are packed with cheese or meat and doused in salsa before being cooked, giving them a delicious gooiness. To make tamales, the *masa* is wrapped in corn husks or plantain leaves with stewed meat, fish or vegetables, and slow-steamed.

   Here's a rule of thumb. *Antojitos* are best purchased from the stand of an old lady on a street corner, rather than ordered at a fancy restaurant. Just look out for smoking cooking pots and queues of locals. Mexico's tamales come wrapped in banana or plantain leaves in tropical areas, or corn husks elsewhere; Oaxacans chow down on tamales served with one of their renowned moles; shellfish are common fillings on the coast. Mexico City office workers might grab a *guajolota* (a tamale inside a roll) accompanied by *atole*, a corn-and-fruit drink. The country is well known for its *enchiladas suizas*, made with stringy Swiss cheese, evidence of a surprising French influence on this classic street food.

⊛ WHERE TO EAT TAQUERIA EL PASTORCITO
4503 LORENZO BOTURINI, COLONIA 24 DE ABRIL, MEXICO CITY
This open-fronted joint causes traffic jams. Experience 'real' Mexican food with locals as chefs carve slivers of pork to stuff into tacos with a choice of vats of salsa.

ABOVE Authentic tortillas are best sampled with the locals, cooked over an open fire and filled with meat, fish, vegetables, and sometimes cheese

ENCHILADAS
Enchiladas are wonderfully versatile. Essential ingredients are tortillas, salsa and a filling: vegetables and chicken in this recipe but you can use anything.

INGREDIENTS
8 tortillas (preferably corn but wheat will do)

150g/5oz white cheese

1 breast of chicken

½ small onion

3 to 6 chillies (fresh serranos ideally, depending on your heat threshold)

1 cup salsa

1 tbsp of oil

PREPARATION METHOD
Begin by making a *guiso* (stew) of the chicken, onion, and chillis. Chop finely and sauté in oil (*manteca,* or lard, is more authentic) until the chicken is cooked and the onion soft.

Heat the tortillas on a flat pan and then put 2 to 3 tablespoons of the stew into the tortilla. Roll them up in an oven-proof dish, top with salsa and the cheese, then cook under the grill until the cheese melts.

FRENCH REVOLUTION
The five-year rule of Maximilian, installed by Napoleon III, was Mexico's most gluttonous period. Feasting was continuous in Maximilian's Chapultepec pad: until he was dispatched by Juárez in 1867. No surprise then that French lavishness was the preferred dining style in Mexico's upper echelons during the 19th century, and that Mexico's first cookbook was influenced by French cooking techniques. Today, the French culinary impact can still be tasted in Mexican foods ranging from the *baño-maria (bain-marie)* cooking style used for meat sauces to those savoury rolls eaten at breakfast, *bolillos* (aka French rolls).

⸻

CHEESE & MEAT
WILD WEST DELICACIES FROM THE NORTH

If you've travelled through northern Mexico, you'll have seen cowboys relaxing in the plazas, and cowboy country means beef country. *Carne asada* (marinated grilled meat) is widely consumed here, as is *machaca*: marinated beef that has been shredded and dried for preservation with chillies – perfect for long stints in the wilderness. The quality of grazing grass around Monterrey means *cabrito* (goat) is at its most succulent here, and the city also gave Latin America the much-loved braised *arrachera* (flank steak). Other disparate peoples have also settled in the north, not least the Mennonites of Chihuahua and Durango states, who were invited over by the Mexican government for their agricultural prowess. The invite reaped dividends: among other foodie treats, Mennonites rustle up Mexico's finest cheeses.

Eating out up north isn't wildly different from the south, and for this reason food lovers often overlook the region. Street food is less prevalent and wheat (shock horror!) is sometimes used over maize as a staple. But a sit-down meal here is still a taste-bud tingler. Beef, either *asada* or *machaca*, frequently fills tacos. With the moistness of the lime marinade and the thin cut of the meat, the lasting impression is lightness rather than the stodginess of taco-filling imitations found outside Mexico. But you will struggle to find the best beef dish of all in any Western recipe book: *el norteño*, a muddle of beef with Mennonite cheese, cooked in a skillet. Durango presents Mennonite cheese in another enticing way: for dessert with *ate* (quince), for which the city is famous.

⸻

🍽 WHERE TO EAT RESTAURANTE MOCHOMOS
MORELOS 701, HERMOSILLO, SONORA

Beef it up in the heart of cowboy country at this intimate restaurant in Hermosillo's Zona Hotelera, where you can enjoy meat-themed delights such as *cabrera*, Sonora's signature T-bone steak fillet.

LEFT Harvesting the agave in the state of Jalisco is back-breaking work **ABOVE** Diners won't be complaining about portion size when they eat their *carne asada* (grilled meat) at this Fiera del Caballo near Mexico City

TEQUILA

There's more to tequila than the slammer. As single-malt whisky is to Scotland, so tequila is to Jalisco state. The potent liquor has Designation of Origin (DO) protection, meaning that all true tequila worldwide heralds from one province in central southern Mexico (and in limited quantities from four other Mexican states). The key ingredient in tequila, and the similar drinks of mezcal and pulque, is the agave plant. Tequila is easily the most sophisticated of these uniquely Mexican spirits, made only with the beautiful blue agave, which photogenically lines Jalisco's fields.

To make tequila, the blue agave heart is steamed for several days to release the *aguamiel* (honey water): the best tequilas use only this and water in fermentation. Look for the 100% agave label on the bottle: if it's not there, sugar-cane spirit or other sugars have been added in the fermentation process and the result will be, well, memorable in a bad way. If you remember anything at all. An agave plant takes about 10 years to mature, which explains the price difference between mixed and true tequilas.

But it's maturation in oak barrels that makes the tequila. The duration (anything from two months to five years) and the type of barrel make for a huge array of tastes. An extra-añejo, aged three years, is the connoisseur's choice, and is best served with a cube of ice. Mexicans are proud of their national drink and will soon show you that, far from a quick intoxicant, tequila is a pleasure to be sipped not slammed. And most bartenders are only too happy to initiate another to the sophisticated side of the notorious party drink.

MOLE VERDE

It's laborious but there is no greater sense of accomplishment than making your own *mole*. The most famous is the *mole poblano*. *Mole verde* (green *mole*) is one of the simpler, fresher varieties.

INGREDIENTS

2 large chicken breasts
1 small onion, diced
½ cup pumpkin seeds
1 can plum tomatoes
1 small chilli jalapeño, stems and seeds removed
2 chilli serranos, stems and seeds removed
6 lettuce leaves
½ medium onion, chopped
2 cloves garlic
½ cup coriander
Pinch cumin
Pinch black pepper
½ tsp ground cinnamon
1 clove
1 tsp vegetable oil

PREPARATION

Cook the chicken and onion in 6 cups of boiling water, skimming scum from the top until the breasts are nearly done. Remove the chicken, strain the broth. Toast the pumpkin seeds on a flat pan without burning. Cool then mash in a blender until powdery.

Add cup of the broth. Remove from blender. Drain the canned tomatoes and toss them in the blender with the chillies (remove the seeds to reduce the heat). Add lettuce, onion, garlic, coriander, ground cloves, cinnamon, pepper and cumin. Blend until smooth. Heat oil in the pan then heat the pumpkin/broth sauce for 4 to 5 minutes, stirring constantly until thick and dark. Add the vegetables and stir.

Gradually add about 2 cups of chicken broth (depending on thickness), and simmer for 25 to 30 minutes. Season. Before serving, return the chicken to the sauce until it heats through.

MOLE
HOLY MOLY!

Mexican food has soul, and at the heart of that soul is *mole* (pronounced 'moh-leh'). The word is thought to originate from the Nahuatl *molli*, meaning 'concoction', but there's a better story.

Back in the colonial heyday, nuns from Puebla heard that the archbishop would soon be visiting them. With their cupboards running low on stock, they produced what they could for an honorary dinner: chillies, old bread, some chocolate and spices, blended together and served over a turkey that had been kicking around. Its hotchpotch nature is the essence of mole: an enigma with anything from 15 to more than 40 ingredients that can take days to prepare, and is the nation's unofficial, yet universally accepted, number-one dish.

The common note in a *mole* is chilli, but with a wealth of seasonings contributing, the lasting impression might be a sweet tang or the lingering smokiness of garlic. *Moles* can be broken into four further component parts: sourness (often from the addition of tart green tomatillos), sweetness (by adding dried fruit, chocolate or sugar), spiciness (with cinnamon, cumin or cloves as regulars), and a thickening agent (often nuts). The accompanying meat is almost academic, acting merely as the stage on which the *mole* performs. And *mole* is an aesthetically pleasing dish too: its colour spectrum can range from orange through ruby-red to black.

Even Mexicans will agree that *mole* mecca is that 'land of seven moles', the state of Oaxaca. And the most sought after of the seven *moles* is *chichilo negro*, made with endemic chilhuacle negro chillies.

🍽 WHERE TO EAT CASA OAXACA
CONSTITUCIÓN 104A, OAXACA CITY

One of Oaxaca's classiest joints, Casa Oaxaca is the perfect *mole* initiation, run by an award-winning chef and offering unique regional dishes in an atmospheric courtyard.

ABOVE While Mexican cuisine is experiencing a surge in popularity in the West, preparing mole from scratch may become a dying art, with more Mexicans prefering the convenience of pre-made foods

ぃ

HUACHINANGO A LA VERACRUZANA
SOMETHING FISHY FROM VERACRUZ

The port of Veracruz enjoys a privileged culinary location: Mexico's major Gulf Coast city, it was historically best equipped to turn the eclectic seafood hereabouts into edible fare. It was also quite literally the first port of call for newly arriving conquistadors. As a result, food here displays some mouth-watering European and Caribbean influences. The flagship *huachinango* (red snapper), prepared in a Veracruz speciality sauce of tomatoes, capers, onion, crushed garlic and the state's very own jalapeño chillies, is perhaps Mexico's best advertisement for a nationally distinctive fish dish.

Cloves, cinnamon, garlic, capers: these Old World flavourings queue up to be added to this dish from the port where they were first unloaded into *nueva España* (New Spain). And it's the delicious, spicy fragrance that hits you while the sauce is still simmering away in the kitchen. *Huachinango a la Veracruzana* is usually served on Veracruz-grown rice, but the dish's secret ingredient, if you're lucky, electrifies your palate: the vanilla pods that are one of the main exports from Veracruz. Many recipes utilise a sauce made with sherry, another Spanish-introduced ingredient, which enhances the slightly sweet taste all good *huachinango a la Veracruzana* should have.

🍽 WHERE TO EAT ULÚA FISH
RUIZ CORTINES 2, VERACRUZ
A trendy cafe masterminded by a chef who has written a cookbook about the local seafood, this is a logical place to start savouring huachinango, served here in mango salsa.

ABOVE First, trap your snapper: the principal ingredient of Veracruz's signature fish dish is caught in the Gulf Coast and tropical waters worldwide

FESTIVALS
FERIA DE LA UVA Y EL VINO
Parras, Coahuila
Sporting several important wineries, Parras goes mad for wine in August. Celebrations include a massive two-day bender in Latin America's oldest winery, Casa Madero.

EL SABER DEL SABOR
Oaxaca
Created especially to showcase Oaxacan food, this September event draws top chefs from across Mexico.

FESTIVAL DEL MOLE
San Pedro Atocpan, Mexico State
This October festival in the town producing most of Mexico's mole is a veritable feast, with myriad mole varieties for sampling.

TOURS & EXPERIENCES
RUTA DEL VINO
Baja California
What the Napa Valley is to California, the Ruta del Vino (centring on Valle de Guadalupe) is to its neighbour, Mexico's wine-growing capital Baja California. The winery trail is near Ensenada, and signposted from there.

COFFEE
Coatepec
Veracruz state has Mexico's best coffee and Coatepec is the focus of coffee-producing activity. There are many great cafes in town and *fincas* (farms) just outside, along with El Café-tal, a coffee museum/cafe with hands-on coffee-making demonstrations and tastings.

TEQUILA
The town from which tequila got its name and other towns around Guadalajara such as Amatitán and Tlaquepaque do a thriving business in tequila 'experiences', including distillery tours and tastings. You can explore them with Guadalajara tour agencies such as Experience Tequila.

~~~ CHOCOLATE

Latin America's most sensual gift to the culinary world – the cacao bean – is the basis for these mouth-watering chocolate experiences.

BELGIUM

Belgians love chocolate as much as they love beer – a lot. Belgium produces 172,000 tonnes each year, sold in more than 2000 shops. And it's not just any old chocolate: Flanders boasts some of the planet's most imaginative chocolatiers. Look out for Hans Burie's flamboyant creations in Antwerp and Laurent Gerbaud's Orient-inspired offerings in Brussels.
Hans Burie; Korte Gasthuisstraat 3, Antwerp; Laurent Gerbaud; Centre Dansaert, Rue d'Alost 7, Brussels.

GHANA

Next time you eat a bar of chocolate, think of Tetteh Quarshie. The man who arguably did the most for modern chocolate production brought seeds of Theobroma cacao home from the island of Fernando Pó in 1876. Planting them in Mampong, he made Ghana a primary cocoa exporter – Ghana still produces 21% of the world's cocoa.
Visit Ghana's first cocoa plant at Quarshie's farm.

SOUTHERN BELIZE

In the beginning there was the pod, and the pod was good... Before Columbus lost his way to the East Indies, the Maya of Central America were tucking into *xocolatl* and *kukuh*, bitter, spicy drinks concocted from cacao beans. Today, Belize's cacao growers have a new lease of life due to Green & Black's, whose Maya Gold bars are based on the *kukuh* recipe. Visit Cyrila Cho's plantation to taste chocolate as 'pod' intended.
Visit Cyrila's plantation via the Toledo Cacao Growers Association

BOURNVILLE, UK

It's not Willie Wonka's Chocolate Factory but Birmingham's Cadbury World lets us drool over big vats of brown liquid loveliness and watch naked bars whizz through wrapping machines. The 1879 factory was revolutionary; with the popularity (and affordability) of cocoa, the Cadbury family moved production from the city centre to the suburbs, building a minitown that provided houses, education and pensions for its workers – a sweet social experiment.
Cadbury World is a 15-minute walk from Bournville train station.

TURIN, ITALY

Ever since Duke Filiberto introduced to Turin's court the sweet Aztec drink he'd discovered on his conquistadoring in the late 16th century, the city's been mad for cocoa. Top-notch chocolate shops are numerous along the grand boulevards and piazzas. Pop into Guido Gobino's emporium (Via Cagliari, 15b) for a taste – he's a master of the *gianduja*, a sensational hazelnut-chocolate combo and Turin's culinary symbol since 1867.
Cioccolatò, Turin's three-week chocolate festival, is held every March.

SWITZERLAND

You can't grow cocoa in the Alps. Yet this compact nation has the highest per-capita chocolate consumption in

the world, spawning some of the most famous makers: Lindt, Nestlé, Suchard and Toblerone. Visit the Nestlé-Calliers site near Gruyères, or for handmade pralines and truffles try one of the Sprüngli outlets – the company has crafted cocoa since 1836.
Sprüngli shops in Zürich, Basel, Zug, Winterthur and Glattzentrum

HERSHEY, PENNSYLVANIA
Welcome to the self-declared Sweetest Place on Earth! This chocolate-scented town, HQ of the Hershey's empire, is as saccharine as the all-American movies that caused kids across the globe to demand the iconic brand. The institution has spawned a resort of choco-entertainment.
14 East Chocolate Av. Pennsylvania

GRENADA, CARIBBEAN
Drive from St George's through the misty forest of Grand Etang National Park to reach remote Hermitage St Patrick's –

home to arguably the best chocolate in the world. The tiny Grenada Chocolate Company makes award-winning bars and cocoa in the most ethical fashion: beans are grown, picked, processed and packed in the factory-cum-family-abode. Stroll amid the cacao plants then taste it for yourself. Supermarket chocolate won't be the same again.
Hermitage St Patrick's, Grenada

PARIS, FRANCE
Chocoholics, you've found heaven. Check out the top-end goods with a visit to one of Robert Linxe's Maison du Chocolat stores. Then stop for refreshment at a chocolate cafe (try Chez Angelina) before booking in at the Lenôtre Culinary School for a cocoa

cooking class. The Salon du Chocolat festival hits Paris in October.
Lenôtre, 10 Champs-Élysées, Paris

VENEZUELA
Purists know that the finest of the three varieties of cacoa bean is the *criollo*, with its lingering aftertaste of vanilla, caramel and nuts. Venezuela, and specifically the Paria Peninsula – known as the 'Chocolate Coast' – is the origin of the most sought-after beans. The best are grown on family-run farms such as Hacienda Bukare. The Esser family offers tours of their plantation and tasty samples.
Hacienda Bukare is above Río Caribe; Via Playa Medina, Chacaracual, Venezuela.

Family and friends
enjoying a welcoming
meal in a Marrakesh riad

MOROCCO

Pierce the pastry of a pigeon b'stilla – which captures the essence of Moroccan cuisine with its meltingly tender meat, aromatic ingredients and theatrical presentation – and you'll be hooked.

An undercurrent of Berber and Arab flavours flows through Moroccan cuisine, but its source lies over the Mediterranean in Andalusia, from where such essential ingredients as olives, almonds, oranges and plums were carried by the Moors. Morocco's quintessential, savoury-sweet technique of cooking meat with fruit and nuts was also forged in Spain.

Olives, fruit and nuts appear in such specialitles as couscous, a fluffy semolina traditionally served on Fridays, and in spiced roast lamb, or *m'choui*. Another Moroccan staple is *harira*, a thick, often lamb-based pulse soup flavoured with tomato, onion, parsley and coriander, and finished with a squeeze of lemon juice. Tagines, those slow-cooked, highly flavoured stews of meat or fish cooked in conical earthernware pots over coals, say Morocco in a mouthful, starring the country's spiced lamb or beef. And of course, meat in Morocco is ubiquitously prepared as kebabs.

Morocco has an enormously long coastline, both Mediterranean and Atlantic, so you can expect some superb fish options. The most exciting array of seafood can be found at the open-air fish stalls at Essaouira's port, where black lobsters, spiny sea urchins, creamy oysters and long-legged crabs vie for attention with dorade, john dory, sardines and swordfish. Make your choice, and it will be simply and deliciously prepared in situ, and served at an alfresco table shared with other customers. *Chermoula* is a favourite when preparing fish – a flavoursome mixture of spices or finely chopped herbs – and every cook has a different recipe. The fish might be marinated in the mixture or rolled in it before frying.

Moroccans have a discerning sweet tooth. They relish fine gazelle's-hornspastries with sweet mint tea, and deep-fried pretzels dripping with honey called *chebakiyya* are served with *harira* soup during Ramadan. Snack on doughnut-style *sfeng* or *baghrir* pancakes between meals, and complete a feast with a crispy *b'stilla* pastry filled with custard.

MRUZIYYA (TAGINE)

This dish is traditionally prepared for Aid el Kebhir, or the 'feast of the lamb'. Because of the over-supply of lamb at this time, the cooking of the meat in spices, butter and honey means that it keeps well and can be eaten over a number of days. The Moroccan spice mixture, ras-el-hanout is a prominent taste in this dish, but a mixture of cinnamon, ginger and black pepper suffices.

INGREDIENTS

1kg/2lb of lamb leg cut into pieces
Salt to taste
3–4 tsp *ras-el-hanout*
Pinch of saffron strands
1 stick cinnamon
200g/7oz unsalted butter
1 tbsp olive oil
2 tbsp honey
250g/9oz raisins
200g/7oz blanched almonds

PREPARATION

Rub *ras-el-hanout* into the meat pieces and put the meat, saffron, cinnamon stick, butter and oil into a pot, adding water to cover. Bring to the boil and simmer for about 90 minutes.

Check from time to time that there is enough water to keep the meat from sticking to the pan.

After simmering, add raisins and honey. Cook for 20 to 30 minutes or until sauce is reduced to rich syrup.

Grill the blanched almonds brushed with butter or oil until they are slightly browned. Before serving, sprinkle almonds over tagine.

Serve piled onto a shallow terracotta dish. Serves four to six.

To keep this dish for a number of days, put it into a terracotta or glass container. Make sure that the meat is well covered with sauce, which will form a protective layer once it cools.

꙳

TAGINES
LIFTING THE LID

Conical-lidded tagines bubble away at pavement cafes across Morocco, but you'll also find them in the country's most prestigious restaurants. All you need as an accompaniment is a fresh round of *khobz* (bread) to scoop up the delicious sauce.

It's in the tagine that the subtlety of Moroccan spices comes to the fore. It might be a gentle blend of ground ginger and coriander, a pinch of cumin, a dash of paprika, a hint of chilli or a smidgin of cinnamon. Signature flavourings might be preserved lemon rind or dried fruits and nuts – maybe dried apricots, figs, dates, prunes and almonds. And tagines are always liberally sprinkled with freshly chopped parsley and coriander before serving.

Classic recipes in the tagine cookbook include chicken with preserved lemons and olives, lamb with prunes, beef with almonds or *kefta* meatballs in tomato sauce with eggs. Each has its own blend of spices, highlighting the ingredients' subtle flavours. Look out for more unusual combinations like lamb with baby quinces and okra, fish *mchermel* with its sauce of herbs and spices, and *kamama,* beef with cinnamon and a confit of onion and tomato.

A variation on the theme is a *tangia,* traditionally cooked by bachelors. Take a wander through the produce market bearing this elongated terracotta pot, and as you stroll, fill it with chopped onion, garlic, a pinch of Morocco's signature spice mix, *ras el-hanout*, some cubed lamb or beef, a drizzle of olive oil and garnish of fresh coriander. Top it with foil and leave it at the hammam, where the attendant will place it in the coals to simmer gently. Six hours later, you'll have the most delicious, meltingly tender concoction for dinner, scooped up with plenty of fresh bread.

It's likely you'll be bringing home your own tagine after a stroll around the souk: the plain ceramic ones are for cooking, while those with pretty painted designs and silverwork are for serving.

ABOVE The word tagine can refer both to the earthenware pot and the stew cooked in it **RIGHT** The shape of the tagine keeps the meat moist and tender

MAISON CORDON BLEUE

Fez

Chef Tariq Hadine hands down family recipes. Start the day in the souk to search out fresh local ingredients, then begin your cooking session and finish with dinner. Epicurean experiences are also on offer, including wine tasting in Meknes, couscous-rolling in a Middle Atlas village, and seasonal excursions.

L'ATELIER FAIM D'EPICES

Near Marrakesh

You'll be picked up at your guesthouse, whisked off for blind spice tasting and lessons in bread making, salads, tagines and desserts, then finish the day eating what you've cooked. It's in the countryside just outside Marrakesh.

A WALK THROUGH THE SOUK
THE MARVELLOUS MARKET

Moroccan markets will mesmerise you with shiny mountains of produce. Glorious seasonal fruit and vegetables, bunches of fragrant fresh mint, whole spices and coffee beans waiting to be ground, the freshest fish and live chickens, pigeons and rabbits... You'll be asked to taste an olive, a date or a sliver of soft white cheese before you buy. Look out for some of these more unusual items to tantalise your taste buds on a walk through the souk.

HONEY

Morocco produces a wide range of honey from different plants. Head for the souk, where you can taste around a dozen different varieties: with aromatic herbs from the Atlas such as thyme, lavender or rosemary; delicate mountain flowers or orange blossom, heartier eucalyptus or carob; and, our favourite, euphorbia with its back-of-the-throat kick. And yes, it's used medicinally to soothe sore throats.

RAS EL-HANOUT

To achieve a true Moroccan flavour on kebabs or in tagines, you have to source the quintessential spice mix *ras el-hanout*. Every spice merchant has their own tried and tested blend and no two concoctions are the same. The fragrant mixture can have up to 40 ingredients and should be ground as you buy it. It will contain cinnamon, star anise, mace flowers, turmeric, nutmeg, black pepper, coriander seeds, dried rosebuds and plenty more.

ABOVE LEFT Moroccan produce is usually harvested by hand when ripe and bought directly from farmers in the souks **ABOVE RIGHT** Picking up some sweet Morrocan pastries at a souk stall

BESSARA

Start the day with a hearty bowl of pale green *bessara,* as the market stallholders do. Made from dried broad beans (fava beans), it's somewhere between a soup and a dip in consistency, and fortified with plenty of garlic. It's served sprinkled with cumin and a swirl of olive oil, with fresh *khobz*.

CAMEL MEAT

OK, so a camel's head on a butcher's hook might not look too appetising, but the meat is definitely worth a try. It's cholesterol-free and very tasty. Heston Blumenthal swears by a camel-hump pastie.

 WHERE TO EAT CAFÉ CLOCK, 7 DERB EL-MARGANA, FEZ

If you're feeling adventurous, try a camel burger at Café Clock in Fez.

ARGAN OIL

Unique to Morocco, argan oil is produced in the south of the country between Essaouira and Agadir. The oil is pressed from the hard nuts of the argan tree. Traditionally these were passed through the digestive tract of a goat before being pressed! Two types of oil are available: a fine, odourless version that's invaluable in skin and hair care; and the delicious oil made from roasted nuts that's used in salad dressings or to give a glistening finish to a tagine.

WHERE TO EAT DOUAR BOUZAMMA

Some of the argan oil produced today is made at cooperatives run by rural women, such as Douar Bouzamma in Ougard, near Essaouira. July is a good time to visit: although it's hot, the goats are allowed to jump up into the trees – a great photo opportunity.

LEARNING

ATELIERS DE CUISINE DE LA MAISON ARABE
Marrakesh

Learn from a *dada*, a professional Moroccan female cook, in this riad guesthouse. She will teach the finer points of the traditional Moroccan meal. Finish by eating your efforts.

L'ATELIER MADADA
Essaouira

A former warehouse is the setting for this cookery school. Learn the secrets of tagines and couscous in the morning, or Moroccan patisserie in the afternoon.

CLOCK KITCHEN
Fez

Souad at Clock Kitchen in Fez will take you to buy ingredients in the souk before helping you whip up a delicious lunch.

⸎
MINT TEA
MOROCCAN CUPPA

In Morocco, any time is mint-tea time. The refreshing sweet tea is served throughout the day, all across the country. You'll see cartloads of fresh mint on every street corner in the souks. Whether it's for breakfast, to accompany a meal or to smooth the purchase of a carpet in the souk, the inevitable silver teapot will appear on its tray, along with pretty tea glasses. If you find the tea too sweet, learn the phrase, '*Shwiya sukkar*', (just a little sugar) – your dentist will thank you.

Making the tea is quite an art form. A metal pot is always used, as it needs to heat on the stove or gas ring, and gunpowder tea and sugar cubes are added once the water has boiled. When the water has returned to the boil, add as much spearmint as you can cram into the pot, and let it rest. Pour a glass, and return the tea to the pot. This is done a couple of times to make sure the tea is absolutely perfect. Now pour from on high so that a foam, known as the *keshkoosha*, sits on top of the tea in the glass. *D'saha* (your health)!

ABOVE Mint tea, the hallmark of Moroccan hospitality, is a sit-down affair that takes around half an hour

STREET FOOD
GO LOCAL

Here's a tip: just watch where the Moroccans queue up to be served, and make for the same pavement cafe or food stall to be sure of an excellent feast. You might find yourself asking for snails in a spicy broth, or hollowed-out *khobz* stuffed with cooked-to-order fillings such as chicken cubes dusted with spices, *kefta* (meatballs) or *merguez* (spicy sausages). Or perhaps you'll come away with delicious *maqouda*, deep-fried potato cakes dipped in chilli-hot *harissa* sauce.

In Fez, head for the snack stalls around the produce markets in R'cif, on Tala'a Kebira near Bab Boujloud or down in Achebine. Kebabs sizzle away, glistening chickens spin browning on a spit, steamed sheeps' heads peer out at you from enormous copper pans – and everything is served with spicy *harissa*, chips and bread.

For dessert, try some of the delicious nougat piled picturesquely for sale on carts throughout the souks. Creamy white, pistachio green or rose pink, stuffed full of peanuts, almonds or sesame seeds, it's flavoured with orange flower water or rosewater. Dodge the bees and ask for a taste before you buy.

⚓ WHERE TO EAT DJEMAA EL-FNA, MARRAKESH

For the best street food in Morocco, you can't beat Djemaa el-Fna in Marrakesh. From around 6pm, the huge square fills with portable kitchens and tables and benches. Tempting aromas begin to permeate the square and it's not so easy to make a choice. You'll find sheep's heads, snails, kebabs, tagines, fish, couscous and all manner of salads. And for something to drink, there are dozens of stalls around the square selling freshly squeezed *aseer limoon* (orange juice).

ABOVE Use your bread to scoop up the food: it's the way the locals eat and it's more hygenic than using utensils briefly rinsed in cold water

COUSCOUS

What Berbers call *seksu*, and food critic Craig Claiborne called one of the dozen best dishes in the world, couscous is a pale, grain-sized, hand-rolled pasta that's lightly steamed in an aromatic broth until toothsome and fluffy, served with vegetables and/or meat or fish in a delicately flavoured reduction of stock and spices. You know those yellowish grains that come in a box, with directions instructing you to add boiling water and leave to stand for three minutes? Well, that's not the couscous you'll discover here!

Couscous isn't a simple side dish either, it's the main event of a Moroccan meal, whether heaped with lamb and vegetables in Fez, or served with tomatoes, fish and fresh herbs in Essaouira. When in Fez, don't miss the legendary couscous with quail and candied fruits served in the medina at Palais Sheherazade. Vegetarians need not despair: many dishes come without meat, including the pumpkin couscous of Marrakesh and the savoury High Atlas version with stewed onions.

While the meat and vegetables are cooking, Moroccan cooks steam the couscous over the pot for maximum flavour. To assemble the dish, the couscous is heaped over the meat in a pyramid shape, and vegetables are pressed artfully into the sides. A bowl of rich broth is served separately, and poured over the lot. In a Moroccan home, the couscous is served on a platter in the centre of the table for everyone to dig into with their own spoon. Guests will be given the choicest pieces of meat and encouraged to *kool, kool* (eat, eat).

And if you really can't manage any more? Pat your stomach and tell your host, *'Baraka, l'hamdullillah'*, ('That's enough, thanks be to God').

AFRICA

By name, there's no doubt that Africa is not synonymous with
great eating experiences, but don't judge a book by its cover: there are of course wonderful
dishes to be found, some of which have travelled and can be enjoyed all over the world.
Here's a selection to have on your radar.

INJERA AND WATS, ETHIOPIA

Just like your first kiss, your first taste of *injera* is an experience you'll never forget. It's the national staple and the base of almost every Ethiopian meal. It is spread out like a large, thin pancake, and food is simply heaped on top of it. The overwhelmingly sour taste can be a challenge at first but give it another few mouthfuls and it'll grow on you. The sour taste contrasts beautifully with the fiery sauces it's normally served with. Use it like a like a pancake, wrapping it around small pieces of food and mopping up juices.

The ubiquitous companion of *injera*, a *wat* is Ethiopia's version of curry and can be very spicy – fortunately the *injera* helps to temper the heat. In the highlands, *bege* (lamb) is the most common constituent of *wat*. *Bure* (beef) is encountered in the large towns, and *figel* (goat) most often in thearid lowlands. Chicken is the king of the *wat* and *doro wat* is practically the national dish.

KUSHARI, EGYPT

Kushari is a delectable, any-time-of-day, year-round whole that is far more addictive than the sum of its humdrum base parts: pasta, rice and lentils. The magic finish comes from a spicy tomato-sauce topping and garnish of fried onions, all enhanced by garlic-vinegar or chilli. This cheap, filling and healthy national dish is so popular that some restaurants in Eygpt, particularly Cairo, specialise in this alone. Although *kushari* was the first Egyptian fast food, little seems known about its genesis. Educated conjecture suggests that it may have been created out of poverty – filling fare for people who couldn't afford meat – or that it was influenced by the vegetarian diet of fasting Coptic Christians. Whatever the case, meat – such as small pieces of fried liver, chicken or lamb – is now sometimes back in the bowl.

PIRI-PIRI CHICKEN, MOZAMBIQUE

As the sun sets over Mozambique's capital, Maputo, your thoughts turn to food. There's only one choice for your first dish in this sliver-shaped nation in southeast Africa: *piri-piri* chicken, or Mozambique on a plate. Portuguese colonists imported chillis from South America but Africa created a super-hot variety, lent it the name *piri-piri*, and sent it back to Portugal. This freewheeling fusion of Old and New Worlds sums up Maputo and Mozambique, a place where jazz-loving South Africans side-stepping apartheid's restrictions partied in colonial splendour on the fringes of the Indian Ocean. The national dish is a charcoal-grilled chicken marinated in a hot chilli sauce, cooled with coriander and best enjoyed with a cold beer and fries in a restaurant on Maputo's seafront.

WALKIE-TALKIES, SOUTH AFRICA

Walkie-talkies are gluten-full feet and protein-packed heads. Literally. Perhaps they're not the most appetising-looking stewed chicken parts, but in South African townships, walkie-talkies are low-priced, lipsmacking, pluck-giving delights. The 'walk' in walkie-talkie are cooked chicken feet ('walkies') and chicken heads are the 'talk'. A large quantity is boiled together to facilitate the removal of chewier bits. The pieces are then seasoned and cooked according to taste. They are cheap year-round treats that are flavourful and high in protein.

RED RED, GHANA

The only thing better than Ghanaian dishes may be their names. Hot, sweet and spicy, *red red* pairs beans with fried plantains and *zomi* (red palm oil), putting the 'red' in red red. Zomi is a palm oil with a rich nutty taste. Onions and chilli (also red) are fried in the *zomi* and added to black-eyed peas, then topped with more *zomi* and *gari* (fermented, dried cassava powder). Sweet, ripe plantains (*koko*;

another red) – thickly sliced, salted and deep-fried in vegetable oil – accompany the beans. Everyone loves *red red*, but it's a favourite of the Ewe ethnic group and may have migrated from Ewe country in eastern Ghana (the Volta Region) and Togo. There, as in Accra, beans are an inexpensive protein, which makes red red Ghana's national cheap lunch. Over time, gari was added for texture and, since it expands with water, as a cheap stomach-filler; *shito* (peppery fish sauce with spices) was added for heat.

BRIK, TUNISIA

A simple and savoury pastry packet, the *brik* is a study of compatible contrasts: crispy and soft, fresh and salty, mild and tangy. It's a mouthful of all that's Mediterranean. It is a deep-fried, triangular 'turnover' generally filled with a whole egg, tuna, onion, harissa and parsley. Other stuffings include minced (ground) meat, potato, anchovies and capers. The casing is a thin semolina-based pastry sheet called *malsouka*, often described as a cross between filo pastry and egg/spring roll wrapping. The *brik* is a quick snack enjoyed year-round and at any time of day. The origins of the Tunisian *brik* can be traced to the Turkish *börek* (from which its name is also derived), an ancient invention that migrated to Anatolia with the people from central Asian Turkistan hundreds of years ago. Today, according to Tunisian tradition, if a young man spills any yolk of a special *brik* prepared by his prospective wife's mother, he may not be allowed to wed.

Rural life in South Korea
revolves around the
seasons and the harvest

South Korea

**Is food a metaphor for a nation's character?
It is in South Korea, where the words 'spicy and robust' could be
used to characterise both the cuisine and the people.**

Temperament parallels seasoning in this finger of land inhabited by 49 million people, where the local cuisine is known as *Hansik*. Comparatively mild flavours are common in northern cities like Seoul, where genteel folk speak the standard language and comport themselves in a way that reflects Confucian ideals of restrained public decorum. Further south, you'll find zesty fare, salty language and ebullient discourse.

Though sandwiched between two Asian culinary superpowers, *Hansik* draws little from China's stir-fry tradition and shows minimal interest in Japan's refined presentation. More introspective than worldly, *Hansik* is a melange of ancient customs and values fused with contemporary priorities: a pinch of ancient oriental medicine, a sprinkle of Buddhist vegetarianism and a healthy dose of modern Korea's pugnacious hurry-hurry

approach to everything. The result on the dinner table is earthy soup, wholesome grains, fresh vegetables, two or three *kimchis*, pungent seasonings and protein from the sea or farm, all served at once in a banquet-like setting. And to finish the meal, there's usually a light dessert, fruit, coffee or tea.

South Korea's regional cuisine is shaped by mountain contours and inspired by jagged coastlines. Roots and leaves hand-picked from steep slopes transform everyday standards into local delicacies like *sanchae bibimbap* (spicy rice and mountain vegetables) or crunchy *deodeok kimchi* (spicy bellflower root). Baked, stewed, raw or processed, the catch from three seas permeates coastal cooking. Anchovies and mackerel are kitchen staples, while squid, eel, hairtail and octopus are commonly found in oceanfront restaurants and bars.

BIBIMBAP

INGREDIENTS

450g/16oz rice

300g/10.5oz young pumpkin

200g/7oz bellflower roots

120g4oz beef (top side)

200g/7oz soaked bracken (optional)

2 eggs

2 tbsp of oil

FOR THE SAUCE

1 tbsp soy sauce

½ tbsp sugar

2 tsp minced green onion

1 tsp minced garlic

1 tsp sesame salt

pinch ground black pepper

1 tsp sesame oil

FOR THE RED PEPPER PASTE

5 tbsp red pepper paste

20g minced beef

2 tsp minced green onion

1 tsp minced garlic

6 tbsp water

1½ tbsp sugar

1½ tbsp sesame oil

PREPARATION

Julienne the pumpkin and bellflower roots into 5cm/2in slices. Add a pinch of salt, tumble with hands, wash, then dry. Julienne the beef into 5cm/2in slices. Wash the bracken and slice into 5cm/2in strips. Blend the sauce ingredients in bowl and marinade the beef and bracken. Fry the egg for garnish. Bring the rice in water to the boil then continue to boil for another five minutes then simmer for ten. Stir-fry pumpkin in a preheated pan on high briefly and cool. Stir-fry bellflower roots on medium heat then stir-fry the beef and bracken on for three minutes. Stir-fry the minced beef, green onion, garlic and half of the sesame oil for a couple of minutes. Add red pepper paste, sugar and sesame oil, stir-fry for five minutes. Add water, stir-fry again to make fried red pepper paste. Serve with steamed rice and the fried egg and red pepper paste on top.

BIBIMBAP
SPEED, SPICE AND HEALTH

Bibimbap is essential *Hansik* in a single bowl. Rice and fresh vegetables mixed vigorously with a splotch of *gochujang* (red chilli sauce, see p143) create a meal in minutes. Restaurants tend to fiddle with the presentation, of course. Most start with a six-pack of vegan-friendly ingredients: carrots, cucumber, spinach, bean sprouts, shiitake mushrooms and bracken fern.

The holy grail of *bibimbap* comes from Jeonju. This cornucopia of taste and texture served in a brass bowl stacks 30 ingredients – like sesame oil, ginkgo nuts and mungbean jelly – on a rice bed cooked in beef broth, topped with *gochujang*, steak tartar and egg. More titillating than complex, *sanchae bibimbap* (spicy rice with mountain vegetables) is Korea's version of a chef's surprise. You never really know what to expect because it's made with seasonal roots and leaves from nearby mountains. *Dolsot bibimbap* is rice, spice and vegetables in a sizzling stone pot. Resist the urge to dive in and start mixing. Let the pot work its magic and you'll add a bottom layer of crispy rice to a near-perfect dish.

☙ WHERE TO EAT GOGUNG
DEOKJIN-DONG, DEOKJIN-GU, JEONJU

This restaurant put *bibimbap* on the world map. Once the food of kings, the full-course option is an opulent spread of side dishes and *moju* (fermented rice wine and medicinal herbs).

ABOVE *Bibimbap* is usually mixed at the table right before eating **RIGHT** *Bibimbap* as served in a restaurant

NEOBIANI

Neobiani uses the same sauce as *bulgogi* but the meat is thicker and there are no vegetables. To tenderise the meat and give the same texture as steak, small knife cuts are made all around the meat, and after marinating in a sauce, it is grilled over an open fire or in a pan.

INGREDIENTS

500g/17.5oz beef (sirloin)

2 tbsp powdered pine nuts

1 tbsp cooking oil

FOR THE SAUCE

½ cup soy sauce

2 tbsp sugar

2 tbsp starch syrup

2 cups water

2 tbsp garlic, crushed

2 tbsp green onion, chopped

2 tbsp rice wine

4 tbsp pear juice

2 tbsp onion juice

Black pepper

2 tbsp sesame oil

PREPARATION

Cut the beef into thick slices after removing fat then make thin cuts in the meat. Blend the sauce ingredients to make the marinade.

Marinate the sliced beef in the sauce for about two hours. Spread cooking oil lightly over a hot pan and fry the one side of the meat for three minutes in high heat and the other for two minutes.

Garnish the cooked beef with powdered pine nuts. Serves four.

BARBECUED MEAT
SEARED SIRLOIN

Tantalisingly aromatic when grilled over charcoal, *bulgogi* (marinated sirloin) and *so-galbi* (beef ribs) are South Korea's celebrated beef dishes. *Samgyupsal* (fatty bacon) is the country's popular pork cut, while black pig from Jeju-do is a renowned regional favourite. Long ago penned under outhouses, these black-haired beasts gained notoriety for feeding on human waste, a practice discontinued in the 1960s to the detriment of its taste, some claim.

Mongols and Buddhists helped shape South Korea's beefy traditions. Thirteenth-century Buddhism, the principle social philosophy of the time, accentuated vegetables and discouraged beef consumption. Some historians believe cattle slaughter was banned outright. Later that century, Mongols hacked their way down the peninsula, pillaged the villages and brought a dynasty to its knees.

On the bright side, the Mongols re-established cattle farming and introduced foods now considered standards, like *mandu* (dumplings), noodles and grilled beef. Interestingly, renewed beef consumption at the time didn't supplant the vegetable- and fish-rich diet; it merely augmented the array of choices, a tradition that continues to this day.

WHERE TO EAT DONSADON
JEJU CITY, JEJU ISLAND (WWW.DONSADON.COM)

Here's a dining tip. The quality of meat in a restaurant often varies inversely with the quality of the decor. Like this place. Well known for tender black-pig pork and the occasional celebrity diner (the entertainer Rain ate here), it's a Jeju institution.

ABOVE Food for sharing: Korean barbeque is not just a meal, it's a social occasion
ABOVE LEFT *Neobiani* is a basic Korean barbecued meat dish

GOCHUJANG
CHILLI HEAT

Red chillies provide the heat in *gochujang*, South Korea's spicy staple sauce made with fermented soybean and rice powder. Store bought, commercially processed *gochujang* has nearly vanquished the time-consuming, time-honoured homemade stuff, a sterling example of how progress is putting South Korean traditions on the shelf.

Indeed, you can look to the lowly chilli to open a window on the changes rippling through the fabric of South Korea's dynamic society. In rural communities, chilli farmers nearing retirement age and young people alike have been abandoning their home towns for big-city opportunities, making agriculture's future look sketchy. And it seems that few Korean women – educated and mobile – choose life on the farm any more.

Tied to the land and committed to farming, rural men were isolated and lonely, until a pipeline of mail-order brides opened up. Since 2000, tens of thousands of women from China, Vietnam and the Philippines, among other countries, have moved here. It's an unparalleled demographic shift that's changed the make-up of rural society, and challenged attitudes towards biracial children and the country's sometimes harsh patriarchal family structure.

♨ WHERE TO EAT MALBAU TRADITIONAL MARKET
BUK-GU, GWANGJU, JEOLLANAM-DO

Explore farm-fresh produce as you wade through dense crowds at this lively market. Close to South Korea's agricultural heartland, it has many hard-to-find products such as Sunchang *gochujang*, an all-natural hot chilli paste. The market opens on dates ending with 2, 4, 7 and 9.

ABOVE Traditionally, Korean families would make their own *gochujang* and it would be left outside the house to age in a pot for several weeks

····· 143 ·····

KIMCHI

Served at every meal, fire-engine-red *kimchi* is the flagship of *Hansik.* It hasn't always been so. Prior to the 1600s, seasonal vegetables like *mu* (white radish) were salted to ensure a winter food supply. Flaked red chilli – modern-day *kimchi's* main seasoning – probably came to Korea via Japan when Toyotomi Hideyoshi's invaders stormed the mainland in 1592. Two hundred years later, this zesty red fruit was a key food preservative. Coincidentally, *napa* cabbage (the base for today's most popular *kimchi*) took root on the peninsula at the same time. By the mid-1800s, cabbage and chilli had married and a food legend was born.

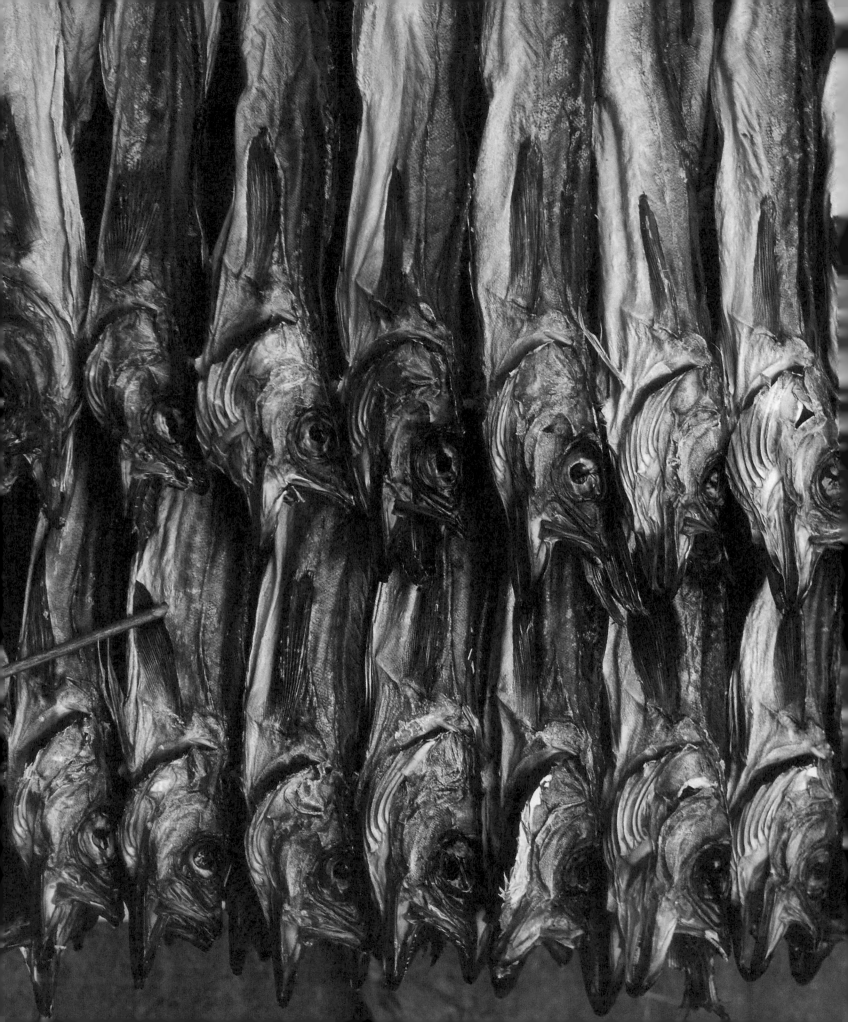

♨
HOE
BOUNTY FROM THE SEA

More than a staple, seafood is the culinary cornerstone of many South Korean social customs. Middle-school students find respite at sidewalk fishmeal stalls en route to a 9pm maths class. Bar owners stimulate customer thirst with salty dried squid, and managers build organisational camaraderie with *hoe* (sliced raw fish), the jewel of Korean seafood.

A *hoe* dinner starts with appetisers like oysters or octopus. A platter of thinly sliced *hoe* without rice is the main course; rockfish and sea bream are popular species. Fish is dipped into a saucer of *chogochujang* (watery red chilli sauce) or soy sauce mixed with wasabi. The meal is typically finished with rice and a pot of *maeuntang* (spicy fish soup). *Hoe* aficionados adore the slightly tough, rubbery texture when accompanied with *soju* (vodka-like hooch).

🍽 WHERE TO EAT DUNGDAE HOEJIB
JAGALCHI HOE CENTER, BUSAN

Don't be put off by the owner's brusque demure. Busan, much like the city's food, is famous for its salty character. Sit next to the floor-to-ceiling windows and nosh on *hoe* while watching the sun set over Busan harbour.

LEFT Drying fish **ABOVE** Seasoned fish makes a tasty and easy-to-eat street (or cinema) snack
ABOVE RIGHT Tofu, one of the ingredients in *doenjang jigae*, is a dietary staple in many Asian countries

SOYBEAN PASTE STEW

Kimchi may be the starlet of *Hansik*, but *doenjang jigae* (soybean paste stew) is the country's everyday staple. An earthy stew with an unmistakable aroma, it's eaten any time of day. Anchovy stock and a dollop of soybean paste topped off with soft tofu and sliced zucchini is the starting point.

Coastal villages serve the heartiest version, thanks to a ready supply of clams, shrimp and crab legs, and it doesn't get much better than postcard-pretty Namhae-do, a rustic island where farmers continue to plough fields with oxen. *Mijo*, a port town on the coastal highway, is a convenient pit stop for nourishment but don't bother looking for a spick-and-span restaurant. It doesn't exist. What you will find though is an enchanting collection of yesteryear buildings daring you to explore country cooking amid faded yellow linoleum floors and unisex toilets that seemingly predate the Korean War. In other words, the classic rural eating experience. One of the best places to sample this stew is Dajeong Sikdang in Mijo, in Namhae County, Gyeongsangnam-do.

If you can't find this eatery, ask for directions at the village police station. In Korea, police officers always know where to find cheap and delicious *doenjang jigae* – which is probably a healthier on-the-job snack than doughnuts.

SAMGYETANG SOUP

Samgyetang is a chicken soup made by boiling a stuffed young chicken that is typically filled with sticky rice, ginseng, jujube and garlic. *Samgyetang* is usually eaten during the three hottest days *(sambok)* in the summer to overcome the heat.

INGREDIENTS

4 young chickens

1 cup/180g sticky rice

milk vetch water: 20g (4 roots) milk vetch roots and 3L/100fl oz water

4 roots fresh wet ginseng

4 cloves garlic

4 jujube

1 egg

1 tbsp salt

Pinch of ground black pepper

20g/1oz green onion

PREPARATION

Trim fats and halve the chickens through abdomen and wash. Wash the glutinous rice and soak in water for two hours.

Drain water on a strainer for 10 minutes. Wash the milk vetch roots and soak in water for two hours. Wash and clean the fresh ginseng and preparing by cutting the top.

Wash and clean garlic and jujube. Set aside for later. Wash green onion and chop finely. Put milk vetch roots and water in the pot and boil on high heat for 20 minutes.

Lower the heat to medium, and simmer for 40 minutes. Filter to make milk vetch stock. Stuff chicken cavity with the rice, ginseng, garlic and jujube. Tie crossed legs to hold stuffing inside of chicken.

Put prepared chicken and milk vetch water in the pot and boil for 20 minutes on high heat. Reduce the heat down to medium and simmer for 50 minutes until the soup turns milky white.

Serve with chopped green onion, salt and ground black pepper. Serves 8.

MEDICINAL FOOD
CULINARY ELIXIRS

Koreans' long-standing view that food is a tonic explains the popularity of medicinally rich seasonings, and the origins of customs like *boknal*. During the summer's three hottest days, steamy soups are relished for their ability to balance *ki* (life force energy). In Korean traditional medicine, *ki* becomes cold in the summer, an imbalance that can be corrected with hot soup. The perennial favourite is *samgyetang*, a whole young chicken served in a stone pot of piping hot broth. Dig inside the bird's cavity and you'll release an aromatic cloud of earthy goodness with hints of ginseng, garlic, ginger, jujubes and rice. Available year-round in speciality restaurants, it's often accompanied by *insamju*, a ginseng-flavoured fermented rice wine nicknamed 'the elixir of life'.

WHERE TO EAT TOSOKCHON SAMGYETANG CHAEBU-DONG, JONGNO-GU, SEOUL

Arguably Seoul's most popular *samgyetang* restaurant. Housed in a traditional *hanok* building, the outstanding soup is seasoned with 30 ingredients. The only drawback is the lunchtime queue of 50 or more hungry, patient patrons.

ABOVE The ginseng in *samgyetang* is believed to have medicinal properties **RIGHT** Feeling good: Koreans believe that certain foods have healthy benefits

Trimming ginseng roots at the Insam Festival in Geumsan

FESTIVALS & EVENTS

Regional Korean cuisines evolved in isolation from each other, thanks to the mountainous landscape. But each region has a festival showcasing its speciality and there's no better way to get an insight into what lies beyond South Korea's cities.

MAY

Korean Food Festival, Jeonju
Sip fermented rice wine, sample new *kimchis* and eat *bibimbap* in Jeonju, the birthplace of South Korea's iconic rice and vegetable dish. The November festival is held in several venues including Jeonju Hanok Village, a community of 800 homes with traditional architectural designs.

Wild Tea Festival, Hadong
Hadong is famous for being the first tea plantation in Korea and continues to produce high-grade tea using traditional methods. Visitors can sample a variety of Hadong's tea for free and buy some at bargain prices.

SEPTEMBER

Insam (Ginseng) Festival, Geumsan
Explore the effects of ginseng at this festival, which takes place in an area surrounded by ginseng and medicinal herb markets. Check out the ginseng cooking contest, the song contest, or take the chance to learn how bake rice cakes.

Songi (Pine Mushroom) Festival, Yangyang
Songi mushrooms, known to many as 'golden mushrooms', grow naturally under old pine trees but are strictly protected from public picking. However, at the Yangyang Songi Festival, visitors may tour the habitat of these precious fungi, pick them, and sample dishes made with them.

OCTOBER

Traditional Drink & Rice Cake Festival, Gyeongju
Go to Gyeongju to quaff home-brewed liquor and nibble delicacies from all regions of Korea. A highlight of this festival is participating in the ancient royal tea ceremony, and learning traditional dining culture. You can also tour crucibles of Korean Buddhism like Bulguksa Temple and Seokguram Grott in Gyeongju, both Unesco World Cultural Heritage sites.

Hanu Festival, Hoengseong
Hoengseong County is cattle country and the Hanu (Korean native cattle) Festival attracts people who want to try the usually expensive Hoengseong *hanu* beef at affordable prices, along with another speciality of Hoengseong County, *deodeok* (mountain bellflower). In addition to food sampling, this is the place to see some Hanu rodeo action.

Namdo Food Festival
Namdo province celebrates its famous foods every October. Stalls feature local delicacies such as *mokpo nakji* (octopus), and *suncheon yeomso-tteokgalbi* (grilled marinaded goat meat). The festival is held at Naganeupseong Folk Village, which is worth exploring.

Rice Cultural Festival, Icheon
Icheon's claim to fame is that it produces the best rice in Korea. The rice is so good that it used to be served to the king of Korea. This festival celebrates the famed rice with tributes such as a reenactment of the parade that transported rice to Hanseong (as Seoul was formerly known) for presentation to the king, and a huge rice cauldron that is capable of feeding thousands of people.

World Kimchi Culture Festival, Gwangju
Yes, there's a festival to celebrate this fermented vegetable dish. Visitors try a wide range of *kimchi* varieties, and can learn how to make it at *kimchi* workshops. While you're in the area, tour Gwangju, known as 'the home of delicacies'. With wide plains and access to the waters of Seohae (West Sea) and Namhae (South Sea), Gwangju cultivates rice and seafood.

DECEMBER

Green Tea Plantation & Light Festival, Boseong
In this southern corner of South Korea, green tea plantations have thrived for at least 1500 years, cascading down green hillsides. This festival runs from December to January. The best tea leaves are picked in April and May and spring is an ideal time to visit the year-round plantations: fragrance fills the air and the harvest is in full swing.

Olive trees in Andalucia's
parched landscape

SPAIN

With celebrity chefs emerging from their kitchens and laboratories to strut the world stage, and the export of tapas all around the globe, Spain has been the culinary star of the decade. *¡Viva la Revolución!*

It's taken centuries of diverse cultural and historical influences to create the Spanish cuisine we admire today. From the Romans came a love of olives and wine. Seven centuries of Islamic rule can be traced through the liberal use of saffron, cumin and other spices, in desserts dominated by honeyed sweets, and through the privileged place afforded to almonds and fruit.

Later, Spain ruled over a vast empire, and from its colonies in the Americas were bequeathed a tasting platter of vital ingredients that ranged from the basic (garlic, onions, potatoes and tomatoes) to the exotic (coffee and chocolate), leaving us wondering how on earth the kitchens of Europe functioned without them.

For all the innovation of today's Spanish chefs, and the complexity of the country's culinary origins, simplicity remains the cornerstone of Spanish cuisine. In fact, it's the lack of fuss and tweaking that lies behind its enduring appeal. While the rest of the world was developing sophisticated sauces and methods, Spanish chefs remained true to the basic laws of Spanish cooking: take the freshest ingredients, interfere with them as little as possible, and let the flavours of the finest ingredients speak for themselves.

The tapas, rice dishes and cooling gazpachos of Spain's Mediterranean coast most closely resemble the stereotypical view of Spanish cooking, but there's much, much more to explore. From Galicia comes seafood like *pulpo a la gallega*, then there's *bacalao* and steak from the Basque Country, and the same mix of maritime and mountain fare from Catalonia. Madrid is meat country, specialising in lamb and pork, and hearty chickpea stews and soups.

Little wonder then that the Spaniards spend more per capita on food than other Europeans, and that food stands at the centre of daily life. They talk about food endlessly. They plan their day around eating, and spend hours relishing every last bite. And then they spend the rest of their time dreaming about their next feast.

TORTILLA DE PATATAS
Tortillas make delicious tapas.

INGREDIENTS
250g/9oz potatoes (a waxy variety)

1 small red onion

5 eggs

Olive oil

PREPARATION
Peel, quarter and slice the potatoes thinly. Halve the onion and slice thinly. Heat olive oil in a medium-sized, non-stick frying pan and fry the onion over a medium heat.

Add the potato slices and cook for 10 minutes without letting either go brown. Remove the onion and potatoes and most of the oil. Beat the eggs, season and fold in the potato and onion. Return to the oiled pan to cook gently. Finish under a grill or flip the tortilla by covering the top with a large plate and turning the pan upside down. Serve hot or cold.

TAPAS
PUT A LID ON IT

Tapas fuses the ideas of a snack, a starter and the elements of a larger meal all in one – the secret to its success lies in this versatility. It can be the prelude to a more substantial meal, or the main event itself. It can be the tiny serving of food that miraculously appears whenever you order a drink, or it can be an entire menu given over to *raciones* – large plates of food to share.

In the Basque Country, tapas (or *pintxos* as they're known up north) consist of small slices of bread topped with all manner of niceties (anchovies, capsicum, *tortilla de patatas* are favourites) in various seductive combinations. In Barcelona, you're far more likely to be served high-quality seafood from a can. All of these – and all manner of variations in between – can be called tapas. Thus it is that tapas enables you to range across (and sample) a diverse collection of tastes during the courses of a meal or over the course of an evening.

That an idea so simple as tapas could change gastronomic history is a mark of culinary genius. But where does the idea come from? One story – quoted most often in Andalucía, it must be said – asserts that the word *tapa* (which means 'lid' in Spanish) attained widespread usage in the early 20th century when King Alfonso XIII stopped at a beachside bar close to the southern city of Cádiz. When a strong gust of wind blew sand in the king's direction, so the story goes, a quick-witted waiter rushed to place a slice of *jamón* atop the king's glass of sherry. The king so much enjoyed the idea (and the *jamón*) that, wind or no wind, he ordered another and the name stuck.

Another version goes back much further to another king named Alfonso – Alfonso X in the 13th century – whose doctors advised him to accompany his wine-drinking between meals with small morsels of food. So enamoured was the monarch with the idea that he passed a law requiring all bars in Castile to follow suit. Yet another legend attributes the birth of tapas to medieval Iberian innkeepers who, concerned about drunken men on horseback setting out from their village, developed a tradition of putting a *tapa* of food atop each glass of wine or beer. The purpose was partly to keep the bugs out, but primarily to encourage people not to drink on an empty stomach.

Tapas serves a similar purpose today and may partly explain why the streetside bar and cafe culture of Spain is so much more civilised than that of certain northern European nations. And since Spaniards don't sit down to a main meal until late into the night, they need something to keep the conversation and wine flowing.

☙ WHERE TO EAT SAN SEBASTIÁN'S PARTE VIEJA

The art of tapas has reached a point somewhere close to perfection in San Sebastián, a graceful seaside town with more Michelin stars than Paris. The bars in San Sebastián's *parte vieja* (old quarter) groan under the weight of *pintxos* (often served with *txacoli*, a sharp white Basque wine) that showcase an astonishing array of ingredients and combinations of the same.

ABOVE LEFT In San Sebastián's tapas bars just point to the morsel you want to order next
ABOVE RIGHT Bite-size inspiration: San Sebastián's chefs take a creative approach to tapas

SHERRY

Sherry, Andalucía's fortified wine is found in every tapas bar and when slightly chilled is the perfect companion to savoury tapas. Dry sherry, called *fino*, begins as a fairly ordinary white wine of the Palomino grape, but is 'fortified' with grape brandy. This stops fermentation and gives the wine taste and smell constituents that enable it to age into something sublime. Sip sherry as an *aperitivo* (aperitif) or as a table wine with seafood. Amontillado and Oloroso are sweeter sherries, reserved for after dinner. Manzanilla is grown only in Sanlúcar de Barrameda on the coast of southwestern Andalucía and develops a slightly salty taste that's very appetising. Most of the big sherry bodegas in Jerez de la Frontera – including Sandeman and Harvey's – are open to the public.

JAMÓN
EVERY PART OF THE PIG

A Spanish food critic in Barcelona once told us that 'the only thing that keeps Spain together is the *jamón*. Not language, not culture, not anything else. Just *jamón*'. Or if you prefer an earthier indicator of the local obsession with *jamón*, consider the oft-heard Spanish saying that 'in this country, we eat every part of the pig, except the walk'.

According to legend, the Spanish passion for ham began with a noble Roman, Cato the Elder, who introduced it to Iberia through his tome *De Re Rustica*. There are many offshoots of his fine idea, among them chorizo, *salchichón* and *lomo*. But none has the prestige or pedigree of *jamón*. Unlike Italian prosciutto, Spanish *jamón* is a bold deep red, well marbled with buttery fat. At its best, it smells like meat, the forest and the field, and is usually served sliced paper thin as tapas.

Spanish *jamón* (like wines and olive oil) is subject to a strict series of classifications. *Jamón serrano* refers to *jamón* made from white-coated pigs introduced to Spain in the 1950s. Once salted and semidried by the cold, dry winds of the Spanish sierra, most *jamón serrano* now goes through a similar process of curing and drying in a climate-controlled shed for around a year. *Jamón serrano* accounts for approximately 90% of cured ham in Spain.

Jamón ibérico – more expensive and generally regarded as the elite of Spanish hams – comes from a black-coated pig indigenous to the Iberian Peninsula and a descendant of the wild boar. Gastronomically, its star appeal is its ability to infiltrate fat into the muscle tissue, thus producing an especially well-marbled meat. If the pig gains at least 50% of its body weight during the acorn-eating season, it can be classified as *jamón ibérico de bellota,* the most sought-after designation for *jamón*.

The *jamón* from Salamanca (particularly around Guijelo) and the Andalusian province of Huelva (around Jabugo) are considered Spain's finest. *Jamón* from Extremadura and the Teruel region of Aragón are also highly regarded.

LEFT Refuelling with tapas for the San Fermín bull run in Pamplona: *jamón* is dried for six to 12 months, then hung for up to two years **ABOVE** Slicing *jamón* requires a sharp knife, working from the rump first

WINE PRIMER

Rather than grape variety, Spanish wines are labelled according to region or classification such as Denominación de Origen (DO; Denomination of Origin). There are more than 60 DO-recognised wine-producing areas in Spain, based on meeting strict standards and covering all aspects of planting, cultivating and ageing.

An outstanding wine region gets the much-coveted Denominación de Origen Calificada (DOC). This is a controversial classification – many in the industry argue that it should apply only to specific wines. At present, the only DOC wines come from La Rioja in northern Spain and the small Priorat area in Catalonia.

Other signs of quality (labelled on the bottle) depend on the length of time a wine has been aged. The best wines are designated as *crianza* (aged for one year in oak barrels), *reserva* (two years ageing, at least one of which is in oak) and *gran reserva* (two years in oak and three in the bottle).

LA RIOJA AND CAVA

Spain's most widespread red wine comes from La Rioja, where the principal grape is tempranillo, believed to be a mutant form of pinot noir. La Rioja's wines are smooth and fruity, and rarely as dry as their French counterparts. Not far behind La Rioja are the regions of Ribera del Duero (in north-central Spain), Navarra and the Somontano wines of Aragón.

Another Spanish classic, sparkling cava, is from the Penedès area of Catalonia. It's the traditional drink for Spaniards at Christmas. For other whites, the Ribeiro wines of Galicia are well regarded. Also from the area is one of Spain's most charming whites: crisp, refreshing Albariño, which is designated by grape rather than region.

PAELLA

'Paella' is the name of the pan in which this dish is cooked. It's wide with a flat bottom, designed for balancing on an open fire. A large frying pan is fine. Paella arrived in Spain with rice farming and it's the rice that should be the focus. Short-grained *bomba* and *calasparra* varieties, which absorb stock, are best but arborio can do the job in a pinch. Traditional paella is not a fancy dish, using just chicken and green beans; a seafood paella lets the cook be more adventurous.

INGREDIENTS

300g/11oz paella rice

200g/7oz green beans, halved

300g/11oz chicken thighs or rabbit

750mL/25fl oz chicken stock

2 large tomatoes (peel and deseed)

2 garlic cloves

1 red onion, finely chopped

1 red pepper, in strips

Pinch of saffron

Bunch of parsley

Lemon

Olive oil

SEAFOOD VERSION

200g/7oz prawns

200g/7oz calamari

12 mussels

PREPARATION

Heat olive oil in a large frying pan and cook the chicken thighs (do not bone) until golden. Remove and add more oil to the pan and simmer the finely chopped onion, tomato and garlic with a little stock. This is the *sofrito*. Add the pepper and green beans, the rice and enough of the chicken stock to cover the rice. Add the seafood if you're doing *paella al mariscos*. Simmer for about 20 minutes until the rice has absorbed the stock. Add stock if required but don't stir. The consistency should be drier than a risotto. Add the saffron, stir in the cooked chicken and serve with a wedge of lemon and lots of parsley.

PAELLA
SPAIN'S NATIONAL DISH

Paella was born in Valencia and it's in this sun-drenched city that the best, most authentic paellas are to be found. There's no meal better suited to an afternoon spent with friends overlooking the sea than this sumptuous rice dish, which somehow captures the essence of the Mediterranean table.

The problem with paella enjoying such fame, however, is that it can be extremely difficult to find a good one. If we can impart two tips for tracking down a paella as it should be cooked and served, it would be the following. First, stick your head in the door of a restaurant and listen – if Spanish or Catalan dominates the conversation, it might be worth sticking around. And at the first available opportunity, buy some saffron. Smell it. Its delicate yet pervasive aroma is unmistakeable and unforgettable. If that aroma isn't wafting up at you from the pan, you've been served a counterfeit. You'll find that in all but the better paella restaurants, saffron (which is extremely expensive) is often substituted with yellow dye number 2.

The true *paella valenciana* is cooked with chicken, beans and sometimes rabbit, but more often you'll find the popular *paella de mariscos* (seafood paella) on menus. The base of a good paella always includes short-grain rice, garlic, parsley, olive oil and saffron. The best rice is the *bomba* variety, which expands in an accordion fashion when cooked, allowing for maximum absorption while remaining firm. Paella should be cooked in a large shallow pan to enable maximum contact with the bottom of the pan, where most of the flavour resides. And for the final touch of authenticity, the grains on the bottom (and only on the bottom) of the paella should have a crunchy, savoury crust known as the *socarrat*.

For many of the Mediterranean seaboard's inhabitants, paella is just one rice dish among many. From Barcelona in the north to Murcia in the south and the Balearic Islands of Mallorca, Menorca and Ibiza out in the east, rice dishes (often served with lashings of *aioli*, or garlic mayonnaise) are very often things of beauty and excellence. In the Balearics and Catalonia, they invariably arrive laden with seafood; a rice dish with lobster can be expensive but utterly magnificent, while *fideuá* (like paella but with noodles) is a Catalan variation on the theme. In Murcia, the rice is often served bathed in a rich stock with few other visible ingredients to distract you from the main event.

Catalonia deserves a special mention as the Basque Country's rival when it comes to culinary superstar status. Both rely on the same combination of *mar y montaña* (sea and mountain), albeit with subtle differences. In Catalonia, sauces have migrated across the border from France, and *suquet* (fish and potato stew) in particular is a star performer. And the high-altitude Pyrenees have brought their own special touches to the Catalan table in the form of *jabalí* (wild boar), *conejo* (rabbit) and *caracoles* (snails, especially in Lleida).

⚓ WHERE TO EAT LA PEPICA
PASEO NEPTUNO 6, LAS ARENAS, VALENCIA

You could choose any rice and seafood restaurant along Valencia's Las Arenas waterfront, but Hemingway for one chose La Pepica. You won't get a better paella in Spain.

RIGHT A paella party in Palma, Mallorca: usually, paella is a meal cooked by families at the weekend

BACALAO AL PIL-PIL

Plan this Basque classic carefully: not only to source the bacalao (dried cod; the tender throats are highly prized) but to de-salt it. Soak the fish for about 48 hours or until it no longer tastes salty. Change the water regularly.

INGREDIENTS

1kg/2lb salt cod
8 garlic cloves, sliced
2 chillies, sliced
250mL/8.5fl oz olive oil

PREPARATION

Drain and dry the de-salted cod. Check it for bones. In a heavy-bottomed skillet or, ideally, a clay cazuela, the dense Spanish cooking vessel used on or in ovens, gently heat olive oil to a depth of 5 to 10mm. Add garlic and chillies and fry until golden. Remove the garlic and chilli. Put the cod into the warm oil, skin side up, and return to a low heat. Do not fry the cod but allow it to cook slowly. After 10 minutes, remove and drain the oil into a jug. Return the cod to the pan with some of the oil, keeping the heat low. Without letting the pan sizzle (remove it from the heat if it does) gently rotate the pan in a circular motion so the oil makes a 'pil-pil' sound as it laps over the cod. This frequent shaking helps the oil emulsify with gelatine from the fish, creating the sauce. Gradually return all the oil to the pan, where it should change to a creamy consistency. Serve hot, garnished with some of the garlic and chilli.

SPANISH STEAKS

The Bay of Biscay and the seas beyond dominate Basque tables, but the steep green hillsides of the interior also provide the raw materials for a regional cuisine of great depth and diversity. Steaks – always cooked rare and dressed in little more than rock salt – are essential elements in any Basque chef's portfolio.

BACALAO
GLORY BE TO COD

If Spanish culinary excellence has a true spiritual home, it would have to be the Basque Country. Many of Spain's most celebrated chefs hail from here, which may have something to do with the fact that if Spaniards elsewhere in the country love their food, the Basques are obsessed with it – culinary excellence is seen here as a basic human right.

Making the most of their Bay of Biscay location, Basque chefs have perfected the art of cooking seafood, but their love affair with fish begins and ends with *bacalao* (dried and salted cod). Like so many modern culinary stars (oysters spring to mind), *bacalao* was once considered food for the poor. Now it's the centrepiece of a Basque meal, and the ability to cook *bacalao* well is a fundamental skill required of any Basque chef. The most famous manifestation of this love for cod is *bacalao al pil-pil* (salted cod in garlic and oil). The simplicity of the dish's ingredients belie an extremely complicated technique – with the pan poised over a low heat, the chef must gently but constantly move the pan back and forth to ensure that the garlic and oil emulsify and thicken to exactly the right texture.

Basque fishing fleets have roamed the seas as far as Newfoundland and the North Atlantic for centuries in search of cod, salting their catch and then carrying the rock-like fish back home. Once back on Spanish shores, soaking the cod several times in water rehydrates it and relieves the cod of its salt content.

🍽 WHERE TO EAT ARZAK
AVENIDA ALCALDE JOSE ELOSEGUI 273, SAN SEBASTIÁN

Arguably the most decorated of Basque chefs, Juan Mari Arzak has been at the forefront of *nouvelle cocina vasca* for more than a decade and has three shining Michelin stars to show for it. The menu is wildly creative, so you probably won't find *bacalao al pil-pil here,* but you will find dishes inspired by the signature Basque creation.

ABOVE San Sebastián, on Spain's northwest coast, is one of the best places to experience Basque cuisine: it's home to everything from secret gastronomic societies to exclusive sit-down restaurants

⌇⌇
OLIVE OIL
THE GOOD OIL

Where would Spain, and indeed the world, be without olive oil? Forget Italy and Greece – more olive oil is produced in Spain than anywhere else on the planet. There are over 100 million olive trees in Andalucía alone, and a remarkable 20% of the world's olive oil originates in Jaén Province, which produces more olive oil than Greece. In fact, Jaén's 4500 sq km of olive trees constitute the world's largest manmade forest.

Southern Spain's olive groves were originally planted by the Romans, but the production of *az-zait* (the juice of the olive), from which the modern generic word for olive oil, *aceite*, is derived, was further developed by the Muslims.

The best olive oils are those classified as 'virgin' (which must meet 40 criteria for quality and purity) and 'extra virgin' (the highest quality olive oil whose acidity levels can be no higher than 1%).

The most common type of olive used for making olive oil is the full-flavoured and (sometimes) vaguely spicy Picual, which dominates the olive groves of Jaén Province and accounts for 50% of all Spanish olive production. It takes its name from its pointed *pico* (tip), and is considered ideal for olive oil due to its high proportion of vegetable fat, natural antioxidants and polyphenol; the latter ensures that the oil keeps well and maintains its essential qualities at a high cooking temperature.

Another important type of olive is the Hojiblanco. Its oil, which keeps for less time and should be stored in a cool dark place, is said to have a taste and aroma reminiscent of fruits, grasses and nuts.

ABOVE Olive harvest time affects the flavour and appearance of the oil – early-harvest olives make a green oil with a sharp flavour while late-harvest olive oil is golden in colour and smoother in flavour

CHURROS CON CHOCOLATE
Use a light olive oil in which to fry this decadent Spanish dessert.

INGREDIENTS
Light olive oil

1 cup water

½ cup butter

pinch of salt

1 cup all-purpose flour

3 eggs

¼ cup sugar

1 tsp cinnamon

FOR THE CHOCOLATE
100g/3.5oz dark chocolate, chopped

850mL/30fl oz milk

1 tbsp cornflour

4 tbsp sugar

Pinch cinnamon

PREPARATION
Heat 3cm/1in of oil in a pan. To make churro dough, heat the water, butter and salt to rolling boil in a large saucepan. Add the flour. Stir vigorously over low heat until the mixture forms a ball (about one minute). Remove from the heat.

Beat the eggs until smooth and then stir into the mixture. Spoon mixture into a piping bag with large star tip. Squeeze 10cm/4in strips of dough into the hot oil.

Fry three or four strips at a time until golden brown, turning once, about two minutes per side. Drain on paper towels. Mix the sugar and cinnamon, roll churros in the mixture or dump it on the pile of churros.

Place the chocolate and half the milk in a pan and heat, stirring until the chocolate has melted.

Dissolve the cornflour in the remaining milk and whisk into the chocolate with the sugar. Cook on a low heat, whisking constantly, until the chocolate thickens (about five minutes). Remove and dust with cinnamon. Pour into cups or bowls then get dunking!

‹‹
PULPO A LA GALLEGA
TASTY TENTACLES

The Galician obsession that is *pulpo a la gallega* – slightly spicy boiled octopus – is not just a Galician staple, it's such a fabulous dish that it crops up on restaurant menus around the country. Its constituent elements – octopus, oil, paprika and garlic – are simplicity itself, but its execution is devilishly difficult and ruthlessly unforgiving of mistakes. The trick is in the boiling: the process of dipping the octopus into the water, then drawing it out and dipping it in again cooks it at just the right rate.

Octopus may cast all else into shadow in Galicia, but other much-loved shellfish in this part of Spain include *navajas* (razor clams), *coquinas* (large clams), *percebes* (goose barnacles), *mejillones* (mussels), *berberechos* (cockles), *almejas* (baby clams) and *vieiras* (a form of scallop), whose shell has become the symbol of the Camino de Santiago pilgrimage.

With its dramatic Atlantic coastline, Portuguese-sounding regional language and Celtic musical traditions, Galicia can feel like nowhere else in Spain, and this culture of difference extends to the world of food. Partly that's to do with supply – the fish and seafood emerging from Spain's corner of the Atlantic simply don't swim elsewhere. But it's also a mindset, a culture in which the sea laps at so many areas of Galician life. Countless Galicians still set out to sea before dawn, casting their nets into the inky blackness. These village fishing fleets – so far from the commercial fleets that dominate the world's oceans – are the heart and soul of Galicia's story, and its favourite dish, *pulpo a la gallega*.

🍽 WHERE TO EAT FESTA DO MARISCO

Held in mid-October in the small town of O Grove on Galicia's southwestern coast, this seafood festival is the perfect place to sample *pulpo a feira* ('octopus in the style of the fair') and witness its role at the heart of local life. More than 125,000 plates of seafood are served in just 10 days.

LEFT *Pulpo a la gallega* means 'Galician octopus' **ABOVE** Oysters at Vigo's seafood market in Galicia **ABOVE RIGHT** A bowl of *fabada asturiana* would keep rural workers fed for the day

PESCAITO FRITO

Down south, Andalusians eat fish in a variety of ways, but they're famous for their *pescaito frito* (fried fish). A particular speciality of Cádiz, El Puerto de Santa María and the Costa de La Luz, fried fish Andalusian-style is an art form with more subtlety than first appears. Just about anything that emerges from the sea is rolled in chickpea and wheat flour, shaken to remove the surplus, then deep-fried ever so-briefly in olive oil, just long enough to form a light golden crust that seals the essential goodness of the fish or seafood within.

GALICIAN NEIGHBOURS

Galicia's neighbours Asturias and Cantabria add some much-loved dishes to Spain's menu. *Anchoas de santoña* (anchovies caught off the Cantabrian village of Santoña) are considered Europe's finest. Asturias turns to the mountains of the Cordillera Cantábrica for inspiration – *queso de Cabrales* (untreated cow's milk cheese) and *fabada asturiana* (a stew made with pork, blood sausage and white beans) washed down with local cider is a meal for which Spaniards will cross the country.

FIESTA DE LA SIDRA NATURAL

Asturias' renowned cider flows straight from the barrel at this late-August festival in Gijón, when Asturians' passion for cider takes over an entire city.

SALMOREJO

Debate rages over the inclusion of bread in traditional gazpacho but the answer is to serve salmorejo from Córdoba, a thicker cousin of gazpacho that is still chilled and definitely uses bread. Both soups were invented by outdoor labourers using what meagre ingredients that they found in the fields – vegetables, water, bread – but where gazpacho is a summer-only soup, salmorejo is substantial enough to eat all year.

INGREDIENTS

100g/3.5oz stale white bread
1kg/2lb ripe tomatoes
2 garlic cloves
2 tbsp sherry vinegar
1 egg
Jamón
Olive oil
Salt, pepper

PREPARATION

Soak the bread in cold water then squeeze the water out. Peel the tomatoes by slitting the skin and blanching them in boiling water briefly. Quarter the tomatoes and discard the seeds.

Blend the garlic, bread and tomatoes in a food processor. Add a slug of olive oil and the sherry vinegar and continue to mix. Season to taste with sea salt and pepper. Pour into a large bowl, cover and chill in the fridge.

Hard boil the egg, peel and chop roughly. Decant the salmorejo into individual bowls, add some egg and strips of *jamón* to each. Serves four.

GAZPACHO
SUMMERTIME SOUP

In this country where seasons and climate play such a pivotal role in determining eating habits, Andalucía's climate looms larger than most. Summer arrives here with a ferocity unmatched elsewhere on the peninsula, especially in Seville, Córdoba and surrounding areas. While temperatures well above 40ºC may come as a shock to first-time visitors, locals learned long ago that there's no better way to keep cool than with a *gazpacho andaluz* (Andalusian gazpacho), a cold soup with many manifestations.

Its base is almost always a blended mix of tomatoes, peppers, cucumber, garlic, breadcrumbs, oil and (sherry) vinegar. Aside from climate, history played a significant role in its popularity here: it's a legacy of the New World, when Columbus brought back tomatoes and capsicums from his travels.

The basis for gazpacho developed in Andalucía among the *jornaleros,* agricultural day labourers, who were given rations of oil and (often-stale) bread, which they soaked in water to form the basis of a soup, adding the oil, garlic and whatever fresh vegetables were at hand. The ingredients were pounded together using a mortar and pestle, and a refreshing and nourishing dish was made that would conquer the world. It is sometimes served in a jug with ice cubes, with side dishes of chopped raw vegetables such as cucumber and onion.

A thicker version of gazpacho is *salmorejo cordobés,* a cold tomato-based soup from Córdoba where soaked bread is essential; it's served with bits of *jamón* and crumbled egg. *Ajo blanco* is a white gazpacho, a North African legacy, made with almonds, garlic and grapes instead of tomatoes.

Of course, you probably won't find gazpacho on offer in the cooler winter months, when warmth rather than a refreshing temperature is required.

ABOVE LEFT Now an essential part of Spanish cuisine and the base of *salmorejo,* tomatoes were introduced to Europe in the 16th century **ABOVE** Cordoba's former mosque: the Moors brought architecture to Andalucia

Cocido
HOT POT HIT

The cuisine of the Spanish interior is the antithesis of refreshing summer soups and lightly cooked seafood. That's because up here on the *meseta*, the high plateau that dominates central Spain, the climate is either bitterly cold or fiercely hot – *'nueve meses de invierno, tres meses de infierno'* (nine months of winter, three months of hell), as the saying goes. In such a climate, at least for nine months of the year, the culinary story is one in which necessity takes primacy over pleasure. And if one dish sums this up, it's *cocido*.

Disdained by the snooty gastronomes of coastal Spain, *cocido* (appropriately, the name is simply the past participial form of the verb 'to cook') is a hot pot stew of considerable girth. Chicken, beef, chorizo, *jamón*, potatoes, cabbage, chickpeas, a noodle broth – all of these can (and usually do) make an appearance in a *cocido*, a dish which is a particular speciality of Madrid and León but is found on menus throughout inland Spain.

There are almost as many ways of eating *cocido* as there are variations on what to include. Many Spaniards like the formality of maintaining the set order of things, eating first the soup, then the cabbage and chickpeas, and finally the meats, each as a separate dish, each in its own place and never the twain shall meet. At the other extreme, others like it all thrown in together, a catch-all dish in which the broth serves as a base for everything that follows. Just to confuse things further, in the *cocido maragato*, the *cocido* of choice in the northern Castilian town of Astorga, the meal's constituent elements are served in reverse order, with the soup bringing up the rear.

While few doubt its power to agreeably fill the stomach and warm the heart on a bitterly cold winter's day, *cocido* is rarely held up as Spain's tastiest dish. We say that with some caution, because most *madrileños* won't hear a bad word said against it. Most dream of it whenever they're away from home. They even love it so much that they compose songs celebrating its charms – one 1950s hit song contained the lyrics:

> *For what keeps me awake of a night*
> *my food of charm and delight*
> *is the one made with a woman's love*
> *and that's cocido madrileña*

There is, of course, more to interior Spain's cuisine than *cocido*: the region's perfectly cooked roast meats (roast suckling pig in Segovia and surrounds, spring lamb just about everywhere else) have a nationwide following.

☕ WHERE TO EAT RESTAURANTE SOBRINO DE BOTÍN
CALLE DE LOS CUCHILLEROS 17, MADRID

Not only is this the world's oldest restaurant (it opened in 1725 and they've a certificate from the Guinness Book of Records to prove it), they also cook a fine *cochinillo* (roast suckling pig) and *cordero asado* (roast lamb) in wood-fired ovens.

LHARDY
CARRERA DE SAN JERÓNIMO 8, MADRID

Serving Madrid's great and good since 1839, Lhardy is another venerable Madrid landmark and one of the best places in the city to try *cocido a la madrileña*.

LEARNING

ALAMBIQUE
Madrid
Mostly Spanish-language cooking classes from one of Madrid's longest-running cooking schools.

CATACURIAN
El Masroig
Three- to 10-day wine and cooking classes in Catalonia's rural wine region of Priorat.

COOK & TASTE
Barcelona
Cooking school where qualified chefs share their secrets on how to cook tapas dishes, paella and a local Catalan dessert.

KITCHEN CLUB
Madrid
Some of Madrid's most respected young chefs demystify Spanish and international recipes.

L'ATELIER
Mecina Fondales
Award-winning vegetarian chef Jean-Claude Juston runs vegetarian cookery courses in the Alpujarras valleys of Andalucía.

APUNTO – CENTRO CULTURAL DEL GUSTO
Madrid
Creatively conceived classes. Most are in Spanish, but you'll find a few conducted in English.

FINCA BUEN VINO
Sierra de Aracena
A wonderfully quiet B&B in the Andalusian hills with six cooking courses a year.

FOSH FOOD
Palma
Join chef Marc Fosh for occasional courses in his Mallorcan restaurants.

Holy Week in Valencia is an opportunity for lavish processions — and feasts

SPANISH FESTIVALS

Time your pilgrimage to Spain with a fun-filled food fiesta.

JANUARY
Madrid Fusion, Madrid
Spain's best chefs converge on Madrid in late January for a gastronomy summit that sees public cooking demonstrations by the masters (tickets can be hard to come by), as well as the chance to sample tasting menus in a number of top-end restaurants.

MARCH
Mostra de la Cuina, Palma
Explore Mallorca's unique local cuisine and wines at this long-running festival. Then follow the island's mapped food routes around local producers and restaurants.

APRIL
Feria del Queso, Trujillo
This orgy of cheese tasting in late April or early May in this medieval Extremaduran town is one of the most prestigious cheese competitions in the country – make your contribution to the popular vote by trying every one.

MAY
Feria del Vino del Ribeiro, Ribadavia
Close to the Portuguese border, Ribadavia in Galicia's south hosts the region's biggest wine festival – learn why Galician whites are ranked among Spain's best.

JUNE
Batalla de Vino, Haro
La Rioja is so blessed with fine wine that on 29 June in Haro they have a wine fight with the rest. Bring a change of clothes or stay on the sidelines and drink the good stuff.

JULY
Albariño Wine Festival, Cambados
Galicia's most decorated white is worshipped at the end of July in this infectiously joyful shindig – join the predominantly local crowd in paying homage to one of Spain's least-known, best-loved wines.

AUGUST
Certamen de Queso, Arenas de Cabrales
A pungent cheese festival in late August in Asturias, this get-together is an excuse for celebrating Spain's love affair with Asturian foods – sample it all to see what the fuss is about.

SEPTEMBER
Fiesta de San Mateo, Logroño
La Rioja's grape harvest is celebrated with grape-crushing ceremonies and tastings, starting on 21 September. The festival draws serious-minded vintners and ordinary punters – feel free to join whichever applies to you.

RELIGIOUS FESTIVALS
During Semana Santa (Holy Week), this once-devoutly Catholic country reacquaints itself with the sacred as hooded penitents bear heavy floats through the streets during haunting Good Friday processions. Before they do, many breakfast on *bacalao a la vizcaína* (dried and salted cod with chillies and capsicum). Easter is also an important time for families and friends to come together to eat. Dishes often served include *monas de pascua* (figures made of chocolate), *torta pascualina* (spinach and egg pie), *cordero pascual* (spring lamb) and *torrija* (French toast).

   At Christmas, *turrón* is a country-wide favourite. It's a uniquely Spanish kind of nougat, whose recipe goes back to the 14th century and incorporates honey, almonds and sugar.

Bangkok's floating markets are a modern-day reminder of the importance of river life in traditional Thai food culture

THAILAND

You think you know Thai cuisine: it's been a restaurant staple for years, you've pounded your own curry pastes in a giant mortar, and fresh galangal and turmeric grow in the garden. But then you arrive in Thailand ...

It is a foodie destination par excellence, no question about it. The golden Buddhas, elephant sanctuaries, white-sand beaches and longboat rides will be brief flirtations before the main event – eating!

And you won't be alone: the Thai themselves get just as excited as tourists when faced with a well-prepared bowl of noodles or when seated at a renowned hawker stall. This unabashed enthusiasm for eating has created one of the world's most fun food scenes, one where, over the centuries, indigenous basics have fused with imported ingredients to produce a distinctive native cuisine. Thailand stands at the crossroads of ancient cultural traditions dominated by India, China and Asian Oceania, and has adapted cooking techniques and ingredients from all three of these major spheres of influence.

Regional diversity is another aspect of Thai food that grabs your taste buds' attention. Despite having evolved in a relatively small geographical area, Thai cuisine is anything but a single entity, and takes a different form every time it crosses a provincial border.

Central Thai food is the most ubiquitous and refined, greatly influenced by both royal-court cuisine and foreign cooking styles, from Chinese to Malay-Muslim. Sweet and rich flavours rule in central Thai dishes.

Northeastern Thai food is Thailand's most rustic regional cooking style, hinting at what the ethnic Thai people have been eating for hundreds, if not thousands of years. Spicy, tart flavours and simple cooking methods such as grilling and soups take charge in the northeastern kitchen.

The most obscure regional cooking style in Thailand is found in the north. Meat, in particular pork, bitter and hot flavours and deep-frying play important roles. Southern Thai cooking is the spiciest of Thailand's regional cooking styles. It can also be very salty, and not surprisingly, given the south's coastline, seafood is the star. Wherever you go, prepare to bring back some new ideas about Thai cuisine.

TASTY TRAVEL

Thailand's cuisine is intensely regional and virtually every town is associated with a specific dish that's unavailable (or at least not as more-ish) outside the city limits. The following are some of Thailand's more famous regional specialties:

AYUTHAYA – *kuaytiaw ruea* (boat noodles)

Rice noodles served with a dark, intense spice-laden broth.

CHIANG MAI – *nam phrik num* and *khaep muu* (roast chilli 'dip' and deep-fried pork crackling)

Available at virtually every market in the city, the two dishes go wonderfully together, ideally accompanied by parboiled vegetables and sticky rice.

HAT YAI – *kai thawt Hat Yai*

The city's namesake fried chicken is marinated in a dried-spice mixture, which gives it a distinctive red hue.

KHON KAEN – *kai yang*

Marinated free-range chicken grilled over hot coals – a northeastern speciality that's said to be best in this town.

LAMPANG – *khao taen*

Deep-fried sticky-rice cakes drizzled with palm sugar are a popular treat in this northern town.

NONG KHAI – *naem neuang*

This Vietnamese dish of balls of pork served with rice paper wrappers and a basket of herbs has found a home in northeastern Thailand.

PHETCHABURI – *khao chae*

The best version of this odd but delicious dish of chilled fragrant rice served with sweet and savoury sides hails from this central Thai town.

TRANG – *muu yang*

Roast pig, skin and all, typically eaten as part of a dim-sum brunch, is a speciality of this southern town.

KUAYTIAW
NOODLE SOUP FOR THE SOUL

If you see a steel rack containing four lidded glass bowls or jars on your restaurant table, it's a good bet it serves *kuaytiaw*. Typically, these containers offer four choices for seasoning your noodle soup: sliced fresh chillies in vinegar, fish sauce, dried red chilli and plain white sugar. The noodle-eater will add a teaspoonful of each one of these condiments to the noodle soup, except for the sugar, which in sweet-tooth Bangkok usually rates a full tablespoon.

Originally introduced via labourers from China, who popularised the dish during the early 20th century, this noodle soup is hands-down the most common street food in Thailand today. *Kuaytiaw* vendors span the most diverse spectrum of Thai eateries, from gritty, open-air, street stalls to flash air-conditioned restaurants. Likewise, the dish functions equally well as breakfast, a late-night snack or anything in-between.

Thai-style noodle soup can take a variety of forms, but the most common version is a simple combination of rice noodles, pork broth and pork or fish balls garnished with chopped coriander, bean sprouts and a dash of white pepper. Variations on the dish are numerous, and range from northern Thai and Thai-Muslim versions using a curry-like coconut milk-based broth to central Thailand's so-called 'boat noodles', served with braised meat and a rich, spice-laden broth.

WHERE TO EAT YEN TA FO JC, SOI SALA DAENG 2, BANGKOK

One of Bangkok's most popular noodle dishes is *yen ta fo*, noodles served in a red, slightly sweet broth, with fish dumplings and cubes of blood. And one of the city's most famous vendors is Yen Ta Fo JC, a streetside stall in the city centre that's known as much for its gruff owner as its delicious noodles.

ABOVE In Bangkok, *kuaytiaw* is usually served with pork, but northern versions often include offal
RIGHT The best places to eat in Thailand are often the most unassuming

COCONUT MILK

Some newcomers to Thai cuisine mistakenly believe that 'coconut milk' means the juice contained inside a coconut. Although this juice does make a favourite thirst-quencher in hot weather, it possesses neither the sweetness nor the thickness needed to make a good base for a Thai-style curry.

To make coconut milk – known in Thai as *kathi* – a fully ripe coconut is husked, then split open to expose the thick white meat lining the inside of the shell. The dry coconut meat is then grated from the hard shell and soaked in very hot water for around 15 minutes until the water is lukewarm. The meat is then strained through a muslin cloth to produce the *kathi*. The first straining is considered 'thick' coconut milk, while the second is thin.

After the coconut milk sits for an hour or so, it will separate. The thicker section at the top is the coconut cream, while the rest of the milk below is coconut milk. Most Thai curry recipes begin with the cooking of the spice mixture in coconut cream, after which the other ingredients, including the coconut milk, are added to the pot and simmered.

KAENG
SIAM'S SOUPY CURRIES

Some of the best dishes in Thailand come served in bowls. In Thai, *kaeng* (it sounds somewhat similar to the English 'gang') is often translated as 'curry' but it actually describes any dish with a lot of liquid, and can refer to soups as well as the classic chilli-paste-based Thai curries we all love so much.

The preparation of curries and soups begins with a *khreuang kaeng*, created by mashing, pounding and grinding an array of fresh ingredients with a stone mortar and pestle to form an extremely pungent and rather thick paste. Typical ingredients include dried chilli, galangal, lemon grass, Kaffir lime zest, shallots, garlic, shrimp paste and salt. Specific combinations of ingredients are the base for various Thai curries, ranging from the coconut-milk-rich *kaeng khiaw waan* and the (in)famous green curry to *kaeng paa*, a herb-laden spicy soup known as 'jungle' curry.

Another food celebrity that falls into the soupy category is *tom yam*, Thailand's ubiquitous spicy and sour soup. Fuelling the fire beneath *tom yam*'s often velvety surface are fresh tiny chillies or, alternatively, half a teaspoonful of a roasted chilli paste. Lemon grass, galingal, Kaffir lime leaf and lime juice give *tom yam* its characteristic tang.

WHERE TO EAT

One of the best places to find *tom yam* and spicy Thai soups are the restaurants known in Thai as *raan ahaan taam sang* (food-to-order shop). This type of restaurant can often be recognised by a large display of raw ingredients – Chinese kale, tomatoes, chopped pork, fresh or dried fish, noodles, eggplant, spring onions. As the name implies, the cooks prepare just about any dish you can name, from soups to salads to stir-fries. Such restaurants are found in virtually every Thai town, are usually open-air, with seating being little more than plastic stools at the side of a street, and are largely run by Thais of Chinese origin.

ABOVE Thai food is all about the balance of four flavours: sweet, sour, salty and spicy **ABOVE LEFT** Coconut milk is a key ingredient in most Thai *kaeng*

YAM
SALAD WITH A KICK

Standing cheek by jowl with curries in terms of Thai-ness is the ubiquitous *yam*, hot and tangy 'salads' typically based around seafood, meat or vegetables. Lime juice provides the tang, while the abundant use of fresh chilli generates the heat. Most *yam* are served at room temperature or just slightly warmed by any cooked ingredients. The dish functions equally well as part of a meal, or on its own as snack food to accompany a night of boozing.

Without a doubt, *yam* are the spiciest of all Thai dishes. A good *yam* to start off with if you're not so chilli-tolerant is *yam wun sen*, bean-thread noodles tossed with shrimp, ground pork, coriander leaves, lime juice and fresh sliced chillies. Another tame *yam* that tends to be a favourite among Thais and foreigners alike is *yam plaa duk foo*, made from fried shredded catfish, chillies and peanuts, with a shredded mango dressing on the side.

⚑ WHERE TO EAT CHOTE CHITR, 146 THANON PHRAENG PHUTHON, BANGKOK

The banana blossom salad at this long-standing six-table restaurant is one of Bangkok's most sought-after *yam*. The dish's primary ingredient is slightly astringent *hua plee*, a large 'flower' holding long thin buds that will eventually grow into fully fledged bananas. At Chote Chitr, it's parboiled before being combined with ground pork, shrimp and a mild dressing that includes coconut milk.

ABOVE Yam can be based around any number of ingredients: vegetables, seafood, noodles, rice...
ABOVE RIGHT Fish are laid out on wire racks to be dried by the sun

YAM PLAA MÈUK

With squid being inexpensive and available all year round, this is a common Thai *yam*. The secret to cooking tender, not rubbery, squid is to parboil it quickly.

INGREDIENTS

5 fresh *phrik khii nuu* (mouse-dropping chilli)

5 garlic cloves, crushed

¼ cup fresh lime juice

4 tbsp fish sauce

500g/1lb squid

½ cup mint leaves

2 shallots, thinly sliced

1 cup Chinese celery, cut into 3cm/1.5in lengths

1 red *phrik chii faa* (sky pointing chilli), thinly sliced

PREPARATION

Pound the garlic and *phrik khii nuu* into a paste with a mortar and pestle. Blend it with the lime juice and fish sauce to form a dressing. Set aside.

Carve a cross-hatch pattern into the squid and slice into 2-sq-cm pieces.

Drop the squid pieces into boiling water and parboil for no more than a minute. Remove with a wire strainer.

Toss the squid with the mint, shallots, Chinese celery and *phrik chii faa*, then add the dressing and toss again.

Serve on a plate covered with lettuce leaves. To give this *yam* a completely different flavour, leave out the Chinese celery and substitute one tablespoon of sliced Kaffir lime leaves and 2 tbsp of sliced lemongrass. Serves 4.

PHAT THAI
IMPORT, EXPORT

Phat thai, **which** allegedly dates back to the 1930s, is a relatively recent introduction to the Thai kitchen and, despite the nationalistic name, is in many ways more a Chinese than a Thai dish. Both noodles and the technique of frying are Chinese in origin, although *phat thai* was invented in Thailand and its seasonings are characteristically Thai. Today the dish is quite possibly the country's most popular culinary export. Domestically, it remains a popular one-dish meal, particularly in Bangkok and central Thailand.

To make *phat thai,* thin rice noodles, seasoned with fish sauce, tamarind extract (and/or vinegar) and sugar, are fried with bits of tofu, dried shrimp, salted radish, shallots and egg. The fried noodles are then topped with ground peanuts, Chinese chives and bean sprouts, and served with a slice of lime and a side of crunchy vegetables. Sometimes, crispy green papaya is used instead of the usual rice noodles from Chanthaburi Province.

WHERE TO EAT THIP SAMAI
THANON MAHACHAI, BANGKOK

Bangkok's Thip Samai has been serving *phat thai* for nearly 50 years. It does a classic yet slightly sweet take on the dish, or for something a bit different, try the delicate egg-wrapped version or the *phat thai* fried with *man kung,* decadent shrimp fat.

LEFT Chinese immigrants have been influencing Thai cuisine for centuries, introducing both woks and noodles to the country **ABOVE** Golden goodness: *Phat thai* is one of the national dishes of Thailand

PHAT THAI

The ingredients for phat thai are available from any good Asian supermarket. Prepare them before you start cooking as things move fast when the heat is on.

INGREDIENTS

4 tbsp tamarind concentrate

6 tbsp palm sugar

2 tbsp fish sauce

300g/11oz fresh rice noodles or 250g/9oz of dried rice noodles, blanched

60g/2oz tofu, cubed

8 shallots

3 duck eggs (or chicken)

5 tbsp peanut (or groundnut) oil

2 tbsp dried prawns, rinsed and dried

1 tbsp salted radish, rinsed, dried and chopped

2 tbsp roasted peanuts, chopped

2 handfuls bean shoots

1 handful Chinese chives, sliced into 2cm/1in lengths

Extra bean shoots, peanuts, chillies and lime to garnish

PREPARATION

Mix the tamarind concentrate with the palm sugar and fish sauce until the sugar dissolves. Set aside. Heat the oil in a wok over medium heat. Fry the shallots until they begin to colour.

Crack in the eggs and stir them until they resemble scrambled eggs. Turn up the heat and add the noodles.

Add the tamarind mixture and let simmer for a few minutes until the noodles have absorbed some of the sauce.

Stir in the tofu, dried prawns, radish and peanuts and continue stirring until most of the sauce is absorbed. Add the bean shoots and chives and stir for a few minutes.

Transfer to a bowl, top with more bean shoots and roasted peanuts and serve immediately with fresh chillies and lime wedges on the side. Serves 4.

NAM PHRIK

Generally regarded as more home than restaurant food, these spicy chilli-based 'dips' are among the most emblematic of all Thai dishes. Typically eaten with rice and steamed or fresh vegetables, they're also among the most regional specialities – in fact, you could probably pinpoint the province you're in by simply looking at the *nam phrik* on offer.

The most common and most pungent variety is *nam phrik kapi,* made by grinding shrimp paste *(kapi),* palm sugar, garlic, lime and fresh *phrik khi nuu*, the hottest of the Thai chillies, in a granite mortar and pestle. In addition to parboiled vegetables, *nam phrik kapi* is usually eaten with deep-fried mackerel.

Certain kinds of *nam phrik* contain the essence of *maengdaa,* a large flat water beetle commonly found in rice fields. Foreigners often mistake this bug for the cockroach when it is sold in markets. The bugs are thoroughly mashed into the paste, so you're unlikely to know they're there, but if you detect a fruity aftertaste reminiscent of menthol, the dip probably contains *maengdaa.*

Head to the northern Thai city of Chiang Mai to try *nam phrik num,* slender long chillies that have been grilled, along with shallots and garlic, and mashed into a spicy, stringy dip that's considered one of the country's most legendary *nam phrik.*

AMERICAN FRIED RICE
HI G.I.

Khao phat amerikan, or 'American fried rice', is served up in restaurants across Thailand. Taking the form of rice fried with ketchup, raisins and peas, sides of ham and deep-fried hot dogs, and topped with a fried egg, the dish is, well, every bit as revolting as it sounds. But at least there's an interesting history behind it. American fried rice dates back to the Vietnam War era, when thousands of US troops were based in northeastern Thailand. A local cook decided to take the typical 'American Breakfast' (also known as ABF; fried eggs with ham and/or hot dogs, and white bread) and make it 'Thai' by frying the various elements with rice.

Such culinary cross-pollination is only a recent example of the Thai tendency to pick and choose from the variety of cuisines at their disposal. Other (more palatable) examples include *kaeng matsaman*, 'Muslim curry', a now classic blend of Thai and Middle Eastern cooking styles, and the famed *phat thai*, essentially a blend of Chinese cooking methods and ingredients (frying, rice noodles) with Thai seasonings (fish sauce, chilli, tamarind).

Foreigners have been impacting Thai food for centuries, but the single largest influence has come from the Chinese, who since the 19th century have introduced the wok, several types of one-plate dishes and many varieties of noodle dishes. Muslims have also had a significant impact, and are thought to have first visited southern Thailand during the late 14th century. Along with the Qur'an, they brought with them a meat- and dried-spice-based cuisine from their homelands in India and the Middle East. Today, a walk down a typical Thai street can reveal opposing stalls selling chicken biryani and pork noodle soup – culturally disparate dishes that are today considered integral parts of Thai cuisine.

🍽 WHERE TO EAT NEW LIGHT COFFEE HOUSE
426/1–4 SIAM SQ, BANGKOK
Sample American fried rice at this 1960s-era Bangkok diner that's changed little.

ABOVE American fried rice is rarely found outside Thailand **ABOVE LEFT** As well as fresh chillies, many Thai dishes use dried chillies, either whole or ground

ℳ FRUIT
A TROPICAL ABUNDANCE

Fresh fruit is everywhere you look in Thailand, from pyramids of orange papaya on market stalls and strings of yellow bananas hanging from the eaves of shops to the panoply of cubed colours stacked behind the glass panes of roaming fruit carts. The omnipresent *phonlamai* (literally, 'fruit of the tree') testifies not only to Thailand's tropical abundance, but also to the Thais' great fondness for fruit, which they consume at every opportunity.

The watchful visitor could almost fix the calendar month in Thailand by observing the fruits – sweet mangoes in March, mangosteen in April, custard apple in July, golden-peel oranges in November amd so on. There are 20 types of bananas alone, and other popular year-rounders found throughout the kingdom include coconut, guava, jackfruit, lime, Kaffir lime, tamarind, mandarin orange, papaya, pomelo, watermelon and pineapple. All are most commonly eaten fresh, or sometimes dipped in a mixture of salt, sugar and ground chilli.

Dubbed the king of fruits by Southeast Asians yet despised by many foreigners, the durian is a member of the aptly named Bombacaceae family; the heavy, spiked orb resembles medieval munitions. Inside lie five sections of pungent flesh whose ammonia-like aroma is so strong that many Thai hotels ban the fruit. Connoisseurs have laboured to describe the flavour. Perhaps the best description is from 19th-century British natural historian Alfred Russell Wallace: 'custard flavoured with almonds, intermingled with wafts of flavour that call to mind cream cheese, onion sauce, brown sherry and other incongruities...neither acid, nor sweet, nor juicy, yet one feels the want of none of these qualities for it is perfect as it is.'

☯ WHERE TO EAT OR TOR KOR MARKET
THANON KAMPHAENG PHET, BANGKOK

The recently remodelled Or Tor Kor Market is known for its impressive fruit – think mangoes the size of toddlers – not to mention some of the country's best durian.

ABOVE Rambutan is closely related to the lychee and is named from the Malaysian word *rambut* (hair)

📖 LEARNING

Having consumed everything Thailand has to offer is one thing, but imagine the points you'll rack up if you can make the same dishes for your family or friends back at home. A visit to a Thai cooking school has become a must-do addition to a Thailand itinerary, and is often a highlight of the trip.

Courses range in price and value, but a typical half-day course should include at least a basic introduction to Thai ingredients and flavours, and a hands-on chance to both prepare and cook several dishes. Nearly all lessons include a set of printed recipes and end with a communal lunch consisting of your handiwork.

Some recommended cookery courses across Thailand:

BLUE ELEPHANT COOKING SCHOOL
www.blueelephant.com
Courses from US$90 in Bangkok and Phuket

HELPING HANDS
www.cookingwithpoo.com
Courses from US$40; Bangkok

BAAN THAI COOKERY SCHOOL
www.cookinthai.com
Courses from US$30; Chiang Mai

KHAO COOKING SCHOOL
www.khaocookingschool.com
Courses from US$48; Bangkok

CHIANG MAI THAI COOKERY SCHOOL
www.thaicookeryschool.com
Courses from US$50; Chiang Mai

SAMUI INSTITUTE OF THAI CULINARY ARTS
www.sitca.net
Courses from US$65; Ko Samui

MOM TRI'S BOATHOUSE
www.boathousephuket.com
Courses from US$70; Phuket

A sound like machine-gun fire fills the streets, the air is opaque with grey-brown smoke, and men and women traipse along blocked-off city roads, their cheeks pierced with skewers and knives, or, more surprisingly, tree branches and lamps. Some have blood running down their fronts or open lashes across their backs. No, this isn't a war zone, this is the Vegetarian Festival, one of most important events on this Thai island.

The festival, occupying the first nine days of the ninth lunar month of the Chinese calendar (late September or October) marks the start of 'Taoist Lent', when devout Chinese abstain from eating meat. More obvious to the outsider are the daily processions winding their way through town with floats of ornately dressed children, armies of flag-bearing young people and men and woman engaged in acts of self-mortification.

Phuket's Chinese community claims that the festival was started by a theatre troupe from China that stopped off in the Phuket town of Kathu around 150 years ago. The story goes that the troupe was struck seriously ill because the members had failed to propitiate the nine emperor gods of Taosim. The nine-day penance they performed included self-piercing, meditation and a strict vegetarian diet.

During the festival, restaurants decorated with yellow flags with Chinese writing serve meat-free food. Inside, you'll find most of the Thai-Chinese standards – served with soy-based meat substitutes – as well as some dishes only available during the festival, such as thick wheat noodles fried with dried mushrooms and vegetables.

PHAK BUNG
MORNING GLORY

Also known as water spinach, morning glory, water hyacinth and swamp cabbage, *phak bung* seems to have been tagged with more English names than any other vegetable in Thailand. Botanists know it by the even less appetising name of water convolvulus. This ubiquitous, vine-like plant grows copiously wherever there is standing water and seems especially fond of shallow ponds, canals and drainage ditches, where enterprising locals collect it by the armload to take home or to market.

The vegetable, high in iron and vitamin A, tastes delicious whether eaten raw as a cooling accompaniment to spicy dishes or stir-fried on its own. To make *phak bung fai daeng* (literally, 'red fire water spinach'), one of the most popular dishes in the country, Thais dribble vegetable oil into the wok, turn the gas flame all the way up, toss in handfuls of *phak bung*, sliced chillies and mashed garlic cloves, and stir-fry the lot for less than a minute. The oil that splashes down the sides of the wok catches fire and tall flames usually leap over the edge of the wok, licking the inside and adding a smoky flavour to the dish that can't be obtained any other way.

To add more drama to what is already an impressive performance, cooks in some parts of Thailand have invented an alternative known as *phak bung lawy faa* (sky-floating water spinach), often advertised in English as 'flying vegetable'. In this variation, the cook fires up a batch of *phak bung fai daeng* in the wok, then by swinging the wok by one handle, flings the *phak bung* across the market area to a waiting server who catches it on a plate. Now that's service!

🍽 WHERE TO EAT
For *phak bung loy fa*, head to the northern Thai city of Phitsanulok, where a string of open-air riverside vendors specialise in the dish.

ABOVE Vegetarianism is not very common in Thailand and most vegetarian dishes are Chinese in origin
RIGHT Thailand's markets are a great place to get a feel for local culture

THE WORLD'S BEST FOOD MARKETS

Hitch a ride with Sarah Baxter across Europe, Australia, North America and Southeast Asia, filling your shopping basket and belly with everything from organic olives to skewered scorpions, ripe dragon fruit to kangaroo salami, at 10 of the top food markets across the planet.

BOROUGH MARKET, LONDON, UK

Traders have been hawking their wares on Borough High Street since the 13th century – though what those rustic Middle Ages shoppers would make of today's boutique-style incarnation is anyone's guess. London's oldest market showcases exquisite produce: a quality-control panel tests the wares on offer at each of the 100-odd stalls (what a job!), to ensure all those exotic fruits, rare-breed meats, artisanal breads, fiery chutneys and fresh fish are up to scratch.
8 Southwark St, London, England; Thu 11am–5pm, Fri noon–6pm, Sat 8am–5pm; www.boroughmarket.org.uk

QUEEN VICTORIA MARKET, MELBOURNE, AUSTRALIA

Even fussy eaters can't fail to be sated at Queen Victoria Market: 1000 stalls spread over the equivalent of 19 football pitches tout an array of produce from Asian vegetables to Polish pierogi and Turkish pastries. Serving Melburnians since 1878, it's still the foodie heart of the city. Join a guided tour for two hours of tasting heaven.
513 Elizabeth St, Melbourne, Victoria, Australia; Tue & Thu 6am–2pm, Fri 6am–5pm, Sat 6am–3pm, Sun 9am–4pm; www.qvm.com.au

MERCAT DE SANT JOSEP DE LA BOQUERIA, BARCELONA, SPAIN

Good food truly is sacred in this corner of Catalonia: not only is Barcelona's premier marketplace named after a saint, La Boqueria is a kind of culinary cathedral, its wrought-iron roof protecting a permanent harvest festival of fresh fruit, meat, offal and all sorts. Locals, tourists and pickpockets converge here, so hold onto your wallet and nibble away.
Rambla 91, Barcelona, Spain; Mon–Sat 8am–8.30pm; www.boqueria.info

MERCADO DE LA MERCED, MEXICO CITY, MEXICO

As befits a metropolis of 20 million people, Mexico City's Mercado de la Merced is simply enormous and colourful as a Latin fiesta. Bowls of multifarious moles (chilli-chocolate pastes) and tortillas and tamales tempt empty bellies. Just beware the Red Savina habanero chilli, one of the hottest in the world...
Cnr Anillo de Circunvalación & General Anaya, Mexico City, Mexico; 8am–7pm daily

VANHA KAUPPAHALLI & KAUPPATORI, HELSINKI, FINLAND

The Finnish capital's historic Kauppahalli (covered market) has a distinctly north European flavour. Expect salted liquorice, cured moose and reindeer meat, salmon in numerous states of smokiness and a bounty of beautiful berries. The nearby Kauppatori (market square) is a more

alfresco affair. In summer, food stalls set out chairs, while October is best if you've a hankering for herring..
South Harbour, Helsinki, Finland; Mon–Fri 8am–6pm, Sat 8am–4pm, Sun (summer only) 10am–4pm; www.vanhakauppahalli.com

SPICE BAZAAR, ISTANBUL, TURKEY

In its heyday, Istanbul's Misir Carsisi – otherwise known as the Egyptian or Spice Bazaar – was the last stop for camel caravans that had traversed the Silk Route. Though centuries have passed, this retail climax is barely less exotic today. Here, you'll find vibrant pyramids of multicoloured spices and bricks of fragrant lokum (Turkish delight) – not to mention a mass of herbal elixirs, good (allegedly) for everything from ear ache to impotence.
Misir Carsisi, Eminönü, Istanbul, Turkey; Mon–Sat 8.30am–6.30pm

ST LAWRENCE MARKET, TORONTO, CANADA

If only all 'supermarkets' could be like this. The St Lawrence bundles butchers, bakers, baristas, chocolatiers, nut-roasters, fishmongers, fruit-preservers and pasta-makers under one historic roof. The building, dating to 1845, used to be part-retail hub, part City Hall; now it's given over almost entirely to food. On weekdays browse South Market for speciality cheeses, organic candy and peameal bacon (a Torontonian favourite). On Saturdays, cross the street to North Market for the weekly farmers' fair.
92–95 Front St East, Toronto, Canada; Tue–Thu 8am–6pm, Fri 8am–7pm, Sat (South Market & Farmer's Market) 5am–5pm; www.stlawrencemarket.com

CAI RANG FLOATING MARKET, MEKONG DELTA, VIETNAM

When you live amid a channel-riven delta, it's easiest to sell your wares on the water. Six kilometres from Can Tho, Cai Rang is home to the biggest such retail confab on the Mekong. Hundreds of boats gather here before dawn, each vessel declaring its bounty by hoisting a sample on a bamboo pole. Board a small boat to get in on the action or grab a strong coffee from the equivalent of a floating Starbucks and watch the show.
Cau Dau Sau boat landing, Mekong Delta, Vietnam; 5am–noon daily

MARCHÉ LES ENFANTS ROUGES, PARIS, FRANCE

The French capital's not short on markets – every neighbourhood has one. However, the Marché des Enfants Rouges, squirreled away in the trendy Marais, has the greatest heritage. This is Paris's oldest covered market (inaugurated in 1628), and one of its tastiest. There are stalls selling delicious supplies (from pumpkins to olive oil and interesting wines), but also many where you can actually eat. It's a cosmopolitan offering too: stop at the chequered tables not just for French fare but also heady tagines, hot curries and fresh sushi.
39 Rue de Bretagne, Paris, France; Mon–Sat 3am–2pm & 4pm–8pm, Sun 9am–2pm

DŌNGHUÁMÉN NIGHT MARKET, BEIJING, CHINA

Skewered seahorse, anyone? This bustling night market in the Chinese capital is a nose-assaulting, eardrum-sizzling, belly-churning Noah's Ark of eating, packed with leftfield menu options – think scorpions on sticks, crunchy cicadas, snake meat and unidentifiable innards. Not feeling brave? There are spring rolls and noodles for those who like their cuisine a tad more conservative, plus signs are in Mandarin and English so you know exactly what you're munching.
Dong'anmen Dajie, near Wangfujing, Beijing, China; 3–10pm daily

Turkish delight: pistachio nuts, and figs stuffed with walnuts, are some of the specialities you'll encounter

TURKEY

Seasonal produce, rich traditions, culturally diverse influences – drawing on flavours from the steppes of Central Asia to Arabia and the Balkans, the Turkish menu is a meze platter of delights.

Turkey's culinary repertoire may have begun with the basic fare of nomads, but over the millennia it evolved to reflect the sprawling reign of the Ottoman Empire; the sultans' kitchens influenced cuisines from Lebanon to Bulgaria, North Africa to Israel.

The Ottoman cooks brought together the saffron and spices of the Silk Road, seafood from the Mediterranean, and the seasonal fruits and grains of the Black Sea and Aegean. Turkish menus continue to beckon the hungry with meze to be shared and lingered over, hearty soups and stews, skewered kebaps, fish sizzling on the grill and sweets drizzled with honey syrup.

Turkey is one of the world's few countries to boast a food surplus. Throughout the year, markets and bazaars overflow with produce pulled fresh from the fields. In winter, it's the citrus fruits of the Aegean; in summer, it's a mouth-watering array of plump tomatoes, capsicums, grapes, stone fruits and melons.

Most of these vegetables are chopped then sautéed with olive oil to retain their flavour, freshness and texture. Tomatoes, eggplants and zucchinis might be stuffed with rice and meat to become *dolma,* then baked to a melting sweetness. Vine leaves stuffed with rice and herbs are the quintessential *dolma* and the perfect finger food.

Turkish fruit is of such stand-alone brilliance that it is rarely presented any way other than in its naked glory. A platter of seasonal fresh fruit concludes most meals.

Food preparation is a measured process in the Turkish kitchen. Turkish cooks take their time to plan a meal, to choose the freshest ingredients and to present a meal as a work of art. Similarly, dining is an event to be savoured, involving several courses, each unfurling with great ceremony. Joyful, celebratory and always communal, meals are an opportunity to bring people together – family, friends, guests, even passers-by – to discuss life, love and the affairs of the day.

FRUITS OF THE SEA

Facing Homer's 'wine-dark' Aegean, the Turks have incorporated the bounties of the seas into their culinary traditions, swooning at the idea of grilled fish accompanied by fresh salad and white cheese, eaten with glasses of chilled *raki*.

Fish is often sold at specialised bazaars, usually positioned at the fishing dock, so the catch can be bought literally net fresh when the trawlers return from the sea. Fishermen and connoisseurs alike know that with the change of season comes a different catch: the fat *hamsi* (anchovies) of the Black Sea are most bountiful during winter, while the arrival of the flounder-like *kalkan* (turbot) heralds the oncoming spring.

Other favourites are *kılıç* (swordfish) cut into hearty steaks and grilled over hot coals, and pink *barbunya* (mullet) rolled in a simple batter of egg yolk and flour then lightly fried. *Uskumru* (mackerel), the core ingredient of the Istanbul institution *balık ekmek* (grilled fish, lemon juice and salad in a crusty roll wrapped in butcher paper and eaten on the hoof), is cooked on boats on the Bosphorus and served up to eager crowds at all hours.

Along the Aegean or Marmara coasts, you may see a man carrying a wooden stool, sporting an apron and balancing a round tray on his head. Chances are he's selling *midye dolması*, mussels stuffed with rice and herbs. Setting his stool down, he will prepare a selection of his salty wonders for you. Dressed with a squeeze of lemon, these morsels are like sampling the essence of the sea one mouthful at a time.

⠰ KEBAPS
SIZZLING AND SUCCULENT

Kebaps may be associated with low-brow fast-food joints in the West, but in Turkey the tradition of kebap-making stretches back centuries. Thought to have originated as the skewered meat that nomads roasted on their campfires, kebaps have evolved to include regional and seasonal variations. Here, kebaps take on a new level of complexity and refinement.

The *döner,* accompanied by fresh tomato, lettuce and garlic sauce, is as ubiquitous in Turkey as in the West, but for Turks the king of all kebaps is the *Iskender*. This rich combination of sizzling lamb mince smothered in yoghurt, tomato paste and butter sauce, all resting on a bed of crumbled pide bread, originated in Bursa.

Other regional variations are the skewered *Tokat* kebap of cubed meat, tomato, garlic and eggplant. Spiced to perfection, the zesty *Adana* kebap is cooked directly over coals and guaranteed to leave your mouth zinging with chilli and paprika.

The *ocakbaşı* (fireside) kebap restaurants are the most fun places to dine. Recalling the nomads of old who gathered by the campfire, patrons sit around the sides of a grill and watch their dinner being prepared and cooked. Talking directly with the chef and fellow diners creates a sense of camaraderie, and here a simple kebap meal becomes a surround-sound sensory experience as the heat of the embers, ribbons of tangy smoke and the crackle and spit of meat over the coals heighten the anticipation of the assembled diners.

☕ WHERE TO EAT TRABZON MANGAL DÜNYASI
ATATÜRK ALANI, TRABZON

On the Black Sea coast, Trabzon Mangal Dünyası feeds the hungry masses with fiery kebaps, fluffy flatbreads and grilled vegetables served straight from the hot plate.

ABOVE Hot coals, smoke and the sizzling of browning kebaps on Turkey's version of the barbecue are a ubiquitous scene here – take some lightly grilled flat *pide*, add some condiments and make yourself a meal

~~~
KÖFTE
FLESH IN THE PAN

Turks are enthusiastic carnivores and you'll find menus replete with meaty options across the country. According to Islamic law, pork is not consumed, but *kuzu* (lamb), *tavuk* (chicken) and *dana* (beef) feature in myriad recipes.

Meat is generally prepared diced or minced rather than served in large cuts, and it is rarely regarded as a meal in its own right. Generally, you'll find meat is cooked up with fresh vegetables, grains and spices to create wholesome and hearty amalgams, or served with a garnish or vegetable side dish. *Saç kavurma* is cubes of meat fried on the *saç* (a convex pan, like an inverted wok), usually in combination with tomatoes, onions, garlic and varieties of capsicums, while *guveç* is meat and vegetables stewed together in a clay pot in the oven.

One stand-alone meat dish you'll find everywhere is *köfte:* perhaps for this reason, it's one of the few meals that Turkish men are happy to make. A combination of ground meat, onion and breadcrumbs grilled to perfection, *köfte* is said to have originated as the quintessential nomadic food, when horsemen carried ground meat in their saddle bags. One version, not for the faint hearted, is *çiğ köfte*, raw ground lamb that's kneaded with chillies and cracked wheat for hours to create a zesty, meaty compote, then served with lettuce and a squeeze of lemon.

🍴 WHERE TO EAT TARIHI KÖFTECISI SELIM USTA
DIVAN YOLU 12, SULTANAHMET, ISTANBUL

In Istanbul's old town, this place has been briskly serving nothing but succulent *köfte* (with white-bean salad and grilled-pepper accoutrements) to hungry locals for donkeys years.

ABOVE You'll be hard pressed to get discover the exact mix of meat, bread crumbs and spices to make the perfect *köfte*, everyone has their own closely guarded recipe.

HÜNKAR BEĞENDI

Commonly translated as 'sultan's delight', this is a mouth-watering dish of lamb stew on a bed of puréed eggplant.

INGREDIENTS

1kg/2lb cubed lamb (beef or veal can be substituted)

2 tbsp butter

2 onions, finely chopped

2 cloves garlic, finely chopped

3 tomatoes, diced

Salt and pepper

½ cup chopped parsley

FOR THE EGGLANT PURÉE

6 medium eggplants (aubergines)

125g/4.5oz butter

4 tbsp flour

500mL/17fl oz warm milk

Juice of half a lemon

100g/3.5oz grated *kaşar peyniri* (sheep's milk cheese)

Salt

Nutmeg

PREPARATION

Soften the onions and garlic in butter then add the cubed lamb. Sauté for about five minutes, until the meat turns brown. Add the tomatoes, salt and pepper and sauté until mushy. Add a cup of hot water, cover and cook for 45 to 60 minutes until the meat is tender.

Char the eggplants over an open flame until the skin is black. Scrape off the skin, discard stalks and seeds and mash the flesh with the lemon juice. Set aside. Melt butter in a saucepan, add flour and stir constantly into a smooth yellow paste. Slowly add the milk, stirring all the while, until it forms a thick, smooth sauce. Add the eggplant mixture, cheese, salt and nutmeg. Cook the mixture for 15 minutes on a low heat. Pour the hot eggplant purée into a serving dish, make a well in the centre and pour in the meat. Garnish with parsley.

YAPRAK SARMA

Get your fingers wrapping classic Turkish stuffed vine leaves.

INGREDIENTS

500g/1lb drained vine leaves
250mL/8.5fl oz olive oil
2 large onions, finely chopped
200g/7oz rice
4 tbsp pine nuts
4 tbsp currants
250mL/8.5fl oz water
1 cup parsley, coarsely chopped
1 cup dill, coarsely chopped
Salt and pepper
2 lemons

PREPARATION

If using fresh vine leaves, boil for two minutes, remove carefully and drain. If the leaves are preserved in brine, rinse them in hot water. Heat the olive oil in a large pan. Gently fry the onions and the pine nuts until golden brown. Add the rice and fry for five minutes. Add the currants and water. Stir briefly then cover and simmer for 15 minutes or until the liquid is absorbed (the rice will be undercooked). Stir in chopped parsley and dill. Let cool.

Lay the leaf out, matte side up, stem pointing at you. Place a glob of stuffing near the base of the leaf and fold the stem over. Fold both sides of the leaf in towards the centre then roll it all up, cigar style. Arrange the parcels stem side down in a saucepan. Cover with water and weigh down with a plate. Simmer for about 30 minutes until the rice is tender. Let cool and serve with lemon wedges.

‹‹‹
MEZE
MANY ARE THE MEZE

Ideally, Turkish meals begin with a meze course, a series of tasting plates, often shared and enjoyed at a leisurely pace, much like Spanish tapas or Italian antipasto. So numerous – and delicious – are the varieties of meze that it's possible to forego a main course and simply continue dipping into a succession of these tasty morsels until you are completely satisfied.

Legend states that the meze tradition was brought to Turkey by Süleyman the Magnificent after campaigning against the Persians, where tasters were employed by royalty fearing poisoning. Süleyman, similarly fearful, appointed a taster to sample small plates of food in his palace, and soon the practice took off among the broader populace, leading to the creation of one of Turkey's great dining experiences. Meze dishes include cold varieties such as cheese plates, olives and dips such as eggplant, hummus and *çacik* (cucumber and garlic with yoghurt). Other standouts include *yaprak sarma* (stuffed vine leaves), vegetables sautéed in olive oil, hot dishes like *kalamar* (calamari), stuffed mushrooms and the signature *börek,* a rolled pastry filled with cheese and herbs.

No self-respecting Turk would think of ordering any meze without washing them down with *raki* (aniseed-infused grape brandy, similar to Greek ouzo). The best place to sample both *raki* and meze is in a *meyhane* (tavern), where the combination of good food, convivial company, busking musicians and potent alcohol can contribute to a 'lively' atmosphere.

Some of the best *meyhane* are found in Beyoğlu in Istanbul.

🍽 WHERE TO EAT SOFYALI 9
SOFYALI SOKAK 9, BEYOĞLU, ISTANBUL

Just off the main thoroughfare of Istanbul's Beyoğlu neighbourhood, Sofyali 9 is always buzzing with merrymakers choosing from trays of succulent meze brought fresh to the table.

ABOVE Sharing plates bring people together to graze on hot and cold dishes at a leisurely pace
ABOVE LEFT *Yaprak sarma*, stuffed vine leaves the Turkish way

❧
BAKLAVA
BETTER THAN TURKISH DELIGHT

Associated with a kind heart, and a must at any celebration, sweets are consumed with gusto in Turkey. Turkish delight has won an international reputation since its invention in 18th-century Istanbul, but the sultan of all sweets is baklava, its layers of buttery filo goodness, crunchy nut filling and sticky sweetness as addictive as any narcotic.

Classic baklava should be made with up to 40 layers of *yufka* (filo), but some fanatical (and genius!) baklava chefs will try to layer up to 100 sheets. Baklava is the ultimate midafternoon sugar hit, and the quintessential closer to a Turkish meal.

Other pastry and fruit concoctions that get taste buds working include *sütlaç* (rice pudding), baked to perfection, cooled and dusted with cinnamon. *Helva* (ground sesame seeds) is flavoured with anything from rose water to pistachio – every region, village and household seems to have its own distinctive version, enjoyed at afternoon tea or at the end of the evening meal.

The pudding of dried fruit and nuts called *aşure* is said to have been invented by Noah's wife on the Ark. It's traditionally served during the first 10 days of the month of Muharrem in the Islamic calendar.

♨ WHERE TO EAT IMAM ÇAĞDAŞ
KALE CIVARI UZUN ÇARŞI, GAZIANTEP
Achieving cult status amongst aficionados, Imam Çağdaş in southeastern Anatolia draws excited crowds with its swoony *fıstıklı* (pistachio) baklava.

ABOVE Ask who invented baklava and you'll get a different answer from every country in the Middle East – Turkey's baklava is renowned for its imperial origins

BAKLAVA
A melt-in-the-mouth classic for the sweet-toothed traveller.

INGREDIENTS
Pack of ready-rolled filo pastry
200g/7oz butter, melted

FOR THE FILLING
500g/1lb walnuts
2tbsp sugar
4tsp ground cinnamon

FOR THE SYRUP
300g/10oz granulated sugar
150mL/5fl oz water
Rose water, to taste

PREPARATION
Preheat the oven to 180°C/350°F and grease a large, shallow baking tray. Chop the nuts. You could use a mixture of walnuts, pistachios or almonds. Combine in a bowl with sugar and cinnamon.

Working quickly so the pastry doesn't dry out, lay half the sheets across the baking tray, folding in any excess. Brush with a light layer of the melted butter. Add the nut mix then the rest of the pastry sheets, and another layer of butter. Fold the whole thing over on itself so it doubles in thickness, and brush the surface with more butter. Spare nuts can be sprinkled over the top after cooking.

Make criss-cross cuts in the pastry to form diamond shapes just under an inch in diameter. Place the tray on the top shelf of the oven and bake for 15 to 20 minutes, until the top is golden.

To make the syrup, the ratio of sugar to water should be at least 1½:1. Put both in a saucepan and heat very slowly. Add tiny quantities of rose water to taste. Allow the syrup to boil for no more than two minutes to avoid the sugar crystallising when cool. When the baklava is done, remove from the oven and pour the hot syrup over it. Leave to cool, then cut fully into pieces.

Make a date at a sweet shop in Istanbul's spice bazaar, which dates from 1664

BITE-SIZE DIVERSIONS

Turkey boasts a wealth of dining experiences.
The street food and side dishes are often as delicious as the
silver service offerings. Here are some of our favourites.

IMAM BAYILDI

Translated as 'the priest fainted', this dish of eggplant stuffed with onion, garlic and tomato is so named because in popular folklore a cleric who once tried it passed out at the sheer pleasure of it. In its simplicity, freshness and full-bodied flavour, it encapsulates all that is great about Turkish cookery.

PIDE

So much better than mass-produced pizza, Turkish *pide* is pulled piping hot from the oven, drizzled with lemon juice, then sliced into fingers and garnished with rocket.

HÜNKAR BEĞENDI

This hearty dish is a sublime combination of sautéed lamb, puréed eggplant and béchamel sauce.

PASTRY SHOPS

To complement Turkey's many savoury delights, sweet-tooths can choose from a drool-worthy array of cakes, cookies or syrup-laced concoctions.

YOGHURT

Common enough worldwide, but in Turkey it is especially delicious – creamy, rich and tangy. Turks serve it as an accompaniment to just about everything, and why not when it is this good?

SEASIDE DINING

Nab a table with a view of the Bosphorus or the Mediterranean, or the Aegeanand revel in great food and ambience as the sun sinks below the horizon on a balmy night.

DONDURMA

Made from goat's milk, sugar and powdered orchid root, Turkish ice cream is so thick and gelatinous you can cut it with a knife. Vendors in embroidered waistcoats ring cowbells and churn chunks of this creamy goodness to drum up business.

MANTI

Originating in Central Asia, these pasta packages – similar to ravioli – are served filled with meat or cheese and drizzled with garlicky yogurt *à la Turka*.

REGIONAL FRUIT

Certain cities specialise in particular fruits. Diyarbakır is famed for its watermelons, ruby segments of which, served fresh, crisp and sweet, are the perfect ending to summer meals. Malatya produces the plumpest, golden apricots sold dried, pitted or au natural, while Giresun, on the Black Sea coast, is Turkey's cherry capital, and is reputedly where the cherry was first encountered.

MARKETS

Shopping is great fun in Turkey, where the markets are lively, colourful and convivial, and afford a view of the inner life of the country. Here you'll see Turks of all walks of life at their gregarious best. Farmers bringing their produce to town, wandering pedlars calling 'boyurun' (an untranslatable come-one-come-all sales pitch), local schoolchildren running errands, grandmothers in headscarves haggling with gusto.

Star in your own road movie in the USA, starting at a diner on Route 66

UNITED STATES OF AMERICA

From the melting pot of New York City to the pineapple plantations of Hawaii, US cuisine is all about diversity. Specific cuisines for the northeast, southwest and the Deep South are the tip of a tasty iceberg.

Take a stash of home-grown bounty: the salmon, clams, corn, potatoes, beans, squash, wild berries and rice enjoyed by Native Americans. Add the culinary twists of early colonists from England, France, Spain and the Netherlands, and you have a pattern of culinary innovation that still defines the way Americans eat today.

In this country of immigrants, pockets of people from around the globe have created distinct regional cuisines within urban neighbourhoods: Norwegians smoking freshwater fish; Chinese families making dumplings; Italians rolling out pasta; Mexicans pressing corn *masa* into tortillas; and Russians boiling borscht. The result is a country where, in the big cities at least, you can order a plateful of just about any kind of global cuisine you choose.

Grains are sourced from the flat and fertile Midwest, where corn and wheat fields stretch to the horizon. Seafood feeds the populations in the northeast, south and along the West Coast, while Western ranch lands produce the beef.

Twentieth-century technology played its part in creating a distinctive US cuisine, with the combination of reliable transportation and food preservation gifting the world a culture of culinary convenience, from 1950s TV dinners to fast-food restaurants that became global corporations. A counter movement based on the idea of slow cooking started in the 1960s with the American chef Julia Child, who introduced Americans to cooking French food at home. In the '70s, California became the centre of a new focus on eating natural, seasonal, locally grown foods.

The culture of food increasingly fascinates America, evidenced by the rise of celebrity chefs and televised cooking that demonstrates how to make Japanese sushi, Indian naan and the rubs and sauces that feature in the nation's pride and joy, barbecue. And to help US home cooks stay abreast of culinary trends, many grocery stores carry what were once considered exotic ingredients, from heirloom tomatoes to Chinese bean paste.

RUB ME TENDER

Competitive barbecue – yes, there is such a thing – is a tale of two cities. Memphis and Kansas City both claim to cook up the yummiest ribs. Make up your own mind with their signature rubs

MEMPHIS
INGREDIENTS

4 tbsp paprika

2 tbsp powdered garlic

2 tbsp mild chilli powder

1 tbsp ground black pepper

1 tbsp salt

½ tbsp celery seed (crushed)

½ tbsp dried oregano

½ tbsp dried thyme

½ tbsp whole allspice

2 tsp yellow mustard seed

1 tsp ground coriander

KANSAS CITY
INGREDIENTS

½ cup brown sugar

¼ cup paprika

1 tbsp ground black pepper

1 tbsp salt

1 tbsp chilli powder

1 tbsp garlic power

1 tbsp onion powder

1 tsp cayenne pepper

PREPARATION

Mix the rubs in a bowl. Apply to the ribs (beef or pork). Barbecue low and slow. Serve with cold beer.
Disclaimer: use these recipes as a starting point. The barbecue experts in each city will have their own top-secret blends.

BARBECUE
SLOW-COOKIN' PERFECTION

Americans love to throw a barbecue, inviting people over to share a meal cooked outside on the grill. But for many, the real down-home barbecue is the kind that requires slow cooking, culinary pride and a hefty dash of loyalty to a particular barbecuing style. This type of barbecue draws the crowds, not only at homes but at commercial barbecue joints (of which there are legions) and tailgate parties held in stadium parking lots as a prelude to football games. There are even barbecue contests from coast to coast, where contestants compete for serious prize money with their individual takes on sauces, rubs and cooking techniques.

Ask an American what 'barbecue' means and you'll get a range of answers across the country, from mustard-sauced pulled pork to beef ribs rubbed with Cajun spice. Usually 'barbecue' describes meat – such as beef brisket, pulled pork, chicken wings and ribs – that has been grilled over coals or gas flame and/or smoked, which helps create tenderness and smoky flavours. But the seasonings are what divide barbecue-lovers; everything from spice rubs to vinegar sauces create distinct zings and nuances.

The barbecue cooking style originated in the South, and Texas, Memphis, Kansas City and North Carolina are the nation's barbecue hubs, each with its own distinct style favouring pork or beef, ribs or pulled meat.

In Kansas City, hickory-smoked ribs are slathered with a sweet molasses and tomato sauce, while Memphis specialises in chopped pork sandwiches and baby back ribs. In North Carolina you might be offered pulled pork with a spice and vinegar sauce. Texas has four distinct barbecue regions, including beef cooked West Texas cowboy-style over mesquite, and the German-style slow-cooked brisket of Central Texas. In true American fashion, barbecue cooking has migrated to all parts of the country, so you'll find it everywhere from Seattle to Sarasota.

Eating barbecue-style is a chance to get messy and eat with your hands. But don't be shy about using utensils for traditional side dishes like corn on the cob, collard greens, potato salad, coleslaw and cornbread.

⚘ WHERE TO EAT SMITTY'S MARKET
208 SOUTH COMMERCE, LOCKHART, TEXAS

Located in Lockhart, a town many consider to be an important source of Texas-style barbecue, Smitty's is a smoky, rough-hewn spot that takes meat seriously. Order oak-smoked brisket, pork ribs or sausage, all of which come served on butchers paper (no plates or forks). Patrons eat at long, communal tables, with sides of white bread and sweet pickles.

ABOVE LEFT The best Texas barbecue is found in the country at family-owned places that have used the same recipes for generations **RIGHT** A key component of barbecue is the rub, which can be either wet or dry

THE RISE OF THE FOOD TRUCK

When a Korean taco truck in Los Angeles has 100,000 followers, you know that something zeitgeist-y is happening.

Visit any major metropolitan area in the US and you're likely to come across a food truck, a mobile vehicle fitted out with a kitchen and a window where customers can place orders. But we're not talking common or garden hot dogs or bagels. In Portland, Oregon, for example, more than 400 carts dot the culinary landscape, serving everything from phat thai to grilled cheese.

The food-truck trend is synonymous with a Los Angeles chef named Roy Choi. His Kogi carts, which serve Korean- and Mexican-fusion dishes, including the famous beef short-rib taco, have developed a fanatical following, most notably on Twitter, where the chef announces where the trucks will be located each day. The Kogi BBQ food trucks are at the front of a bandwagon that includes 6000 other trucks in Los Angeles. All revved up, the food trucks have somewhere to go: out of Latino districts and into upscale neighbourhoods where hungry young things (read: Twitter-using hipsters) descend on them. All Choi does is broadcast where his truck will be and what's on the menu. LA's food trucks even have their own lobby group, La Asociación de Loncheros.

On the east coast, munch *churros* or *empanadas* from trucks in Miami. And in New York, gourmet options include top-notch burgers from Frites 'N' Meats, couscous or kofte from Comme Ci Comme Ça and falafel from the black-painted truck of Taïm. Happy hunting.

HAMBURGERS
QUINTESSENTIAL AMERICANA

If the US had an emblematic food, it would be the hamburger. In its purest form, a burger is simply a patty of cooked ground beef slipped inside a bread bun – the perfect symbol for a country with a Midwest breadbasket and a love for the Wild West and its cattle-herding cowboys. The quality of the meat and what accompanies sets the gourmet burger apart.

The hamburger arrived in New York City with German immigrants in the late 19th century. Named after the German city, Hamburg steak was a shredded-beef dish that used cheap cuts of meat and was eaten by the less well-off. The burger can now be found at most fast-food joints and even in traditional Chinese and Mexican restaurants. Since around 2000, it's been de rigueur for high-end restaurants to feature their own signature burgers made with high-grade aged and imported beef cooked to order. Celebrity chefs have elevated the dish to gastronomic heights and price tags, notably Daniel Boulud and his famous DB burger made with short-rib meat braised in wine and stuffed with foie gras and truffles. Restaurants like the Shake Shack chain and the Spotted Pig gastropub in New York City also serve memorable burgers.

Burger fetishism has created an infinite number of interpretations of the classic. While purists may still worship the standard American cheese-tomato-pickle-onion-and-ketchup combo, you're just as likely to come across burgers composed of focaccia and Roquefort as well as onion rings, fried eggs, pickled beets and bacon.

🍽 WHERE TO EAT **IN-N-OUT BURGER**

This out-West chain, which first opened outside Los Angeles in 1948, is famous for outstanding burgers made with top-quality ingredients – rare indeed. Menus are basic: burgers, fries and shakes. A 'secret', unprinted menu includes upgrades like 'animal style', which is a patty cooked in mustard and topped with a slathering of secret sauce.

ABOVE Like most American dishes, the hamburger has many regional variations, such as New Mexico's green chilli burger

PIZZA
IMPORTED FROM ITALY

Do you prefer New York or Chicago? Or perhaps, California? No, we're not talking vacation spots but pizza. Most Americans have distinct ideas about what constitutes a good 'pie', be it one with a thin crust that oozes grease or a bready deep-dish layered with pepperoni.

At the turn of the last century, American immigrants co-opted the Naples-born pizza, a basic Italian peasant dish, and took it to new heights. Since then, the standard Neapolitan Margherita, a pizza topped with tomato sauce, slices of fresh buffalo mozzarella and basil, has been invented and reinvented across the country.

Dozens of styles of pizza have emerged in the US over the years, but a few distinct versions dominate. Often served by the slice, New York–style pizza has a thin, chewy crust topped with a thin layer of tomato sauce and a heavy layer of cheese. New Haven, Connecticut, claims a more Neapolitan-style pizza that comes with a blackened, blistered crust. In Chicago, pizzas are more like bready casseroles, with thick 'deep dish' crusts heavily loaded with toppings, cheese and sauce (fork and knife worthy). California-style pizza usually means untraditional toppings, such as barbecue sauce and chicken, goat's cheese, avocado or smoked salmon.

🍽 WHERE TO EAT SAL AND CARMINE PIZZA
2671 BROADWAY, NEW YORK CITY

This unpretentious family-owned joint has been making slightly crisp yet chewy pizzas since 1959. This isn't the place for exotic accoutrements, like Brussels sprouts or pancetta, but you will find straight-up slices topped with a tangy tomato sauce and a generous layer of cheese and tried-and-true toppings like pepperoni. This is the kind of pizza you eat by the slice, folded in half, with a pile of napkins nearby.

ABOVE The first pizzeria in America opened in New York City in 1905

FOOD LOVER
RUTH ROGERS

I first went to Italy in 1973. When I started cooking, it was the food that made me go 'Wow! This is what I want to cook and eat'. It lets the ingredients speak for themselves without sauces or pastry. I remember having a grilled seabass with lemon and olive oil and thinking it was the best thing I'd ever eaten. That was how we started the River Café – it was about the best ingredients not disguised or diminished by others.

In Florence, around 1975, I had some bruschetta, a piece of really good toasted sourdough rubbed with garlic and olive oil that had been pressed two weeks before.

In Puglia, they do **an amazing chickpea soup,** *zuppa di ceci,* with chilli. It's very southern.

Most inspiring ingredient? Olive oil, whatever you do with it.

I'm a fan of the New York restaurateur Danny Meyer but **I love the city's food trucks,** where you can get anything from a great piece of cake to a taco.

Chef Ruth Rogers set up the River Café in London with Rose Gray.

CALIFORNIA CUISINE
LOCAL, ORGANIC, SEASONAL AND FRESH

Long recognised as the country's trendsetting hub of health, California has played a major role in current attitudes about eating organic and locally grown foods. And why not? It's easy to eat local if you have a long, luscious coastline, plenty of fertile farmland and varied microclimates that support everything from citrus to fig trees. California also grows avocados, almonds, grapes, strawberries, artichokes, dates and olives.

In the 1970s, Alice Waters, who later influenced a generation of chefs and home cooks with her book *The Art of Simple Food*, helped ignite a movement to support local farmers, ranchers and food purveyors through her landmark Berkeley restaurant, Chez Panisse. The breadth of fresh, naturally produced ingredients made for some delicious results. A succession of other star chefs, including Wolfgang Puck, helped popularise California cuisine, which emphasises lighter fare, Asian and Latin American fusion, and of course, local ingredients. Think burgers topped with a tall portion of sprouts and avocado slices; artisan goat's cheese; sourdough bread; Thai-style pizzas; and Baja fish tacos.

It's not only food that California does well. Out of the state's wineries come world-class red, white and sparkling wines (see p194). And, in Anchor Brewing of San Francisco, it has one of America's original craft brewers. Health and hedonism: a very Californian combo.

🍽 WHERE TO EAT CHEZ PANISSE
1517 SHATTUCK AVE, BERKELEY, CALIFORNIA

Genuflect at the temple of Alice Waters, the enduring doyenne of modern California cuisine. The temple of the revolution, the restaurant remains at the pinnacle of Bay Area dining, with its legendary prix-fixe meals that can include everything from grilled lamb stuffed with green olives to Meyer lemon éclairs. Upstairs, the more casual cafe offers fresh lettuce salads, oysters on the half-shell and braised meats.

LEFT Seasonal eating has hit the mainstream, but in California it started 40 years ago **ABOVE** Chez Panisse's kitchen **ABOVE RIGHT** Getting fresh: ingredients from local farmers feature in Jim Denevan's dishes

GO ALFRESCO

Californians seem to have more than their fair share of bright ideas. Take Jim Denevan, a surfer, artist and chef born and raised in Santa Cruz. What better way, he thought, to put people in touch with their local farmers than host alfresco dinners at their farms? The first Outstanding in the Field outdoor banquets took place in 1999 and matched organic or small-scale farmers with a local chef and a guest winemaker from the region. 'It's not every day that you get to sit next to the person who planted the beans, raised the lamb and shaped the cheese on your plate', says Denevan.

Today the Outstanding in the Field May to December road trip, in a vintage red bus, makes more than 80 stops across North America, from California to Kentucky. Diners pay up to $200 for a seat. They're no picnics, although walking boots might be required to get to the location; settings for supper have included mountain tops and sea caves. The trestle tables are set with white linen, cutlery and glassware. Menus feature the best locally grown, seasonal produce. The effect is to reconnect diners with the land that produces the food on their plate – in a fun way. As Denevan and his band of gourmet gypsies continue their inspirational journey, where else could it have started but under the big blue skies of California?

JAMBALAYA

Nothing epitomises the cultural mix of European, Spanish and Cajun cuisines than jambalaya, a rich rice-based stew of seafood, meat and vegetables. Native to New Orleans, the dish originated as a filling one-pot meal, similar to Spanish paella. Unlike its cousin, jambalaya mixes ingredients that were available in the South with culinary traditions from Europe, Canada and the Caribbean. The result is a dish that often includes green peppers or okra, cayenne pepper, tomatoes, chicken, sausage and shrimp or crawfish. Predominant flavours can be spicy or smoky, depending on who's cooking, and most Southerners know what style they prefer. Its spiritual home is in Louisiana; start at Coop's Place in New Orleans' French Quarter on Decatur Street.

SEAFOOD CHOWDER
ONE-POT WONDERS

Seafood has always played a starring role in New England's cuisine. The early settlers who landed here in the 1600s took the abundance of cod, clams, mussels, oysters and lobsters and created the staple seafood stew called chowder, a hearty and delicious way to stretch any kind of seafood into a one-pot meal. The first chowders were catch-alls, stews for poorer people making do with what was available. The word may have originated from the French *faire la chaudière,* which translates as 'to make the cauldron', the vessel that held such a hearty, peasant stew. In the US, however, chowder came to mean a chunky stew made primarily with clams – one of the country's most famous founding foods.

Even as overfishing depleted many fish populations off the eastern seaboard (most notably Atlantic cod, which has been fished to near extinction), chowders survived as mainstays. Traditional New England chowders include a base of milk or cream, chunks of potato, clams and a bit of bacon. The broth-based Manhattan-style clam chowder includes tomatoes. Either way, crackers are the standard garnish. In the Pacific Northwest and California, the orangey-pink flesh of salmon tastes great in the West Coast version of seafood chowder. Most salmon chowders are made with the same ingredients as a classic New England–style chowder, with the addition of chopped dill. Every Fourth of July weekend, 'chowdah' (as pronounced in the local vernacular) fanatics flock to Boston for Chowderfest, a cook-out as patriotic as the 'Star Spangled Banner'.

ABOVE LEFT Martha's Vineyard, the largest island in New England, remains untouched by the commercialism of the mainland **ABOVE RIGHT** The traditional clam bake is a true New England experience

LOUISIANA GUMBO

Gumbo is the Deep South's soupy one-pot wonder. Cajun or Creole versions can both use shellfish or poultry; add duck for a twist.

INGREDIENTS

2 chickens, cut into quarters

3 garlic cloves, crushed

1 small onion, peeled

10 tbsp unsalted butter

100g/3.5oz flour

1 large red bell pepper, diced

1 large green bell pepper, diced

2 onions, diced

2 stalks celery, diced

2 (15oz/420g) cans diced tomatoes

5 tbsp Worcestershire sauce

2 tbsp Tabasco sauce

2 tbsp tomato paste

1 bay leaf

2 tsp dried thyme leaves

2 tsp dried oregano leaves

1 tsp ground cayenne pepper

1 tsp ground white pepper

2 cups fresh okra, sliced

6 cups chicken stock

Sea salt to taste

Freshly ground pepper to taste

6 cups cooked rice

Filé powder

Pepper sauce

PREPARATION

Simmer the chickens in 8 cups (2L) of water with the garlic cloves and the small onion for about an hour. Remove the chicken parts from the pot and discard the garlic and onion. Skim all the fat from the chicken stock. (If you have the time, the easiest way to do this is to put it in the refrigerator overnight and lift off the solidified fat in the morning.) When the chicken has cooled, remove the meat from the bones and discard the bones and skin.

In a large, heavy soup pot, make a roux by melting the butter over medium heat and stirring in the flour. Whisk or stir constantly over medium heat until the roux becomes a very dark brown color (for about 20 minutes). If black flecks appear in the roux, you have burnt it. Start over. When the roux is the desired colour, turn off the heat and add the peppers, onion and celery, and sauté until the vegetables are soft (about five minutes). Add the tomatoes, Worcestershire, Tabasco, tomato paste, bay leaf, thyme, oregano, cayenne, and white pepper. Stir thoroughly. Whisk in the skimmed chicken stock a little at a time making sure there are no lumps. Cook over a medium heat for 30 minutes. Add the okra and chicken meat and continue cooking for another 30 minutes. Season to taste. The gumbo should be fairly thick.

To serve, mound a half a cup of rice in the middle of a bowl. Ladle gumbo around the rice. Serve with pepper sauce and filé powder. Serves 12.

CALIFORNIA WINES

California has a long tradition of winemaking that began with Native American tribes cultivating grapes in the region's rich soils. Today, Napa and Sonoma counties feature hundreds of top-ranking wineries that produce big reds (cabernet sauvignon, merlot and zinfandel) as well as chardonnay and some pinot noir. The two counties' varied climates and geography produce wines with a range of flavour profiles to entice the taste buds of wine-loving visitors, who flock to the tasting rooms to sample the range and take in the fields planted with rows of vines.

Californian wine came of age in Paris, 1976, when a pair of local wines – one red cabernet sauvignon and one white chardonnay – trounced their French opponents in a tasting competition known as the Judgement of Paris. This was a shock to the organiser Steven Spurrier, who imported French wines. The winning red was from Stag's Leap winery in Napa Valley. It beat Bordeaux's biggest names, including Haut-Brion and Mouton-Rothschild. Spurrier's white nemesis was a chardonnay from Chateau Montelena, also in Napa.

But there's more to wine-tasting in the Golden State than Napa and Sonoma (north of San Francisco); more than 2000 wineries pepper the state from cool-climate top to the dry foot. Continue north from Napa to reach Russian River Valley and Mendocino. South of San Francisco lies Santa Cruz. And in the film Sideways, the characters take a road trip through Santa Barbara and Santa Ynez wine regions in search of the perfect pinot noir (although zinfandel is California's signature grape).

҉
BEER
HIP HOPS

Americans love to drink beer. In fact, more Americans like to drink great beer – at least that's what stats from the Brewers Association tell us. In 2011, turnover by craft brewers grew by 15%, with more than 11.5 million barrels sold. While Prohibition destroyed many of the country's earliest commercial breweries back in the 1920s, brewing bounced back in a big way once the Volstead Act was overturned. Large-scale breweries thrived, morphing into giant brewing conglomerates like Anheuser-Busch InBev, MillerCoors and Pabst, the companies that now produce the majority of American beer. In the 1980s, small-scale craft breweries began popping up in the Pacific Northwest and the idea caught on nationwide. Craft breweries have allowed brewers to experiment with styles and ingredients, resulting in everything from super-hoppy India pale ales (IPAs) to chocolate espresso stouts.

Although the nation's big brewers have a knack for producing characterless lagers, America's microbrewers have built an enviable reputation for world-class beers, driven by passion and the discerning palates of a growing number of American beer lovers. Events to look out for include the American Craft Beer Week in May and the Great American Beer Festival in October. Here are five of the best little brewers around the country:

BOSTON BEER CO., MASSACHUSETTS
Now a mainstream brewer, Boston Beer's Samuel Adams Boston Lager remains a very drinkable beer, made to a family recipe dating back to the 1870s.

SIERRA NEVADA BREWING CO., CALIFORNIA
Sierra Nevada's fragrant, malty Pale Ale is a classic craft brew. The brewery at 1075 East 20th St in Chico is open for free tours every afternoon.

NEW BELGIUM BREWING CO., COLORADO
New Belgium's iconic Fat Tire Amber Ale marks founder Jeff Lebesch's 1989 European bike trip, bringing back ideas and ingredients. His Fort Collins brewery is open Tues–Sat.

BROOKLYN BREWERY, NEW YORK
Award-winning brewmaster (and author) Garrett Oliver crafts perennial favourites such as Brooklyn Brown Ale and seasonal specials. Tour the brewery at 79 North 11th St.

GREAT LAKES BREWING COMPANY, OHIO
Founded in 1988, a few years after the last of Cleveland's 30 breweries had closed, Great Lakes creates muscular ales, porters and lagers. It has a brewpub on Market Ave.

WHERE TO DRINK OREGON
Some of the country's first small-scale craft breweries were born in Portland, Oregon. Today, the city boasts about 40 breweries, the highest number in a single city in the world. Some have pubs that serve food, others offer tastings and tours. On the last weekend in July, the Oregon Brewers Festival attracts beer lovers from around the globe.

A couple of hours' drive southeast of Portland, Bend has a population of 80,000 and more than 10 breweries, drawn to the area not only by the rugged scenery but the soft water. One of the nation's pioneering craft brewers, Deschutes, has a public house on Bond Street where you can taste its pale ales, porters and stouts. Guided tours of Deschutes Brewery on Simpson Ave take place every afternoon.

RIGHT Rogue Ales, one of Oregon's many craft breweries, was founded in Ashland in 1988

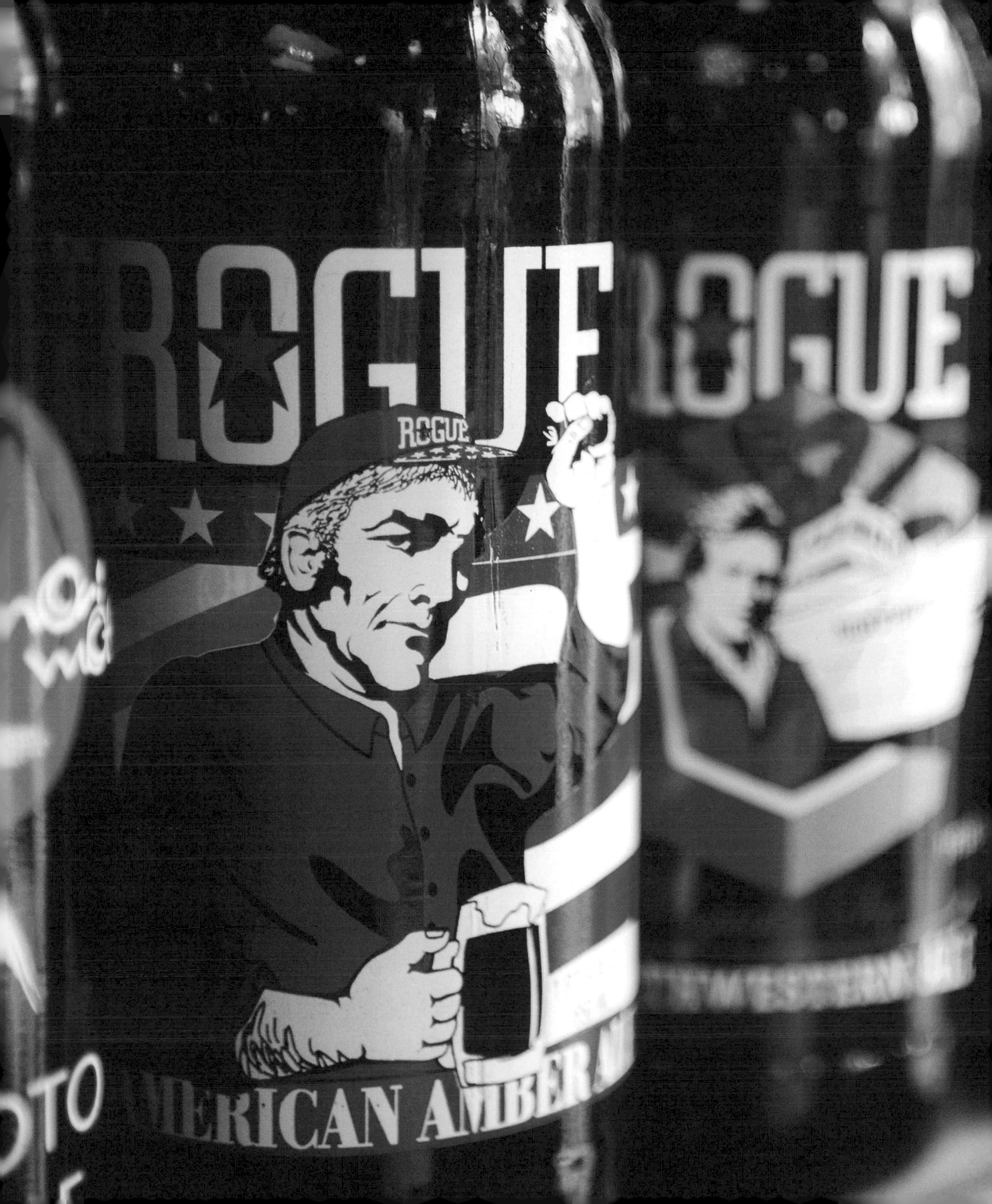
ROGUE
ROGUE

Gone fishin': catch your supper in Lake Clark National Park, Alaska

BITE-SIZE DIVERSIONS

Wherever you're on the road in the USA, there'll be a tasty snack nearby to keep you going until the next stop.

SAN DIEGO, CALIFORNIA
Sampling Baja-inspired fish tacos: grilled or fried fish, shredded cabbage, slices of avocado, fresh salsa and a white sauce folded inside a corn tortilla.

NEW YORK
Noshing on a New York City bagel, the chewy, ring-shaped bread introduced to the US by Polish Jews. Purists claim a true NYC bagel can only be made in the city, because of the properties of the local water, in which an authentic bagel is boiled before baking.

WISCONSIN
Nibbling on artisan cheeses from the growing group of small-batch cheese-makers in a state long known as a dairy and cheese-making powerhouse.

MIDWEST
Popping into one of hundreds of summertime country fairs for a taste of classic American apple pie. Choose from homemade pies, pie-contest winners and, best of all, fried pies.

ASPEN, COLORADO
Rubbing shoulders with celebrity cooks, food industry insiders and dedicated amateur foodies at the weekend-long Food and Wine Classic, the country's most famous food festival. Claim an early seat at the cooking demonstrations and superstar chef Q&A sessions, which are the most popular events.

FORT VALLEY AND BYRON, GEORGIA
Slurping the sweet juices of a fresh Georgia peach during the fruit's prime season (June) at the Georgia Peach Festival. The state grows more than 40 varieties of peach, harvesting more than two million bushels of the fruit. And did you know that the peach is part of the rose family?

ALASKA
Catching your own fresh salmon between May and September, when at least one kind of salmon is always swimming upstream: chinook, sockeye, keta or coho. Prepare for a fight: chinook can grow up to 1.5m and weigh 60kg, Anglers also take to the ocean in pursuit of huge halibut.

NEW YORK
Learning how to do everything from butchering a pig or baking a cake to cooking veal seven ways during the single-day courses at the Institute of Culinary Education.

HAWAII
Cooling off with a shaved ice, a mound of soft, fluffy ice drowned in sweet syrups of guava, mango, pineapple and coconut.

WALLA WALLA, WASHINGTON
Touring vineyards and tasting rooms along the border with Oregon in one of the country's hottest emerging winemaking regions, known for cabernet sauvignon, merlot and syrah (shiraz) wines.

Restaurants Of The World

Stars, dispensed by Michelin and reviewers, are not the only way to rank restaurants. An elite group of classic restaurants has survived the twists and turns of fashion, seen generations come and go, and defied definition. When you're eating your way around the globe, save some room for a meal at one of Tom Parker-Bowles' selection of the world's must-eat destinations.

CONTRAMAR, ROME

Fish is at the heart at Contramar, spanking fresh, piled high on tacos, marinated in lime juice and smothered in chilli. Octopus tostadas mix crisp crunch with cephalopod so soft and sweet it brings a tear of greedy joy to the eye. The *pescado a la talla,* a whole fish grilled with red and green salsa, is the sort of dish that should be placed on a pedestal and worshipped as a god.
Calle Durango 200, near plaza Cibeles, Rome, Italy

TETSUYA'S, SYDNEY

Tetsuya Wakuda mixes classical French and Japanese techniques and ingredients, following the seasons yet never enslaved by them. Each mouthful zings with flavour, and each tiny piece of silken sea urchin or sea cucumber makes perfect culinary sense. This is food to wake the senses and turn on the taste buds. It may be Michelin-starred haute cuisine, but being in Sydney it's also a place to talk, drink and share the pleasures of the table.
529 Kent Street, Sydney, Australia

VICTORIA SEAFOOD, HONG KONG

OK, there's not too much to love about the garish, over-lit room, poised halfway up a Hong Kong tower. But forget your surroundings, for this experience is all about the classic Cantonese food. As the name suggests, it's all things piscine that makes Victoria Seafood a Hong Kong classic. Don't forget to order the freshly steamed flower crabs in Chinese yellow wine and chicken oil – silken and seductive, they're possibly the finest thing to pass your lips in this Titan of culinary capitals.
Citic Tower, Fifth Floor, 1 Tim Mei Avenue, Hong Kong

LE GAVROCHE, LONDON

The 'Gavver' is unmoved by passing fancies and transient trends, instead concentrating on flawless service and high-end Gallic cuisine that still dazzles and delights. There might be a little less butter and cream in the sauces than back in the days when culinary legends Albert and Michel Roux ran the joint. But this is still some of the finest cooking in London, from the cheese-drenched bliss of soufflé Suissesse, a true Gavroche classic, to Le Caneton Gavroche, a whole duck complete with bowls of delicate consommé and three different sauces.
43 Upper Brook Street, London, UK

NOMA, COPENHAGEN

Too often, restaurants such as René Redzepi's Noma are drowned in a maelstrom of their own hype. But despite all its accolades, the atmosphere is laidback and unpretentious – and the food? Exciting, innovative and downright delectable. Live prawns, hauled from the fjords hours before; beef tartare spiked with wood sorrel; edible soil and foraged treats. Redzepi trained all over the world, yet Noma represents the very quintessence of its Danish terroir.
Strandgade 93, 1401 Copenhagen, Denmark

DA MICHELE, NAPLES

Purists will argue for years about exactly where the finest pizza can be found, but true Neapolitan pizza perfection is easy to sniff out. Just follow your nose to Da Michele in the winding backstreets of Naples. The menu is short to the point of curt – Margherita or marinara in three sizes. Tomato sauce is freshly made and spread thin, the mozzarella dotted in molten, alabaster pools. The crust is the true star: a narrow, putted-up rim, speckled with black blisters. There's a slight crack as you bite, then a wonderfully dense chew.
Via Cesare Sersale, 3, Naples, Italy

ST JOHN, LONDON

The restaurant that proved there was more to British food than soggy vegetables, jellied eels and deep-fried Mars bars was opened 18 years back, and the pared-back prose of its menu matches the cool, clean white walls of this iconic Smithfield space. No cut or organ is overlooked here at St John, the home of British nose-to-tail eating. Bone marrow, baked until wobbling, is slathered on sourdough toast, anointed with good salt and eaten with a mouthful of sharply dressed parsley salad. Lamb's tongue comes with butterbeans and green sauce, ox heart with horseradish. This is a place for bonhomie, and food that continues to inspire.
26 St John Street, London, UK

JOE'S STONE CRAB, MIAMI

Joe's is only open from mid-October until mid-May, when the famed stone crabs are in season and the crowds flock to this legendary Miami Beach joint. Be prepared to wait, as there's no booking. Joe's has been here, in one form or other, since 1913, and while its fried green tomatoes, hash browns and creamed spinach are the stuff of edible dreams, it's the stone crab claws, piled high and served with a mustard sauce, that are the main event.
11 Washington Avenue, Miami Beach, USA

DA CALOGERO, PALERMO

To many, the sea urchin is little more than an object of spiky abuse. But cut through that fearsome carapace, and sweet bliss awaits. At Da Calogero in Mondello they sell them by the dozen. Hauled from the deep waters of the coast, they're sliced open to reveal the bright orange roes within. A dozen eaten raw, gazing out at the sea, is a good start – no lemon needed – then a plateful of pasta, the roes melting among the steaming strands.
Via Torre 22, Palermo, Sicily, Italy

PRINCE'S HOT CHICKEN SHACK, NASHVILLE

A sign painted on the window is the only evidence of the greatness hidden in this nondescript row of shops, a few yards from the main Nashville highway. And the smell of chicken too, fried in vast iron skillets, blacked by years of use. Walk up to the small hatch at the back and order anything from leg to whole bird. Medium, hot or extra hot. A few minutes later, a golden piece of chook arrives, with a crisp, burnished crust, sitting atop two slices of cheap white bread alongside cheap chopped pickles. The flesh is filled with juice, the crisp coating joyously crunchy. Mild is spicy with cayenne pepper, medium pretty fiery, hot eye-wateringly so. As for the extra hot –'this ain't chattin' food,' I was told with a smile. It will take your head off. So proceed with caution. That said, this is the best fried chicken you'll ever taste. Just beware the Extra Hot.
123 Ewing Drive, Nashville, USA

CHEZ GEORGES, PARIS

Forget those foams and smears that seem so drearily de rigueur in the hushed world of three Michelin stars. Chez Georges is a proper Parisian bistro, a place where menus are written anew each day in a florid purple script, where the chequerboard marble floors match the black dress and white apron of the waitress. Their *steak au poivre* mixes real peppery punch with lashings of cream, while *oeuf en gelée* sees a perfect *oeuf mollet* (a six-minute boiled egg) wrapped in a slice of ham and encased in a jewel-like jelly.
1, rue du Mail, off Place de Victoire, 7th, Paris, France

REGIONS

Sheep, here grazing on New Zealand's South Island, outnumber New Zealanders by about 10 to one

AUSTRALIA & NEW ZEALAND

Australia and New Zealand are both praised for their wine, lamb and beef. What sets the two countries' palates apart is their indigenous and Pacific flavours, local ingredients and idiosyncratic twists.

If you could zap a regular 1950s Aussie or Kiwi into the 21st century and take them out to lunch, you'd have one bamboozled time-traveller on your hands. The food enjoyed by modern Australians and New Zealanders bears little resemblance to the fare their forebears ate only a few decades ago. There would be a few classics our visitor from the '50s might be relieved to see – a roast lunch with gravy; a meat pie with sauce; fish and chips wrapped in paper, with plenty of vinegar. But for the most part, you'd be translating the menu for them.

So what happened? In a word: immigration. Old favourites like stews and roasts were shipped out with the first immigrants, the British, Irish and Scots who settled in Australia and New Zealand in the 19th century. They persisted with their bland northern European cuisine, with its overcooked vegetables and heavy puddings, despite the much warmer antipodean conditions.

The Australian gold rush of the mid-19th century saw the first incursions into that tradition, as an influx of Chinese immigrants came, stayed and cooked, leaving their mark with the 'Australian-Chinese' restaurant you'll find in almost every country town.

The next wave, and the best thing to happen to Australian palates in 100 years, was the post-WWII immigration of thousands of European immigrants, particularly from Italy and Greece. Basic foodstuffs like olive oil, pasta and garlic – all but unknown to Australia's still British-influenced populace – started to appear, along with pizza restaurants, espresso coffee and souvlaki shops.

Just as Australia began to enjoy its more cosmopolitan dining scene, along came the great wave of Asian immigration in the 1970s, and all of a sudden, Australia had a real cuisine, dubbed 'Mod Oz', and heavily influenced by the ingredients and cooking styles of Vietnam, Thailand and Japan. Across the Tasman Sea, something similar was happening as New Zealanders embraced the cuisine of their Pacific Island neighbours, along with that of Southeast Asia, to create what's commonly described as Pacific Rim fusion.

SCHOOL OF FISH

Australia and New Zealand is home to several weird-and-wonderful seafood species. Here's how to enjoy five of the best.

FLATHEAD

It won't win prizes in a beauty contest but the flathead's flesh is sweet, firm and stands up well to zesty Asian flavours of ginger, lime, lemon grass and coriander. The fish inhabits estuaries around Australia in what are considered sustainable wild populations.

GREEN-LIPPED MUSSELS

Growing up to 25cm in length, New Zealand's pumped-up native mussels don't make the best eating (at that size!) but produce extracts used in alternative health supplements. For cooking, select smaller mussels and steam in a deep saucepan with several glugs of cider, butter, shallots and garlic, as they do in Normandy, France. Stir double cream into the broth and serve.

BARRAMUNDI

Wild barramundi are caught along Australia's north coast and the hump-backed fish are exceptionally good to eat, so long as they've not dawdled too long in brackish backwaters. Fillets can be pan-fried, roasted or steamed.

MORETON BAY BUGS

They may look like throwbacks to a prehistoric era (and actually they are) but grilled in their shells these small slipper lobsters are a popular addition to any Australian barbecue.

KING GEORGE WHITING

Along Australia's south coast, the King George whiting rules. The small fish have a delicate flavour that merits a simple approach: pan-fry fillets in butter or olive oil.

SEAFOOD
SWIMMING BENEATH THE WAVES

Both Australia and New Zealand have moved on from the cuisines of their early settlement days, but perhaps the biggest departure is their shared love of fish and seafood. Even the once-revered Christmas lunch of ham and turkey now more often features prawns, lobster and perhaps a couple of dozen Bluff or Sydney rock oysters. The two countries are blessed with generous coastlines, and native species abound: green-lipped mussels, Tasmanian salmon, Moreton Bay bugs (a flathead or slipper lobster), barramundi from Australia's north, and wild brown and rainbow trout from New Zealand's streams and rivers.

Ocean fish is a New Zealand speciality, with kingfish, gurnard and terakihi some of the favourite varieties. You'll find the freshest of these – along with lobsters and mussels – sold from roadside stalls around the coast. An iconic West Coast snack is whitebait fritters, made with tiny whole fish netted from rivers. The influence of early Scottish settlers can still be tasted in the tradition of smoking fish, and the classic smoked-fish pie.

You'll find seafood on the menu of most Australian dining establishments, from cafes to fine-dining restaurants, but wherever you dine, it will be simply prepared to allow the quality of the fish to shine through. The humble fish-and-chip shop was of course imported from Britain, but it has had local tweaks: flake (gummy shark) instead of cod, accompanied by potato cakes (a battered round of fried potato) and dim sims (a low-brow yet beloved bastardisation of a fried Chinese dumpling). Battered scallops and oysters are also on offer – beware though, as a potato cake is called a scallop in New South Wales, resulting in severe disappointment as out-of-towners open their steaming paper packages.

In classic Aussie pubs, the 'fisherman's basket' is an iconic menu item which in its purest form includes battered fish and calamari rings and a couple of crumbed prawns and scallops; the presence of a fresh oyster connotes a pub making a tilt at gourmet dining. And in the best restaurants, high-end seafood features. On the menu at Tetsuya's, the eponymous Sydney restaurant of one of the country's most respected chefs, you might find sea-urchin custard, confit ocean trout or steamed spanner crab with foie gras.

Seafood is also essential to Australia's fusion and ethnic cuisines. Enormous Queensland king prawns might be served in a Thai-style curry. Fish tacos are on the rise as Australia's major cities discover Mexican food. Sashimi – usually salmon, ocean trout, tuna or kingfish – is common, and its workaday cousin, the sushi hand roll, is a ubiquitous lunch option during the working week. And for the old-school but still popular oysters Kilpatrick – provenance uncertain – oysters are topped with bacon and Worcestershire sauce and grilled.

⚓ WHERE TO EAT SYDNEY FISH MARKET
BANK ST, PYRMONT

Take a tour, watch the Dutch auction (at which 50 tonnes of seafood changes hands each day), attend seafood school or just marvel at the array of scaled, shelled and carapaced creatures from all the country's coasts, including snapper, blue swimmer crab, Balmain bugs and Sydney rock oysters.

RIGHT Moreton Bay bugs are sometimes confused with Balmain bugs, a different species of slipper lobster found in Australia – both are eminently edible, though the Balmain version has a stronger, fishier taste

LOCAL
COOKED

FRESH
COOKED
WEST
AUSTRALIAN
CRAYFISH
$1990

THE BARBECUE
BRING ON THE BARBIE

The Great Aussie Barbecue is more than just a way to eat, it's a way of life that speaks of Australian culture more generally: casual, easygoing, and out-of-doors.

Once upon a time, the script for a barbie ran reliably thus. A group of people – family, friends, in fact any social gathering – would arrive at a home or public space like a park or waterfront (where free or coin-operated barbecues are often strategically placed by thoughtful local authorities), and reduce to a charry mess a number of meaty favourites: rissoles, 'snags' (sausages) and chops. Salads – supplied by the ladies of the group – would be green, potato and coleslaw (the more adventurous might experiment with a pasta or rice salad). Men would stand around the barbecue, prodding the meat with a variety of metal implements. Beer would flow.

While gender roles in Australian society have changed remarkably in recent decades, and the gender stratification of the barbie ritual is not as rigid as it once was, you're still guaranteed to see a group of men standing around the barbecue prodding meat with metal implements (and the beer still flows). But the edible components of the event have certainly changed. Lamb chops might be prepared Greek-style with olive oil, lemon and oregano. Prawns might be skewered and marinated with Asian flavours rather than just 'thrown on the barbie'. Snags will come in a variety of exotic flavours. Whole fish wrapped in foil are increasingly popular, and even – shock! – vegetables and Greek cheeses like haloumi are making their way to the grill plate. Salads can be anything and everything depending on the season, with ingredients like asparagus, beetroot, bitter greens, walnuts and goat's cheese among an ever-changing list of favourite gourmet ingredients. It's a long way from wilted lettuce and a can of three-bean mix.

While New Zealanders also love a barbecue, the nation's most distinctive cooking style is the *hangi*, where both meat and vegetables are cooked in an underground pit for several hours with heated stones, and covered in earth. This traditional Maori method is now most often used at large gatherings and celebrations, and can also be experienced at Maori cultural centres.

♨ WHERE TO EAT TAMAKI MAORI VILLAGE

In Rotorua, a strongly Maori city in central NZ, Tamaki holds cultural evenings including a tour of a *marae* (community centre, including carved meeting house), traditional dances and a meaty *hangi*.

LEFT Traditions may evolve over time, especially with an increasingly multi-ethnic population, but the Australian barbecue retains some consistent themes: casual, friendly and celebrated with cold beers

HOW TO LAY A HANGI
Building a Kiwi *hangi* – the Koro Hunt way.

INGREDIENTS
Stones (large)

1 cubic metre firewood

Meat

Vegetables

Chickenwire baskets (the kids can weave these; you'll need chickenwire, pliers and sticking-plasters)

Cloths, sheets, hessian sacks

Bucket of water (large)

Shovels

Beer

PREPARATION

This takes about six hours, mostly waiting. Cover an area 1m square with large river stones and build a big fire on top. The stones must get red hot, so feed fire for 2-3 hours. Note: the 'wrong type' of stones may explode when heated to red hot. You can tell they're the 'wrong type' of stones when they explode.

Building the fire is thirsty work. Have a beer around now.

As the stones heat, dig a hole 1m deep, and 1m square, nearby. Prepare the food: wrap meat and vegies in old, wet tea towels. Put it in wire baskets. When the stones have heated for a couple of hours, pull the wood aside, and drag red-hot stones into the pit with rakes. Do *not* fall into the pit at this point.

Put the food in the pit on top of the stones, meat first, then vegies. Lay old sheets then sacks on top. Pour a bucket of water over everything. This will produce a lot of steam. (Flush steam burns with cold water.) Fill all the dirt back in so no steam escapes. Wait. After three hours, dig it all up. Do not put a shovel through food. Unwrap food, serve. If timed correctly, the sun is setting and no-one can tell if any of the food is a bit raw. Accompany with a cold beer. Once dark, it's traditional for a few people to fall into the pit; leave the now-cold stones to break their fall.

FOOD LOVER
DAN HUNTER

All chefs cooking and working in the New World are influenced on some level by some or all of the major cuisines – French, Italian, Cantonese, Thai, Japanese. That's the beauty of living and working in a multicultural society – you can be exposed, sometimes quite subliminally, to different techniques and flavour profiles that are true to a cuisine that you haven't actually trained in.

Living in Spain and **two years in the Basque country** was a memorable experience. I worked in a restaurant that had a worldly outlook but the thought behind the food came from a very Basque viewpoint. It gave me a chance to get in touch with a cuisine that I had no previous knowledge of and to look through a different pair of glasses for a while.

Just picked, unrefrigerated vegetables are the most inspiring ingredients, such as **raw wild mushrooms,** particularly Slippery Jacks. They are found around pine trees in autumn in southeastern Australia.

I'll always remember a soup (Tom Yam) I ate for breakfast in Thailand in 1998. **It was cooked on a stove attached to a bicycle.** It cost A$.05 and is still one of the most captivating and perfectly balanced dishes I've ever eaten.

Dan Hunter is chef at the Royal Mail Hotel, Dunkeld, Victoria

NEW WORLD WINES
BUBBLES TO ROSÉ

Even if you've never eaten a macadamia nut, a kangaroo fillet or a huhu grub, you've most likely consumed produce from Australia and New Zealand in the form of wine. Australia alone exports almost 800 million litres a year (as the fourth-largest exporter after France, Italy and Spain), and drinks about 500 million.

After claiming the bottom of the market in the 1980s, with the help of the invention of the wine cask (or 'bag in box' packaging), Australia began to win acclaim for its big, fruit-driven, high-alcohol shiraz and cabernet sauvignon styles from the Barossa and Coonawarra regions of South Australia. The maturing of the industry saw a massive increase in varieties and regions being planted – from pinot gris and pinot noir in Tasmania, to Italian varietals like nebbiolo and arneis in Victoria's King Valley.

When you think of New Zealand wine, you're probably thinking of sauvignon blanc. Never has an entire industry owed so much to one humble grape. Sauvignon blanc from Marlborough, in the north of the South Island, exploded onto the world stage in the 1990s and won credit from many critics as the world's best. Since then, other regions and varieties have emerged, with Martinborough at the bottom of the North Island producing fine pinot noir and reisling; while Waiheke Island, a 35-minute ferry ride from Auckland, is a hot, dry microclimate perfect for Bordeaux reds, shiraz and rosé.

WHERE TO DRINK BAROSSA VALLEY
Australia's oldest growing region, the Barossa is a must-visit for wine buffs. German settlers planted the first vines in 1842, and remnants of their heritage – unusual for Australia – are still seen in Gothic church steeples and a taste for wurst and pretzels. There are around 80 vineyards and 60 cellar doors to visit; among the best are Penfolds (home of the famous Grange Hermitage), Henschke, Rockford and Peter Lehmann.

ABOVE Spared phylloxera, a disease that decimated French vineyards, the world's oldest shiraz vines grow in the Barossa Valley **RIGHT** Taste wines in the Yarra Valley, just two hours outside Melbourne

AUSTRALIANA & KIWIANA FOODS

While it's true that Australia and New Zealand are home to sophisticated modern cuisines, there's still plenty of room for nostalgically beloved foods from the past. Australia's chicken 'parma' (a bastardisation of the Italian *parmigiana*) is a crumbed, usually plate-sized schnitzel covered with tomato sauce, ham and cheese, and a staple of any respectable pub menu.

New Zealand's old favourites betray the country's national sweet tooth: lemon delicious pudding, Anzac biscuits, pavlova. The last is claimed by both nations but Australia must cede its invention to New Zealand (the origins of the Anzac are also sketchy but the argument is not so hard fought, perhaps as a mark of respect for the WWI soldiers for whom it's named).

In return, Australia claims the lamington, a small chocolate-and-coconut-covered sponge, also beloved of both countries. Another iconic Australian foodstuff is Vegemite, an unbearably (to visitors) salty paste, produced as a by-product of beer manufacturing and best consumed spread on warm toast with lots of butter.

INDIGENOUS CUISINE
NATIVE TUCKER

Most of the dishes eaten today in Australia and New Zealand have their origins in foreign lands – Britain, Europe, Asia. But the indigenous cultures of both countries had their own favourite ingredients, which to varying degrees have made their way onto modern tables.

In New Zealand, early Maori settlers imported kumara (sweet potato) from the Pacific Islands over a thousand years ago, while baby fronds of the pikopiko fern – one of the few edible ferns – are now known as bush asparagus. The manuka tree – named 'tea-tree' when discovered by Captain Cook's botanist Joseph Banks in 1769 – is best known as the source of acclaimed manuka honey.

Many of the Australian indigenous ingredients known as 'bush tucker' are herbs and spices, with only the native macadamia nut winning widespread appeal. Plants such as lemon myrtle, wattleseed and quandong (wild peach) are finding their way onto more adventurous menus. More controversial is the consumption of the 'coat of arms' (kangaroo and emu) and other native animal species. While proponents argue that eating wild kangaroo, for example, is far more environmentally sustainable than the large-scale grazing of introduced livestock, it seems a national queasiness has prevented it being widely accepted.

And despite being staples of the countries' respective indigenous people, neither New Zealand's huhu grub nor Australia's witchetty grub have crossed over successfully into mainstream consumption.

🍽 WHERE TO EAT OCHRE RESTAURANT
43 SHIELDS ST, CAIRNS

In northern Queensland, the Ochre Restaurant dishes up all sorts of local beasts and plants with a Mod Oz slant. Dishes like crocodile wontons, kangaroo terrine, wallaby topside and wattleseed pavlova allow adventurous diners to get a real taste of Australia.

ABOVE LEFT Despite their disputed origins, Anzac biscuits are perfect with afternoon tea on either side of the Tasman **ABOVE** Most Australians are only just waking up to the flavours of native bush tucker

PAVLOVA
DESSERT FOR A DANCER

This seemingly innocuous (though delicious) white, puffy, super-sweet dessert created a trans-Tasman feud unequalled until the battle for birthright of Russell Crowe. What's not disputed is that pavlova is named for legendary Russian ballerina Anna Pavlova; nor that it is a large meringue (the addition of cornflour to the egg whites and castor sugar giving it a crispy exterior and marshmallowy centre) topped with whipped cream and fresh fruit.

Both Australia and New Zealand claim to have invented the dessert to honour the famed dancer on one of her antipodean tours in the 1920s. Australian claims centre on Perth in Western Australia, where the chef of a local hotel is said to have invented the dessert in 1935. However the most in-depth scholarly research (for an entire book dedicated to the sweet, read *The Pavlova Story*) uncovers a recipe in a NZ dairy magazine dating to 1929 – fully six years before the first Aussie pav is sighted.

While Australians retort loudly that all culinary invention is evolution and what does it matter anyway, New Zealanders continue to smother their pavs generously with kiwifruit and claim it as their national dish. The Great Topping Debate – kiwifruit versus passionfruit – is another combat zone for this battle-scarred sweet. Actually, toppings vary widely and are limited only by the imagination of the maker – berries are classic, mango slightly exotic, pomegranate seeds firmly new-wave. Crumbled chocolate bars win approval from both kids and grown-ups (usually Flake or for an even more retro flavour, Peppermint Crisp).

Whichever nation owns its genesis, pav is the ultimate easy-to-make, impressive-to-serve festive dessert, beloved of both Aussies and New Zealanders.

And Russ? He's a Kiwi, too.

ABOVE Pavlova with strawberries may be traditional but toppings have come a long way: New Zealanders love kiwifruit but inventive dessert chefs are pushing the pav boundaries with new fruits and old-school sweets

LAMINGTONS
These coconut-dusted cakes are often cooked for Australia Day.

INGREDIENTS
100g/3.5oz butter , softened

100g/3.5oz caster sugar

2 eggs, beaten

140g/5oz self-raising flour

1 tsp baking powder

2 tbsp cocoa powder

2 tbsp milk

FOR THE ICING
100g/3.5oz plain chocolate, in pieces

25g/1oz butter

100g/3.5oz icing sugar , sifted

100g/3.5oz desiccated coconut

PREPARATION
Heat oven to 180°C/350°F. Butter and line the base of a square baking tin. Beat together the butter and sugar until pale and creamy, then beat in the eggs. Add 1 tbsp of the flour if the mix starts to curdle.

Sieve in the flour, baking powder and cocoa and fold in with a metal spoon. Stir in the milk. Scrape mix into the tin and level the top. Bake for up to 20 minutes or until the cake springs back when pressed. Allow to cool in the tin.

To make the icing, put the chocolate, butter and 4 tbsp water in a pan and gently heat until melted. Allow to cool slightly, then beat in the icing sugar.

Remove cake from tin and peel away paper. Cut into squares. Dip the squares into the icing, then roll in the coconut. Allow to set on cooling rack.

BUZZ ABOUT THE BEAN
Coffee's antipodean evolution has taken the beverage from tea's poor cousin, to popular brew adopted from Italian immigrants, to lifestyle marker with tasting notes similar to those of fine wines. To witness the apotheosis of coffee at one of its modern temples, try a flat white at Melbourne's Auction Rooms cafe or Auckland's Altezano.

Drinking in the sights: in the lee of Sydney Opera House with a view of Sydney Harbour Bridge

OPERA BAR

ANDREW WATSON :: LONELY PLANET IMAGES ©

︎ ︎ ︎
BITE-SIZE DIVERSIONS

A focus on fresh produce and an inclusive approach to cuisines mean the lands down under want for nothing when it comes to eating.

AUSTRALIA

QUEEN VICTORIA MARKET
Get a sense of the variety of Australian produce at Melbourne's Queen Victoria (or simply 'Vic') Market. The Deli Hall, with stands selling Polish sausages, French cheeses, native meats and fresh pasta, is an instant insight into the city's culinary melting pot.

TASTE FESTIVAL
Hobart's Taste Festival, held on the waterfront at the end of each year, is a great way to sample the produce of the island state – Pacific oysters, Bruny Island cheese, Tasmania's celebrated wines and locally brewed beers.

QUAY
There are fine-dining options aplenty in Australia, but the restaurant most often acclaimed as the country's best is Quay on Sydney Harbour, with sweeping views from the Bridge to the Opera House. Rare and local ingredients are prepared with stunning creativity and an emphasis on textural variety. The nectarine 'snow egg' dessert has celebrity of a status rarely achieved by a plate of food.

MINDIL BEACH MARKET
Darwin's Mindil Beach market is a unique edge-of-Australia experience. Locals bring along fold-up chairs and eskies full of beer and settle in for a tropical evening feast from stalls featuring cuisine from, among others, Japan, Thailand, Timor, Indonesia, the Philippines, Malaysia and Cambodia.

MULTICULTURAL EXPERIENCE
For a vivid snapshot of the vitality injected into Australia's food scene by immigration and multiculturalism, visit Sydney's Cabramatta or Melbourne's Footscray. Hubs of the cities' respective Vietnamese communities, they're packed with people, inexpensive *pho* restaurants, fresh food markets and groceries bursting with exotic goods.

AGRARIAN KITCHEN
One of Australia's top cooking schools, Tasmania's farm-based Agrarian Kitchen offers holistic, immersive garden-to-table classes, the most popular of which involves making 16 different dishes over two days from a whole Wessex saddleback pig.

NEW ZEALAND

WILDFOODS FESTIVAL
Self-proclaimed as the country's 'most outrageous food experience', Hokitika's Wildfoods festival is a celebration of extreme eating (as well as silly dress-ups and plenty of beer). On offer might be magpie pies, roasted possums and sheep's testicles; the less adventurous can try whitebait fritters, venison burgers and maybe muttonbird (a type of shearwater), a traditional Maori favourite named for its taste.

MAKETU PIES
Famous for their take on an icon of old-school New Zealand cuisine, Maketu Pies does standards like lamb 'n' mint as well as Kiwi classics like mussel pie and smoked-fish pie.

AKAROA COOKING SCHOOL
Based in a quaint seaside town on the South Island, this cooking school runs gourmet road trips exploring the Banks Peninsula, visiting local salmon and mussel farms, goat's cheese producers and olive groves, and foraging at the seashore; delicious meals are created from the results.

Wasdale in England's Lake District:
rural landscapes have been shaped
by farming over many centuries

THE
BRITISH ISLES

Seasonal, wild and surprising – British cuisine has been reinvented in the last decade or so. With British beef, Welsh lamb and Galway oysters on the menu, food lovers have plenty to celebrate across these isles.

If your only experience of British food has been fish and chips in a chintzy theme pub, prepare your palate for a surprise. The focus of Modern British cuisine is on seasonal ingredients, wild foods, traditional breeds and surprising herbs and spices borrowed from Britain's diverse population, reclaiming the character that was sapped out during the lean years of rationing during and after WWII.

British food of old had a reputation for being starchy, stolid and seasoned with nothing more exotic than salt and pepper. This midcentury culinary black spot has been swept away by a food revolution that's transformed humble staples like carrots and peas into fabulous fusions of flavour.

The rediscovery of flavour has permeated every corner of the British Isles, from the southern tip of Ireland to the remote Scottish islands. In Orkney, diners feast on lamb raised on a diet of seaweed. In Anglesey, locals lunch on freshly caught scallops and smoked sea bass. And in Dublin, Michelin-starred chefs create magic with free-range pheasant and wild chestnuts.

Cooks across the nation are experimenting with elegant ingredients like fennel, celeriac and wild mushrooms, while the craze for old-school ingredients finds its peak in the concept of nose-to-tail eating, a joyous celebration of offal and the cuts in-between.

REAL ALE

Forget the frosty fizzy pop served on the Continent – the British like their beer pulled by hand from the barrel, topped with just the right amount of foam and always served at room temperature. And it happens that this style of brew is the best suited to soothing the flames of a curry of an evening out on the town.

Brits have had brewing in the blood since at least the Dark Ages, when beer was put forward as a safe alternative to polluted river water by inebriated monks. Today, real ale comes in a kaleidoscope of hues, from the coffin-black stout imbibed in Ireland to the amber-coloured Indian Pale Ales (IPA) that fortified the busy men of the British East India Company.

When it comes to finding Britain's best pubs, trust the opinion of the Campaign for Real Ale (www.camra.org.uk). Their top pub for 2012 was the Bridge End Inn, a family-run microbrewery serving home-brewed nut-brown ales in the village of Ruabon near Wrexham. Look for a Campaign for Real Ale sticker in the window of the best pubs.

Otherwise, the mark of a good pub is a long line of beer taps bubbling with guest ales – and there are increasing numbers of these from top to bottom of the British Isles thanks to a boom in independent brewers. Some names to look out for are Sharp's from Cornwall, Hop Back in Wiltshire, Hook Norton in Oxfordshire, Meantime in London and Harviestoun in Scotland.

British real ale is consumed at something close to room temperature and is a drink to savour. Sip, don't swig, and swirl the liquid across your palate to separate the subtle flavours. Try an ale with a packet of salty pork scratchings for the full pub effect.

໒ຯ
CURRIES
CURRYING FLAVOUR

With histories intertwined since 1619, it's no surprise that Britain and India have a shared culinary heritage. Cinnamon, cloves and pepper from the Subcontinent were favourite spices in the Tudor kitchen, ever since the first English ships returned from the Spice Islands with their fragrant cargo. By 1747 early recipes for curry had been published in Hannah Glasse's *The Art of Cookery*. And in 1926 Veeraswamy restaurant opened on Regent St in London – and it's still serving Malabar lobster curry and other classics today.

But the great meeting of minds came in the 1950s, when migrant workers from India, Bangladesh and Pakistan introduced Indian cooking to the British masses. Chicken tikka masala (boneless chicken in a dense coriander and tomato sauce) has since become Britain's unofficial national dish, the favourite finish to any big night out.

The menus of British-Indian restaurants – mostly owned and staffed by Bangladeshis – form an interactive map of the Subcontinent – tandoori dishes from the Punjab, Parsi-inspired *dhansak* (sour lamb curry with lentils) from Mumbai, rogan josh (richly spiced lamb with tomatoes) from Kashmir. Back in India, however, where dishes are known by their cooking technique, the word 'curry' wouldn't even be recognised.

⚓ WHERE TO EAT LADYPOOL RD, BIRMINGHAM

Along with the classics, there are Indian dishes that have never been served in India – head to Ladypool Rd in Birmingham to enjoy Britain's greatest contribution to the Indian culinary canon, the balti, a sizzling spectacular cooked in an iron pan and served with a giant *karack* naan bread.

ABOVE British inventiveness meets Indian spices in the chicken tikka masala

⌇⌇
CORNISH PASTIE
A MOVEABLE FEAST

Eating down a mine presents certain logistical challenges. It's dark, it's dusty, there's hardly room to swing a sauce bottle, and it's a mile to the surface if you drop your fork.

In Cornwall, the solution was the portable pastie – a nourishing stew of minced beef and slithers of swede and potato, stuffed inside a glazed pastry shell with a thick pinched seam along one edge, creating a natural handle. Sometimes the pastie provided two courses, with a savoury filling at one end and something sweet at the other. After the filling was consumed, the doughy handle was tossed aside, along with the toxic dust that accumulated on the fingers of Cornish lead and tin miners.

The earliest known reference to a pastie was discovered in a stack of government papers from 1510, sparking a fierce debate between Devon and Cornwall over who actually invented the pastie. Regardless, the pastry parcel has some exotic relatives, including Argentinian *empanadas* and the calzone of Italy. These days, gourmet pasties are all the rage – look out for sophisticated ingredients like Cornish asparagus and creamy St Endellion Brie alongside the traditional fillings.

⛉ WHERE TO EAT ANN'S PASTIES
SUNNY CORNER, BEACON TCE, THE LIZARD, HELSTON

Every village baker in Cornwall claims to serve the best pasties, but Ann Muller, owner of Ann's Pasties can draw on recipes honed by her mum (Hettie Merrick), the author of the much-loved *The Pasty Book*. Arrive for lunch when the pasties come hot from the oven. Her recipe includes onion, turnip, steak and potato.

ABOVE The Cornish pastie, crimped by hand here, is now a snack for city commuters not miners
TOP RIGHT A serving of slow-cooked Lancashire hot pot would greet a hungry northerner after a day's work

LANCASHIRE HOT POT

A nation founded on collieries, seafaring and agriculture needs a filling foundation for the day. While the French were searing scallops and pan-frying sweetmeats, the English put their efforts into creating a perfect one-pot feast that could simmer all day on the hob while the populace engaged in honest toil. Enter the Lancashire hot pot, a working-man's casserole as inexorably linked to the north of England as whippets and flat caps.

Forget the bland version served in chain pubs; a proper hot pot should be homemade, with ingredients sourced within sight of the kitchen: hill-raised lamb, ideally marbled neck fillet and kidneys, cooked in a stock with garden-raised leeks, onions and carrots, and topped with a golden crust of sliced potatoes, like a savoury *tarte aux poivres*. The lamb should fall apart into soft flakes, and the potato topping caramelised to a crisp.

Serve with real ale, then roll up your sleeves, turn your flat cap backwards and forge yourself a plough. Or if that's too prosaic for your tastes, at Northcote Manor in Langho Michelin-starred chef Nigel Haworth does a spruced-up hot pot with pickled red cabbage and lamb raised on hill-farm heather.

FOOD LOVER
FERGUS HENDERSON

Italian cuisine has influenced me greatly. I came back from Italy going **'We must put less on the plate'…** you order a roast rabbit, and that's what you get on your plate. No confusion.

On the first night of my honeymoon, my wife Margot fell asleep in her steak tartar, so I quietly ate my grilled pig's trotter. The cementing of two relationships.

A pig's trotter is still the most inspiring ingredient for me.

A clear apricot eau-de-vie I had in Budapest years ago **made an unforgettable impression!**

When I was young, my father took me to Le Pré Catalan in the Bois de Boulogne in Paris. **We ate a sea-urchin soufflé,** my first experience of the musk, beautifully served in the severe spiny shells. That was another great impression.

Chef Fergus Henderson is the co-founder of St John restaurant in London, and has also opened a bakery and hotel in the city. As the author of *Nose to Tail Eating: A Kind of British Cooking,* he is regarded as the godfather of modern British cuisine.

WELSH LAMB
DINING WITH ST DAVID

Lleyn, Llanwenogg, Beulah: no, those aren't misprints, they're the names of Welsh sheep breeds. There are many more – the Black Welsh Mountain, the South Wales Mountain, the Welsh Hill Speckled, the Llandovery Whiteface Hill, the Hill Radnor and the Badgerface Welsh – because Britain, according to the Rare Breeds Survival Trust, has the widest range of native sheep breeds in the world. And Wales has more than its share, all hardy varieties bred to cope with life foraging on cold, rainswept hillsides, as their names suggest. Due to its unique heritage, Welsh lamb was granted Protected Geographical Indication status in 2003.

With such regional specialities as laverbread (a seaweed dish) and *bara brith* (a sweet and spicy bread) the Welsh have plenty to bring to the culinary map of the British Isles. Take *cawl,* a hearty broth made from bacon, lamb, cabbage, potato and leeks (the national vegetable), traditionally ladled out on St David's Day. Track down *cawl* in public houses decorated with daffodils anywhere in Wales on 1 March. This Welsh delight is elevated above its humble ingredients by the use of flavoursome cuts of meat – bacon on the bone and well-marbled lamb breast or neck. And what lamb! Raised on a diet of wild grasses and heather on seasonal salt-marshes and the abundantly watered Welsh hills, it has a sense of place as unmistakeable as the sheep's unpronounceable names.

WHERE TO EAT VAUGHAN'S FAMILY BUTCHERS PENYFFORDD

Native breeds and a diet of sweet hill grasses are only part of the Welsh lamb story. It takes an expert butcher to elevate this celebrated meat to gourmet perfection. Tucked away in the North Wales village of Penyffordd, Vaughan's Family Butchers looks modest from the outside, but owner Steve Vaughan has a list of trophies as long as his butcher's apron, including the coveted award for Best Butcher in Wales.

RIGHT Rush hour in the Welsh countryside **ABOVE** Roast a leg of spring lamb with rosemary and garlic then serve with seasonal vegetables, such as new potatoes and asparagus

BEEF WELLINGTON

It's not delicately engineered but a fillet of beef, encased in puff pastry with a layer of mushroom, is a show-stopping addition to the table. As with many traditional dishes – coq au vin, bolognese – simplicity is key. Don't over-complicate the ingredients with unecessary hams or pâtés; spend the money on the finest fillet of Aberdeen Angus. Known as *boeuf en croute* in France, the dish is thought to mark the Duke of Wellington's victory at the Battle of Waterloo in 1815. He also had a rubber boot named in his honour.

INGREDIENTS

500g/1lb Aberdeen Angus fillet

250g/8oz mixed mushrooms, wild, fresh or rehydrated, chopped

sprig of thyme or parsley

200mL/7fl oz white wine (or Madeira, which adds a pleasant sweetness)

2 tbsp double cream

250g/8oz puff pastry

1 egg

Butter and mild olive oil

PREPARATION

Allow the beef to warm to room temperature. Pre-heat the oven to 200°C/400°F. Cook the finely chopped mushrooms with butter or mild olive oil in a pan. When soft, turn up the heat and add a generous splash of wine or Madeira, until it burns off. Remove from pan, stir in the cream.

Wipe pan, add oil and sear the fillet on all sides. Roll out the pastry, brush with beaten egg and smooth over the mushroom mixture. Roll the beef in pastry, brush the outside of the pastry with egg and place on roasting tray, seam side down. Cook for 30 minutes.

As the beef rests, deglaze the pan with wine or Madeira and reduce a beef stock to make a sauce. Serve with potatoes and green vegetables. Serves four.

ABERDEEN ANGUS BEEF
BEST OF SCOTTISH

The best British meat always has an address. Take seaweed-fed Ronaldsay lamb from the Orkney Islands, Aylesbury duck, Gloucestershire Old Spot pork – and the king of them all, Aberdeen Angus beef, the pride of the butchers' block north of the border.

The history of this famous breed can be traced back to just two animals – Old Jock and Old Granny – raised on the country estate of pioneering 19th-century breeder Hugh Watson of Keillor. With deeply marbled meat that rivals Japanese Kobe beef (at least according to local carnivores), Angus cows make for fabulous roast beef – the favoured dish of the *rosbifs* (English), as any Frenchman will tell you. Most beef in Britain is grass-fed (unlike imported US beef), which benefits the animals' flavour and quality of life.

Prime cuts for roasting are rib, sirloin, top rump and fillet, but the meat should be dry hung for at least two weeks to allow the natural process of postmortem tenderisation to take place. Even the off cuts find their place. Oxtail soup is a popular winter-warmer, and pressed ox-tongue remains a much-loved treat throughout the north of England.

🍽 WHERE TO EAT RULES
35 MAIDEN LANE, COVENT GARDEN, LONDON

With a pedigree dating to 1798, and its own country estate perched high in the North Pennine hills, Rules is a prime spot to sample British game. Roe deer, rabbit, hare, trout, grouse, ptarmigan, capercaillie and crayfish all grace the menu in season; the rest of the year, enjoy hearty dishes prepared using rare Belted Galloway beef. And, of course, Aberdeen Angus rib roast.

ABOVE Make friends with your local butcher and get to know where the meat is sourced and how to prepare it

ARBROATH SMOKIE
A FISHY BUSINESS

It's an early start to the day for Iain Spink, the fifth generation of his family to smoke haddock in Arbroath, a village on the east of Scotland where there's the tang of smoke and salt in the air. He's up at 6am preparing fish for the smoker by de-heading, cleaning, dry-salting and then washing off the salt before the their tails are tied and they are smoked hanging from struts over an open whisky barrel or pit of woodchips. After about 30 minutes each haddock has been transformed into an Arbroath smokie – 'Simply some of the most delicious fish I've ever had', according to Jamie Oliver. So unique is this creamy, savoury, cured fish to the area around Arbroath village that it was granted Protected Geographical Indication (PGI) status in 2004 by the European Commission. Just don't call them kippers, which are smoked herrings.

'The Arbroath smokie began its life in Auchmithie, a small village three miles up the coast', says Iain. 'It was there that Viking settlers landed centuries ago, bringing with them their fish preservation techniques.' Before the 20th century's refrigerator, knowing how to keep fish edible for months was essential to survival. Years ago, most Arbroath smokies would have been haddock caught off the tiny village, but today most come from Peterhead, 100 miles north. Their journey might be longer but they don't hang around for long once smoked; those that aren't greedily gobbled straight from the fire are served for breakfast from Aberdeen to London's finest hotels. 'Today's Arbroath smokies have much lower levels of salt and have a much lighter smoking process', says Iain. 'This gives them a much more delicate flavour.' Smokies can also be substituted for plain old smoked fish in recipes such as kedgeree, risottos and the iconic Scottish soup Cullen Skink.

ABOVE Nordic knowledge: the Vikings brought smoked fish to Britain but Scots invented the Arbroath smokie

CULLEN SKINK

A smokie adds another layer of flavour to Iain Spink's version of this Scottish fish soup. The soup was traditionally prepared with a 'finnan haddie', another type of lightly-smoked haddock, this time from the north-east tip of Scotland.

INGREDIENTS

450g/16oz (1 pair) Arbroath smokies
300mL/10fl oz water
2 onions, chopped finely
3 large potatoes, peeled and sliced
Pinch cayenne pepper
¼ tsp turmeric
475mL/16fl oz whole milk
25g/1oz butter
Salt

PREPARATION

Place the flaked smokie in a medium-sized saucepan with the water. Bring gently to the boil and immediately set aside from the heat. Do not break the flakes further. After 10 mins, using a slotted spoon, lift the fish from the water and set aside on a plate.

Strain the cooking liquid into a bowl. Clean the saucepan and return the cooking liquid to it.

Add the onions, potatoes, turmeric, and cayenne. Cover the pan and cook until the potatoes are soft (about 20 minutes).

When the potatoes are cooked, remove the pan from the heat. Mash the potatoes with the onions and the cooking liquid. Gradually add the milk, stirring constantly, until it is blended with the potatoes. Return the pan to low heat.

Add the flaked smokie and butter. Cook the mixture until it is hot, gently stirring, but do not boil. Taste and add salt if necessary

Just before serving in a soup bowl, pour a swirl of cream to the centre, and garnish with some chopped fresh parsley.

OYSTERS

A food's desirability can change over the centuries. Before they were a symbol of sex and luxury, oysters were a basic food for the poor of London and New York. The 17th-century diarist Samuel Pepys consumes barrels of them; 18th-century author Dr Johnson fed his cat on oysters. In Ireland, oyster shells have been found amid the ruins of Mesolithic stone huts, and the Celts were certainly partial to the odd oyster or dozen. Oyster-opening contests, on the other hand, are a relatively new phenomenon.

At the legendary Galway International Oyster Festival, champion shuckers gather from across the globe to separate native Irish oysters from their knobbly dwellings. The record, in case you wondered, is 30 oysters in a minute and a half. The newly evicted shellfish don't go to waste – revellers knock back thousands the traditional Irish way: raw with lemon juice, a slice of brown bread and a big swig of stout. *Sláinte!*

<ιιι>

FISH 'N' CHIPS
A DEEP-FRIED FEAST

Battered cod has never achieved the gastronomic recognition of tempura or pimientos de Padrón (Spain's famous deep-fried chillies), but fish and chips is still the pride of the British Isles. Indeed, the Brits eat a staggering 500,000 tonnes of the stuff every year. More surprise then that the English national dish was actually introduced by Jewish refugees. New arrival Joseph Malin opened the first recognisable fish-and-chip shop in London in 1860, launching a fad that soon became a national obsession.

So popular, in fact, that overfishing to satisfy the Brits' insatiable appetite for fried fish led to a catastrophic collapse in cod stocks in the 1990s – these days, the flakes of fish beneath the batter are as likely to be haddock, pollock, coley, plaice or ray.

The best way to sample the nation's favourite is still a fill-you-up-to-the-gills portion from a seaside takeaway, served in paper with all the trimmings: tartare sauce, salt and vinegar, mushy peas, pickled onion, gherkins and a pickled egg.

⏾ WHERE TO EAT SENIORS
91 FLEETWOOD RD N, THORNTON

If you don't fancy working through plate after plate of soggy chips to find the perfect portion, the National Fish & Chip Awards has been showcasing the nation's best chip shops for 25 years. Old-fashioned Lancashire chippie Seniors in Thornton took the crown in 2012, with special guests like sea bass and John Dory joining haddock and plaice on the menu.

TOP LEFT Classic combination: fresh oysters and a pint of Guinness stout **ABOVE** A modern interpretation of fish and chips; the street-food version is served in a folded sheet of newspaper and doused in malt vinegar

ιὶ
SAUSAGE
THE BRITISH BANGER

Step aside chorizo. Move over *andouillettes*. The British banger is about to take the stage!

Served at least once a week in nine out of 10 households, British sausages are stuffed with myriad combinations of pork, lamb, beef, bacon, apples, chestnuts, Stilton, leeks and wine, then steamed, fried, stewed, roasted or cooked into blocks of Yorkshire pudding in the inimitable toad in the hole.

Every part of the British Isles has a sausage to call its own. Spiral sausages from Cumberland combine coarse-chopped pork and pepper. Oxford sausage blends pork and veal with lemon, cloves and mace. In Lincolnshire, the magic ingredient is sage. Scented with nutmeg, parsley and thyme, Newmarket sausage has been the Royal Family's favourite since 1907.

And as for the name 'banger'? Blame the butchers of WWI, who bulked up their sausages with water, making them explode in the pan.

🍲 WHERE TO EAT O'HAGAN'S SAUSAGE SHOP
THE WOOLPACK INN, 71 FISHBOURNE RD WEST, FISHBOURNE, CHICHESTER, WEST SUSSEX

The English like to insist that the local butcher serves better sausages than anyone else – and in Chichester, they're right. O'Hagan's Sausages was voted Britain's best sausage-maker by the Sausage Appreciation Society. Owned by newspaper-editor-turned-master-stuffer Bill O'Hagan, they certainly come up with the most imaginative varieties – Goan pork curry, anyone?

ABOVE Bangers and mash served with onion gravy: gourmet sausages and colcannon add an appetising twist

COLCANNON

Transport yourself to a stormy night on the west coast of Ireland. The wind howls like a banshee, an appropriate metaphor in these ancient hills where the bean sí (women of the burial mounds) are said to roam. Rain batters the windows; clouds race across the sky like galleons. It takes a special kind of comfort food to compete with such an inclement climate, so thank St Patrick for colcannon, a creamy blend of seasonal vegetables that defines the taste of home in Irish cookbooks.

Potatoes have some negative connotations on this side of the Irish Channel, but colcannon takes this troubled tuber and coddles it in homely ingredients: butter, cream, scallions, chives, parsley and chopped curly kale, which comes into season as winter storms start to lash the Irish coast. Think of it as posh mash, made according to Slow Food principles, long before it became cool to cook hearty meals with seasonal, local produce.

Traditionally served as a side to boiled ham, colcannon comes into its own on the evening of Halloween, when secret items are hidden inside its creamy mass to help predict the future. Find a coin, the legend goes, and wealth will follow. Find a ring, and marry soon. Unlucky souls who find a bachelor's button or an old-maid's thimble can expect a lifetime of dinners for one. To the relief of medics who specialise in choking, this custom is fast disappearing.

Colcannon is still served on St Patrick's Day, across Ireland and anywhere the Irish settled. You may be lucky enough to hear the colcannon song, with its rousing, nostalgic chorus: 'God be with the happy times, when trouble we had not, and our mothers made colcannon, in the little skillet pot'.

SUMMER PUDDING

The foolproof solution to a glut of garden berries, this dessert is best served with a dollop of double cream on a warm and sunny afternoon.

INGREDIENTS

500g/1lb raspberries
125g/4.5oz red currants
125g/4.5oz sugar
white bread, sliced

PREPARATION

Stew the berries very briefly – until soft and no more than 3 minutes – in a large saucepan. Leave them to cool but don't strain.

Line a deep dish or bowl with slices of white bread about 1cm/½in in thickness. Remove the crusts first to ensure a non-leaky fit.

When the whole bowl is lined, spoon the cooked fruit in, reserving some of the juice. Cover the bowl with some more slices of bread and compress with a plate weighted with whatever you have to hand.

Refrigerate overnight. Before serving, turn the bowl upside down and the pudding should slide from its mould. Pour over the saved juice and cut.

FORAGE FOR A FEAST

Nature serves up a feast in these rain-soaked islands, but you need to know where to look. Learn the art of wild-food foraging at the Wild Food School in Cornwall, and gain the skills required to sort the tasty treats from the fatal fungi. In London, Andy Overall leads mushroom-hunting expeditions over Hampstead Heath and out as far as Wimbledon Common and Epping Forest. You'll be surprised at the number of varieties you'll find and Andy will explain which can be eaten and those to avoid. Hedgerows and suburban streets are also fertile hunting grounds for seasonal berries and fruits.

ξ⟨ξ
SUMMER PUDDING
JULY IN A BOWL

The ingredients of this quintessential English pudding are so simple they only just qualify as a recipe: British berries, sugar and sliced, slightly stale white bread. And that's it. So why does it taste so darn good? Perhaps it's the way it distils all the glory of the English summer into spoon-sized chunks. Fresh raspberries, bursting with flavour, gathered in the back garden. Tantalisingly tart redcurrants, whitecurrants and blackcurrants, that spill from the case like glistening pearls. Hedgerow blackberries, plucked by hand from among the prickles on a country lane. Doused in fresh cream, each mouthful is a tantalising reminder of a vanished summer afternoon.

Where other British puddings offer year-round delight, summer pudding is only around for those fleeting weeks of summer when the fruit become ripe. Pressed into a bowl lined with soft white bread, the berries burst and release their pectin, staining the case a rich blood-red and transforming what is essentially an upscale fruit sandwich into something sublime.

With the first slice, mingled juices spill out across like the plate like a misadventure at the ice rink – enjoy with champagne and friends on long summer evenings.

🍲 WHERE TO EAT

Summer pudding is one of those dishes that cries out to be eaten outdoors at a British garden party in midsummer, when the sun lingers late on the lawn like sweet muscat dessert wine lingers on the palate. Make yourself available for invitations from July, when the redcurrants start to ripen on the bush, or win friends by bringing a plump summer pudding as your dinner contribution.

ABOVE A perfectly formed summer pudding should be served chilled with cream, preferably outside
RIGHT Love all: strawberries and cream is a fixture of Wimbledon tennis championship

Whisky has been distilled
on the Isle of Islay, Scotland,
since the 1700s

BITE-SIZE DIVERSIONS

They might be compact but there's enough packed into the British Isles to keep the hungriest visitor happy.

BOROUGH MARKET, LONDON

Trying before you buy from the nation's finest range of home-grown produce at London's Borough Market. Artisan suppliers are carefully selected and include bakers, cheesemongers, butchers, grocers and producers bringing local honey and hand-made delicacies. The market is open on Thursday, Friday and Saturday but London's chefs beat the rush and get there early.

LUDLOW FOOD FESTIVAL

Unleashing your inner gourmet at Ludlow's Food Festival – the perfect feast in a postcard-perfect English country village every September. Attractions include demonstrations from chefs, local producers and food trails around the town

CHEDDAR CHEESE

Biting into the tart tang of a mature, crumbly cheddar cheese, best sampled at the source in the farmhouse creameries of Somerset.

FORAGING

Combing the countryside for wild food: hedgerow blackberries in August and September, wild plums, rose hips for jelly, sloe berries for gin, chanterelles and penny-bun mushrooms, sea spinach and salty marsh samphire leaves. Most areas have organised tours if you're unsure about what's safe to eat.

FESTIVE FARE

Testing the principle of 'all you can eat' at an English Christmas dinner – just leave enough room for the brandy-steeped, steamed Christmas pudding. It's no coincidence that gym memberships peak in January.

WHISKY

Picking out the characteristic notes of peat and malt in the historic distilleries that line Scotland's Whisky Coast. The Malt Whisky Trail along Speyside takes in Glenfiddich and Glenlivet. Once you've acquired basic tasting skills, it's time to graduate to the smoky, peaty flavours of Islay's distillers: Caol Ilha, Ardbeg, Bowmore, Bunnahabhain and Laphroaig.

DOUBLE GLOUCESTER

Chasing a round of Double Gloucester cheese down a hill at the Coopers' Hill Cheese-Rolling Festival, then eating it afterwards.

CORNISH SEAFOOD

Diving into a seafood feast – dressed crab, potted shrimp, boiled cockles, raw oysters – on the cove-studded coast of Cornwall. Padstow is the personal fiefdom of chef Rick Stein and his presence has raised standards across the county.

BREAKFAST FRY-UP

Starting the day with the gut-busting glory of a full English – or full Scottish, or full Welsh, or full Irish – breakfast. For the addition of black pudding, an oatmeal and blood-filled sausage, the Scottish breakfast gets our vote.

CELEBRITY CHEFS

Tasting how the other half eat at Heston Blumenthal's Fat Duck or Dinner venues and Restaurant Gordon Ramsay in England, Martin Wishart and Tom Kitchin's restaurants in Scotland or Patrick Guilbaud's place in Dublin.

THE CARIBBEAN

A mashup of cultural influences, Caribbean cuisine rides a roller-coaster of West African, Indian, Dutch, French and Spanish flavours. And as ubiquitous as the sparkling sea is the region's iconic, but deceptively potent, rum.

If at first you're a little agog at the strange and eclectic flavours and dishes that come to you in the Caribbean, it only takes a quick island-hop to make sense of it. Conversing with locals on such a jaunt would require mad multilingal skills – in a flash you'll hear at least six different languages – English, French, Haitian Creole, Dutch, Spanish and Papiamento (a Portuguese/Spanish Creole). It's this multicultural jumble that gives Caribbean cuisine its colour and flair.

Former slave-holding colonies such as the Bahamas and Barbados show their West African colours in dishes like *benne* cakes (sesame-seed cookies) and *cou-cou* (a dish of cornmeal and okra). Countries with a substantial Indian population, such as Trinidad and Tobago, have a South Indian slant to their cuisines – roti flatbread stuffed with meat or curried vegetables is an omnipresent snack. The people of the Dutch 'ABC islands' (Aruba, Bonaire and Curaçao), meanwhile, chow down on many of the foods you'd see in Amsterdam, such as *bitterballen* (spiced meatballs) and *frikandel* (a fried sausage).

Many Caribbean people still make their living fishing, so it should come as no surprise that seafood dominates local cuisine. Look for spiny, putty-pink rock lobsters, chewy conch (a type of ocean-dwelling mollusc), flying fish, grouper, crab, shrimp, snapper and tuna. Seafood is served a thousand different ways – in stews, in sandwiches, fried, raw – from roadside stalls to ultra-luxe hotel restaurants.

Other local bounty includes tropical fruit like pineapple, soursop, banana, mango, tamarind, lime, coconut and guava. Starchy side dishes are a menu must – rice and beans (rice 'n' peas in the Bahamas and Jamaica, *Moros y Cristianos* in Cuba, *diri ak pwa* in Haitian Creole etc), macaroni and cheese, fried plantains, cornmeal mush, stewed sweet potatoes. Last but not least, sugar cane remains an important crop on the islands, and much of it still goes into making an essential cocktail ingredient: rum.

CARIBBEAN RUM
ISLAND SPIRIT

The image of lounging on a beach with a fruity drink in hand doesn't come from out of the blue. Every Caribbean nation has its very own classic cocktail (or five). Some are enjoyed by locals, while others are concocted strictly for the tourist trade.

The basis of many of the region's most iconic cocktails is smooth, sweet and deceptively strong Caribbean rum. This local firewater is made from sugar cane, first brought to the Caribbean by Christopher Columbus himself. Later on, sugar cane became the basis for a system of servitude, with enslaved or indentured workers brought from West Africa and India to work the fields. Many islanders today are descended from these workers.

WHERE TO DRINK OLD TAVERN COFFEE ESTATE
THE BLUE MOUNTAINS, JAMAICA

If you're looking to wind up rather than down, skip the rum and sip some of Jamaica's legendary Blue Mountains coffee instead – or combine the two in a shot or three of coffee-flavoured Jamaica rum cream on the rocks. Coffee grown on the mountains' cool, damp slopes is considered some of the best in the world, though it's almost all for export and nearly impossible to find in Jamaica's own coffee shops. Connoisseurs should email ahead to the Old Tavern Coffee Estate, a Blue Mountains farm that produces Jamaica's only single-estate beans. The English owners will be keen to show you around.

SIGNATURE TIPPLES

THE BAHAMAS
Goombay Smash (rum, coconut rum, pineapple juice, orange juice);
sky juice (gin, coconut water, nutmeg)

BRITISH VIRGIN ISLANDS
Painkiller (dark rum, coconut cream, orange juice, pineapple juice, nutmeg)

CUBA
Mojito (rum, lime juice, mint, sugar, soda water); **daiquiri** (rum, lime sugar)

CURAÇAO
Curaçao (a startlingly blue liqueur made with a local citrus fruit)

HAITI, MARTINIQUE, GUADELOUPE
Ti' Punch (rum, lime, cane syrup)

JAMAICA
Planter's Punch (dark rum, lime juice, grenadine, Angostura bitters, various fruit juices)

PUERTO RICO
Piña Colada (rum, coconut cream, pineapple juice)

ABOVE Draining rum from a barrel at a distillery in Puerto Rico **ABOVE LEFT** Piña colada means 'strained pineapple' in Spanish **RIGHT** Mixing mojitos, a favourite drink of Ernest Hemingway, in a bar in Havana, Cuba

MOFONGO

The taste of traditional home cooking in Puerto Rico and the Dominican Republic, mofongo can be served as a main or a side dish, along with a huge variety of meat or seafood.

INGREDIENTS

4 green plantains
500mL/17fl oz canola oil
6 garlic cloves
2 tbsp olive oil
500g/1lb *chicharrón* (crisp pork rinds)
250mL/8.5fl oz chicken stock
salt

PREPARATION

Peel the plantains and cut into 2.5cm/1in slices. In a deep saucepan or deep-fat fryer, heat the oil. Add the slices of plantain in batches, cooking for five or more minutes, until golden but not brown. Drain on paper towels.

With a mortar and pestle crush the garlic cloves and add the salt and olive oil. Continue to blend then transfer to another bowl.

In the mortar (or the larger bowl), crush some of the fried plantain with some of the *chicharrón*, some of the garlic mixture and add a dash of chicken stock. Repeat until all the plantains are crushed and combined.

Shape the mixture into four balls and top with more *chicharrón*. Or form small bowls out of the mofongo (using a bowl or cup as a mould) and serve with fillings such as garlic shrimp.

Serves four.

MOFONGO
MOFONGO MADNESS

As beloved a comfort food in Puerto Rico and the Dominican Republic as mac 'n' cheese is in the United States, *mofongo* is a mash of green plantains seasoned with garlic and bits of crispy pork skin, served with a vast variety of seafood, meat and stews. Originally of African origin, it's the kind of dish home cooks love to put their own personal touch to – everyone claims their own mother's is the best.

It's traditionally served in a special tall wooden bowl known as a *pilón*, often with a bowl of broth on the side. The *mofongo* is soft and sticky, the broth hot and savoury, the whole thing studded through with crackling bits of *chicharrón* – delicioso!

Mangú, a Dominican favourite, is similar to mofongo. It consists of mashed boiled green plantains, often served with cheese and sausage as a breakfast side dish. In other parts of the Caribbean, *fufu* is another lookalike side dish, this time made with sweet ripe plantains. It's delicious when served with spicy, peppery vegetable stews.

WHERE TO EAT PIKAYO
999 AV ASHFORD, SAN JUAN, PUERTO RICO

Dine on some of the country's most exquisite *mofongo*, served here with shrimp and saffron broth, among the jet-set crowd at this wildly praised palace of nouvelle Puerto Riqueño cuisine. Inside the San Juan Museum of Art, it's the flagship of celebrity chef Wilo Benet, the island's answer to Gordon Ramsay.

ABOVE Seek out the perfect plate of mofongo in San Juan's Old Town in Puerto Rico
ABOVE LEFT Mofongo is primarily served as a side dish, or stuffed with meat or seafood

STEWS
WINTER DISH FOR SUMMER CLIMES

You might think that a region where summer stretches nearly year-round wouldn't go in for piping-hot bowls of stews, yet they're some of the Caribbean's most common dishes.

Callaloo, a thick stew made from leafy greens and other vegetables, is ubiquitous from the Virgin Islands to St Vincent and the Grenadines to Dominica. Goat is a staple stew ingredient across the islands – curry goat is beloved in Jamaica, goat-head-based 'mannish water' is said to cure impotence in the Cayman Islands, while in Montserrat the local goat soup goes by the less-than-appetising name of 'goat water'. On the island of Curaçao in the Dutch Caribbean, lamb and cucumber are paired off.

In Martinique and Guadeloupe, *blaff* is a popular stew of white fish seasoned with lime, and a similar dish called 'boil fish' is a common breakfast in the Bahamas. Pepperpot, the national dish of Antigua and Barbuda, is a hearty blend of meat and vegetables, commonly served with cornmeal balls called fungi.

☙ WHERE TO EAT GLADYS' CAFE
ROYAL DANE MALL, CHARLOTTE AMALIE, ST THOMAS, US VIRGIN ISLANDS

Hearty bowls of callaloo kick off filling meals at this casual West Indian spot, where owner Gladys is known for belting out Tina Turner tunes while dishing out local favourites like Old Wife (triggerfish), conch and fried plantains.

ABOVE Callaloo varies across the region with different green leaf vegetables used to create the stew depending on location **ABOVE RIGHT** Pepper sauce adds a kick to any or every meal

PEPPER SAUCE

If soaring temperatures aren't hot enough for you, turn up the heat with one of the Caribbean's innumerable hot chilli sauces, called 'pepper sauce' on the English-speaking islands. The sauces' heat levels vary by island – Jamaican pepper sauce will scorch your tongue with the fire of scotch bonnet chilli, Matouk's pepper sauce from Trinidad and Tobago packs a fruity, medium-hot punch, and curry-spiked Mrs Greaux' Hot Pepper Sauce will wallop your palate on St Kitts and Nevis.

Sprinkle pepper sauce on almost everything – breakfast eggs, goat stew, rice 'n' peas and fried fish.

THE SADISTIC SCOTCH BONNET

Packing up to 350,000 Scoville units of heat, the Caribbean's pumpkin-shaped scotch bonnet pepper is one of the hottest chillies fit for human consumption. The jalapeno, by comparison, packs a mere 8000 Scoville units!

BE A JERK

Scotch bonnet chillies provide the fire for Jamaica's jerk seasoning, which is rubbed on everything from goat to fish. Other ingredients in jerk spice rubs include cinnamon, allspice, cloves and nutmeg. The best place to sample jerk-cooked meat is at a jerk stand – wooden shacks where jerk chicken, pork and more are cooked up over old oil barrels.

CONCH
THE CALL OF THE SEA

A staple in every Bahamian home, restaurant and roadside stall, conch (pronounced 'conk') is the de facto national dish of the Bahamas, and the adjacent Turks and Caicos. A type of sea snail with a large cone-shaped shell, it's fished from the shallows then brought live to market. Its tough flesh is comparable to calamari, and takes a good dash of TLC to tenderise – the mark of a top Bahamian cook is the tenderness of their conch.

The most popular conch dishes are cracked conch (battered and fried), conch salad (chopped and tossed with lime juice, onion, tomato and chilli), conch chowder and conch fritters (fried balls of battered conch). Rustic, sandy-floored conch stands are the best places to sample this tasty mollusc – just belly up to the counter, order a cold Kalik beer and prepare to sample some genuine island flavour.

WHERE TO EAT TURKS AND CAICOS CONCH FESTIVAL
PROVIDENCIALES

Try conch cooked any way you please at this annual festival dedicated to the staple sea snail. It's usually held in late autumn in the T&C capital of Providenciales, and features a weekend of parties, contests, charity races and, of course, plenty of chowing down.

LEFT Inspecting the morning fishing haul before heading to St Barts' market **ABOVE** Is there anything more satisfying than finding your own conch in the shallow waters of the Caribbean?

GONE FISHIN'
The people of the Caribbean respect their seafood, and often the best places to sample an island's flavours are the humble seafood shacks and home-style restaurants frequented by locals. Sadly but truly, many upmarket hotels rely on imported 'fancy' fish. We'd just as soon have a piece of fried flying fish at a roadside stall in Barbados than a chunk of frozen salmon at an all-inclusive resort in the Virgin Islands. And if it's fresh fish you're after, the freshest way to get it is to catch it yourself. Fishing charters are a popular activity across the Bahamas, and many of them include a post-fishing cookout.

FRIDAY NIGHT AT THE FISH FRY
Part open-air food court, part neighbourhood block party, the fish fry is a beloved tradition of many English-speaking Caribbean nations, including Jamaica, the Bahamas, the Virgin Islands and the Turks and Caicos. Most towns and villages have their own fish-fry facility, usually a grouping of brightly painted huts that sit vacant during the day. But at night and on weekends cooks haul in oil-drum cookers and begin frying up hearty platefuls of fish, fritters and starchy side dishes. Cold beer or rum starts flowing, the locals start gossiping, and sooner or later a guitar or drum set appears and the whole thing turns into a raucous party.

≈
BITE-SIZE DIVERSIONS

Your taste buds will be jumping as you island-hop your way across the Caribbean, sampling delights from flying-fish sandwiches to many a mojito.

THE BAHAMAS
Snagging a table at one of the many celebrity-chef-run restaurants at Paradise Island's impossibly luxurious Atlantis megaresort. We dig Bobby Flay's Southwestern-spiced Mesa Grill and Nobu Matsuhisa's legendary sushi spot, Nobu.

BARBADOS
Grabbing a flying-fish sandwich at one of the stalls at the famous Oistins Fish Fry. If it's a weekend, prepare to party, local-style, with calypso beats and cold Banks beer.

CUBA
Making like Ernest Hemingway and sucking down a mojito, a classic Cuban cocktail made with local rum, mint, lime and sugar, at one of Havana's many colonial-era bars. La Bodeguita del Medio was Papa's favourite.

JAMAICA
Sampling Jamaica's national dish, a hearty platter of ackee (a red tree fruit related to the lychee) and salt fish (salt cod cooked with capsicum and bacon), served at one of the country's many humble home-style cafes.

PUERTO RICO
Touring the Bacardí Rum Factory, aka the Cathedral of Rum, 50 hectares of distillery buildings and manicured grounds where the famed golden liquor has been made since the 1930s. Don't forget your two free drinks!

GUAVATE
Making the pilgrimage to the Guavate area for a taste of smoky, juice-dripping *lechón asado* (roast suckling pig), one of Puerto Rico's most iconic and drool-worthy delicacies. On weekends, everyone from millionaires to local *jíbaros* (mountain villagers) gathers to feast and listen to old-fashioned troubadours at Guvate's numerous *lechoneras* (lechón restaurants).

ST BARTH
Eating, drinking and partying with *tout le monde* in the haute Creole fusion restaurants favoured by the Hollywood types who haunts this ritzy island. The capital Gustavia is particularly thick with culinary hot spots.

ST MARTIN
Choosing between the humble lolos (open-air food stalls) and haute French bistros that line the seafront road in Grand Case, often called the Gourmet Capital of the Caribbean. Tuesday nights bring out at the locals, who love a stroll before settling down to dine.

ST VINCENT AND THE GRENADINES
Seeing and being seen at Basil's Bar and Restaurant on Mustique, a casual seafront joint more famous for its clientele (think Mick Jagger, Tommy Hilfiger) than its delicious menu of French-inflected Caribbean fare.

TRINIDAD AND TOBAGO
Fortifying yourself with 'bake and shark' (deep-fried shark bits), T&T's quintessential party food, while sucking down rum and whooping it up at the island's legendary Carnival celebration.

You won't go hungry browsing the st
of Budapest's Central Mar

EASTERN EUROPE & RUSSIA

'Eat, drink and loosen your belt.' So goes a favourite Polish aphorism, which indicates how food here works. Rich in meat and hearty soups, the cuisine is varied, inventive and deliciously garlic-laden.

Eastern Europe and Russia have experienced their fair share of tumult, yet nourishing, heart-warming food has been a constant, binding people across generations, politics and cultural gulfs. Rich in calories and strong on flavour, traditional dishes originated with peasants, hunters and herders, who depended on salt for preservation, roots for sustenance and fat for warmth. Harsh winters and brief growing seasons mean that fresh produce is in short supply. But this carnivorous region consumes any animal it can, especially in the form of sausages and stews.

Embracing 20-odd countries and 200 million people from Catholic, Orthodox, Muslim and Lutheran backgrounds, who speak Baltic, Romance and Slavic languages, Eastern Europe is a mosaic. The diversity is indisputable, which is why the many culinary commonalities are so intriguing. The most characteristic elements are drawn from the Czech Republic, Hungary, Poland, Ukraine and the Balkans, but travellers will discover local versions of these specialities in villages and towns throughout the region.

Known as *krestyanskaya* or 'peasant' fare, Russia's traditional food remains firmly based on the ingredients gathered, grown and prepared by rural cooks over the ages: fish, poultry, potatoes, mushrooms, berries, grains and garden fruits and vegetables. Its culinary influences are as sprawling and eclectic as the country's vast territory: *sashlyk* (meat kebabs) from the Caucasus, *lapsha* (noodle soup) from the Tartars, flavoured rice dishes like plov (the Uzbek version of pilaf), seafood from Primorye (the Russian Far East) and game in the unpopulated north. The greatest influence on Russian food, though, is the climate and the country's marked seasonality.

Adventurous eaters are in for a pleasant surprise in Russia and Eastern Europe, while hungry travellers will have their taste buds tantalised and appetites sated by the region's hearty cuisine.

GOULASH

An authentic Hungarian goulash is more soup than stew, with hearty winter root vegetables not tomatoes. You can cook a thicker version by flouring the meat, reducing the liquid and baking in a casserole dish in the oven.

INGREDIENTS

700g/25oz braising steak

2 red onions, sliced

2 cloves garlic, chopped or crushed

1 red pepper

2 carrots, diced

500g/1lb new potatoes, halved if large

3 tbsp paprika

200mL/7fl oz beef stock

Black pepper

Sunflower oil

Soured cream

Flat-leaf parsley

PREPARATION

Gently cook the onion in the oil in a heavy casserole dish until soft. Season the beef to taste, add it to the dish. Turn up the heat so the meat browns. Add it in batches if the dish is small.

Add the garlic and paprika and cook for a couple of minutes. Add the diced carrots and some beef stock (water is fine) to cover the meat and bring to a simmer. Cook slowly with the lid on for about 40 minutes.

Add the potatoes then strips of the red pepper and and cook for another 20 minutes or until the potatoes are done. Ladle into bowls, garnish with a dollop of soured cream and the parsley. Serves four.

GOULASH
GOING HUNGARIAN

Hungary's national dish is a thick soup of meat, vegetables and potatoes, generously spiced with paprika. In Hungarian, *gulyás* means 'herdsman', providing a clue to the origins of this dish.

For centuries, sheep and cattle herders have prepared the hearty soup in a cast-iron kettle, leaving it to cook on the open fire while they are out tending their animals. Many Hungarian cooks believe this is still the only proper way to make a goulash, as the ingredients benefit from a long, slow stew – it's crucial to breaking down the tougher cuts of beef and thickening the potage.

Of course, there are probably as many variations on goulash as there are cooks in Hungary. Some popular add-ins are noodles, sauerkraut, vegetables and kidney beans. The quintessentially Hungarian dish has proved popular throughout the region, too. In Croatia and Serbia, goulash is often prepared with game meats like venison or wild boar. Slovenians eat 'partisan goulash', a version with extra potatoes and little meat that apparently fed Slovenian partisans during WWII. Czech goulash is served with dumplings and beer.

Western countries have altered the recipe, flavouring it with tomatoes and thickening the mixture with flour, resulting in a stew that barely resembles the Hungarian original.

⬧ WHERE TO EAT BORBÍRÓSÁG
CSARNOK TÉR 5, BUDAPEST, HUNGARY

Most traditional restaurants in Budapest give visitors a chance to sample the national dish, often in a kitsch atmosphere with waiters in peasant dress and musicians playing folk music. For a more refined experience, try Borbíróság, a casual but sophisticated wine bar near the Grand Market in Budapest. Traditional dishes such as goulash are prepared with contemporary flare and offered alongside more than 60 local wines.

ABOVE LEFT Lashings of paprika give goulash its warmth and colour
ABOVE Fisherman's Bastion on the banks of the Danube in Budapest, the capital of Hungary

⚶
PRE-LENTEN FARE
FAT TUESDAY

All good Catholic and Orthodox believers enjoy pre-Lenten festivities – at least a day of feasting before the 40 days of fasting leading up to Easter Sunday. Less well known than the Carnivals of Brazil and Italy, the Eastern European celebrations are no less merry. Most predate Christianity, harking back to pagan rituals that ushered in spring. Kukeri in Bulgaria, Karneval in Croatia, Masopust in Czech, Vaslapaev in Estonia and Farsang in Hungary are all variations on this holiday.

Shrove Tuesday is sometimes called 'Fat Tuesday', thanks to the tradition of indulging in the cakes and pastries that are subsequently forbidden until Easter. Every country has its own sweet, buttery specialities to sate sugary cravings for the coming weeks. In many countries, cooks prepare thin pancakes for the special occasion, filling them with honey, jam or sweet cheese. Known variously as *palacinki* or *palacinky* (Serbia, Croatia and Czech), *palacsinta* (Hungary), *nalesnikiyai* (Lithuania) and *nalesniki* (Poland), the crêpes are a common breakfast or snack item. Alternatively, the devout might devour 'angels' wings', which are delicate flaky butter cookies that are sprinkled with powdered sugar.

Eastern Europe's most celebrated pre-Lenten pastry is the irresistible Polish *pączek*, a fried doughnut filled with jam and sprinkled with sugar. Poles line up outside their favourite bakeries for *pączki* (paunch-ki) not on the Tuesday but rather the Thursday before Lent. By starting consumption on Tłusty Czwartek, or Fat Thursday, they have the whole weekend to eat doughnuts, instead of just one day.

⊜ WHERE TO EAT A BLIKLE
NOWY SWIAT 33, WARSAW, POLAND

Poles swear that the best *pączki* come from any hole-in-the-wall bakery but you can't go wrong at A Blikle, an esteemed sweet shop that has graced the Warsaw Old Town since 1869.

ABOVE RIGHT Lager was first brewed in Pilsen and Budweiser Budvar – no relation to the US brand – is one of the world's great beers **ABOVE** Hungarian pastries on St Stephen's Day

BEER

The Czechs drink more beer per person than any other people in the world. This prowess is backed by a millennium of beer-brewing history: the earliest record of brewing is from 933 and the first Czech brewery was founded in 1188. Czech beers are distinctive for the earthy, spicy aroma of the Bohemian hops, known as Saaz.

Since 1842, Pilsner Urquell has been produced at a brewery in Plezň. The world's first 'light' beer, it's had immeasurable impact on brewing in the two centuries since. Aside from its historic value, Pilsner Urquell is still much loved for its hoppy flavour and golden colour.

The Czechs' other famous beer has been produced since 1895 in Čeksé Budějowice, a town that is also known by its German name, Budweiser. The complex lager is not to be confused with the Bud-branded beer of the United States. There is plenty of legal wrangling about which company gets to use which name in which country but there is no confusing the two brews: the Budvar exhibits the characteristic Saaz flavour that defines Czech beer so deliciously.

The local love of beer is obvious across their culture. Jaroslav Hasek's novel, *The Good Soldier Švejk*, features a beloved, beer-drinking protagonist who speculates that any government that raises the price of beer will collapse within the year. The hypothesis has not been tested.

ᘰ
PELMENI
WINTER COMFORT FOOD

When Russian midwinter temperatures plummet, wrap your hands around a bowl of *pelmeni*, breathe in the fragrant steam, and inhale a smidgen of Russia's ancient culinary history. These handmade dumplings were brought to Russia by Mongol invaders in the 13th century. They travelled well in saddle bags, a form of deep-freeze in winter, and made an efficient high-energy snack for hard-working horsemen. Even today, people store batches of *pelmeni* on their apartment balconies in winter – a handmade quick-fix fast food for when the occasion dictates.

   Pelmeni are crafted from an egg-and-flour-based dough, and filled with a blend of beef, pork and lamb mince, garlic and parsley. Learning to fashion these tasty parcels, by getting the garlic, herb and meat mixture and the finicky dough-folding just right, is a Russian girl's culinary rite of passage. A few minutes' hearty boil cooks the dumplings, and they're served either in a clear broth, or heaped in a deep bowl with plenty of *smetana* (like sour cream) and a sprinkle of fresh dill and parsley. There's also a sweet version, *varyeniki,* of Ukrainian origin. Filled with blueberries, cherries or strawberry jam, they're served as a hot dessert with sugar and cream.

   Pirozhki are another doughy cousin of the *pelmeni* family. A Russian snack and party food, the delectable yeast-based buns are stuffed with fillings like mushrooms, meat, cabbage, stewed fruits or cottage cheese; either baked or deep fried, they're served piping hot. *Chebureki*, originally from the Caucasus, are crafted flat into a thin layer of dough – they resemble a stuffed pancake that's deep-fried until deliciously browned and crispy.

🍲 WHERE TO EAT YOLKI PALKI
NEGLINNAYA UL 8/10, MOSCOW

It might not be the most refined of places to dine but this chain serves affordable down-home traditional meals in outlets across the country. The *pelmeni* here are irreproachable.

LEFT Moscow in winter: the gilded domes of the Annunciation Cathedral in the Kremlin **ABOVE** Boiled *pelmeni* (dumplings) topped with *smetana* (sour cream) and a sprinkle of dill is the perfect winter snack

PARTY FOOD

Celebratory eating in Russia is all about grazing. Rather than being served a dish on a plate, you'll be asked to help yourself from a table loaded with an array of salads, cold meats and dry sausage, salted fish, breads and cheeses, marinated mushrooms, pickled cucumbers and *pirozhki*. It's now that the truly classic Russian delicacies are in evidence: no *prazdnichni stol* (celebratory table) is complete without caviar – *ikra*.

   This comes in several kinds: the black sturgeon caviar that's most highly prized – and priced – and the more common (and arguably more delicious) amber-coloured salmon roe that pop like salty beads in the mouth. Salmon caviar is usually spread thinly on buttered white bread. Black caviar is traditionally served with blini, buckwheat and buttermilk pikelets, with a delicious dollop of *smetana*.

CAVIAR

Caviar was once the food of Russian imperial luxury, reserved for tsars and the nobility. The most highly prized was the roe of the Caspian beluga, but sterlet, ossetra and sevruga sturgeon also yield caviar. In fact, Russians tend to call any fish eggs caviar, though technically only sturgeon roe counts as such.

   Centuries of unsustainable harvesting of sturgeon eggs has placed the species under threat of extinction, and trade in caviar is now highly regulated – if you are buying caviar, buy carefully. Make your purchase only from shops (not on the street or at markets), buy it in sealed jars (not loose) and make sure the jar or tin is sealed with a CITES (Convention on International Trade in Endangered Species) label, an international trade-control measure that helps reduce sturgeon poaching.

SLIVOVITZ

Fiery, fruity and as bright as borshch, *slivovitz* is a potent plum brandy produced from the ripe fruit and crushed pits of damson plums, and consumed in great quantities throughout the region.

Eastern European drinkers have long produced their own homebrewed versions of *slivovitz* (which are still the best, purists claim); but this is becoming rarer as production is regulated and moved to community and commercial distilleries.

Known variously as *slivovice* (Czech), *šljivovica* (Serbian), *slivovitsa* (Bulgarian) or *sliwowica* (Polish), the liquor varies in production methods and drinking traditions. But some things are consistent: it is usually served chilled but not on the rocks; and in true Eastern European style, it's not sipped, but rather knocked back as a shot.

Nestled in the foothills of the Balkan Mountains in the tiny town of Orešak, Troyan Monastery is famed for its plum brandy. Monks have been distilling *slivovitsa* from locally grown plums since the monastery's founding in the 14th century. It's transformed in September when the village hosts its annual Plum Festival, which includes much sampling of local varieties. *Nazdrave!*

◈
BORSHCH
RUBY NECTAR

It's winter in Siberia. Outside, the temperature is 40 degrees below zero, and the streets are black with ice under an anaemic winter sun. People huddle in furs, their faces shrouded in clouds of frozen breath and masked behind scarves, for this is flesh-freezing weather.

Come inside and unwrap. The apartment is tropically hot, and from the kitchen floats a deliciously inviting aroma. You're about to try your first real *borshch*, Siberian style. Only after making the journey from the icy outdoors to the homely warmth of the kitchen table can you truly understand the hearty comfort of this pan-Russian favourite.

Borshch is the classic Russian broth: ruby hued and steaming hot, it's a warming blend of beetroot, carrot, cabbage and plenty of garlic. The soup may be vegetarian, or meaty, with the addition of anything from sausage to chicken hearts. It's always served with a dollop of *smetana* (sour cream), and usually a sprinkle of fresh dill and parsley.

Soups are one of the foundations of the Russian diet. They may serve as a first course or, loaded with rich ingredients, they can be a satisfying meal in themselves. As well as this best-known Russian broth, there are a thousand variants on the soup theme. *Shchi* – based on cabbage and carrot, flavoured with sorrel and sometimes with added beef, mushrooms and even nettle leaves – is another winter favourite. A complete contrast is the summer soup *okroshka*, which is served cold. Based on *kvass* (a refreshing fizzy fermented beverage made from rye bread), it's a cooling blend of cucumber, potato, celery and turnips – with green onion, dill, parsley and tarragon for flavouring. *Okroshka* may contain poultry or fish, and is garnished with chopped hard-boiled eggs and smetana.

Whether the soup's hot or cold, you'll be offered beautifully doughy Russian bread – *khleb*. Savour the distinct sourness of the coriander-flavoured rye – and help yourself to plenty of golden-sweet Russian *maslo* (butter).

LEFT *Silvovitz* is served chilled and knocked back in one shot **ABOVE** This is a Ukrainian version of Russia's traditional winter-warming dish: you'll find a pot brewing on the back burner in many homes

SAUSAGES
SPICY SNAGS

If there is one staple common to every Eastern European cuisine, it is the not-so-humble sausage. North Americans use the word *kielbasa* to refer to a specific kind of Polish sausage, but in Eastern European languages it's the generic word for sausage (*kiełbasa* in Polish, *kolbász* in Hungarian, *klobása* in Czech, Slovak and Slovenian). One word and one food, with countless variations in pronunciation, production and ingredients. Speciality sausages from different countries and regions use different kinds of meat, spices and cooking methods, and some are a key ingredient in the region's most distinctive dishes. Sausages are a staple at Polish weddings, Estonian Christmas and Romanian New Year. Indeed, in rural communities across the region, the autumnal pig slaughter is often a multiday, celebratory affair dedicated in part to making sausages. Eastern Europe's love affair with stuffed and smoked meats reflects the Germanic influence in the region, and is typical of countries with meat-heavy culinary traditions. In the attempt to use every last bit of the animal, butchers all over the world learned to flavour the less appetising parts with spices and salt, and stuff them into the animal's intestine for preservation. This explains the sausage's characteristic tubular shape, as well as its lip-smacking, spicy, salty goodness.

WHERE TO EAT KOLBÁSZFESZTIVÁL
BÉKÉSCABA, BÉKÉS, HUNGARY

For centuries, Hungarians and Slovaks from the region around Békéscsaba in Hungary have produced the paprika-flavoured *csabai kolbász,* characterised by its spicy taste and reddish colour. The pork-stuffed intestines are dried and smoked, traditionally in an open chimney fuelled by sweet-corn cobs. The resulting sausage is piquant, chewy, and served on bread or alongside green peppers. To learn more, visit in late October during the *Kolbászfesztivál*, where folk music and wine-tasting frame the centrepiece sausage-making competition.

ABOVE Sizzling sausages wait for hungry customers in a Budapest restaurant

SALO

The aptly named 'fatback' is the layer of fat on the back of a pig. Cut a slab, cure it with salt, pepper and garlic, then store it for a few months in a wooden barrel – and you've got the Ukrainian speciality *salo*. It might be used as an ingredient in soups or sausage, but is most often smothered onto a wedge of black bread and eaten raw, as an accompaniment to vodka or spirits.

It's enough to make health-food fiends wince. But if you can get past the idea of eating pure pig fat, it will make you salivate for more. The fat's rich meaty flavour and melt-in-your-mouth texture are enhanced by the earthiness and chewiness of the rye bread. Nowadays, pigs are raised on special diets of milk and grains to ensure maximum succulence and savour of their salo.

Salo originates in the Eastern European peasant culture, where the consumption of animal fat was crucial to surviving the long, bitter winters. In summer, it nourished the hard-working farmers without need of refrigeration or condiment. Although salo is most closely associated with Ukrainian cuisine, it's a staple in countries throughout the region, and is sometimes treated with paprika or coriander.

Taking a modern approach to this traditional dish, the Salo Lviv Modern Art Museum is part museum and part restaurant. Exhibits showcase an impressive array of *salo* sculpture (seriously), along with other food- and fat-themed paintings, cartoons and multimedia art. The restaurant menu offers edible art, such as ice cream and *salo* in the shape of Marilyn's lips. Thankfully, the menu also includes more traditional *salo* presentations for the novice, including an introduction to a dozen different types of *salo* from around Ukraine.

WILD FOOD

Autumn arrives in Russia with balmy, golden days and the crunch of leaves underfoot – and something appears in the forest that's the foundation of a truly Russian tradition. With the joyful expression *'gribi poshlii'* – the mushrooms have come – families journey to the woods with their wicker baskets in hand.

Russians know their mushrooms: *lisichki* (chanterelles), *veshenki* (oyster mushrooms), *belyi gribi* (porcini) and *ryzhki* (orange milk mushrooms) are common finds. Any mushroom hunt is an excuse for a picnic – vodka and a campfire included – and will provide the raw ingredients for an array of Russian specialities.

Wild berry gathering is a similarly wonderful Russian pastime. Bilberries, lingonberries and wild strawberries pop up in summer, cranberries and blueberries in autumn. *Yagodi* (berries) can be eaten fresh with *morozhenoe* (ice cream), used to fill sweet *varenki* or fashioned into homemade jam.

The tradition of wild food gathering is revered in Russia. Maximising time in the outdoors before the sudden freeze of winter, whether picking berries, fossicking for mushrooms or hunting wild game, Russians approach hunter-gathering with a joyfulness they call *zhizni radost* – a particularly soulful (sometimes vodka-fuelled) Russian brand of joie de vivre.

If you don't want to venture into the woods alone, you can taste hunted and gathered produce at Varvary, a central Moscow restaurant owned by the flamboyant Anatoly Komm. The menu proudly states that only Russian-sourced ingredients are used. In true Komm style, the morel mushroom stuffed with porcini in a white-truffle sauce is exquisite.

⟨⟨⟩⟩
BIGOS
HUNTER'S STEW

Setting out from the manor in the early morn, a hunting party journeys deep into the Białowieża forest, in pursuit of bears, bison, deer and pheasant. The primeval forest is dense and filled with wildlife, which bodes well for extravagant feasting and merrymaking later in the week. The air is crisp during these autumn days, and appetites intensify for the meat that is the hunters' prize. The game will go into a pot with pickled cabbage, simmering for several hours over the course of several days to tenderise the meat and draw out the flavours, allowing the aromas to waft throughout the manor house and tantalise the guests.

Finally, the hour of the feast arrives. The hard-working and long-awaiting hunting party is rewarded with heaping bowls of *bigos*, accompanied by black bread smothered with lard and copious amounts of vodka and ale. Toasting the good King Jagiełło, who apparently first introduced *bigos* to Poland in the 14th century, the celebrants eat, drink and generally make merry until the wee hours.

Usually translated as 'hunter's stew', *bigos* is a tasty, tangy melange of cabbage, meat and vegetables that is popular in Poland, Ukraine and Lithuania. The iconic dish was immortalised by the Polish writer and philosopher Adam Mickewicz, who wrote about the ingredients, aromas and preparation of *bigos* in his epic poem *'Pan Tadeusz'*. More importantly, it has been handed down from generation to generation by centuries of Polish cooks who harbour their own secret recipes for this hearty dish.

There are no fixed ingredients for clean-out-the-pantry *bigos*. It's usually made with both sauerkraut and fresh cabbage; the mixed meats might include pork, bacon and sausage, although a true hunter's stew will also include venison or other game meat; mushrooms, tomatoes, apples or dried plums enhance the flavour, as do pepper and other spices. The only hard and fast rule is that it must simmer on the stove for many hours, preferably over two or three consecutive days.

🍽 WHERE TO EAT POLSKIE SMAKI
UL ŚW TOMASZA 5, KRAKÓW, POLAND

For unbeatable *bigos*, head to Polskie Smaki in the Kraków Old Town. A vaulted ceiling, wrought-iron staircase and stained-glass ceiling give the place more atmosphere than your typical *mleczny* bar, but it doesn't detract from the cooking, which is straightforward, simple and downright delicious.

RIGHT Bialowieza forest, a historic hunting ground between Belarus and Poland, is the last patch of primeval forest in Europe and a final stronghold of the European bison; the bison are protected from hunters now

FESTIVAL FOOD

The Orthodox festivals of *Paskha* (Easter) and *Rozhdestvo* (Christmas) call for the preparation of special sweet dishes. For the festival of Maslenitsa, a week of celebration and feasting before the sober, solemn time of Lent, mountains of *blini* are prepared. For Easter Sunday, Russians bake the saffron-flavoured buttery loaf *kulich*, on which is spread the Easter cheesecake known as *paskha*, a delicious mix of *tvorog* (cheese curd), egg yolks, sugar, butter, *smetana* and vanilla. On Christmas Eve (6 January by the Orthodox Calendar) it is traditional to eat *kutya*, a wheat porridge prepared with poppy seeds, slivered almonds, honey and raisins.

TASTE RUSSIA

Kazarmenny per 4/3, Moscow

If you're keen to take some Russian cooking wisdom home with you, the best thing is to befriend a local and have them show you how to cook a few dishes in the home kitchen – where they originated. If that's not possible, you could sign up for a Russian cooking course, such as those offered at this cosy little cooking school. They'll teach you all the most delicious traditional recipes, as well as national dishes of the ex-USSR: *things like Georgian shashlik, Uzbek plov,* Ukrainian *borshch* and Ossetian cheese and potato pie.

OLIVYE
THE REAL RUSSIAN SALAD

The dish known to the world as Russian salad really does exist, only here it's called *olivye*. A substantial, creamy blend of boiled and cubed potato, carrot, egg, peas and meat, the salad is drenched in a garlic-enhanced mayonnaise and graces dining tables across the country. One of the few staples of Russian cuisine that originated in a restaurant, the salad is named after a well-known chef of the 1860s, Lucien Olivier, whose special recipe was long a well-guarded secret.

There are all sorts of domestic variations on *olivye*, as Russian home cooks are famously inventive – after centuries of making do with whatever's available, they have to be. Of course, *olivye* is just one of the recipes that makes up the Russian salad repertoire. Forget lettuce: salads in Russia are far more exotic and substantial. Served year-round, they rely on ingredients that keep through the winter, or can be frozen or preserved.

Vinegryet is another ubiquitous salad, based on grated beets, carrots, cubed potatoes, onions, marinated cucumbers or sour cabbage; seasoned with garlic, vinegar and olive oil. There's also the strangely named *syelyodka pod shuboi* (herring in a fur coat): salted herring covered with layers of grated boiled potato, carrot, beetroot, onion and mayonnaise. Some variations include a layer of grated apple.

🍴 WHERE TO EAT TSENTRALNY DOM LITERATOV (TSDL) UL POVARSKAYA 50, MOSCOW

Built in 1889, and home to the Union of Writers during the Soviet era, this urbane restaurant serves standout versions of almost every Russian traditional staple – but it's the *olivye* that's said to be the best in the country. The gorgeous carved oak, sandalwood panelling and glittering chandeliers provide just the kind of surroundings where *olivye* would have been savoured when it was an exotic addition to the Moscow culinary scene.

ABOVE LEFT Celebrating pancake week in Russia **ABOVE** *Oliyve* is a creamy potato-based salad, served year-round, often with thick slices of crusty bread

﹌
SHARLOTKA
SWEET SENSATIONS

You've walked your legs off round the glorious, glittering city centres of Moscow or St Petersburg. Your mind is reeling with the history and grandeur of it all, and you need to sit and absorb – and perhaps recharge with some new Russian deliciousness. Order a cup of hot chai (tea) from the samovar, and for something sweet, it's time to try *sharlotka*. This effortless classic – at its best, tart and cakey, light but satisfyingly filling – is a no-fuss five-minute recipe: an egg, flour and sugar batter is simply poured over the tart apples and baked until golden.

Many Russian desserts make use of the bounty of fruits and berries that are available in the short summer – and those that can be jammed, canned or otherwise preserved through the rest of the year. Variations on *sharlotka* (which is not to be confused with the French dessert *Charlotte Russe*) include cherry cakes and blueberry tarts. Visit any *bulochnaya* or bakery, and you'll also encounter all manner of fruit-filled breads, dumplings and sweet *pechyonie* (pastries).

There's no counting calories when it comes to *muraveinik* (which translates as anthill, and is fashioned to look just like one). This dessert is made from a buttery dough that's put through a meal mincer, and then baked until crunchy. Caramelised condensed milk is then added, and the mix is built up into a sweet, golden brown mountain that's refrigerated. *Muraveinik* is served in neat, chewy wedges, perhaps with coffee.

Morozhenoe (literally 'frozen') is the Russian word for ice cream – and Russians love it, summer and winter. The best *morozhenoe* is the simplest, creamiest vanilla sold in cups or blocks from a street vendor. It's not unusual to see an ice-cream cart doing a roaring trade, even when there's snow on the streets and the temperature is below zero. The upside of a Russian winter is that if you're buying *morozhenoe* for tonight's dessert, the vendor will just wrap it in paper and it will stay deep-frozen as you walk home.

WHERE TO SHOP

Buying food in Russia was long an experience in frustration. Food shortages were rife before the coming of communism, and life in the Soviet Union meant yet more shortages, rationing, endless queues, and sometimes little at all to buy. When there was food in the *magazini* (shops) – most of which specialised in selling just one kind of produce – shoppers queued to prepay for each item. Only on presentation of a receipt would they be allowed to make their purchase.

This system has slowly died out in Russia's largest cities and towns, where there are now Western-style supermarkets. However, most Russians are still used to buying their food in neighbourhood corner shops, where people tend to buy a little fresh food every day rather than filling a trolley once a week.

One food-related institution that is alive and well in most Russian towns is the local produce market – or *rinok*. These are often impressive, cavernous halls built for the purpose, and populated with hundreds of vendors selling everything from fruit and vegetables to honey, cheese, caviar or slabs of meat. A market is also the best bet to buy the delicacy *salo* – smoked pig fat that melts wonderfully in the mouth. Wherever you are in Russia, a visit to the local *rinok* provides an insight into the country's food culture. Take along bags and small change – you can haggle if your Russian is up to it.

ABOVE RIGHT Women doing the daily food shopping at a market deli stand **ABOVE** Take tart apples coupled with a batter of eggs, flour and sugar and you have the no-fuss Russian dessert *sharlotka*

Eat your way around the
sun-kissed streets of
historic Dubrovnik

BITE-SIZE DIVERSIONS

Snowcapped spires, dark-hearted forests, baroque buildings; Eastern Europe and Russia have everything for a romantic tour including plenty of wonderful local treats and a very warm welcome.

BULGARIA
Recovering from your mountain hike with a glass of Melnik red. The ruby-coloured vintage was apparently a favourite of Winston Churchill. Sample it at the Mitko Manolev Winery in Melnik, in the foothills of the Purin Mountains in southwestern Bulgaria.

CROATIA
Feasting on fresh seafood straight from the Adriatic along the centuries-old streets of delightful Dubrovnik. Look for lightly breaded, fried squid, or *lignje*, a delectable local speciality.

CZECH REPUBLIC
Touring the oldest and most atmospheric brewpub in Prague, U Fleků (Křemencova 11), and sampling the dark rich lager that has been produced there for 500-plus years. The smooth, chocolaty lager – dark enough to be mistaken for a stout – is enhanced by the accordion music and old-world charm of the brewery.

ESTONIA
Warming up your Baltic winter with *verivorst* (blood sausage) and lingonberry jam. Traditionally served at Christmastime, the sausage is made from a batter of pig's blood and barley, then baked or fried, and served with sauerkraut or jam.

HUNGARY
Indulging in rich decadent tortes, strong coffee and lively scuttlebutt at one of Budapest's historic coffee houses, such as Gerbeaud (Vörösmarty Tér 7-8). Since 1858, Gerbeaud has been enticing visitors with its elegant interior and decadent sweets. Try the towering, triple-layered *kréme*, a quintessential Hungarian dessert of vanilla cream sandwiched between flaky puff pastry and dusted with sugar.

POLAND
Celebrating Easter with a rummy, fruit-sweetened *babka*, a yeast bread rich with eggs and butter. The spongy sweet treat is the traditional way to celebrate the end of Lent. The Polish *babka* is round with an open centre, while the Ukrainian version is tall and cylindrical. The blessing of the parish priest makes it even more delicious.

After a night of drinking and fun in Kazimierz, Kraków, heading to Plac Nowy to nosh on *zapiekanka*, a sort of baguette pizza. The idea is simple: it's half a baguette, topped with cheese, ham and mushrooms. The cheap, filling snack tastes especially delicious after midnight. Indeed, there may be no reason to eat it before midnight – and there's certainly no reason to eat it anyplace other than Plac Nowy.

RUSSIA
Though not the place to come looking for a bargain, Kuznechny Rinok in St Petersburg is one of the best-stocked markets in the country. Browse stalls weighed down with huge cheeses, wade through curtains of dangling *kolbasa* (dried sausage), breathe deep on the scent of dill and sample a dozen types of honey. Enthusiastic vendors will have you tasting everything until you can't say no to buying just a little bit of it all.

Opened in 1901, and decorated in neo-baroque style with columns and elegant chandeliers, Eliseevsky Magazin delicatessen may be Moscow's grandest food-shopping experience. It stocks a stupendous range of Russian foods: pots of caviar, cheeses, breads and pastries in countless varieties, freshly prepared Russian salads and a huge range of handmade Russian chocolate.

SLOVAKIA
Ensconcing yourself in a hidden courtyard in the Bratislava Old Town and digging into a heaping plate of *bryndzové halušky*. These gnocchi-like dumplings, topped with bacon and *bryndza* cheese, are the national dish of Slovakia.

UKRAINE
Visiting the Crimean peninsula to smoke hookahs and sample exotic Tatar dishes like dumplings and *plov*. Don't miss the 'national' dish, the *çiberek*, a deep-fried turnover stuffed with ground beef and onions. Tasty and filling, the half-moon-shaped snack is usually wrapped in a sheet of brown paper and sold from roadside stands and '*cheburechnaya*' joints around Crimea, as well as in Romania and Russia.

UNIVERSAL
Filling your tummy and comforting your soul with stuffed cabbage rolls, whether they are called *gołąbki* in Poland, *holubky* in the Czech Republic and Slovakia or *sarma* in Serbia and Croatia. These 'little pigeons' are made from ground pork and beef mixed with rice or barley, enveloped in a cabbage leaf, then baked until tender.

In the foothills of the Andes, wheat is still harvested by hand

LATIN AMERICA

Spanish and Portuguese conquistadors stamped their authority over most of Latin America, but in the indigenous cuisine they met their match. The result was one of history's greatest culinary shake-ups.

From the Maya in the north to the Inca in the south, Latin America's indigenous cuisine is succulent and delicious, delighting the taste buds of the conquering conquistadors. Small wonder then that the newly arrived colonists diplomatically adapted local traditions to adopt an all-embracing fusion food. The beef and lamb, rice, cheese, tomatoes, garlic, vinegar and wine of the Europeans mingled with the edible delights they discovered in the New World: maize (corn), root vegetables like potatoes, fiery chillies, a tantalising variety of fish and hitherto unknown fruits that the wildly differing climatic zones had fashioned into a thousand shapes, colours and tastes.

African slaves, who were typically given less-appealing cuts of meat and so concocted adventurous seasonings to make meals palatable, introduced the likes of ginger, cashews and dried smoked fish. More recent fragmented settlers like Argentina's Welsh community got in on the action by making tea and cakes a national afternoon institution.

The familiar staples of Latin American cuisine stem from maize, cultivated since ancient times. The tortilla, a cornflour dough cooked on a circular griddle, is a common base or wrap for a meal. A combo of beans and rice is so popular it has become a national dish in some countries. Chicken is Latin America's main meat, but there is also diverse seafood, and possibly the world's best selection of freshwater-fish dishes.

Latin America's topographical variation means culinary variety is often as great within countries as between them. Ask citizens of Colombia, Ecuador or Peru to name their typical dishes and they will give you three sets of answers: one for the coast, one for the mountains and one for the jungle. This means that guinea pig or turtle can liven up menus along with cooking styles like the Inca *pachamanca* method: a bake inside a heap of hot stones.

And to finish? Latin Americans have a notoriously sweet tooth, and the most distinctive flavouring is the caramel-like *dulce de leche*, gracing desserts region-wide.

SEMANA SANTA SNACKS

It's well known that no one does Easter like the Latin Americans, but the food produced for this ultimate fiesta is less talked about. This time of year traditionally kick-started Central America's ice-cream season and this, along with *raspados* (cones of flavoured shaved ice), features prominently on vendors' carts.

Fish replaces meat for most traditionalists at Lent (or at least on Good Friday), when fish soup explodes in popularity. *Torrejas* (Spanish French toast with a cinnamon-and-sugar batter) are a favourite Easter hunger-buster in El Salvador and Honduras, while Ecuadorians get helped through meat-free times with broth made from 12 different grains and beans (one per Apostle) called *fanesca*.

Antigua has Guatemala's most famed Semana Santa festivities and is the hub of its sweets industry too. These gaudily coloured delights, made with figs, nuts, honey and condensed milk, even manage to tempt eyes away from the city's one-of-a-kind procession during Easter when they decorate food stands in droves.

ιιι

PRE-COLUMBIAN FOOD
FROM CUY TO CEVICHE

Back in preconquistador days, Latin America had no cows, sheep or pigs: llama and guinea pig were South America's meaty alternatives. In Central America seafood was often relied upon, and marinated or dried for preservation. Today, *cuy* (guinea pig) and ceviche (lime-marinated fish) are two of the region's famed foods.

Indigenous cuisine relied extensively on root vegetables. Peru is the original home of the potato, and the fellow native root cassava is also commonly used in Latin American food. The maize of the Mayans and Incas still forms the bulk of the region's cuisine – from straightforward corn on the cob (smeared these days in butter, mayonnaise, cayenne, paprika or cheese) to tortillas (used to wrap everything from meat to beans) and the culturally important corn-fermented *chicha* drink. Also crucial to ancient diets were grains and pulses, still blended into stews and soups today. It's possible that the nutrition-rich grains quinoa and cañahua, only recently discovered by the outside world, were as important to the success of ancient empires as maize.

But the real power of pre-Columbian cuisine is delivered courtesy of those who make it. Food purchasing is a memorable experience: peoples like the Maya and Quechua still wear traditional dress, often speak only their own language, and cook more or less as they've cooked since the mists of time.

⚓ WHERE TO EAT INTI RAYMI, CUZCO, PERU

Inti Raymi, Cuzco's big party commemorating the Incan sun god, is the perfect introduction to pre-Columbian grub. The main celebration on 24 June unfolds at Sacsayhuamán, an Inca ruin outside Cuzco, but there's tasty food city-wide, including the distinctive ancient Andean dishes of *cuy*, llama, alpaca and food slow-cooked *pachamanca*-style, as well as abundant *chicha*. Calle Plateros, northeast of the Plaza de Armas, has particularly great eats.

ABOVE LEFT A young girl joins a procession of worshippers **ABOVE** Peruvians in colourful costumes mark Inti Raymi, or Festival of the Sun, during the winter solstice with food offerings

TAMALES
THE ARCHETYPAL TAKEAWAY

It's a safe bet that street-food junkies traversing Central or South America will inevitably sample tamales before too long. Dating back to the Mayan empire that stretched from Mexico to Honduras, this steamed maize-based delight mixed with meat or fish and served in a plantain leaf casing is among the most popular portable foods hereabouts. Variants fed Inca armies and Amazon tribespeople on river trips, and were soon gobbled up by conquistadors too. The heart of the Mayan world, Guatemala, is characterised by its tamale diversity, while fillings region-wide veer from almonds or prunes to boiled eggs.

You can make your version of tamales by pressing (rolling) a tortilla dough until papery thin (the thinner the better). Fill the small square with ingredients you have to hand, for example beef or pork with a hint of mole sauce (see p124), or simply some shredded pork that has been cooked with garlic and chilli; let your imagination run and add fruit or spices such as cumin or cinnamon. Fold like an envelope to seal and place fold-side down on a cornstalk leaf that has been soaked (and thus softened) overnight.

Wrap each leaf securely – you can tie an extra strip around the tamale for presentation purposes – and steam the parcels for 10 to 15 minutes or until the dough is cooked. Consume greedily without delay. If cornstalk leaves aren't available, an alternative is to wrap the tamales in banana leaves. Or travel to Latin America to try the real thing.

♟ WHERE TO EAT NICARAGUA

Nicaragua's pride and joy is its very own tamale, out-trumping even Mexico's versions. Nacatamales are larger than Mexican tamales and come with meat, vegetables (potato and tomato), olives and rice along with the corn *masa* (dough).

ABOVE Traditionally wrapped in cornstalk leaves, tamales are sometimes presented in banana leaves, and wrapped securely before steaming

EMPANADAS

Argentina's empanadas – small, stuffed parcels of spiced and minced meat – are the more stylish cousin of Britain's Cornish pastie. They share a similar purpose: filling food packaged for convenience on the go.

INGREDIENTS

500g/1lb lean minced beef
2 red onions
20g butter
2 eggs, hard-boiled
150g green olives, pitted
1 tin chopped tomatoes
Vegetable stock cube
2 spring onions, sliced
1 tsp paprika
1 tsp cumin
Olive oil

FOR THE DOUGH

600g/21oz plain flour
300g/11oz butter
Salt
Water

PREPARATION

Sauté the onions in the oil and butter in a large frying pan. Add the minced meat, crush the stock cube over the top and cook lightly. Pour in the chopped tomatoes, add enough to moisten the mixture without making it too liquid. As it cooks, add the spices, the olives and the chopped hard-boiled eggs. When thick, cool then refrigerate, ideally overnight.

To make the dough, sift the flour into a bowl and incorporate the butter until it forms a breadcrumb. Add the water gradually, with salt to taste, until the dough forms a ball. If it becomes too sticky, flour your hands and continue kneading. Roll it into a ball and let it chill. Roll out on a floured surface until thin (about 3mm) and using a saucer, cut into circles. Place a tablespoon of filling onto each disc and crimp them closed. Brushing with melted butter or egg yolk will glaze the top. Bake in a preheated oven at 200°C/400°F) for about 15 minutes or until golden.

CEVICHE

In this dish, the citric acid in the lime juice essentially 'cooks' the fish. Most types of fleshy white fish work well (avoid oily fish such as salmon and sardines), but freshness is paramount. Look for fish with clear, bright eyes, shiny skin, bright, red gills and a smell that reminds you of the ocean rather than fish necessarily. For a novel, but distinctly Brazilian twist, add a shot of cachaça to your lime juice marinade.

INGREDIENTS

500g /1lb firm white fish fillets, skinned and thinly sliced
8 limes, juiced, plus wedges to serve
1 red onion, sliced into rings
Handful pitted green olives, finely chopped
2–3 green chillies, finely chopped
2–3 tomatoes, seeded and chopped
Bunch of coriander, roughly chopped
2 tbsp extra-virgin olive oil
Pinch caster sugar

PREPARATION

In a large glass bowl, combine the fish, lime juice and onion. The juice should completely cover the fish; if it doesn't, add a little more. Cover with cling film and place in the fridge for 90 minutes.

Remove the fish and onion from the lime juice (discard the juice) and place in a bowl. Add the olives, chillies, tomatoes, coriander and olive oil, stir gently, then season with a good pinch of salt and sugar. This can be made a couple of hours in advance and stored in the fridge. Serve with tortilla chips to scoop up the ceviche and enjoy with a glass of cold beer.

CACHACA

Also called pinga or aguardente, cachaça is a high-proof sugarcane alcohol produced and drunk throughout Brazil. It can be cheaper than water (literally) or as dear as whisky, and yes, price definitely signals a difference in taste and effect (and aftereffect!).

CEVICHE
'COOKED' RAW FISH

There's no better example of fusion cuisine from Guatemala to Chile than this marinated fish dish: raw fish 'cooked' in a lime marinade with red onion, garlic and chilli flakes, and served alongside sweet potato and clumps of corn on the cob.

Ceviche's popularity has spread all along Latin America's Pacific coast, but Peru, with a national holiday in honour of the fishy dish, is usually deemed its birthplace. Marinades were used by the Inca, but with maize-based *chicha* rather than lime, which was introduced by the Spanish. Corvina, the fish of choice used, has been consumed across the region for millennia, but it was a Japanese chef, Dario Matsufuji, who pioneered a new recipe in the 1970s that reduced marinating time from hours to minutes and did wonders for boosting the cooking technique's popularity. Origins of ceviche are a hot topic. Did it derive from the Quechua word for the dish, *siwichi* or from the Spanish *escabeche* (a fish or meat dish with an acidic marinade)? Or could Arabic peoples have had a hand in its origins, seeing as *sakbāj* in Arabic means 'meat cooked in vinegar'?

But it's the way the fish absorbs the flavours of the other ingredients to produce an assault on the eyes as well as the taste buds that makes it so special. Take Peruvian ceviche: crisp red onion and the country's distinctive, flavoursome yellow-red chilli, *aji limo*, adding to the zing of the lime to counteract the soft, juicy sensation of the corvina as it breaks apart inside your mouth.

🍽 WHERE TO EAT

The ceviche family is extended indeed. Ecuadorians prefer a tomato-heavy version while Panamanians eat ceviche in a pastry shell. Replacements for the corvina could be freshwater dorade in the Amazon and shrimp or lobster among Central Americans. Perhaps most distinctive of all, folk in El Salvador use black clams.

ABOVE Ceviche's colours are as vibrant as its flavours
RIGHT The fresher the better: buy your fish straight from the dockside

STEAK
THE BIG GRILL

Few would dispute it: the world's best beef heralds from Latin America's far south. Brazil might be the number-one exporter, but it's Argentina's beef, grass-fed on the country's vast pampas and Patagonian wilderness, that has the most succulent reputation. There's even a national institute ensuring beef's top-quality standards are maintained. And Argentines enjoy beef; they're superseded in per-capita consumption by neighbouring Uruguay alone.

Of course, you don't have to grill a steak barbecue-style in South America, but an *asado* is the classic excuse for a get-together, popularised by the continent's prime cattle-rearing country in Argentina and Uruguay. *Asado* might be Patagonian tenderloin, or perhaps *anticuchos*, skewered, grilled meat popularised in Peru. Take advantage of tasting *chimichurri* sauce with your steak, an ancient Andean-Spanish blend of parsley, garlic and vinegar with chilli and oregano combining into the region's signature seasoning. Or serve with an all-purpose salsa. In Brazil, grill-ups are called *churrascos*, with saltwater-basted beef, seasoned chicken, lamb or fish and chorizo-like *linguiça* cooked on skewers. Here, the barbecue, or *churrasqueira*, often lacks the usual griddle and just has skewer slots.

♦ **WHERE TO EAT ESTANCIA HUECHAHUE, AP. ESP. 12, JUNIN DE LOS ANDES, NEUQUÉN, ARGENTINA**
This 600-sq-km working *estancia*, which rears its own Hereford cattle, offers guests lodging here exceptionally meaty dinners, where the beef, cured pork and wild boar all come from its gorgeous estate. It rustles up frequent *asados*.

LEFT Home on the range: Argentinian gauchos herd Hereford cattle on an *estancia*
ABOVE Only a man-sized barbecue will do when this much meat is on the menu

SALSA!
Steak in Latin America excels without exotic flavourings. At most, it's rubbed with pepper and salt. But it is often accompanied by salsa criolla or chimichurri. This salsa criolla recipe zings with raw onion and lime brings a fresh edge to a charred and juicy steak. The salsa can be served with a wide variety of meat dishes.

INGREDIENTS
3 large tomatoes (deseeded)
1 large red onion
1 green or yellow chilli
3 tsp fresh flat-leaf parsley
1 tsp red wine vinegar
1 tsp lime juice
Olive oil

PREPARATION
Peel, halve and then finely slice the red onion so the strips are curved. Peel, halve, deseed and slice the tomatoes. Finely slice the chilli and the parsley.

Mix these ingredients in a large bowl. Add the red wine vinegar, the lime juice and a splash of olive oil, stir and leave to marinate in the fridge before the steak is cooked.

CHIMICHURRI
Garlicky *chimichurri* is the standard sauce for steaks in Argentina.

INGREDIENTS
1 bunch of flat-leaf parsley
Sprigs of oregano
6 garlic cloves
Dried red chilli flakes
125ml/4fl oz olive oil
Red wine vinegar

PREPARATION
Finely chop the garlic cloves. If using a food processor, add the parsley and oregano leaves and give a quick pulse so they're not chopped too smoothly. Otherwise, chop the leaves and add to the garlic with the olive oil, a splash of red wine vinegar, a pinch of dried red chilli flakes to taste and seasoning. Mix and serve at once with steak.

A PISCO PRIMER

It is Peru's national beverage: pisco, the omnipresent grape brandy served at events from the insignificant to the momentous. Production dates back to the early days of the Spanish colony in Ica, where it was distilled on private haciendas and sold to sailors making their way through the port of Pisco. In its early years, pisco was the local firewater: a great way to wake up the following morning feeling as if you had been hammered over the head.

By the early 20th century, the pisco sour (pisco with lime juice and sugar) arrived on the scene, and with the assistance of a few skilled bartenders at the Gran Hotel Bolívar and the Hotel Maury in Lima it became the national drink.

In recent decades, production of pisco has become increasingly sophisticated. The result is excellent piscos that are nuanced and flavourful (without the morning-after effects). The three principal types of Peruvian pisco are Quebranta, Italia and *acholado*. Quebranta (a pure-smelling pisco) and Italia (slightly aromatic) are each named for the varieties of grape from which they are crafted, while *acholado* is a blend that has more of an alcohol top-note (best for mixed drinks). There are also many small-batch specialty piscos made from grape must (pressed juice with skins), known as *mosto verde* or *mosto yema*. These have a fragrant smell and are best sipped straight.

The most common brands include Tres Generaciones, Ocucaje, Ferreyros and La Botija, while Viñas de Oro, Viejo Tonel, Estirpe Peruano, LaBlanco and Gran Cruz are among the finest. Any pisco purchased in a bottle that resembles the head of an Inca will make for an unusual piece of home decor – and not much else.

⁂

CHICHA
EXPECT THE UNEXPECTED

If there was a liquid equivalent of the enigma that is Latin America, *chicha* would most certainly be it. Even when you think you know what chicha is, you'll have no idea what to expect when you're offered it. The region's most diverse drink, *chicha* has a place at the heart of Latin American culture. Across the continent, chicha was used for rituals and food preservation. It can be served as a child's chilled fruit drink or as part of an alcoholic debauch at fiestas. It varies from a purplish colour in Peru to having a sharp apple tang in Chile. Typical *chicha* is corn-fermented but Amazonians use cassava as the base and in Venezuela the drink is made with rice. A range of fruit from pineapple to grapes gets used as flavourings, and favoured do-it-yourself traditional methods mean that whatever *chicha* experience you have, it's unlikely to be conventional (the *chicha* maker's saliva is sometimes the source of enzymes to kick off the ferment). You'll find *chicha* drunk more in unofficial back rooms than bars; commonly at festivals but rarely in supermarkets.

According to recent studies by Lima's San Marcos University, some *chicha* has curative powers. The purple corn in Peruvian *chicha morada* can supposedly reduce blood pressure and act as an anti-inflammatory: no wonder the Incas, who invented the drink, lasted so long. Want to make it yourself? *Chicha morada* is not fermented and can be boiled with spices and flavourings such as pineapple juice to make a fruity punch without an alcoholic kick.

ABOVE A squeeze of lime adds extra zing to the purple maize in your glass of do-it-yourself *chicha morada*

⟨⟨⟨
STEWS
LATIN AMERICA'S COMFORT FOOD

It's not easy to explain the popularity of stews in a corner of the world that's usually so sweltering, people often ice their wine and take several hours off in the midday heat. There are chilly high altitudes a-plenty, but stew hot spots aren't specific to cold climes. It's possible that, as elsewhere, the stew was a poor man's dish. Meat would need to go further, particularly in traditionally impoverished mountain areas, and stews could easily disguise less-desirable cuts.

Mayan *Kak'ik*, a tempting turkey soup-broth, is one of Guatemala's incredible number of stews. Look for vats of the stuff bubbling away in marketplaces. Then again, there's no better way to break an Andean bus journey than with a steaming platter of *lomo saltado*: strips of beef served with red onion and potato, arranged around a cake of rice.

Thin stews are often known as *caldos*; thicker stews are called *recados*. Either way, they'll go down a treat.

🍲 **WHERE TO EAT LA COCINA DEL OBISBO**
27 CALLE 3A OTE, SAN JUAN DEL OBISPO, GUATEMALA
Enjoy a phenomenal selection of the afore-mentioned stews, set in a tranquil plant-filled garden, in this little village near Antigua. It's only open at weekends.

ABOVE Cooking up a pot of *caldos* **TOP RIGHT** Peru's national dish, *lomo saltado*, traditionally seasoned with a sprinkle of yellow chilli *aji amarillo*

LOMO SALTADO
Fittingly for the country that was the source of the humble tuber, potato fries are an essential part of Peru's national dish of lomo saltado. If you can't find the Peruvian yellow chilli *aji amarillo*, use a large, mild red chilli.

INGREDIENTS
3 large tomatoes (deseeded)
1 large red onion (or 2 medium)
3 garlic cloves
3 large potatoes (waxy)
500g/1lb sirloin steak
200g/7oz rice
1 yellow chilli (aji amarillo)
Cumin
Oregano
Soy sauce
Red wine or red wine vinegar
Vegetable oil

PREPARATION
Peel, chip into 1cm/½in wide lengths and fry the potatoes. Finely chop the chilli and garlic. Peel and slice the onion and tomatoes.

Rinse the rice and put into a saucepan of boiling water with a third of the garlic. While it is cooking, cut the steak into strips of 5cm/2in and fry in some vegetable oil. Remove while still tender.

Add the garlic, chilli, onion and tomato to the pan and cook until golden. When done, return the steak strips to the pan, add a sprinkle of cumin and oregano and a generous splash of red wine and soy sauce.

Season to taste and remove from the heat before overcooked. Serve with the rice and a side of fries. Serves 4.

Celebrating the good life
and the body beautiful on
Ipanema Beach

BITE-SIZE DIVERSIONS

Fish cooked in lime juice, the planet's best chocolate, strange fruit from the world's most biodiverse forests...here are Latin America's most sense-enriching foodie experiences.

HONDURAS
Savouring Central America's best seafood on the idyllic Bay Islands, where their unique Caribbean influence contributes something special to delicacies like conch chowder (conches being sea snails).

EL SALVADOR
Chowing down at a *pupusería*, a Salvadoran eatery that specialises in the country's eclectic cheesy, doughy snack, the *pupusa*: a maize flour disc-shaped tortilla packed with cheese, *frijoles* (refried beans) and *chicharrón* (fried pork).

COSTA RICA
Slurping up one of the world's greatest caffeine fixes in the region that makes half of the planet's coffee, and staying a while on to enjoy the local produce on a shaded coffee plantation in Finca Rosa Blanca, near Heredia.

ECUADOR
Touring a cacao plantation in the country producing the highest percentage of top-quality chocolate, or indulging at an affiliated chocolate shop like Quito's Kallari Café.

AMAZON REGION
Immersing yourself in the vivid furore of an Amazon market, where you can browse among ingredients that include everything from diverse rainforest fruits and berries to weird-and-wonderful freshwater fish.

PERU
Partying in one of the region's most cuisine-rich cities at Lima's massive food festival, Mistura, which happens each year in September. Among the delicacies on offer here you might find *cuy* (guinea pig), ceviche (citrus-marinated fish) or *juane* (steamed rice with fish or meat trussed up in a jungle vine).

BOLIVIA
Acclimatising to mountainous Bolivia with (legal) Andean coca leaf tea – a mild stimulant (similar to tea or coffee) said to help prevent altitude sickness – that will leave you feeling sky-high.

ARGENTINA
Sampling the heated debates, wicked coffee and effortless class of San Telmo, the traditional cafe district of Buenos Aires. Sit and linger until teatime: a custom introduced by the British, which is celebrated with cakes concocted with *dulce de leche* (caramel-like sweetened milk).

BRAZIL
Freshening up with juice from a Rio juice bar, often concocted with rare jungle fruits and packed with guarana, an energy-boosting bean with twice the caffeine levels of coffee.

CHILE
Partaking of this leading Latin American wine-growing region with a vineyard tour and a glass of rich Maipo Valley cabernet sauvignon in pastoral Valle Central.

ζζζ
COFFEE

Most of us need a jolt of caffeine to get things firing. Wherever you find yourself waking up, here the rules for ordering the perfect coffee.

VIETNAM

Take a seat – a plush chair in Hanoi's Metropole bar; a pavement stool, anywhere – and order a *cà phê*. Now wait. Some paraphernalia will eventually arrive: a tiny glass (containing a splash of sweet condensed milk) with a curious aluminium pot on top. Slowly – drop by oil-slick drop – the java falls... The French did a good thing, introducing coffee to Indochina in the 1800s; the invention of condensed milk sealed the deal – a dairy product that could survive the tropics! A match made in hydration heaven.

THE RULES

* Don't bother ordering coffee strong (*manh*) – it just comes that way. You can try ordering it weak (*nhe*), but it'll get you bouncing anyway.
* Foreigners get a thermos of hot water with which to dilute the brew – but it's better enjoyed the unadulterated Vietnamese way.
* Take slow, tiny sips. Let the flavour resonate on your tongue. Feel alive.

TURKEY

The Ottomans liked a brew to accompany their Turkish delight; Istanbul's first coffeehouse opened in 1640. Now, as then, it all starts with a copper pot, the *cezve*, in which the super-fine beans simmer. The smell is divine. Sugar is added (unless you ask not), and the thick, dark liquid is poured into a glass, but only experts can deliver the perfect foam head on top.

THE RULES

* Order according to your sweet tooth: *az şekerli* (a little sugar); *orta şekerli* (some sugar); *çok şekerli* (lots); *şekersiz/sade* (none).
* In eastern Turkey, try *mırra* – 'old-fashioned coffee', flavoured with cardamom.
* Don't drink the sludge left at the bottom of your glass – it tastes bad, and can be used for fortune-telling.

ETHIOPIA

Caffeine addicts: welcome to the Motherland. Ethiopia is the birthplace of buna (we thank an ancient goatherder for the tree's discovery). Fresh black, cappuccino and latte-style brews are served countrywide (we thank occupying Italians for injecting style). An Ethiopian coffee ceremony is the best way to drink it, a slow-burning ritual in which you accept three, progressively weaker cups, culminating in the *berekha* – or 'blessing'.

THE RULES

* Pick your poison: *beu/ya leu skwar* (with/without sugar); *beu/ya leu weu teut* (with/without milk).
* Know the accompaniments: coffee might come with butter or herbs rather than milk and sugar.
* When offered coffee at a ceremony, nod your head in appreciation.

INDONESIA

That's right: the man wants you to pay top dollar for coffee that's been pooped by a cat. *Kopi luwak* has been the world's most prized brew since the 18th century, in spite of its production process. It's made from beans that have passed through the digestive tract of the palm civet; the animal's enzymes reputedly make the beans smoother and less bitter. Which you can test, if brave/rich enough to try it.

THE RULES

* *Kopi luwak* is the world's most expensive blend: if you see it sold cheap, it's likely fake.
* *Kopi luwak* is produced mainly on Sumatra, Java, Bali and Sulawesi, as well as the Philippines and East Timor.
* Don't fancy it? Try local specialities *kopi telur* (raw egg and sugar, topped with coffee) or *kopi jahe* (coffee with ginger) instead.

ITALY

You want *caffè* Italian-style? Then stand up, people! This is no time to dither. You hit the bar, you order, you drink (no sipping!), you go. This is fast fuelling – but done oh-so-well, and in so many ways. In truth, you can sit and savour if you like, just expect to pay more for the privilege.

THE RULES

- Don't order espresso – the short shot is called *caffè* here, served with a tawny crema on top.
- As well as the familiar options, look for *ristretto* (very short black), *doppio* (long, strong, black) and *corretto* (with a dash of liqueur).
- It's bad form to order coffee with milk after a meal – Italians reckon it monkeys with digestion.

AUSTRALIA

If it weren't for the postwar wave of Italian migration, Australians might still be making coffee with bottled essence. Nowadays, no city cafe would survive without its espresso machine and well-trained staff. Invented Down Under, most beloved is the flat white: coffee mixed with microfoam (non-frothy steamed milk).

THE RULES

- Be picky if you like: Aussie baristas are used to orders for skinny-soy-decaf-lattes. You want choc sprinkles with that?
- The flat white is a point of pride. What to say: 'Bonza brew, mate!'. What not to say: 'Didn't the Kiwis invent this?'
- If ordering coffee in the dust-blown outback, don't ask for cappuccino. They might spit in your instant.

USA

Pike Place Market, Seattle, 1971: ground zero of US coffee culture. This is where the first Starbucks opened its doors – and the hot-beverage-service world changed forever. It's a complicated world now, too. The coffee shop giant reckons there are 87,000 ways of ordering one of its frappuccinos. Don't know what a frappuccino is? Boy are you in trouble...

THE RULES

- A frappuccino is coffee blended with ice and whatever else you fancy: milks, syrups, creams, sprinkles...
- Other handy vocab: no fun (decaf), double no fun (double decaf), speed ball (regular coffee with shots of espresso).
- Consider your waistline: grande sizes and sweet extras can turn your caffeine fix into an obesity problem. A Starbucks venti dark berry mocha frappuccino (!) contains more than 500 calories.

MIDDLE EAST

Middle Eastern cooking blends a bounty of East-meets-West flavours to create a distinctive cornucopia of dishes all its own, which play a pivotal role in age-old hospitality rituals and traditions.

The best known Middle Eastern food is Levantine, drawn from the region's heartland of Syria, Lebanon, Jordan, and Israel and the Palestinian Territories. The delicate weaving of culinary influences takes its inspiration in part from the rich tapestry of trade routes that criss-crossed the deserts and mountains of this region, stretching out to India, ancient Persia and the many cultures that once made up the grand Ottoman Empire. The most common dishes – those ubiquitous kebabs and mezze spreads – are eaten throughout the region in one form or another.

Middle Eastern cuisine is also heavily influenced by its own nomadic desert roots and ancient history. The origins of some of the most beloved regional specialities are said to have their origins as far back as Pharaonic Egypt, while Bedouin dishes are still commonly eaten at celebrations and large gatherings across the Gulf countries, Jordan and Egypt's Sinai.

Throughout the region, the simple act of sitting down to share a meal is a crucial element in the continuation of culture. Take, for instance, the practice of *Iftar* (the sunset meal) in the Muslim month of Ramadan, the ceremonial Seder meal on the first night of the Jewish Passover, and the vast picnics held on Sham el-Nessim (Egypt's springtime holiday) to celebrate the first Monday after the Coptic Christian Easter. And no matter the religion or nationality, all will have a family recipe for *warak enab* (stuffed vine leaves) and will slow-cook their eggplants in the same way, to achieve the smoked and creamy perfection of *baba ghanoush*.

In a part of the world that's often riddled with conflict, where the three monotheistic religions have their roots, it is food that binds the region together.

LEBANON'S WINE TRAIL

Lebanon's arrival on the wine world stage may have only just begun, but winemaking has a long tradition here. Viticulture was first practised by the Phoenicians and exported by them to ancient Carthage. All of the following wineries have guided tours for visitors:

KSARA

The granddaddy of Lebanon's modern winemakers; Ksara's vineyards were founded by a mission of Jesuit brothers in 1857. The cellars, a series of subterranean Roman-era caves first discovered by the Jesuits in 1898, are a highlight of any visit here.

MASSAYA

Massaya may be a young winery but it's probably the best known abroad, as its wines have found acclaim internationally. Come on Sundays for the brunch, where you can indulge in the best of Lebanese mezze while sampling their award-winning tipples.

KEFRAYA

Kefraya has the most in-depth wine tour, making it a must for anyone interested in the ins and outs of Middle Eastern winemaking.

MEZZE
MORE THAN A STARTER

Artistically arranged with a flourish of parsley or swirl of olive oil and spice, the mezze's host of hot and cold morsels, dips and salads are the cultural dynamo of Middle Eastern dining. A mezze is not meant to be eaten alone, nor should it be scoffed in a hurry. It is a carnival of flavours and textures to be savoured, passed around and leisurely meandered over. With the table groaning under the weight of a succession of tiny plates, brought out in stages of five or so dishes at a time, a mezze spread provides the backbone to a long evening of socialising.

The pinnacle of Middle Eastern feasting, the mezze has survived as a menu tradition in nearly all of the nations that once formed the vast Ottoman Empire. But it is in the countries that make up the old Levant that mezze holds the highest pedigree. Here, a mezze is presented as something of a culinary art form, bursting with the rich colours of fresh ingredients and brimming with all the tantalising flavours of the East.

And what can you expect at a Middle Eastern mezze? Plenty. To start, bowls of tart olives sit alongside simple peasant salads of ruby-red tomatoes and crispy cucumber. There's *tabouleh*, the heavy-on-the-parsley Lebanese bulgur salad, and *fattoush*, the Syrian salad with a minty zing and the satisfying crunch of fried pita-bread wedges. A medley of dips are scooped up straight from communal bowls with fresh-from-the-oven flatbread – nutty-flavoured hummus sprinkled with pine nuts, and the pungent smoked taste of eggplant in the *baba ghanoush*. And Seinfeld's George Costanza needn't be worried: there are no rules against double-dipping here!

Then more substantial dishes arrive, though all still delicate in their arrangement. There are *makdous*, piquant eggplants filled with walnuts and garlic, and soaked in oil. Tiny bowls of stewed okra, or *bamia*, and green beans known as *fasulye*. Platters are laden with bite-sized *felafel* balls and *fatayer* pastries jam-packed with cheese and spinach. Delicate fingers of vine leaves known as *warak enab* are stuffed with rice. The mezze favourite of *kibbeh,* minced meatballs wrapped in bulgur, will nearly always be invited to the table – deep-fried, they're deceptively light with a subtle aftertaste of spice.

And then there are the seasonal delicacies for the braver eaters; *asafeer*, tiny birds drenched in tart lemon, velvety fried brains and fried liver.

🍽 WHERE TO EAT ZAHLE, LEBANON

Every evening during the balmy summer months, the strip of restaurants strung along the trickling Berdaouni River in the Lebanese town of Zahle is packed full of diners, drawn here by the famous mezze spreads. This is the place to sample the full caboodle of dishes available and to do it the way the Lebanese do, so grab a group of friends, order a groaning weight of plates and stagger your mealtime to last maybe three or four hours as families socialise around you.

ιι

MOLOKHEYA
MIDDLE EASTERN SOUL FOOD

Molokheya has a history that reaches back to the Pharaonic era, but its modern name – which stems from the Arabic word for 'royal' – is said to have been gained due to the Fatimid Caliph Al-Hakim's great love for the dish. He was so obsessed with it that he supposedly banned Egypt's *fellaheen* (peasants) from eating it, reserving the dish for royal consumption only.

Al-Hakim would have no luck trying to ban his subjects from enjoying the soup today. This glutinous stew of mallow leaves is now a favourite dish across the Middle East, and the home cook who can make a good *molokheya* is admired by all. *Molokheya* cooks will tell you the secret boils down to a certain well-timed gasp. Just after adding the *taqleya* (a combination of coriander, garlic and butter), while the pot of mallow leaves is slowly simmering on the stove, the cook will pause for a moment to sharply inhale. It's this act, they'll assure you, that will transfer the cook's soul into the food. Without it, the molokheya will be a failure.

Spiked with a heady punch of garlic, your first spoonful of *molokheya* is always a sensation. Its viscid character and earthy taste have a surprising depth that seem to summon the homespun flavours of an earlier age. This is hearty, peasant-style fodder – just make sure the cook hasn't forgotten to gasp.

♧ WHERE TO EAT ABOU EL-SID
SHARIA 26TH OF JULY, ZAMALEK, CAIRO, EGYPT
You'll sample a feast fit for a pasha at Egypt's premier spot for stylish Egyptian dining. Tuck into your *molokheya* amid hanging lamps, low tables and scattered cushions, and find out why everyone adores this farm-style dish.

ABOVE Sample traditional Middle Eastern dishes such as *molokheya* at Khan El Khalili souk, in Cairo, Egypt
TOP LEFT A little bit of Bordeaux in Lebanon: the stone cellar of Chateau Musar in Ghazir, Mount Lebanon

MOLOKHEYA
Molokheya leaves are available fresh, frozen or dried in specialist Middle Eastern stores.

INGREDIENTS
1 rabbit
8 garlic cloves
750g/126oz fresh/frozen *molokheya* leaves or dried equivalent
1 tsp ground coriander
50g/12oz plain flour
2 lemons
1 large onion, halved
3 tbsp ghee or butter
2 bay leaves

PREPARATION
Wash and prepare the rabbit by removing any organs (or have your butcher do this). Joint the rabbit into five pieces, roll them in flour and place in a large bowl. Mix 1 tbsp of crushed garlic, the juice of one lemon, and salt and rub this marinade into the floured rabbit. Leave for at least one hour.

Melt 2 tbsp of ghee (or butter) in a large frying pan, add the rabbit and brown the meat. When browned, put the rabbit in a large saucepan of boiling water, with bay leaves, salt and the onion.

Cook for 30 minutes until the meat is tender. Then remove the rabbit, saving the water. Heat more ghee or butter in the frying pan, add salt, pepper and garlic and fry the rabbit until the skin is crisp and golden.

Bring five cups of the stock back to the boil and add the *molokheya* leaves. Simmer for 10 minutes. Add more water if the mixture becomes too thick.

As the *molokheya* cooks, heat the remaining ghee (or butter) in a small saucepan, add the remaining garlic (approximately half), the coriander and stir until golden. Add this garlic sauce to the *molokheya*. Taste, season and cover the mixture for a minute or two. Serve the rabbit separately or with the *molokheya* in a bowl.

۶۶
MANSAF
THE BEDOUIN INFLUENCE

Mansaf is a Bedouin speciality, and Jordan's national dish, anchored in the nomadic traditions of Arabia. The slow-cooked meal of gently spiced lamb is boiled in a sauce of *jameed* (fermented dried goat's milk yoghurt). Once cooked, the meat is laid over a layer of flatbread and rice, the yoghurt sauce is ladled on top, and almonds and pine nuts are sprinkled to provide a nutty crunch.

To the uninitiated *mansaf*-eater, your first sight of this dish can be unappealing. The overriding shade of beige isn't particularly inviting, and the peculiarly sharp and distinctively robust aroma of *jameed* is also a little off-putting. But go with it, for this is a meal to be eaten the old-fashioned way, presented on a communal tray. Sit yourself down on the surrounding floor cushions and using your right hand, scoop from the overflowing bowl.

The yoghurt sauce suffuses the meat with a strange but enticingly tart flavour, while the meat itself is so tender it falls straight from the bone. The rice and bread, oozing with sauce, have a slightly sticky-soggy texture, aiding you to eat the mixture more easily with your hands.

This is comfort food the Bedouin way, the sort of meal that sticks to your sides as your hosts ply you with more until you lean back on your cushion in defeat.

🍲 WHERE TO EAT
Although traditionally eaten at large family celebrations, *mansaf*'s status as a culinary cultural icon in Jordan means that it is now on menus across the country. For a real-deal Bedouin feast, head out into the desert, to TE Lawrence's fabled Wadi Rum, and eat *mansaf* at night with your Bedouin hosts in a traditional *beit shar* (house of hair) tent.

ABOVE Palestinian Bedouins prepare *mansaf* near the city of Hebron
LEFT Flat breads such as *lavosh* are constant companions for the Middle East food explorer

FLATBREADS
Middle Eastern flatbreads are among the world's oldest forms of bread, their origins stretching back to antiquity in this region where wheat was first cultivated. During Egypt's Pharaonic era, the builders of the pyramids of Giza were even paid partly in bread. Today, *khobz* (bread), in one form or another, is rarely missing from a Middle Eastern table.

In Egypt, where bread is so important that it's known as '*aish*' (the Arabic word for 'life'), the most common flatbread is *aish merahrah*. Shaped into discs, these pita-style loaves have a rustic texture in Cairo, where bread deliverers do their daily circus act on the crowded streets. Weaving through the traffic on their bicycles, they balance a wooden tray stacked precariously high with loaves on their heads. Eat your *aish* hot for an Egyptian breakfast with *torshi* (pickles) and *fuul* (mashed fava beans).

In the nations of the old Levant, a wafer-thin flatbread is the traditional bread of choice. It's known as *shrak* in Jordan and *markook* in Syria, Lebanon, Israel and the Palestinian Territories. Cooked on a *saj*, a hot iron griddle, the dough is flipped over so that it bubbles evenly. Sniff out the aroma of slowly roasting meat in the alleyways of Aleppo's old city souk to eat yours as the wrapping for a hearty lunchtime *shwarma* (meat carved from a vertical spit).

Abud is the desert nomad's age-old flatbread, still cooked by Bedouin herdsmen. It's made by mixing flour and water, then burying the dough beneath the embers of a fire to cook. Break off a chunk to sample the densely heavy loaf around the fire on a silent Sinai night, then fall asleep under a blanket of stars.

UMM ALI
Make this celebrated dessert – an Arabic bread pudding – with everyday ingredients.

INGREDIENTS
1 packet filo pastry
30g/1oz butter
50g/2oz sugar
2 cups single cream
2 tbsp coconut flakes
3 tbsp ground hazlenuts
3 tbsp ground almonds
3 tbsp sultanas

PREPARATION
Preheat oven to 200°C/400°F and bake pastry in a generously buttered baking dish until it is flaky.

Remove from oven and layer flakes of pastry in the dish, sprinkling the nuts, sugar, coconut flakes and sultanas between each layer until the ingredients are used up.

You can add or subtract sugar and nuts according to taste.

Pour the cream over the flaked pastry and return the dish to the oven (same temperature), until the top is golden, which should take no more than 15 minutes. Serve hot.

LEARN TO COOK THE MIDDLE EASTERN WAY
BEIT SITTI

Beit Sitti cooking school dishes up a unique cultural cooking experience, allowing participants to delve into the secrets of traditional Middle Eastern food. Come here for brunch to learn how to make Jordan's favourite breakfast fuel, *maneesh zaatar*, or dive into a three-course lunch or dinner lesson featuring the best of Jordanian cooking.

16 Sharia Mohammed Ali Al Sa'di, Jebel Weibdeh, Amman, Jordan

UMM ALI
THE REGAL DESSERT

One of the Middle East's most scrumptious desserts is a decadent bread pudding. Its intriguing origins are linked to the bloodthirsty tale of revenge and power centred on the life and death of Egypt's last female ruler, Shajar al-Durr, at the end of Ayyubid rule.

According to the old story, the pudding made its first appearance on the culinary scene after Shajar was battered to death (using hammam slippers!) by al-Mansur Ali and his mother Umm Ali so that he could take the sultan's throne. Supposedly, Umm Ali then created this dessert to celebrate Shajar's death.

Although the legend of Umm Ali's creation may well be apocryphal, this sweet treat's taste is lavish enough to celebrate a royal battering. Your first spoonful is a wildly luscious mix of velvety cream, coconut, sultanas and cinnamon, infused with the crunchy aftertaste of liberal sprinklings of almonds and pistachios. Dig a little deeper into the bowl and you'll find layers of filo pastry, sumptuously softened by being steeped in milk.

This is an indulgently sinful dessert that pulls out all the stops. Even better, these days you don't need to whack someone over the head with a hammam slipper to make it.

🍽 WHERE TO EAT EL-MALKY
19 SHARIA GAMIAT AD-DOWAL AL-ARABIYYA, MOHANDISEEN, CAIRO, EGYPT

Since 1917, this specialist dessert-restaurant has been dishing out calorific, sugar-laden treats to the Cairo crowd – you certainly wouldn't want to bump into your dentist here. El-Malky's Umm Ali pudding is renowned to be as authentic as it can get, and its added richness is due to the chefs' adherence to only using buffalo milk.

ABOVE The Todra Gorge, Southern Morocco, where almonds for Umm Ali are harvested in spring
RIGHT The traditional drink *karkade*, made from dried hibiscus flowers

A Bedouin family enjoys a
break in the Wahiba desert

‹‹‹

BITE-SIZE DIVERSIONS

Middle Eastern hospitality is famous for good reason – you'll never lack for a snack or a drink in your hand.

BAKDACH ICE CREAM PARLOUR
Souq al-Hamidiyya, Old City, Damascus, Syria
Come here to sample *booza* (pounded ice cream), made from *sahlab* (orchid root) and *mastic* (resin from the mastic tree).

SOFRA
Sharia Mohammed Farid, Luxor, Egypt
Set in an old house festooned with antique chandeliers and oriental furniture, Sofra dishes up a menu of traditional Egyptian favourites.

MOUNIR
Off Broummana Main Road, Broummana, Lebanon
This massive restaurant in the hills above Beirut is renowned for its Levantine cuisine of mezze and kebabs. In summer, when the tables spill outside, it's a wonderful spot for leisurely lunching.

ST GEORGE WINE TOURS
Jordan
The Zumot family first started out as vintners in 1954 and have since gone on to produce Jordan's award-winning St George–label wines. Wine tours of their Sama vineyard, in the north of the country, can be booked through their website.

SOUK EL-TAYAB FARMER'S MARKET
Trablos St, Beirut Souks, Beirut, Lebanon
Focused on supporting small-scale, organic producers across Lebanon, this weekly market is a great opportunity for visitors to pick up spice mixtures, preserves and other foodie treats. It's held every Saturday from 9am to 2pm.

HASHEM
Al-Amir Mohammed St, Amman, Jordan
It may be a modest restaurant of scruffy tables that sprawl across an alleyway, but everyone who's anyone in Jordan (including the king himself) has eaten hummus here.

ABOU RAMY
Opposite Sidon Sea Castle, Corniche, Sidon, Lebanon
Is this the perfect felafel sandwich? The jury's out but we rate the delectable combination of chickpea goodness, crunchy salad and divinely tangy tahina sauce, all wrapped up in super-fresh bread, from this hole-in-the-wall shop.

MAHANE YEHUDA MARKET
Off Agripas St, Jerusalem, Israel
Known locally as 'the Shuk', this is a sprawling Neverland of fresh produce, artisan bakeries, cheese-makers, fine wine sellers and sweet-makers. Fossick amid its winding alleyways, all named after fruit and nuts, for gourmet delights and then put your feet up at one of the many surrounding chi-chi cafes and restaurants.

ABDUL RAHMAN HALLAB & SONS
Rue Tall, Tripoli, Lebanon
One for the sweet-tooths. This bakery has been pumping out the finest in Arabic pastry concoctions since 1881.

TAYBEH OKTOBERFEST
Taybeh, Ramallah, Palestine.
The Middle East's first microbrewery, based in Taybeh in the Palestinian Territories, celebrates its beer making (along with music and dishes to feast on) over two days every October.

JEWISH DISHES

Jewish cuisine is the original fusion fare, influenced by geography, symbolism and culture. Traditions vary from country to country, reflecting the local food and customs of the lands in which Jews have lived over the centuries – from Egypt to Spain, Poland and beyond. The only common element, of course, is that it must be Kosher, abiding by Jewish dietary laws (Kashrut), Sabbath laws (Shabbat) and festival rituals. Denise Phillips leads the way.

CHALLAH

Challah is the traditional plaited bread served on a Friday night and at other festivals. The dough is enriched with egg and sugar to form a soft sweet loaf, and blessed after kneading. Two loaves are blessed at the start of Shabbat and enjoyed with the Friday-night family dinner. At Rosh Hashanah (Jewish New Year), the *challah* is formed into a round to symbolise the circle of life, and is eaten dipped in honey to remember the sweetness of life.

CHICKEN SOUP WITH MATZA BALLS

The number one favourite in Jewish households, this nurturing soup is known as the Jewish penicillin. Made from the carcass of a chicken and an abundance of fresh vegetables including onions, leeks, carrots, parsnips, turnips and swedes, the soup is simmered for about three hours. An Ashkenazi (Eastern European) recipe, it is the traditional dish served on a Friday night or at festivals with *knaidlach* (matza balls) and *lokshen* (vermicelli). Every Jewish mother has her own twist, and Friday night just wouldn't be the same without it.

CHOLENT & HAMEEN

The best-known Shabbat dishes, these one-pot hot meals consist of various meats, grains, beans, eggs and vegetables, all cooked together in a very slow oven. The cooking process starts on the Friday on a very low heat, continues overnight and is served after the synagogue service for Shabbat lunch, along with potato *kugel*. The dish for Sephardic Jews is called *hameen* and includes plenty of spices – cinnamon, turmeric, ginger and cardamom, along with rice. *Cholent* is favoured by Ashkenazi Jews and features beans, barley and potato.

CHOPPED LIVER

Chopped liver is regularly eaten as an appetiser on Friday night prior to chicken soup. Enjoyed with *challah* or matza crackers, it is made with chicken livers, fried onion, hard-boiled eggs and lots of seasoning. The dish may originally have been an Eastern European recipe that was adapted to meet a kosher palate, and is now embraced by Jews worldwide.

GEFILTEFISH

Popular amongst Ashkenazi Jews, *gefiltefish* was originally a whole carp stuffed with the minced fish, but over the centuries it has evolved into fried or boiled fish balls. Raw minced white fish is mixed with seasoning, onion, matza meal and egg.

Rolled into balls – anything from the size of a walnut to the size of a tennis ball – they are then either simmered in fish stock or deep-fried. *Gefiltefish* is often served with *chrain,* beetroot-flavoured horseradish sauce. Boiled *gefiltefish* is traditionally served topped with a slice of carrot.

TZIMMES

The classic *tzimmes* recipe is an Ashkenazi Eastern European dish made with slowly baked carrots, honey and dried fruits. Some recipes include meat, dumplings and onion. Carrots are eaten at Rosh Hashanah because they look like coins – may your pockets never be empty in the year to come! *Tzimmes* recipes vary from household to household but they're all sweet and they all contain the vital ingredient of carrots.

KUGELS

Kugels are a baked Ashkenazi Jewish pudding that can be either sweet or savoury. The German word *kugel* means 'sphere, globe or ball', and they were originally cooked in a round *kugelhupf* tin. *Kugels* have always been popular for the Shabbat meal, either for the Friday-night meal or Shabbat lunch. The most common *kugel* is potato, the ultimate in Jewish comfort food. The secret of the potato *kugel* is to squeeze out any excess water from the raw potatoes, add baking powder and don't skimp on the seasoning. The result will be a crisp, tasty and light-textured dish.

CHEESECAKE

Israel is known as the 'land of milk and honey', renowned for its dairy products. Celebrating the Biblical story of the receiving of the Torah, when the Israelites ate only dairy foods, the festival of Shavuot is known as the cheesecake festival. A range of cheesecake flavours are served at Shavuot, including the ever-popular vanilla and lemon baked with a sour cream topping.

LATKES

Latkes are crispy potato pancakes served at Chanukah (the festival of lights), when fried foods are favoured. Chanukah celebrates the miracle of the rededication of the Temple in ancient Israel – the oil remaining to light the holy *menorah* (candelabra) was sufficient for one day, but it miraculously lasted for eight. The secret to making the perfect crispy *latke* is to make sure that all excess liquid has been squeezed out of the grated potato and onion, and that the oil is piping hot. This will guarantee that your *latkes* don't turn out soggy or greasy.

HOLISHKES

These stuffed cabbage leaves are a traditional dish for Sukkot, the autumn harvest festival. Versions of this dish have long been enjoyed by Jewish communities in the Middle East, Europe and Russia, and the addition of chopped apricots gives the tradition a great twist. The cabbage leaves are stuffed with a mixture of minced lamb or beef and rice, and cooked with a tomato sweet-and-sour sauce. For a stylish presentation, keep the outside of the cabbage leaf on the *holishkes.*

Bars and restaurants line the waterways of Copenhagen

NORTHERN EUROPE

Traditional Northern European food was hunted, gathered, cured, smoked, pickled and preserved. These signature tastes are now celebrated by today's much-feted New Nordic chefs.

f one word could be used to describe the cuisine of this vast region, it would be seasonal. In these northern climes where the winter night may last for months on end and the summer sun barely sets, the seasons wholly dictate what's for dinner. Diurnal extremes are most characteristic of more northerly latitudes, but even in Denmark the midsummer festivities are lit with 17 hours of sunlight, while the middle of winter sees only seven hours of daylight each day.

In the Arctic regions of Greenland and northern Scandinavia, indigenous peoples survived for thousands of years on the resources of land and sea, as hunters, fishermen and reindeer herders. Traditional preserving techniques saw the bounty stretched to cover lean times.

Although every Arctic town now has a supermarket stocking everything from boil-in-the-bag seal meat to microwaveable burgers, traditional meat fresh from a hunt is still prized above all else.

In recent years, the Northern European region has been re-evaluating its culinary habits and boldly reinventing its gastronomic traditions. The resulting culinary movement, known as New Nordic cuisine, has become the food world's latest crush. The food media, trend-makers and gastronomes are worshipping at the altar of the new cuisine, which flaunts local, seasonal ingredients, often in mind-bending ways. Copenhagen in particular is seen as an essential destination for anyone interested in food – but can they land a reservation at Noma?

DRINKING

The long winter darkness can strain even the most optimistic soul, which helps explain why the vast bulk of Northern Europe belongs to the Vodka Belt, an informal grouping of countries with a long tradition of vodka manufacture and consumption (Russia is its spiritual capital, of course).

Finland's drinking culture is the stuff of legend, where beer and vodka work their wicked ways to break down the famously silent reserve of the natives. The joke goes that Finns invented mobile-phone texting (courtesy of Finnish company Nokia) so they didn't have to speak to each other, but one look at Helsinki's buzzing outdoor beer terraces on a long summer night and you'll see that the stereotype doesn't always match the reality.

Finlandia is a well-known brand on the international vodka market, but the best way to loosen inhibitions like a local is to partake of uniquely Finnish drinks like *salmiakkikossu*, which combines dissolved salty-liquorice sweets with the iconic Koskenkorva vodka, or *fisu*, which does the same but with Fisherman's Friend pastilles (menthol-flavoured cough drops). Acquired tastes, certainly. Alternatively, get in touch with the true Suomi spirit with beers and sausages after a lakeside sauna with new Finnish friends. *Kippis!* (Cheers!)

MEAT & FISH
FROM PECULIAR TO PROSAIC

Food in far Northern Europe was once about simple subsistence, and any animal in the vicinity was fair game – and every skerrick of the beast was put to good use (meat, hides, oil, bones – everything from a steak to skins for a kayak or a pair of natty boots). Over time, agriculture and farming have seen the menu broaden hugely, but there's still a strong tradition for simple foodstuffs sourced from the sea, the forest and the lake.

Inuit Greenlandic culture means eating from the top of the food chain (whale, seal, musk ox), with little room for sentimentality. Reindeer herding ties the indigenous Sami people to the lands of their ancestors in Lapland. Elk (moose) and bear make appearances on menus (the latter primarily in Finland), while seabirds such as puffin frequently wind up in Icelandic and Faroese cooking pots (for the curious, puffin meat looks and tastes like calf's liver).

But it's the Icelanders who take the prize for gastronomic bravery. Born from centuries of near-starvation, their traditional dishes reflect a 'waste not, want not' mindset that pushes new boundaries. Specialities include *svið* (singed sheep's head complete with eyeballs), *súrsaðir hrútspungar* (pickled rams' testicles) and *hákarl* (putrefied shark meat, buried and rotted for months to make it digestible).

Lest you start thinking all Icelandic dishes are better suited to horror-film props, rest assured that the local lamb is hard to beat. During the summer, sheep roam free to munch on chemical-free grasses and herbs in the highlands, before being corralled for the winter. The result of this relative life of luxury is very tender lamb with a lightly gamey flavour.

Danes, on the other hand, prefer to get some pork on their fork – they consume more pork than any other national, in the form of *leverpostej* (liver pâté), *frikadeller* (meatballs) and various incarnations of roast pork and pork chops. Danish bacon is a major export item – as is Danish butter, to further delight taste buds while hardening arteries.

Fish and seafood play a vital role in the cuisine of every country in the region, and the choices are plentiful – beyond the ubiquitous herring are delicacies such as snow crab, Norwegian fjord trout, langoustine and all-important salmon, popularly served grilled or smoked. The Scandinavians will keep you on your toes with some local variations, however: *surströmming* is a northern Swedish dish of fermented Baltic herring (so pungent it is only eaten outdoors), while *lutefisk* is a glutinous Norwegian dish of dried cod treated in lye solution.

WHERE TO EAT REYKJAVÍK, ICELAND

Nowadays, traditional Icelandic dishes are generally only eaten during the pagan midwinter celebration of Þorri. Many Reykjavík restaurants serve Þorri buffets, where *brennivín* (aquavit made from potato, flavoured with caraway seeds and nicknamed 'Black Death') plays a strong supporting role.

The rest of the year, bravehearts can try cubes of *hákarl* at Reykjavík's harbourside flea market, but be warned that the smell alone (heavy on ammonia) makes many foreigners ill!

ABOVE LEFT Flavoured vodkas take away winter's chill; the Ice Hotel in Sweden serves vodka in ice glasses
RIGHT Cod dry during the long summer days on the Lofoten Islands off Norway

FLØDEBOLLER

This delightful Danish dessert is a challenge but rewards cooks with a light, fragrant meringue encased in a crisp chocolate shell.

INGREDIENTS
Whites of 3 eggs
20g/1oz sugar
50g/2oz raspberries
half a vanilla pod

FOR THE SYRUP
50mL/1.5oz water
220g sugar

FOR THE BASE AND SHELL
150g marzipan
20g/1oz almonds (finely chopped)
200g/7oz chocolate (85% cocoa)

PREPARATION
Mix the almonds and marzipan, roll to 5mm thickness and cut out 4cm discs. Place on a wire rack over some paper. Whip the egg whites until stiff, add a heaped tablespoon (20g) of sugar and continue whipping. In a pan, bring the water and sugar to a boil until a syrup forms, Add it to the egg whites gradually while whipping (or use an electric mixer). Mash the raspberries (to remove the seeds push them through a sieve) and add to this mixture, which should become glossy and thick. Fill a piping bag and squeeze a blob onto the centre of each marzipan base, moving the bag upwards as you squeeze. Leave them to cool before melting the chocolate in a *bain-marie.* Let it cool but while runny, pour the chocolate over each meringue until covered. Chill the *flødeboller* before serving.

COFFEE CULTURE
The region's vodka intake – and resulting hangovers – may help to explain its obsession with coffee: in a list of per-capita java consumption, Nordic nations take five of the top six spots. Finns top the table, downing a hefty 12kg of coffee per person each year.

NEW NORDIC CUISINE
ADVANCE BOOKING REQUIRED

Nordic countries are enjoying a resurgence of interest in their traditional food culture, with dynamic chefs giving local dishes a modern reinterpretation, or adding a splash of ingenuity to the seasonal produce. So what's taken a city like Copenhagen from its prosaic pork-and-potatoes tradition to culinary dynamo? Responsibility lies with Copenhagen's young chefs, many of whom have apprenticed with the world's most influential chefs. The young guns combined this experience with a passion for Denmark's raw ingredients – its game, seafood, root vegetables and wild berries – and a reverence for the seasons. They then cast their net to encompass ingredients from the wider Nordic region – produce that is unique to often-extreme climates, landscapes and waters: Greenlandic musk ox, horse mussels from the Faroe Islands, obscure Finnish berries and truffles dug up on the island of Gotland.

Thus, in Copenhagen, Noma's lauded chef René Redzepi eschews non-indigenous produce in his creations (no olive oil, no tomatoes). He plays with modest, overlooked ingredients (pulses and grains) and consults food historians. He forages in the wilderness for herbs and plants. Ingredients are prepared using traditional techniques (curing, smoking, pickling and preserving) alongside experimentation. Until recently, New Nordic cuisine was an exclusive domain, but the style now defines a number of casual, affordable eateries in Copenhagen, among them Marv & Ben, Kødbyens Fiskebar and Relæ. The latter two are headed by ex-Noma chefs, determined to bring top produce and local innovation to a wider range of diners.

🍽 WHERE TO EAT NOMA
STRANDGADE 93, COPENHAGEN, DENMARK

A Holy Grail for gastronauts, Noma topped the 'World's Best Restaurants' list from 2010 to 2013. The name is a contraction of the Danish words *nordisk mad*, meaning Nordic food. At the helm is chef René Redzepi, pushing New Nordic cuisine to breathtaking highs.

ABOVE Overseeing the final touches on another genius dish, internationally-renowned Danish chef René Redzepi with his kitchen staff at Noma

SMORGASBORD
FROM SCANDINAVIA WITH LOVE

The funky flavours of putrefied shark haven't wowed the world but there have been gifts from the Nordic kitchen. Thank you Sweden for the buffet bounty of the smorgasbord. The *smörgåsbord* (from the words *smörgås*, sandwich, and *bord*, meaning table) stems from the 18th-century upper-class Swedish tradition of the *brännsvinsbord*, a table of appetisers put out for gentlemen and polished off with shots of *brännsvin* (aquavit) as said gentlemen (they ate while standing) presumably compared hunting trophies. The *brännsvinsbord's* popularity waxed and waned. In the late 19th century it re-emerged as the *smörgåsbord* buffet, served to travellers in train-station and hotel restaurants. Due to visiting Swedes, the *smörgåsbord* became internationally known at the 1939 New York World's Fair and the waistbands of overexcited diners have been groaning ever since.

All-you-can-eat buffets are a bastardised form of the true *smörgåsbord*. To understand the latter it's handy to know about Swedish concepts of *ordning och reda* (tidiness, good order) and *lagom* (meaning 'just right', neither too much nor too little). The rules mean you'll identify yourself as an outsider if you 1) overload your plate with a bit of everything, and 2) use the same plate on each visit. The horror! Start with herring dishes, with boiled potatoes, crispbread and cheese, accompanied by an aquavit. Grab a clean plate and try gravadlax, eel, salads and charcuterie. From there, it's on to hot dishes: meatballs with lingonberries and *Janssons frestelse* (Jansson's temptation), a rich potato-and-onion casserole loaded with anchovies. Find your dessert pocket for cheese, fruit and sweets.

🍲 WHERE TO EAT GRANDS VERANDA
GRAND HÔTEL, STOCKHOLM, SWEDEN

Snare a window seat at Grands Veranda's famous *smörgåsbord*, offered year-round at lunch and dinner, for views to Gamla Stan. December sees the *julbord*, or 'Christmas table'.

ABOVE More than just pickled fish: a smorgasboard of seafoods can be consumed cured, salted, smoked, or diced and mixed into a cold tangy salad **ABOVE RIGHT** Gravadlax topped with sea salt and dill

GRAVADLAX

Curing a fillet of salmon to create your own gravadlax is not only an easy but satisfying way to create a dinner party starter or preserve a surplus of salmon. Curing the fillets with more sugar than salt makes for a milder taste.

INGREDIENTS

1kg/2lb side of salmon
250g/9oz good quality sea salt
300g/10.5oz sugar
100g/3.5oz bunch of dill
Flavourings can include lemon or lime zest and juniper berries.

PREPARATION

Mix the sugar, salt, chopped dill and flavourings – the zest of a lemon and a lime with a few juniper berries is a good start – in a bowl. Cut the salmon fillet in half widthwise. Check it for bones, which can be removed with tweezers. Cover a strip of cling film (enough to wrap the fish) in a layer of the flavoured sugar and salt mixture and lay the salmon skin side down on it. Cover the flesh with the remaining sugar and salt mix and wrap tightly in the cling film.

Place the wrapped salmon in a tray with a smaller tray or plate on top, weighed down with cans. Store in the fridge for 12 hours, turn over and return to the fridge for another 12 hours. To serve, wipe the salt mixture from the salmon. You might like to rub some freshly cut dill into the surface for aesthetic effect. Slice thinly with a sharp knife and serve with rye bread and wedges of lemon.

Don't lean back on your seats, kids: a summer crayfish party in Sweden's idyllic archipelago

BITE-SIZE DIVERSIONS

In the land of the midnight sun and grim winter darkness, they've learned
to make the most of the seasons by foraging for summer food and celebrating autumn's harvest.
Join the party before winter arrives...

TRUFFLE-HUNTING SAFARIS

Touring truffle-sprinkled woods on the lovely Swedish island of Gotland, where the 'black gold' is the Burgundy truffle, and every bit as good as the French equivalent. Truffle-hunting season is October and November.

GREENLAND GOURMET

Dressing up to eat in the Greenlandic capital of Nuuk at Sarfalik, where an innovative menu blends European cooking methods with traditional, seasonal ingredients – perhaps seal served with pickled and puréed cauliflower, or reindeer fillet with a blackcurrant demi-glace.

ARCTIC MENU

Seeking out a restaurant affiliated with the Arctic Menu scheme in northern Norway, as far north as Svalbard. Members undertake to use the region's natural ingredients – it may be a sauce utilising local berries, an Arctic char pulled from the icy water, local cod, reindeer, seal or whale.

TOUR BORNHOLM

Hiring a bike and hitting the cycling trails of the Danish summer-holiday island of Bornholm – home to traditional fish smokehouses, a brace of fine-dining restaurants and scores of local specialities and treats, from caramel to microbrewed beer.

BERRY NIRVANA

In summer, joining locals to forage for delicious berries (blueberries, wild strawberries and countless more-obscure varieties). Amber-coloured cloudberries are highly prized – they grow one per stalk on open swampy ground and feature in sublime desserts: warm cloudberry jam with ice cream is simply fantastic.

MEET THE LOCALS

Spending an evening in the home of locals, sampling traditional food and learning about the destination straight from the horse's mouth. In Denmark, try the agencies Dine with the Danes; in Finland, contact Cosy Finland.

MEDIEVAL MAGIC

Indulging in a gluttonous feast at medieval-themed Olde Hansa (www .oldehansa.ee) in Tallinn, the fairytale Estonian capital. Juniper cheese, forest mushroom soup and exotic meats (wild boar, elk, bear) are among the delicacies, with candlelit rooms and peasant-garbed servers setting the mood.

CRAYFISH PARTIES

Celebrating (or commiserating) the passing of summer in late August with Kräftskivor (crayfish parties), where people wearing bibs and party hats get together to eat lots of crayfish and drink aquavit.

ICE, ICE BABY

Dining above the Arctic Circle in Sweden's wondrous Ice Hotel, whose restaurant showcases the region's produce. Beautifully presented dishes include grilled Arctic char, reindeer steak and cloudberry mousse, and some dishes are served on plates and bowls made from Torne River ice (the same ice used to construct the hotel).

HELSINKI DINING

Joining the faithful at nostalgic Kosmos, designed by Finnish design icon Alvar Aalto and a local institution, with a menu that dips between Nordic delights (eg reindeer carpaccio with cloudberry balsamico), traditional comfort foods and cross-border influences to the east.

FÄVIKEN MAGASINET

Gourmands on a mission to uncover the next Noma would do well to head to Jämtland, in remote central Sweden (close to the Norwegian border). Here, in a tiny, 12-seater restaurant holed up on a hunting estate, chef Magnus Nilsson is making culinary waves serving up *rektún mat* – 'real food, fit for a man', he says, all sourced locally and exquisitely presented. Due to its location, most guests stay for a night at the estate's lodge.

Stepped rice terraces
near Ubud, Bali

SOUTHEAST ASIA

Four flavours – sweet, sour, salty and spicy – set your taste buds tingling. From Myanmar to Singapore, the Philippines to Aceh, Southeast Asian cuisine is defined by the balance of this sensational quartet.

It's amazing what four simple flavours can do. In Laos or northeastern Thailand, this symmetry of sweet, sour, salty and spicy flavours might be obtained by combining the sweetness of sugar, the tartness of lime juice, the salinity of *paa daek* (a thick fish paste) and a few fresh chillies. In northern Vietnam, the salty flavour might come from soy sauce, which might be countered by a few dried chillies and a strategic splash of vinegar. In the Philippines, a unique sweet-spicy marriage might come from a combination of palm sugar and black pepper. Regardless of the country or the medium, the goal is the same – a favourable balance of sweet, sour, salty and spicy.

The countries of Southeast Asia share other culinary characteristics, including a strong reliance on fish – both as a protein and, in the form of fish sauce, a seasoning. Nearly every cuisine has also taken advantage of the region's fresh herbs, whether they're added as a fresh garnish, ground into pastes and dips, or added to soups or steamed dishes. Foreign influences, from the Chinese wok to the egg yolk-based sweets introduced to Thailand by early Portuguese explorers, have also influenced Southeast Asian cuisine in a profound and irrevocable way. And the cuisines of every country in Southeast Asia are linked by rice – without a doubt, the grain of choice for the entire region.

These links are strong, and their origins similar, but the standout feature of the cuisines of Southeast Asia is not their similarities, but rather their differences. The food of Southeast Asia is anything but a single entity, and from a handful of shared traits has sprung a legion of disparate cuisines that rival just about any region in the world in their diversity and full-flavouredness.

GREEN PAPAYA SALAD

Unripe papaya is spiked with chilli and salty fish sauce in this staple dish of Thailand and Laos.

INGREDIENTS

1 medium unripe papaya

1 large garlic clove

1 tbsp dry-roasted salted peanuts

1 tbsp dried shrimp

2 fresh birds-eye chillies

½ tsp sugar

2 tbsp lime juice

1-2 tbsp *nam pla* (fish sauce)

2 tomatoes (or 8 cherry tomatoes)

250g/9oz green beans, halved (optional)

Pinch of salt

PREPARATION

Pound together into a paste the garlic, salt, peanuts, chillies, sugar and shrimp with a pestle and mortar.

In a large bowl add lime juice and fish sauce to the paste.

Gently crush the tomatoes and green beans and add to the bowl.

Peel then shred the papaya, discarding the seeds and membrane.

Add it to the bowl and mix together with the paste, beans and tomatoes.

Serve in a bowl (which can be lined with lettuce) and sprinkle with a few crushed peanuts.

Serves four.

PAPAYA SALAD
SALAD THAT PACKS A PUNCH

With likely origins in Laos, green papaya salad just might be the most delicious dish in Southeast Asia. Known in Laos as *tam maak hung*, the dish employs crunchy ribbons of unripe papaya, sliced eggplants and tomatoes, all of which are bruised in a clay or wood mortar along with garlic, palm sugar, MSG, lime juice, a thick unpasteurised fish sauce known as *paa daek* and a typically shock-inducing amount of fresh chillies. The Thai version of the dish, known as *som tam*, is generally sweeter (but no less spicy), includes dried shrimp and peanuts, and is seasoned with bottled fish sauce.

In other riffs on the dish, the papaya can be replaced with green mango, cucumber or long beans. Almost always made by women, papaya salad is also primarily enjoyed by women, often as a snack rather than an entire meal – the intense spiciness providing a satisfying 'I'm full' feeling. Although you can order the salad in many Lao and Thai restaurants, it's still largely associated with rickety street stalls and mobile carts. And as is the case with much Southeast Asian–style street food, ordering papaya salad requires a fair bit of pre-emptive discussion, with diners typically stating unequivocally exactly how many chillies or how much sugar they prefer. The dish is often eaten on its own, but is best accompanied with sticky rice.

To eat the dish like a Lao, roll a small ball of the rice in your hand and dip it into the spicy dressing, or pinch both the rice and a bit of the papaya salad with your fingers.

⏚ WHERE TO EAT KHAMBANG LAO FOOD RESTAURANT 97/2 TH KHOUNBOULOM, VIENTIANE, LAOS

This third-generation restaurant – basically an extension of the family's living room – serves the best Lao food in central Vientiane, the capital of Laos. We're confident you could blindly choose from the menu and put together an outstanding Lao meal, but it'd be a pity if you missed the excellent *tam maak hung*, best accompanied by a steaming bamboo basket of sticky rice.

ABOVE The raw ingredients: a green papaya and green beans **LEFT** A green papaya salad makes for a quick, easy and healthy lunch – try frying the papaya for extra flavour

FISH
FRESHWATER CATCH

For the vast majority of the inhabitants of Southeast Asia, fish represents far more than just the one that got away. It's often the most common source of protein, and has been so for millennia. Oft-quoted inscriptions from northern Thailand that date back nearly 1000 years declare, 'There are fish in the water and rice in the fields', implying that these are really the only two elements one needed to survive.

Freshwater fish is the catch of the day for a significant portion of the region, plucked from the countries' lakes and rivers. These range from the giant Mekong catfish – among the world's largest freshwater fish, and an increasingly rare delicacy in Thailand and Laos – to tiny whitebait that are consumed head and all.

One of the most significant sources of piscine protein is Cambodia's Tonle Sap, an immense lake formed by water from the Mekong River that is considered one of the most productive inland fisheries in the world. The oceans, not surprisingly, also serve as important sources of fish for Southeast Asians, although in places such as Indonesia, overfishing is threatening this important resource.

FISH SAUCE

Westerners might scoff at the all-too-literal name of this condiment, but for many of the cuisines in the Greater Mekong area, fish sauce is more than just another ingredient, it is *the* ingredient.

Essentially the liquid obtained from fermented fish, fish sauce takes various guises, depending on the region. In Laos and northeastern Thailand, discerning diners prefer *plaa raa* or *paa daek*, a thick, pasty mash of fermented freshwater fish, salt and sometimes rice. In Cambodia, locals eat a similar condiment known as *prahoc*. In Myanmar, locals love *ngapi*, a fermented fish condiment that Rudyard Kipling famously described as 'fish pickled when it ought to have been buried long ago'.

Elsewhere, where people have access to the sea, fish sauce takes the form of a thin liquid extracted from salted anchovies, such as the famous Vietnamese *nuoc mam* or the Thai *nam pla*. In all cases, the result is highly pungent, generally salty (rather than fishy) in taste, and is used much the same way as a saltshaker in the West.

ABOVE Traditional fishing with a net, an oar and a canoe – a tranquil affair **ABOVE RIGHT** Anchovy, the key ingredient of Southeast Asia's essential fish sauce

GRILLING

The oldest cooking method known to man, grilling is still an important – in some places the most important – cooking method in Southeast Asia.

In Laos, grilling meat or fish over red-hot coals is particularly common, and *ping kai*, grilled chicken, is the unofficial national dish. Another Southeast Asian grilled highlight is the street-side grill stalls that pop up every evening in the cities of Myanmar. Simply point to the skewered ingredients you fancy, and they will be brushed with a spicy oil sauce and grilled to perfection before your eyes.

In Cambodia, grilled catfish or snakehead fish (a type of freshwater fish), often served with bitter herbs, is a staple for many people. And in Hanoi, northern Vietnam, the locals live for *bun cha*, a street favourite that features barbecued pork patties served with thin rice vermicelli, a heap of fresh herbs and green vegetables, and a bowl of sweetened *nuoc mam* (a dipping sauce made with fish sauce and syrup) with floating slices of pickled daikon and carrot.

HERBS

Just as Indian cooking is often associated with the use of dried spices, so Southeast Asian cooking is equally synonymous with the use of fresh herbs. These range from varieties found across the entire region such as mint and Thai basil, to more obscure regional herbs such as pennywort or sawtooth coriander. In particular, southern Vietnamese cooking makes extensive use of fresh herbs, and a platter of several different green leafy things is a typical accompaniment to many dishes.

SATE
MEAT ON A STICK

Grilling was probably the Neanderthal cooking method of choice, but skewered meat cooked over coals and called sate (or satay) is an Indonesian institution. Any meat can be used: goat, chicken, mutton, rabbit, pork, entrails or even horse and snake can find their way on to a sate skewer. Cooking the sate over coals produces aromas delicious enough to lure a vegetarian. Sate is nearly always prepared 10 to a serve with a sweet/spicy peanut sauce and rice or *lontong* (rice steamed in banana leaves).

Indonesian-style sate is often sold from roving stalls known locally as *kaki-lima*, which means 'five legs', for the three wheels on the cart and the two legs on the vendor. Some *kaki-lima* have a permanent location, while others roam the streets, tempting the hungry from their home or place of work In this case, the vendors will call out what they are selling or advertise their provender with a signature tune or sound. Sate sellers may just wail 'Saaateee!', but in some areas they sell sate from a boat-shaped cart with small bells attached that jingle as it's pushed along. At night, the bells and shadow of the boat slinking through alleyways creates an appetisingly eerie scene.

🍽 WHERE TO EAT SAT KHAS SENAYAN
JALAN KEBON SIRIH RAYA 31A, JAKARTA, INDONESIA

Sate is generally associated with street food, but in recent years chain restaurants, such as Sat Khas Senayan, have gained a loyal following.

ABOVE Making sate is child's play, just remember to soak the wood skewers in water before putting them on the heat **RIGHT** Sate is popular throughout Indonesia, Malaysia and Singapore

GINGER TEA

In tropical Indonesia, you wouldn't think you'd need a warming ginger beverage. But high-altitude areas like Dieng Plateau, Brastagi and Lembang are surprisingly chilly and a steaming glass of *bandrek* (ginger tea) provides respite from the cold. On the hill trails around Bandung stand bamboo shelters where a weekend walker can rest, take in the views and down a soothing glass of *bandrek*. Here, *bandrek* is brewed by an *ibu* (mother or older woman), who spikes the drink with pepper. And in largely Islamic Indonesia, ginger tea tends to be less confusing a name than ginger beer.

INGREDIENTS

6 cups water

3cm/1in piece fresh ginger, sliced

5cm/2in cinnamon stick

2 tsp palm sugar (or brown sugar)

10cm/4in piece fresh coconut flesh (or 1 tbsp shredded coconut) per glass

1 tsp black peppercorns

PREPARATION

Combine all ingredients except sugar and coconut in a saucepan and boil for three minutes. Add the sugar and stir for one minute. Place the coconut in glasses and strain the liquid over. Makes four glasses.

BEERLAO
CHIN-CHIN!

Perhaps no foreign culinary introduction, bar chillies, is so widespread in Southeast Asia as beer. Introduced to the region by the Spanish more than 100 years ago, today modern brewing facilities can be found in every country in Southeast Asia, and the amber liquid is quickly overtaking the indigenous rice and toddy-based alcohols as the tipple of choice. Much of the region's beer is brewed in the lager style: a chilled lager is the ideal partner of spicy Southeast Asian food. Many locals enjoy their beer with ice to beat the heat.

One of the most unique brews in the region is Vietnam's *bia hoi*, a rough equivalent to homebrew, and quite possibly the cheapest beer in the world. Another standout is Laos' Beerlao, a relatively obscure brand but considered by many to be the best brew in the region. The beer dates back to 1973, when the then Lao Beer and Ice Factory was founded in Vientiane with the help of French businessmen. When Laos was 'liberated' in 1975, the brewery was taken over by the state and run with the support of brewers from Laos's communist allies in Eastern Europe. With the collapse of the Soviet Union, the brewery was on its own. In a clever move, it decided to introduce rice as malt, rather than rely on expensive imported barley. It also modelled the beer on a classic Czech-style pilsner. The result is today's Beerlao, a light, slightly sweet beer with 5% alcohol.

With ownership divided between Carlsberg and the communist state, Beerlao produces more than 200 million litres of beer per year and commands a 99% market share in Laos. Only about 1% is exported (mostly to Cambodia). The brewery hopes to increase this to 10% in the next decade through word of mouth – which should return the favour.

WHERE TO DRINK

It's hard to beat a bottle (served, of course, on ice) while gazing over the Mekong River on the waterfront promenade in Vientiane, the capital of Laos.

ABOVE French barley, German hops and Laotian rice combine to create a light, crisp beer perfectly suited to the hot climate and food of Laos **ABOVE LEFT** Warm your hands and your heart with a glass of *bandrek*

⟨⟨⟩ CHICKEN RICE
CHINA'S GIFT TO SINGAPORE

Although the dish has its origins on the Chinese island of Hainan, chicken rice has found a second home in Singapore, where many would argue it's the country's de facto national dish. A combination of tender boiled chicken, rice cooked in chicken stock, slices of cucumber, a bowl of clear broth and a variety of dipping sauces (usually ginger and chilli, and soy), chicken rice is available across the island state at all times of the day, in venues ranging from humble hawker centres to swanky hotels.

By the end of the Middle Ages, Southeast Asia had been part of a complex trading network stretching from China for hundreds of years. The northeast monsoon brought Chinese junks laden with silks, porcelain, pickles and other foodstuffs to the Malay Archipelago, as well as to Tongking, Annam and Cochin China – today's mainland Southeast Asia. More recent generations of Chinese labourers and vendors introduced the wok and several varieties of noodle dishes to the region.

The Chinese have also influenced the region's cuisine in other ways: beef is not widely eaten in much of Thailand due to a Chinese-Buddhist teaching that forbids eating 'large' animals. As a result of this long-standing cultural exchange, wheat noodles, fried rice, stir-fries, yum cha and numerous other Chinese culinary contributions are now standards in just about every corner of Southeast Asia.

⚓ WHERE TO EAT TIAN TIAN HAINANESE CHICKEN RICE
MAXWELL FOOD CENTRE, MAXWELL RD, SINGAPORE

It's a contentious – some might say the most contentious – issue, but Tian Tian Hainanese Chicken Rice serves what many Singaporeans consider the country's best dish.

ABOVE Everyone in the know will have their tried and true restaurant or recipe – Hainanese chicken rice is a dish that people get very possessive about.

CHICKEN RICE
INGREDIENTS
1 whole fresh chicken

8 slices fresh ginger

1 garlic clove

2 shallots, roughly chopped

1 tsp sesame oil

Pinch of salt

RICE
3 cups of long-grain rice

Chicken fat (skin and Parson's nose)

1 tbsp peanut oil

Knob of ginger grated

3 cloves of garlic

3 cups of chicken stock

PREPARATION
Bring a pot of water large enough to contain a whole chicken to the boil. Chop three pieces of ginger, garlic and one shallot, blend in a food processor.

Rub mixture inside chicken. When the water boils, turn heat off and place the chicken and remaining pieces of ginger and shallot in the water. Leave the chicken to stand in the water for one hour. After the first five minutes, lift the chicken and drain the water from the cavity. Repeat this process two or three times during the cooking to ensure the chicken cooks inside.

After 30 minutes, turn heat on to bring water back to a simmer. Don't allow chicken to boil. At the end of the hour, remove chicken and rub with soy sauce combined with sesame oil and salt. Cut into bite-sized pieces.

Wash the rice and drain. In a wok, fry chicken fat until oil is released and add the ginger and garlic and fry. Remove from heat and discard the chicken skin. Add the rice and salt and stir-fry briskly for one to two minutes.

Transfer rice into a rice cooker or pot. Add in chicken stock and pandan leaves. Follow instructions for cooking rice. Ladle a small amount of hot strained stock into serving bowls. Add finely chopped shallot. Serve with chilli, ginger and soy sauces.

∿
RICE & NOODLES
HAVE YOU EATEN RICE TODAY?

Rice is so central to Southeast Asian food culture that the most common term for 'eat' in nearly every regional language translates as 'consume rice'. This is not entirely surprising, given that the grain is thought to have been cultivated in the area for as many as 7000 years. Today, Thailand is Southeast Asia's (and the world's) greatest rice exporter, a title it sometimes exchanges with Vietnam. The rice of choice for the vast majority of Southeast Asians is the long-grained variety that is prepared by being boiled directly in water. Just to be different, the inhabitants of Laos and northeastern Thailand prefer sticky rice, short stocky grains that are soaked in water before being steamed in bamboo baskets.

Although strands of rice- or wheat-flour-based dough are probably Chinese in origin, there is hardly a corner of Southeast Asia where you won't be able to find noodles. And given the local fixation on rice, it's hardly surprising that the most popular form of noodles is made from rice flour mixed with water to form a paste, which is then steamed to make wide, flat sheets. The sheets are folded and sliced into various widths, and are sold both fresh and dried.

Another type of rice noodle, particularly popular in mainland Southeast Asia, is produced by pushing a type of rice-flour paste through a sieve into boiling water, much the way Italian-style pasta is made.

The Chinese introduced the region to the ubiquitous round noodles made from wheat flour and egg; they're yellowish in colour and are sold only in fresh bundles. Also popular are the clear noodles made from mung-bean starch and water.

THE UNKNOWN NOODLE

Seen as the country's unofficial national dish, Myanmar's *mohinga* is a comforting noodle soup that exemplifies the earthy flavours of the national cuisine via a combination of indigenous ingredients including lemon grass, shallots, turmeric and freshwater fish. Some suspect that the noodles, which are made from rice via a complicated and time-consuming process that is thought to date back several centuries, are also indigenous to the region.

Generally associated with central Myanmar and that region's predominately Burmese ethnic group, *mohinga* is nonetheless sold in just about every town in Myanmar, typically from mobile vending carts and baskets or basic open-fronted restaurants.

Mohinga vendors are busiest in the morning, and ordering the dish is a simple affair, as the only optional ingredients are a boiled egg and *akyaw*, crispy fritters of lentils or battered and deep-fried vegetables that serve as a topping. A bowl is generally seasoned in advance, but dried chilli and quartered limes are usually on hand to add a bit of spice and tartness.

🍲 WHERE TO EAT MYAUNG MYA DAW CHO
158 51ST ST, YANGON, MYANMAR

If you're in Yangon (Rangoon), head to Myaung Mya Daw Cho, where a bowl of noodles will set you back less than a dollar.

ABOVE Until 2008's Cyclone Nargis, Myanmar was the world's sixth-largest producer of rice
ABOVE LEFT Tea houses are a great place to try *mohinga* **RIGHT** Monks sharing a meal in Mandalay

BANH KHOAI

Also known as 'happy crêpes', these are good for breakfast, lunch or dinner. They require a lot of work, but if you have a large kitchen, invite your friends over and cook these as a group.

INGREDIENTS

1 cup/120g rice flour
½ cup/60g cornflour
¼ cup/30g wheat flour
560mL/18fl oz water
3 spring onions (scallions), green and white parts sliced separately
250g/9oz minced pork
2 tbsp *nuoc mam*
2 cloves garlic, minced
250g/9oz prawns, shelled and split
250g/9oz bean sprouts
1 onion, sliced
10 white mushrooms, sliced
3 eggs, beaten
Vegetable oil

PREPARATION

Combine all the flours and spring onion greens to make a batter.

Combine the pork with half the fish sauce, garlic, spring onion whites and pepper. Combine the shrimp with the remaining fish sauce, garlic, spring onion whites and pepper. Arrange the above, and all the other ingredients, handily near the stove.

Heat a small skillet or an omelette pan to high. Add 1 tbsp of oil, then 1½ tbsp of pork and two to three pieces of shrimp prawn and cook for two minutes. Reduce the heat to medium and add 3 tbsp of batter, 1 tbsp of bean sprouts and a few slices of onion and mushroom.

Cover and cook for two minutes. Uncover and pour 3 tbsp of egg over the crepe then cover again for two minutes. Uncover and fold in half, adding more oil if needed. Continue cooking with the lid on, turning the crêpe from time to time, until crisp. Serve with *nuoc cham*. Serves six.

COLONIAL CONTRIBUTIONS
CLASH OF CUISINES

Try to imagine Thai food without the chillies, Vietnamese cooking without lettuce or peanuts, or Lao papaya salad without the papaya. Many of the ingredients used on a daily basis by the inhabitants of Southeast Asia are in fact relatively recent introductions courtesy of European traders and missionaries. During the early 16th century, while Spanish and Portuguese explorers were first reaching the shores of Southeast Asia, there was also subsequent expansion and discovery in the Americas. The Portuguese in particular were quick to seize the products coming from the New World and market them in the East, and thus very likely introduced modern-day Asian staples such as tomatoes, potatoes, corn, lettuce, cabbage, chillies, papaya, guava, pineapples, pumpkins, sweet potatoes, peanuts and tobacco.

Chillies in particular seem to have struck a chord with the natives of Southeast Asia, and are thought to have first arrived in Thailand via the Portuguese. Before their arrival, Southeast Asians got their heat from bitter-hot herbs and roots such as ginger and pepper.

More recently, colonialism has been responsible for such culinary introductions as baguettes and coffee in former French Indochina (today's Laos, Vietnam and Cambodia), beer in Thailand, China and the Philippines, and in Laos, a thick, meat-based stew served at weddings and festivals known as *lagoo* – yes, none other than the French ragout.

Malaysia's Eurasian community stems from the arrival of the Portuguese, who started a policy of racial integration. Intent on incorporating Malaysia's native cuisine into their own, they combined ingredients of local cuisines (which were already a hybrid of Malay, Chinse, Indian and Arab cultures) with Portuguese cooking methods. Today, Eurasians use tamarind, lemon grass, lime and galangal to create curries, sambal (spicy, chilli-based dips), soups and vegetable dishes. Occasionally they use alcohol to add body to meat and fish dishes. Signature Eurasian dishes include curry *debal* (devil's curry; a spicy Eurasian meat curry) and *feng* (pork curry), a Christmas speciality that's best eaten a day old.

ABOVE Fiery chilli powder – dried and ground chillis – is a common ingredient in Southeast Asian cooking but the plant originated in South America, an example of colonial cross-pollination

℘℘
BANH MI
VIETNAMESE-FRENCH FUSION

The Vietnamese baguette sandwich known as *banh mi* is an early example of Southeast Asian fusion food. The dish's primary ingredients – baguette, mayonnaise and a type of peppery pork liver pâté – show an obvious link with the French, who introduced these foods to the Vietnamese under their tenure as colonial rulers during the early 20th century. Other ingredients, including *xa xiu*, the barbecued pork known in English as *char siu*, have Chinese origins, while the sandwich's herbs and seasonings are distinctively Southeast Asian. The sandwich is now popular around the world, and in 2011 the word *banh mi* was added to the Oxford English Dictionary.

Banh mi begins with a light baguette that has been grilled over coals. After a smear of mayonnaise and a dollop of pâté, the crispy shell is then filled with a mixture of meat (usually more pork), crunchy pickled vegetables and fresh herbs. *Banh mi* is then typically seasoned with a few drops of soy sauce and a spicy chilli condiment.

Banh itself is a word that embraces all sorts of baked goods, including crêpes. *Banh* can be sweet or savoury, wrapped in leaves and steamed or grilled. Each region of Vietnam has its own *banh*; in the north *banh gio* is made from rice flour and pork wrapped in banana leaf. The only common denominator is that *banh* is always a handheld snack.

🍲 WHERE TO EAT PHUONG
NEAR THE CORNER OF BACH ĐANG AND NGUYEN DUY HIEU, HOI AN, VIETNAM

They're prepared on a wheeled cart parked on a nondescript street corner in Hoi An, but the *banh mi* sold from this vendor are considered among the best in Vietnam. If the combination of crispy bread and a meaty, spicy filling aren't enough, revel in the fact that a sandwich at Phuong will set you back a whopping 15,000 dong (about US$0.75).

ABOVE The French left Vietnam in 1954 but *banh mi* stayed behind: the baguettes differ from French baguettes in that they are made from a combination of rice and wheat flour

PHO

Pho is Vietnam in a bowl. It's soul food. It's comfort food. It's beef noodle soup and so much more.

You can have *pho* everywhere in Vietnam, but it is almost a cult in Hanoi. A bowl of *pho* begins its Mayfly life the day before you eat it. A slow simmering of beef shin bones, oxtails and scraps in a deep pot creates a rich, clear consommé. The alchemist adds their herbs, their spices, their family secrets. Chief among them, and you will always know the aroma of *pho* by them, are star anise, ginger and cinnamon.

From a distance, its come-hither smell urges you to reach the *pho* shop. The vendor deftly cuts rice sheets into noodles and slices meat into near-translucent thinness. 'Customer,' he asks, 'what kind of meat do want?'

He immerses a sieve of noodles into hot water for a moment, lifts them out, drains them, and pours them into your bowl. With a florist's eye, he arranges on top a bouquet of white onion slices, tiny yellow shavings of ginger, perhaps something green. And then, red raw beef, in slices about the size of the heel of your hand. He lifts the lid of his stockpot and steam billows out, enveloping you in a gossamer cloud. You know you're about to taste poetry. Ladles of the broth fill your bowl, its heat penetrating the meat, cooking it to perfect tenderness in seconds.

From the garnish tray, add a squeeze of lime. Some bean sprouts. A dash of chilli sauce and garlic sauce or fish sauce. Lastly, sprinkle with coriander, mint or basil leaves. Or all of them. What you have before you is a bowl of yin and yang. It is hearty yet delicate; complex and straightforward; filling but not bloating; spicy and comfortably bland. It is *pho*.

Try the roadside
snacks of Laos

BITE-SIZE DIVERSIONS

Explore how pungent spices and aromatics such as galangal and lemongrass create distinctive dishes.

CAMBODIA
Leave your fried-rice comfort zone and discover *samlor*, the vibrant, herb-laden soups that are the highlight of this culinary dark horse. Eaten with rice and a fish dish, it's the closest you'll come to the quintessential Cambodian meal.

LAOS
Indulge in the legendary Lao culinary triumvirate: *tam maak hung* (papaya salad), *laap* (a minced meat 'salad') and sticky rice. (Throwing a Beerlao into the mix certainly wouldn't hurt either.)

INDONESIA
Think only Americans know barbecue? Challenge the notion with Bali's *babi guling*, spit-roast whole pig seasoned with chilli, turmeric, garlic and ginger. Coupled with coconut rice and spicy sides, it just might be the best barbecue in the world.

MALAYSIA
Experience Malaysia in a bite: *nasi lemak*, the country's unofficial 'national dish'. It combines rice cooked in coconut and served with cucumber, tiny crunchy fish, peanuts, hard-boiled egg and a spicy sambal (a chilli-based condiment).

PENANG
Get stuffed in Penang – dare we say it, Southeast Asia's best food destination – where tasty regional cuisines and some of Southeast Asia's best produce (hello durians!) meet in a more-ish marriage.

MYANMAR
It's not the most attractive dish in the world, and it's often mixed by the naked hand of the vendor, but a taste is all that's needed to become pleasantly addicted to *lephet thoke*, a salad made from fermented tea leaves.

PHILIPPINES
Pluck up the courage to try *balut*, a boiled duck egg containing a partially developed embryo, sometimes with tiny feathers.

SINGAPORE
It may be a tiny island, but mealtime in Singapore means choosing between Southern Indian, regional Chinese, Malaysian, Thai and even European cuisines. Simply put, when it comes to food, Singaporeans are spoilt for choice.

THAILAND
Why let a plump tummy be the only evidence of your trip to Thailand? Recreate those meals yourself after a visit to one of the country's numerous and excellent-value cooking schools.

VIETNAM
You may never look at a bowl of Rice Krispies the same way again after starting the day with a steaming bowl of *pho* (see p301), one of the most legendary noodle soups in the world.

Tea is part of life's daily rhythms at Thangbi Goemba monastery in Bhutan's Chokhor Valley

THE
SUBCONTINENT

A hint of cumin, a whiff of cinnamon, steamy notes of cardamom and cloves, the tang of ginger: cooks here draw on the world's finest spices, transforming every dish into a sublime assault on the senses.

While cultures elsewhere had to trade to get hold of spices, here in the Subcontinent, nature provided the spice rack free of charge: cardamom and cinnamon grow wild in the foothills of the Himalaya, while pepper vines, ginger and turmeric are common as weeds in the plains.

Subcontinental cuisine was also elevated by the clash of cultures – and the clatter of cook pots – that took place along its borders. In the west, invading armies from Turkey, Afghanistan and Persia introduced roast meat, fragrant casseroles and sweetmeats alongside the Qur'an and the onion dome. In the west, invaders from Burma brought seafood stews and hot and sour soups from Southeast Asia. Traders, warlords and refugees from China and Tibet trekked in dumplings, stir-frying and noodles over the ridge of the Himalaya.

Over the centuries, every corner of the Subcontinent pulled a different combination of spices, ingredients and cooking styles from the culinary melting pot. In Sri Lanka, the bounty of the sea is harvested for intense seafood curries and pounded chutneys. The freshwater fish of Bangladesh are simmered in rich sauces scented with poppy seeds and mustard. And the lavish seasonings of the Indian plains collide with the rugged mountain cuisine of the Himalaya in Nepal.

Travel in South Asia is a voyage through flavours and aromas. In bustling bazaars, follow your nose to sizzling skewers, popping *puri* (fried bread puffs) and simmering stews perfumed with aromatic spices. Everything that can be harvested makes it into the cooking pot – plantains, mangoes, sugar cane, okra. Meat-lovers weave magic with lamb, pork, chicken and beef, while vegans and vegetarians cook searing sauces so full of flavour you don't even notice the absence of meat. Could this be the world's greatest cuisine? You decide...

HOPPERS

India's rice-flour dosas are world famous, but Sri Lankan cooks take the rice pancake idea one step further, adding a dash of toddy (palm liquor) to the batter to speed up fermentation overnight. Yeast is sprinkled over warm water, then coconut milk and sugar are added before the yeast mixture is blended with rice flour, sugar, salt and palm wine to form the batter.

Cooked in a round wok-like pan, the resulting hoppers – or *appa* in Sri Lankan – have a pleasing acidity and a light, bubbly texture that compliments the *sambal* (an inferno chutney made from ground fish, coconut and chilli) on the side. For extra protein, seek out egg hoppers, with a whole egg broken into the base of each pancake. Hoppers with extra coconut milk are called *miti kiri appe,* and *idiyappam* (string hoppers) – made from noodles twirled into spirals and then steamed – are the pride of the hopper family and a breakfast staple on the island.

Two-man teams, one to make the batter, the other to serve the hoppers and accompaniments, work the streets of every Sri Lankan town and city. One of the best places to shop for hoppers is the Deliwala/Wellawatta area of Galle Road in the capital, Colombo. Two hoppers is the standard fix: tear off a quarter of the coconut-infused pancake, and dab it in the sharp *katta sambal*. The sweet dough gives way to a mouth-puckering salty-lime sensation before the hit of chilli arrives.

KATTA SAMBAL

This simple salsa of chilli (fresh or flaked), red onion, lime and either Maldive fish flakes or dried prawns for saltiness, is an ever-present condiment on Sri Lankan tables and street stalls.

KOTTU
SRI LANKA'S FAVOURITE STREET FOOD

What's that swirling around on the hot plate? Stir-fried noodles? Phat thai? Chow mein? And what is up with those crazy knives? If any of that sounds familiar, you've probably encountered Sri Lanka's *kottu*, prepared from *godamba roti* (fried flatbread), chopped to ribbons on the griddle with ginger and garlic paste, chilli and the chef's favourite blend of herbs and spices, with a ladle of zingy curry sauce to lubricate the mix. The noise of *kottu* blades clattering on the griddle serves as an impromptu dinner gong across Sri Lanka.

Originally imported from the temple towns of Tamil Nadu, *kottu* has been embraced as the unofficial national dish by Sri Lankans of all backgrounds. It was eaten almost exclusively by Tamils until the second half of the 20th century, when the whole island was seized by the *kottu* bug. Vegetarians sup on *kottu* with mixed vegetables, eggs or *paneer*, smooth-textured curd cheese prepared without rennet to meet the dietary requirements of devout Buddhists and Hindus. Muslim and Christian diners toss in chicken and beef.

What makes *kottu* so good? It could be the ritual of preparation, or the varied textures and flavours. Or perhaps it's the fact that it arrives at the table sizzling hot, with the delectable crispy bits and charred tones that only come from food prepared on a hot plate. If you get a chance, watch a *kottu* chef at work – the machine-gun rat-a-tat-tat of the *kottu* blades on the hot plate is part food preparation, part martial art, part impromptu percussion performance.

🍽 WHERE TO EAT HOTEL DE PILAWOOS
417 GALLE RD, COLOMBO, SRI LANKA

Colombo is Sri Lanka's *kottu* capital. After dark, locals flock to Hotel de Pilawoos for on-the-hoof munchies; when the tables are full, crowds spill out onto the pavement.

ABOVE You may have to queue for *kottu*, but it's worth the wait **RIGHT** Praying at Anuradhapura in Sri Lanka: Buddhists make food offerings at temples and have vegetarian versions of most dishes

STEAK, BUT NOT AS YOU KNOW IT

It might seem a little inconsistent for a Hindu nation to be famous for its steaks, but Nepal has a handy opt-out clause from the religious proscription on eating the flesh of sacred cows. As often as not, the fat, juicy steaks that trekkers fantasise about after weeks of rice and lentils on Nepal's trekking trails are actually water buffalo, with all of the flavour of well-hung beef but none of the religious taboos.

However, it pays to check when you order – increasingly, real steak is appearing on menus in Kathmandu and Pokhara, imported from Kolkata as part of secretive foreign trade deals. The pepper steak at K-Too steakhouse in Kathmandu, followed by fried apple *momos,* has become a post-trek necessity.

BREAKING THE FAST

After a month of assiduous fasting for the holy month of Ramadan, Pakistan's Muslims break the fast with gusto to celebrate Eid al-Fitr, which always falls on the first day of Shawwal, the tenth month in the Islamic calendar.

Giving food as alms is a religious tenet, and rich and poor come together to feast on delights like *bhuna ghost* (dry lamb, pan-fried with spices, then simmered in a cinnamon-scented sauce) and mutton korma, made the authentic Pakistani way with yoghurt and almonds rather than ground cashew paste.

Dessert is celebrated with similar aplomb – as well as myriad *mithai* (South Asian sweets), look out for *seviyan,* vermicelli noodles cooked with sugar, cardamom, milk, fruit and nuts; and *sheer khurma,* the same noodles in a creamy sauce thickened with dates.

৬৬
KEBABS
WHAT'S COOKING IN THE HINDU KUSH?

When Muslim and Hindu armies clashed along the mountain wall of the Hindu Kush, two of the world's great cuisines collided. The barbecued meats beloved of the Turkic tribes were reborn in a crucible of Indian spices, spawning a host of meaty delights – tandoori chicken, lamb *shashlik,* pressed mince *seekh kebabs* – all forged on the Northwest Frontier from Indian seasoning expertise and Persian and Ottoman cooking know-how.

Cross the Khyber Pass today, and you can walk in the culinary footsteps of invading emperors. Mahmud of Ghazni allegedly had a soft spot for spit-barbecued lamb. The Emperor Akbar preferred chicken, particularly when ground and moulded around a skewer with garlic, ginger, onion and fenugreek seeds. Shah Jahan, builder of the Taj Mahal, was said to be partial to flame-grilled fish steaks. In fact, if locals are to be believed, half the dishes in Pakistan were the personal favourite of this emperor or that sultan.

♨ WHERE TO EAT KHYBER BAZAAR, PESHAWAR, PAKISTAN

Carnivores insist that the finest kebabs are served in Peshawar, gateway to the Khyber Pass – just follow the cooking smells to the myriad grill-houses of the Khyber Bazaar. At the gateway from the cantonment to the old city, around the junction of Railway Rd and Bajori Rd, you'll find mouth-watering *boti kebabs,* tender cubes of lamb marinated with garlic, ginger, lemon juice and pounded papaya, and the burger-like *chapli kebab,* a flattened beef patty seasoned with an intoxicating blend of cumin, coriander, mint leaves and chilli.

ABOVE Lamb *shashliks* with onion and red and green peppers, slowly rotated over hot coals in Pakistan

⅊
TANDOORI CHICKEN
EVERYONE'S FAVOURITE SPICY RED CHICKEN

That's not an oven, it's a furnace! In a tandoor, heated to temperatures just shy of 500°C, chicken undergoes a baptism by fire that by all rights should sear it to ashes. Instead, the meat emerges deliciously moist and tender, stained phoenix-red by a lip-singeing marinade of ginger, yoghurt and ground Kashmiri chilli. The tandoor clay oven was first used by prehistoric tribes in the Indus Valley, but the idea of using it to cook marinated chicken is popularly credited to Kundan Lal Gujral, a Punjabi chef who fled from Peshawar to Delhi in 1920 and started serving this inspired combination to the masses.

Today, tandoori chicken is found wherever the word 'nonveg' appears above the door – just look for the hanging skewers of chicken dripping with marinade. By default, tandoori chicken is served in fractions – half, quarter or whole – with steaming-hot naan bread, cooked on the sides of the same clay oven. Locals barbecue the meat on the bone to preserve moisture – the dry boneless cubes of chicken served outside the Subcontinent are a pale imitation. Deep scoring allows the rich flavours of the marinade to permeate the meat, and a squeeze of lemon juice just before serving transforms the dish into an almost religious experience.

ABOVE After deep marinating the chicken is plunged into the searing heat of a tandoori oven

BREAD ON A HOT TIN PLATE

European-style leavened bread never caught on in South Asia. The only lasting legacy of British baking traditions is the omelette sandwich, a railway-station staple made with sweet, sliced white bread. Locals prefer flatbreads, prepared on the spot and served piping hot from the tandoor or hot plate. The delectable naan is what the clay oven was invented for – a soft, inflated pillow that comes plain or buttered, scented with *methi* (fenugreek) or garlic, topped with minced meat or stuffed with dried fruit and nuts, Mughal-style. Away from the tandoor, hot plates – known locally as *tava* or *saj* – are used to crisp up wheat-flour chapatis (aka roti), the default starch for dipping in sauces. Add ghee or palm oil, and you have parathas; deep fry the dough, and you have the puffed-up *puri*. Serve any of the above with curry, and you have perfection.

KARAHI COOKING

A macho, cast-iron variation on the Chinese wok, the *karahi* is the preferred cooking vessel in the parts of the Subcontinent that trace their history back to curly-slippered emperors and sultans. Transferring heat rapidly and evenly to the ingredients inside, the *karahi* is used to roast and fry dry spices, liberating the flavours before the addition of garlic, meat and vegetables. *Karahi* dishes come to the table in the sizzling pan, which is propped up on a wooden stand or metal ring. There are almost as many *karahi* curries as there are cooks who make it – infused with chilli, garlic and ginger, *karahi* chicken is a firm favourite from Cox's Bazaar to Karachi, as well as being the ancestor of the British *Balti*.

MOMO
DUMPLING DELIGHTS

Picture the scene: a lonely, tin-roofed tea house on a remote Himalayan trail. Inside, the dining room fills with steam as the matriarch of the house deposits plates of piping-hot Tibetan dumplings in front of the gathered crew of trekkers, porters and guides. For a time, the only sound is chewing, slurping and appreciative grunts of pleasure. Meet the *momo* – comfort food in a wheat-dough wrapper, pinched together like the spotted handkerchief at the end of a traveller's stick.

Ubiquitous from Lhasa to Thimphu, via Gangtok, Leh and Kathmandu, *momos* come steamed, fried or boiled in soup, with a cornucopia of fillings. Water-buffalo meat blended with onion and coriander is the stuffing of choice for meat-eaters; vegetarians, of which there are growing numbers in Buddhist Tibet, have the pick of yak cheese, potato or freshly harvested mountain vegetables. On popular trekking routes, you'll even find chocolate *momos*, a Himalayan homage to the Scottish deep-fried Mars bar.

Travellers who have explored Central Asia and the Korean peninsula will note similarities to Chinese *jiaozi*, Mongolian *buuz* and Korean *mandu* – all have a similar lineage, tied to the yak caravans that plied their trade across the Himalaya. Whatever the filling, these enticing morsels come with a trio of dips: simple soy, sliced chillies in vinegar, and poker-hot garlic and chilli sauce. After days of lean pickings while crossing high mountain passes, dropping back into the *momo* belt feels like a little bit of heaven.

⊕ WHERE TO EAT SNOWLAND RESTAURANT
4 ZANGYIYUAN LU, LHASA, TIBET

The best *momos* are the ones you find in a farmhouse kitchen on a mountain trail, but if this sounds like too much effort, travellers rave about the potato *momos* at Snowland in downtown Lhasa.

LEFT Rebuilt Taktshang Goemba on a rock face in the Upper Paro Valley, Bhutan **ABOVE** Steamed *momos* with a fiery dipping sauce **ABOVE RIGHT** Yak milk cheese if you please

TIBET'S SWISS CHEESE

Unlikely as it may sound, cheese prepared from *nak* (female yak) milk is a favourite food of the Himalayan tribes. The traditional cottage cheese of the Tibetan plateau has been joined by local interpretations of gruyère and emmental, made in factories founded by Swiss missionaries in the 1950s, along with rock-solid *chhurpi*, sucked like cheese-flavoured hard candy in Sikkim, Nepal and Bhutan. Perhaps the most surprising Himalayan cheese dish is *ema datshi,* an incendiary Bhutanese soup made from pounded chillies, cheese and lava (at least that's what your taste buds keep telling you!).

TIBETAN BUTTER TEA

Sugar in tea is one thing, but salt and butter? That's how they like it on the Tibetan plateau. Once you leave the foothills and enter the Buddhist Himalayan heartland, sweet chai is replaced by soup-like *po cha,* a high-energy hot drink made from steeped Chinese tea leaves, yak butter and salt. This is a beverage born of trade across the Himalaya, when salt from Tibetan lakes was swapped for Chinese brick tea, and grains and spices from the Indian plains. Still prepared in portable churns known as *mdong mo*, Tibetan tea is not so much brewed as beaten into submission. With a puddle of melted butter on top, it takes some getting used to, but with sweat-replacing salt and readily metabolisable fatty acids, this is thermal insulation in a cup.

FUEL OF THE GRAND TRUNK ROAD

The Great Trunk Road snakes across the Subcontinent for 2500km, from Pakistan to Bangladesh, but the legions of truck drivers who ply this mighty artery relish the stretch that passes through the Punjab above all else for the *dhabas* (Punjabi roadhouses) that flank the tarmac on both sides of the border. In Pakistan you'll be offered a full-flavoured mutton curry, while on the Indian side of the border you'll find South Asia's finest samosas, deep-fried wheat-flour triangles stuffed with spiced potatoes and peas. Flash-fried just before serving, samosas make the perfect portable meal, warm, nourishing and easy to eat with one hand while navigating four lanes of highway chaos. Drivers who tire of these tantalising triangles can fall back on pakoras, a panoply of vegetables deep-fried in gram-flour batter – potatoes, eggplant, spinach, cauliflower, onions, chickpeas, or best of all, giant green chillies stuffed with zingy potato mash.

THE VERSATILE LENTIL

Lentils crop up in a staggering variety of dishes as you roam the Subcontinent. In Pakistan and Bangladesh, no meal would be complete without a side order of dhal, slow-cooked black gram lentils, mung beans or pigeon peas, infused with the flavour of chilli, mustard, ghee (clarified butter) and pungent, onion-scented asafoetida. Ground pulses are the key ingredient in *namkeen* – a whole family of spicy, savoury snacks – while *masoor dhal* (red lentils) add texture and taste to *khichdi*, a blend of rice and pulses that is the first solid food eaten by infants and the last food eaten by toothless grandparents.

THE SUBCONTINENT

DHAL BHAAT
NEPAL'S MEAT AND TWO VEG

Can lentils be a national delicacy? They can in Nepal. In fact, *dhal bhaat* – boiled rice with a topping of lentil soup and a side order of vegetable curry – isn't just Nepal's national dish, it's the engine that fuels Nepali society. Once you trek beyond the gastronomic melting pot of the Kathmandu valley, people eat *dhal bhaat* for lunch and dinner, day in, day out, from the cradle to the grave. For a country with more walking trails than roads, it ticks all the right boxes – protein to maintain muscle bulk, broth to replace lost electrolytes, and loads of slow-release carbs for sustained bouts of exercise.

Forget any insipid lentil soups: a good *dhal bhaat* will leave you stuffed, the perfect end to a long day on the trekking trails. The seasonings that go into this Nepali staple depend on what the cook has to hand. Close to the Terai plains, expect complex spice mixes, and mouth-searing side servings of *achar* (chutney), made from pounded chillies, garlic and tomatoes, mangoes or cucumber. At higher altitudes, the soup can be as thin as the rarefied atmosphere, and the job of flavouring is left to the *tarkari*, a fire-cooked curry made from any seasonal vegetables that can be grown, foraged or traded at that elevation. Utensils are provided on mainstream trekking routes; elsewhere, eating *dhal bhaat* is a hands-on affair. Soup is sloshed over the rice and the resulting mix is squished into balls and spooned into the mouth with the fingers of the right hand. For all its merits, a constant diet of *dhal bhaat* can be slightly wearing on longer trekking routes, and many trekkers carry secret stashes of ketchup, cheese and salami to add variety to the menu.

🍽 WHERE TO EAT BHOJAN GRIHA
DILLI BAZAAR, KATHMANDU, NEPAL

To sample *dhal bhaat* without putting in the miles, try the version served at Bhojan Griha, set in an elegant Rana mansion in Kathmandu's Dilli Bazaar.

ABOVE Lentils served with rice and vegetables, *dhal bhaat*, in a Dhukur tea house, Nepal

312

HILSA
KING OF FISH CURRY

Like a South Asian salmon, the *hilsa* (or *ilish*) lives a life full of peril. Born far upstream in the rushing tributaries of the Ganges, this delectable fish spends most of its life at sea in the Bay of Bengal, before beginning the risky migration inland through the waterlogged channels of the Sundarbans Delta to spawn. Dodging sharks, fishing cats, sea eagles and fishermen, a lucky few make it through the mangroves and rapids to spark the next generation; rather more make their final leap into the cooking pot, to be served as *ilish sorshe*, Bengal's favourite fish curry.

The key ingredient in this delta delicacy is *sorshe bata* – a pungent paste made from ground mustard seeds. Some recipes also call for *posto bata*, a similar mix of ground poppy seeds. Sizzled in the pan with mustard oil, chilli, turmeric and aromatic spices, the pastes release their flavours, infusing the fish with the scent and colours of the mustard fields of Bengal. Some cooks take the dish a step further, steaming mustard-marinated *hilsa* steaks in banana leaves to create the lip-smacking *ilish macher paturi*. The flip side to this love affair with *hilsa* is overfishing, which has depleted stocks across the Sundarbans, pushing prices sky high.

⌁ WHERE TO EAT
In Dhaka, seek out this increasingly exclusive treat at Kasturi Garden or Heritage Restaurant in Gulshan.

ABOVE Netting the night's dinner on the Bay of Bengal; there are fewer *hilsa*, the national fish of Bangladesh, than ever before

BITE-SIZE DIVERSIONS

BHUTAN
Supping on *tshoem* (Bhutanese curry) in medieval market squares in Bhutan's Paro Valley.

PAKISTAN
Slurping down the world's sweetest mangoes fresh off the tree during the mango harvest in Sindh.

PUNJAB
Crunching crisp lentil-flour noodles of every shape and size at a bus-station *namkeen* stand in the Punjab.

TIBET
Sipping Tibetan tea with enthusiastic novices at remote Buddhist monasteries on the Tibetan plateau.

KASHMIR
Discovering the real rogan josh (lamb braised with tomato and ground red chilli) in the poplar-lined valleys of Kashmir.

KHYBER PASS
Sharing an impromptu banquet of lamb biryani with Pashtun traders while crossing the Khyber Pass.

CHITTAGONG HILL TRACTS
Snacking on strange meals of jungle mushrooms and fish cooked in bamboo tubes with tribal villagers in the Chittagong Hill Tracts.

SRI LANKA
Celebrating the bounty of the sea with freshly caught prawns in coconut curry at a palm-thatched beach-hut restaurant in Sri Lanka.

POKHARA
Chowing down on buffalo steak beside Phewa Lake to celebrate the end of the gruelling Annapurna Circuit trek.

ACROSS THE SUBCONTINENT
Digesting dinner over a *paan* – a rolled-up betel leaf stuffed with nuts, dried fruit, fenugreek seeds and spices.

INDEX

FOOD *Lover's* GUIDE
TO THE WORLD

PUBLISHED IN OCTOBER 2012 BY

LONELY PLANET PUBLICATIONS PTY LTD

ABN 36 005 607 983

90 Maribyrnong St, Footscray,

Victoria, 3011, Australia

www.lonelyplanet.com

PUBLISHING DIRECTOR Piers Pickard

PUBLISHER Ben Handicott

COMMISSIONING EDITOR &
 PROJECT MANAGER Robin Barton

ART DIRECTION & DESIGN Mark Adams

LAYOUT DESIGNERS Lauren Egan, Paul Iacono,
Carol Jackson, Wibowo Rusli, Nicholas Colicchia

EDITORS Janet Austin, Helen Koehne, Samantha Trafford

IMAGE RESEARCHERS Rebecca Skinner, Nicholas Colicchia

PRE-PRESS PRODUCTION Ryan Evans

PRINT PRODUCTION Larissa Frost

WRITTEN BY Carolyn Bain (Northern Europe); Sarah Baxter;
Andrew Bender (Japan); Joe Bindloss (The British Isles, The
Subcontinent); Lucy Burningham (USA); Austin Bush (Thailand,
Southeast Asia); Janine Eberle (Germany, Australian & New
Zealand); Duncan Garwood (Italy); Will Gourlay (Greece,
Turkey); Anthony Ham (Spain); Jess Lee (Middle East); Zoe Li
(China); Emily Matchar (Caribbean); Gabi Mocatta (Russia);
Tom Parker Bowles; Denise Phillips; Helen Ranger (Morocco);
Sarina Singh (India); Mara Vorhees (Eastern Europe); Luke
Waterson (South America, Mexico); Rob Whyte (Korea); Nicola
Williams (France)

THANKS TO Mark Bittman, Claudia Bowman, Alice Gosnell,
Fergus Henderson, Mark Hix, Errol Hunt, Dan Hunter,
Andrew Kim, Tessa Kiros, Atul Kochhar, Kylie McLaughlin,
Peter Meehan, James Oseland, James Phirman, Eric Ripert,
Ruth Rogers, Curtis Stone, Lisa Supple, Martin Wishart

ISBN 978 1 74321 020 8

© Lonely Planet 2012

© Photographers as indicated 2012

Printed in China

LONELY PLANET OFFICES

AUSTRALIA

90 Maribyrnong St, Footscray, Victoria, 3011

Email talk2us@lonelyplanet.com.au

USA

150 Linden St, Oakland, CA 94607

Email info@lonelyplanet.com

UNITED KINGDOM

Media Centre, 201 Wood Lane, London, W12 7TQ

Email go@lonelyplanet.co.uk